THE VICTOR AND THE SPOILS

WILLIAM L. MARCY
The Pentagon Portrait
(Painted while he was secretary of war, 1845-1849)

THE VICTOR AND THE SPOILS

A Life of William L. Marcy

BY

IVOR DEBENHAM SPENCER

"It may be, sir, that the politicians of the United States are not so fastidious as some gentlemen are, as to disclosing the principles on which they act. . . . They see nothing wrong in the rule, that to the victor belong the spoils of the enemy." (W. L. Marcy, speaking in the United States Senate, January, 1832)

BROWN UNIVERSITY PRESS
PROVIDENCE, RHODE ISLAND
1959

Library of Congress Catalog Card Number: 59-6898

COMPOSED, PRINTED AND BOUND BY

GEORGE BANTA COMPANY, INC., MENASHA, WISCONSIN

TO

JAMES BLAINE HEDGES

superb teacher
and
warm friend

PREFACE

THE CAREER of William L. Marcy has not been an easy one to study. For one thing, his was an extended career. For forty-one years he held public office with but little interruption, rising from humble local posts to be finally the secretary of state of the United States not long before the Civil War. The positions which he held were generally important ones, and for each of these landmarks in his life there survive extensive public or private records. His successive roles were likewise greatly varied. He was now lawyer, now soldier, party organizer, comptroller, judge, senator, governor, receiver of a defunct bank, Mexican claims commissioner, secretary of war, secretary of state, and a prominent candidate for the presidential nomination, to mention only his principal employments.

For many other statesmen, it is true, similarly long lists could be presented. What is startling about Marcy, however, is that he had a fatal genius for taking an office just when its tenure was most hectic. Thus, when he was comptroller, there was the Erie Canal to finish; when he was judge, there were the politically hazardous Masonic cases; when senator, congress had the most difficult session in the memory of its members; when governor, the United States was going through its most difficult crises over banking; and when secretary of war, there was a full-scale conflict with Mexico. To cap it all, his important service as secretary of state (1853-57) came when the United States was going through the excited and exciting era of "Manifest Destiny." Southerners wished the United States to take Cuba, Britain was extending a protectorate along a part of Central America, apparently with an eye to controlling a future canal route, and William Walker was blandly carving out an empire for himself in Nicaragua.

Probably no other figure of comparable importance in the period before the Civil War has been as yet without a biography. John Bassett Moore wrote a brief sketch of Marcy's life for a scholarly journal, entitling it "A Great Secretary of State," and Henry Barrett Learned wrote several chapters on his career, principally for the state department era, for Samuel Flagg Bemis' *The American Secretaries of State and their Diplomacy*. This is the full list. One reason for such virtual neglect, no doubt, has been in the indisputable fullness and complexity of the subject. More important, however, is the fact that Marcy has commonly been classed as a "doughface" or a "northern man with southern principles." This resulted from his participation in two administrations which took one step or another in the direction of freer trade—long a grievous fault in the eyes of those northerners who have so largely written the history of the ante-bellum era—and which acquired lands south of the Missouri Compromise line or its extension, in short, territory in which slavery existed or into which it might possibly spread. Worst of all, he remained in the second of those administrations, the one headed by Franklin Pierce, when it gave its approval to the bill to repeal the Kansas-Nebraska act. This last meant the legalizing of slavery, if settlers wanted it, in an area north of the compromise line.

And, in truth, Marcy was a man who in his later life much too easily assented to steps of which he did not approve, like the Nebraska act. With his great common sense, his high and powerful "intellect," as his friends called it, he usually reached wise decisions when on his own. Of that, there is no doubt. Yet he did have this serious failing of too readily accepting the decisions of the presidents under whom he served. On the other hand, behind his gruff and at times callous attitude in public there were a cultivated mind, informed by wide reading, and an attractively philosophical viewpoint. These qualities make him all the more interesting to study, for the very reasons that he was enough given to introspection to examine his own life with detachment and that he recorded what he observed. Even before he had entered high national position, he had recognized the sinister pull of public office and, like many another public figure, essentially anticipated Lord Acton's phrase, that "power corrupts." It is not merely for his origination of the phrase that "to the victor belong the spoils of office," therefore, that he is an interesting political type.

Apart from all this, Marcy was very certainly a man of large stature. Had he been nominated for the presidency in 1852, as he very nearly was, he would surely have been elected, as any Democrat not too strongly committed on the sectional issues would have been. In such case, he might well have prevented the Civil War from developing, for he would have been better able, as president, to check the foolish Nebraska policy. He was surely the ablest of the men considered for the nomination that year, of larger calibre than both Pierce, who did receive it, and James Buchanan, who won it four years later. As secretary of state, to speak of his crowning office, he showed great talent and wisdom. The "Gadsden purchase" was added to the United States in the southwest, a great treaty for mutual trade with Canada was put through, the historic tolls were lifted from vessels passing through the straits into the Baltic, and important contributions were made in the study of neutral rights. Best of all, however, Marcy was a restraining influence upon the hotheads of the Pierce period, who on more than one occasion might have led the country into a needless war. In conclusion, it was not for nothing that in his last years some contemporaries considered him the leading living American statesman—and that at the time of his funeral an estimated fifty thousand persons marched in the procession or were spectators.

* * *

The writer wishes to acknowledge his indebtedness particularly to the one to whom this book is dedicated. He is grateful to Kalamazoo College for a leave of absence and for grants for summer research and writing. He also desires to express his thanks to Thomas A. Bailey, Paul N. Garber, John A. Garraty, Robert S. Henry, Martin Lichterman, Roy F. Nichols, Julius W. Pratt, Theodore S. Troff, Richard W. Van Alstyne, and Glyndon G. Van Deusen for reading parts of the manuscript and for their suggestions. He is very grateful to Dr. Wen Chao Chen and others of the Kalamazoo College Library staff and to David C. Mearns, Drs. C. Percy Powell and Elizabeth McPherson and Mr. John de Porry of the Library of Congress, Carl L. Lokke of the National Archives, Edna L. Jacobsen of the New York State Library, Douglas W. Olcott of Rensselaer, Catharine H. Miller and J. Harcourt Givens of the Historical Society of Pennsylvania, Alexander P. Clark of the Princeton University Library, Erwin G. Simmons of the Knower house, Altamont, and Arthur B. Gregg of Altamont, Harry C. Newell, Southbridge, Clarence O. Lewis, Lockport, Margaret Butterfield of the University of Rochester Library, and Stephen T. Riley and Winifred Collins of the Massachusetts Historical Society. He wishes to thank Mr. P. Blair Lee and Mrs. James W. Wadsworth for permission to cite material from the Francis Preston Blair and James S. Wadsworth Papers, respectively, The Citadel for permission to reprint parts of chapter I from its *Faculty Studies Bulletin,* and the office of the Assistant Secretary of Defense for authorization to reproduce the War Department portrait of Marcy. He is also very thankful to Mrs. David F. Sadler for editorial assistance and to Eloise Mange, Lura Ann Addy, Sharon Hightower, Margaret Edmonds, Sally Goddard, and Mrs. Howard C. Bush and others who have given devoted secretarial service. Finally and not least, he wishes to thank his wife, Marion Dickinson Spencer, for her repeated assistance.

For a fuller understanding of the footnotes and of the sources, readers are advised to consult the Notes on the Abbreviations and Short Titles used in the Footnotes and the Bibliographical Notes, on pages 416 and 418, respectively.

IVOR D. SPENCER
Kalamazoo College

TABLE OF CONTENTS

I. STURBRIDGE AND BROWN

"Ordinary citizens have a greater love of country than the rich and noble." (One of Marcy's theses at the Brown commencement, September 7, 1808)

PEOPLE who had to go over to the southeastern part of Sturbridge, Massachusetts, in December of 1786 to see Captain Newell about the manufacture of some rakes, or to arrange for the fulling of cloth by the Plimptons, often climbed the long hill eastward after their business was done and took refreshment at Colonel Freeman's tavern. In doing so, they sometimes paused for a moment to catch their breath and to enjoy the view northwards across the river to the hills of Charlton and Dudley. It was a pleasant spot for those who liked to see the good New England orchards and grazing land typical of the area.

Anyone well acquainted with the vicinity, which was later to be incorporated as Southbridge, no doubt was glad to exchange a word or two with Captain Jedediah Marcy, who owned the big house on the summit.[1] It cannot always have been easy to find the captain near the house, for he had a large farm and two mills to care for. Yet it was sometimes necessary to look for him. He was a man of a certain importance, acting now and then as selectman and taking turn and turn about with the other local worthies in the management of the affairs of the local school district. If Jedediah, who was short and thickset, could not be located and there was some item of business to be transacted, one could speak to Mrs. Marcy about it, for she was a keen, vigorous person. She had an imposing manner, but she made a firm friend.[2]

In the month in question, however, business was not particularly

---

[1] The Marcy house stood on the site of the present Church of Notre Dame, at the corner of Main and Marcy Streets, Southbridge.

[2] The descriptions of Jedediah Marcy and his wife are from Mrs. Calvin D. Paige, "The Marcy Family," *Quinabaug Hist. Soc. Leaflets,* No. 11, I, 137. For Jedediah's official services, Sturbridge town meeting records, town hall, 1784-1798 vol., 108, 123, 170; 1798-1824 vol., 28.

good. The general depression following the Revolutionary War, which had ended three or four years earlier, was at its worst, so that the poor farmers of that part of the state were finding it impossible to pay the debts upon their lands. Thousands of legal actions to compel payment had been entered in the county. Fearing foreclosure, the poorer men had in fact grouped together into military companies to stop the processes of the courts. This was the famous Shays' Rebellion. Although the uprising was put down some weeks later, one can perhaps fancy that old wives of the neighborhood later argued that Mrs. Marcy, who was pregnant, unconsciously gave to her expected child a trace of the ruddy hue of that flaming moment, for her son was to grow into a statesman who spent his life in the more radical of the country's two major political parties. Before the uprising was put down, in any case, the town clerk was to record the following: "William Marcy Son to Jedediah Marcy by Ruth his wife born Decem^r 12th 1786." He was their third child. Four more were to follow.

The name "Marcy," it may be explained, is of French origin and is related to "Massey" and "Massie." The Sturbridge bearers of the name, however, were descended from John Marcy, who came to America in the late seventeenth century and is said to have been the son of the high sheriff of Limerick, Ireland. A member of the "ascendancy" Irish and a Protestant, John Marcy joined Elliot's church at Roxbury. He had eleven children, of whom the seventh was the Moses Marcy who in 1732 was one of the founders of Sturbridge. Moses became the leading citizen of the new community. He acquired much land and built the two mills which have been mentioned. He also, by 1740, had erected the fine frame house on the hill overlooking the river. This residence, subsequently enlarged and altered, was to become the birthplace of the secretary of state.

Jedediah Marcy, one of Moses' children, was a merchant who resided most of his life in the nearby town of Dudley and was also, like his father, a leading citizen. It was his third child, another Jedediah, who was to be the father of William L. Marcy. The younger Jedediah grew up in the uneasy years before the Revolution; as a soldier in that war he was in a regiment which took part in the memorable campaign that produced Burgoyne's surrender at Saratoga.

In the year of that British defeat, Moses Marcy died, leaving the bulk of his estate to the elder Jedediah. The latter in 1789 sold most of the Sturbridge inheritance, four hundred acres in all, including the family homestead and the mills, to Jedediah the younger. Three years later, after the fighting had come to an end, the second Jedediah married Ruth Larned of Dudley, a girl of seventeen who was the daughter of Major William Larned of his own regiment. It was a union of two families of a very similar type, both made up of plain, solid farming people whose men were often called upon to serve as town officials.[3]

For a decade or more after William Marcy's birth in 1786, Sturbridge remained the quiet town of orcharding and dairying that it had always been. Some first textile mills, of a crude sort, were established farther along the river, which was the Quinabaug, but they did not essentially alter the character of the place. There were still bears and wildcats in the hills.[4] As to the Marcy household, a reasonably valid glimpse is provided in the inventory of the father's estate. This was made quite a bit later, in 1811, but is none the less rather suggestive. Besides the homestead and the mill property, which latter was valued at only a fraction of the amount for the farm, there was a smaller farm which was seemingly rented out. Among the furniture, there were eleven dining chairs, which reflected the large size of the family, while the expensive eight-day clock, the five Windsor chairs, and the fact that there were enough silver spoons to go around suggested the presence of a modest comfort. On the cultural side, moreover, there were two Bibles and also other books, the latter totalling a value greater than that of the Bibles, in other words, quite a few for a family of yeomen. The large quantities of butter and cheese on hand and the two cheese presses, together with the large amounts of grain and potatoes, showed how the family earned its livelihood. This is to mention only a few of the items listed.[5]

---

[3] Oliver Marcy, *Moses Marcy and his Descendants,* 4, 6; *ditto,* "Record of the Marcy Family," *New Eng. Hist. and Gen. Register,* XXIX, 301-305; Paige, *loc. cit.,* 133-136; will of Moses, July 14, 1777, Worcester Co. Ct. House; deed of Jed. I to Jed. II, *ibid.* For the name Larned or Learned (nearly always pronounced "Larned") and for the Learned ancestry see William Law Learned, *The Learned Family,* 5 and *passim.*

[4] "Southbridge," in *History of Worcester County* (Boston, 1879), II, 790; Holmes Ammidown, *Historical Collections, II,* 232, 360-361; "Bounties on Bear, Crows' Heads," town clerk's residence; town meeting records, 1798-1824 vol., April 2, 1798.

[5] Inventory, Worcester Co. Ct. House.

In an autobiographical sketch written years later, Marcy commented that he was put to work on the farm "at a tender age" and was sent to the little district school, which was open for only three months during the dead of winter.[6] The greatest influence upon him, however, was that of his mother, who, as has been indicated, had a strong character. This explained why it was that in 1796 or 1797, when the town's vital records were copied over, her maiden name of "Larned" was given to him as a middle name—"by the order of the parent [sic]." At some time afterwards, perhaps immediately, an "e" was inserted after the "L," thus giving it the spelling which he was later to use.[7]

A more meaningful result of parental influence, it would seem, was his highly rebellious attitude in these years. Possessed of a very strong body (if we may judge from after life) and of an active mind, he probably needed more outlets for his energies than he had. He may have been held down too much. In any event, by the time he was in his teens he was a very obstreperous youth, as is made clear by a number of anecdotes. One of the more circumstantial of these was given by Salem Towne of Charlton, when ninety-two, many years after Marcy's death. Towne's story and his local reputation as "the man who made Bill Marcy" are not completely credible, but he was a distinguished man and an executor of Jedediah the second's will, so that some credence may be given to the account.

According to it,[8] Marcy was known at school and elsewhere as the worst boy in town. As such, he was the ringleader in producing the expulsion of the teacher, a crude man who relied chiefly on the strength of his fists. Marcy's father, and this is revealing, sympathized more with the teacher than with his own son, and announced that if the new teacher wished to keep the boy out of school for good, that would be entirely all right. As it happened, the new man, Salem Towne, proved to be a young fellow of understanding and common

---

[6] Manuscript autobiography, 1-2, Marcy Papers, Library of Congress, hereafter cited as Autobiography. These papers hereafter will be referred to simply as "M.P."

[7] When Marcy filed his intention of marriage, September 13, 1812, he gave his middle name as "'Learned." For the mother's role, see *Journal*, July 28, 1857.

[8] *Every Saturday*, Sept. 23, 1871, copied from the *Liberal Christian*, whose correspondent had visited Towne; Ammidown, *op. cit.*, 223-224.

sense. He admitted Bill Marcy to school. He also won him over, by
tact and kindness, telling him that there was good in him and that
he expected great things of him after proper instruction. There must
have been an obvious sincerity in Towne, together with other admirable traits. By his own account, he was completely successful and
Marcy studied as never before. This narrative is repeated here because
it jibes with the boy's character as shown afterwards.

Late in 1800 or early in 1801 Marcy went off, "in compliance with
his own wishes," to attend the academy at Leicester, Massachusetts.
He did not plan to go on to college, he said years later. As it turned
out, he did not last long at Leicester, because he was a misfit, politically. The fact was that, at fourteen, Marcy was a devoted adherent
of Thomas Jefferson, and Jefferson, who was about as popular as a
leper in New England, had just been elected president in a heated
campaign. The great Virginian was despised in that area, which was
then still quite puritanical, for his deism, while his party was hated
for its agrarian views. Just why Marcy should have been on Jefferson's
side is not clear. His relatives and friends were all Federalists, i.e.
anti-Jeffersonian, as was Sturbridge as a whole. Very probably his
liberalism arose simply out of his rebellious character. He may have
picked up some of it, however, from one of the rare non-conformists
of Sturbridge, such as the Reverend Zenas L. Leonard. In any case,
when he arrived at the academy and found the other boys overwhelmingly Federalist, he would not keep quiet, although, as he put it
later, "to be a democrat was then generally regarded as a reproach."
The result was that he was denied admission to the school's literary
society—"expressly upon the ground of his political sentiments."
This was too much. He packed up and went home.[9]

In the winter after leaving Leicester, presumably at the end of
1801, he was persuaded by a friend to undertake the job of teaching the village school at Union, Connecticut, which was not far away.
The motive for doing so was to obtain "a winter's amusement," he
said. Certainly there was an amusing side to the matter, for he was
only fifteen and the former "worst boy in town." However that might
be, it was while there that he first became definitely interested in

[9] Autobiography, 2-3. For Rev. Leonard, see Marcy to Manning Leonard, 9 Feb.
1857, M.P.

going to college. Boarding around among the village families, as teachers did, he spent part of the period living at the Edward Fosters', who were relatives of his, and heard much of the erstwhile doings of their son, Eleazer, at Yale. This was Mrs. Foster's favorite subject. Yale affairs proved to be very fascinating to young Marcy. Before long, he was considering a like course for himself; he also concluded that if he did he would go on beyond that, to study law. He considered the matter very solemnly, but did not make up his mind until the following autumn, when he heard an inspiring speech during the exercises at a newly opened academy at Woodstock, Connecticut.[10]

Resumption of his studies came in the spring of 1804, at which time he enrolled in the Woodstock institution. In the meantime he had probably been saving up money. The Woodstock Academy was not in a particularly flourishing condition at the moment, but to Marcy this was of little importance. He had made up his mind to acquire enough Latin and Greek to get into college. And that was what he did. By September of 1805, or after only a year and a half there, he obtained admission to Brown University. That he managed to do so was a tribute as much to the easy standards of Brown in that day, however, as to his own state of advancement. For while the college catalogue called for enough of a mastery of Latin to start Cicero and Virgil in the freshman year, plus enough Greek to begin the New Testament, President Asa Messer of the Providence college was always willing to stretch a point or two in the case of students of ability. In Marcy's case, he not only let him in but made him a sophomore, probably in part in recognition of the fact that he was nineteen. There had been particular trouble in the matter, however, because his teacher at Woodstock had refused to recommend him, apparently on account of his liberal religious views. Messer had suggested, however, that a letter of endorsement be obtained from the Reverend Leonard, who was a Brown graduate, and this was done.[11]

The other great obstacle was financial. Even in a New England flushed by the prosperity of the Napoleonic era, a college education was expensive, while Marcy had but little money. It is true that his

---

[10] Autobiography, 3-8.

[11] Autobiography, 8-9; [S. A. Crane], *Brown University under the Presidency of Asa Messer*, 12-13; *Journal*, cited above; *The Laws of Rhode Island College*, 1803, 3.

father had a good deal of land, but the Marcys' cash income was small and there were also the other children to assist. Young Marcy did receive aid from home, in the form of advances upon an ultimate share in the family estate; these added up to $700 by the time he had finished college and his study of law together, but probably he had only a small part of the total while at Brown.[12] In any event, he was to do some teaching during these college years in order to help pay his way.

If he had a weakness in the classics and occasional financial troubles, Marcy none the less was now in a larger and more stimulating environment than he had known before. The "university" was such in name only, it is true. Its plant consisted chiefly of the "college edifice," a large brick structure that has since been named University Hall. With the exception of the president's house, this building stood all alone in the midst of the great rough field that was the campus. The faculty was likewise modest in size. It included the president, one or two professors, and two "tutors" (who today would be called instructors). The teaching was commonly on the formal side, but President Messer was a man of a good deal of practical ability and the tutors who were there in Marcy's period were all persons who were later to make successful careers of their own. Judge David Howell, the professor of jurisprudence, was only nominally a member of the staff, but Marcy may have become well acquainted with him on the side. Howell was brilliant, well versed in public affairs, and had a political outlook much like Marcy's. As to the president, Marcy became quite attached to him. He was a plain but just man who applied a simple and effective liberalism in his running of the college. When Marcy was asked in 1849 to write a piece on him for the *Annals of the American Pulpit,* he was happy to oblige and called it "a labour of love." He said, in part, that Messer "always met his class . . . with a kindly spirit and manner, and never assumed any offensive judicial airs, or did any thing that seemed designed to impress us with a sense of his superiority."[13]

---

[12] Autobiography, 10. Will of Jedediah Marcy, Aug. 27, 1811, Worcester Co. Ct. House.

[13] Scrapbooks relating to the history of Brown and Rhode Island, p. 61, part 2, B.U.A.; *Historical Catalogue,* 1914 and 1934 eds., *passim;* R. A. Guild, *History of Brown University,* 30; Wm. B. Sprague, *Annals,* VI, 333-334.

Before his first year was more than well under way, Marcy went off to teach for a time. He did this at Newport, in a partnership with Eleazer Trevett, who was a native of the place and somewhat older than himself. The announcement of their program appeared in the *Newport Mercury* of November 16:

Messrs. Marcy & Trevett, Respectfully inform the Public, That they shall open their school, on Monday the 18th inst., in Clarke-street, near Washington-square, late the residence of Mr. William Bridges—where Youth will be carefully and expeditiously taught Reading grammatically, Writing, Cyphering, Geography, Book-Keeping by single and double Entry, etc.— Those who may intrust them with their Children, may depend on the strictest attention being paid to their morals and manner of behavior.—The Latin and Greek Languages will be taught to those who wish it. . . .

Marcy continued in this work until the middle of the following March,[14] thus stretching the long winter vacation of that era into far more than its usual length.

A few weeks after his return to Providence he was very much in the thick of things, for to this period belongs the most interesting event of his college years, the founding of the United Brothers' Literary Society. The fact was that in the previous fall so many new men had, like Marcy, been given sophomore standing that the class had been more than doubled in size. The newcomers who wanted to join the one literary society then existing, the Philermenians, had found that they could not, because it had a limited membership and because the share for the sophomore class had already been filled. Marcy and the other new men were greatly annoyed, since to be in such a club was highly important. Aside from social prestige, it meant the best and almost the only extracurricular activity that there was; there were something like the rituals and fellowship of a twentieth-century fraternity plus an intellectual life which was focused upon debates and speeches. To many of the newcomers, moreover, it was aggravating to learn that generally only Federalists were taken in anyhow.

The result was that Marcy now became one of the leaders in a movement to found a rival body, which was to be predominantly

---

[14] The advertisement ran through March 15, 1806; on the 22nd it was omitted; on the 29th Trevett announced his plans to reopen in association with a different man.

Jeffersonian in its politics. As a first step, he and two other persons were chosen to call upon President Messer and ask his permission. Messer refused, on the ground that dissension might result, but the petitioners were not to be halted so easily. They boldly resolved to have their way or leave the college. Some sixty students signed a declaration to that effect, whereupon the president yielded. During these first moves and in the following period when they were framing a new constitution, they held their meetings in the dead of night, "without a lamp" and with a man on watch at the door. They then turned to the hardest of all tasks, the obtaining of a suitable library. This was uphill work for impecunious youngsters who were trying to go through college quickly, but they did very well. The sum of $120.00 was soon pledged, after which a member was sent off secretly to Boston to spend it all for books. "And the first intimation the Philermenian society had of the existence of its rival," jubilantly wrote the United Brothers' historian, "was the appearance of a dray, freighted with a box of books, directed to the secretary of the United Brothers' Society." The secretary was none other than Marcy himself. And from the way in which this book purchase was handled it seems likely that as secretary he had exerted the really guiding hand in the formation of the club.

No records of the meetings of the new organization for the period 1806-1808[15] have survived. We do have glimpses of his activities, however, in the minutes of the Philandrian Society, which was somewhat more along the lines of a social club. These show that he was continuing to develop his political interest, and along Jeffersonian lines, as, for example, in a debate on the Louisiana purchase, in which he upheld the federal administration. The Philandrian records also reveal that the members thought highly of him. They appointed him, for instance, to deliver the quarterly lecture on politeness at the last meeting before his graduation. Afterwards, a copy of it was requested for preservation.[16] It would appear that Marcy gave these extracurricular concerns a quite ample attention.

---

[15] This account is from the "Early history, constitution and list of members of the United Brothers' Society," 1-6, B.U.A. Marcy supplied some of the information for this history.

[16] Philandrian Society Record, Nov. 12, 1806, March 18, April 8, Nov. 4, 1807, April 27, July 6, 1808, B.U.A. The copy of his lecture is not now to be found.

According to Marcy's own statement to his son Samuel long after, he also put in a great deal of time in leisurely reading in works of his own choosing and by contrast did only the minimum needed for his course work. Systematic study bored him and he lazily put it aside in so far as was possible. He later regretted this,[17] but the inferior methods of instruction were probably as much to blame as he was. In any case, moreover, his idle reading was of much value, for it was done very largely in the great British classics.

We catch some glimpses of his occupations in both of these categories in the literary diary or "commonplace book"[18] which he kept in 1808. Many of the entries were for the first part of January, when he was at home for the winter vacation catching up on his reading, the nearness of graduation having rendered further teaching unwise. He was busy with the scholarly works of Kaim and Hedge, but also with such literary pieces as *Two Gentlemen of Verona* and Johnson's Preface to Shakespeare. His best recorded comments were those regarding the *Notes on the State of Virginia,* written by his idol, Thomas Jefferson, which he termed "a book which has very justly obtained the name of a Philosopher for its author. For depth of thought—philosophic calculation, and political information [it] is not equalled by any American author that I have ever seen." Jefferson's views on the subject of religion, he said properly enough, were:

liberal but not licentious and from reading them we are very strongly convinced of the fell malignity which broods in the hearts of his wicked calumniators.

The great Virginian's predictions had so often come true, Marcy asserted, that they were proof of "his thorough acquaintance with the human heart and the progress of rational passions and propensities."

Originally, at commencement time, it had been the practice for every member of the senior class to have one or more theses or propositions which he must defend if called upon. These had been stated in Latin and the defense had likewise been given in that tongue. The custom of challenging the seniors to defend their theses had long since died out, but the broadsides were still printed.

---

[17] Marcy to his son Samuel, Dec. 3, 1843, M.P.
[18] M.P.

On the broadside of theses for 1808, Marcy was allotted seven. His second was surely his most significant one: "Cives communes amorem patriae majorem quam opulentesque nobiles habent." ("Ordinary citizens have a greater love of country than the rich and noble.") It was a splendid proof of President Messer's liberality—in Federalist New England—that he allowed this ultrademocratic assertion to be included. But then, perhaps the Federalists were not as good at reading Latin as they liked to pretend. Marcy's remaining theses were less arguable. They were all in the field of politics and reflected the natural law philosophy of the eighteenth century and some enlightened theories of law enforcement.[19]

On September 7, 1808, the day of days, as he and his classmates marched down the steep college hill behind the blaring band and the colorfully arrayed militia and entered the white meeting house erected "For the public worship of Almighty God and also for holding Commencement in," sober young William L. Marcy could indulge in a feeling of deep satisfaction. That he occupied "a high (though not the highest)" position in his class, as the number of theses assigned to him affirmed—was an honorable achievement, in view of his inadequate preparation for college. His class was a rather distinguished one, incidentally. His role in the day's festivities came in the afternoon, when he and his friend Jacob Corey of Sturbridge discussed "Is a Delicate Sensibility Desirable?" After they had finished there came another student speaker and then the long awaited conferring of degrees. "On both parts of the day, the assemblies were very numerous and brilliant, and the exercises drew from them a very general applause."

Marcy had not fully overcome his deficiencies in Greek and Latin, despite their vast importance in contemporary higher education. More serious, he had not conquered a deep-rooted ineptness in public speaking. This was striking, in view of the reputation Brown then had for producing able orators.[20] Yet there had been laid the solid foundations of a genuine love for English and other modern litera-

---

[19] Commencement broadside, university archives. The average number of theses per person was about four.

[20] Autobiography, 9; *Providence Gazette,* Sept. 10; Guild, *op. cit.,* 378; Crane, *op. cit.,* 18-19.

ture, and, more important, he had acquired that wide and deep interest in public affairs which was to remain with him forever. Whether in literature, philosophy, or social and political matters, moreover, he was already well started in a course of private reading which was to make him one of the better educated public leaders of his own generation. He was soon to quit New England, putting Providence and Sturbridge behind him, to seek a career in new and different surroundings. Ahead lay legal studies, war, and lifelong preoccupation with the affairs of state.

II. POLITICAL APPRENTICESHIP, WITH
A MARTIAL INTERLUDE

"Which Fame is most valuable that of [the] Warrior, the
Scholar, or the Statesman? Warrior, Marcy. Scholar, Fiske.
Statesman, Barker." (Assignments for a debate before the
Philandrian Society at Brown University, 1807)

MARCY left New England in the fall of 1808. He was determined, as he had long been, to become a lawyer. Yet Sturbridge, the only community where he was really well known, presented little opportunity for practice, while to settle in Providence or
some other good-sized eastern town would call for a long and probably very lean period of building up a clientele. With his political
views as they were, moreover, he would probably never secure the
better paying clients. Whatever his reasons may have been, however,
he had decided to follow the example of other ambitious young
Yankees and move to the West, which then usually meant upstate
New York. He intended to enter a law office in some one of the new
villages there and "grow up with the community." By the time that
he had put in the three years of clerking required of college gradu-
ates, he would know many people in the place, and professional
men were usually scarce in such surroundings anyhow.

As it turned out, Marcy did not hold to his resolve entirely. He
stopped in Troy, New York, barely outside of New England at all
and even then one of the chief towns of the state—a place of tidy
brick warehouses and shops, bustling with Yankee enterprise. It was,
moreover, a Federalist stronghold. It also had an ample supply of
lawyers. His reason for going no further may well have been simply
his shortage of money. As he put it himself, he was "if not un-
provided, very scantily provided" with funds.[1] Nor did he know
anyone there. Yet, in one respect, the choice was excellent. The high-

---

[1] Just how he financed himself in these years is not clear, but he did have some
of the money which has been mentioned before, as an advance upon his share of his
father's estate. He may also have done some school teaching, as has been asserted.

est ranking member of the local bar, "the fountain of legal practice in the county," as a local historian called him, was a Jeffersonian (or "Republican") and also a scholarly, charming, and likeable man. This was William M. Bliss, the clerk of the trustees of the village. Marcy soon decided to seek admission to his office. The entry was granted. From the date of his admission to the bar and the requirement of three years' clerking, it is to be concluded that the time was not later than the middle of October, 1808.

Marcy was soon installed at a desk in Mr. Bliss' office and put to work at such routine tasks as he could handle, reading his law books whenever there was time. The routine work annoyed him, however. He wrote in his commonplace book as follows:

Painful is the reflection that the professional man must withdraw from the field of general Literature—The delightful prospects which just began to amuse his fancy must be forsaken—the fragrance of flowers in the various departments of Learning are no more to regale his senses; but one art must engross his whole attention, and even that is not sufficient unless recurrence is had to certain mechanical rules and systematic processes. . . .

He closed philosophically by quoting the comment that "Life is short [,] art (or science) is long and time is swift." When the tasks of the law office became too tedious, he sometimes played whist with the other young men of the place, often for the stake of a couple of shillings for the game. But his chief outlet was from the start in the heady business of public affairs.[2]

For one with such a leaning, New York state in general was very attractive, for Federalists and Republicans were as a rule fairly evenly balanced, and at the moment the Republicans were actually in control. The enemy was very strong, however, having the unvarying support of the wealthy city merchants and of the great landed gentry who so dominated the life of the Hudson Valley. In Rensselaer County, in which Troy is located, indeed, the party of "the few, the rich and the well born" was still in control. While most dirt farmers could qualify to vote, their fear of the manor influence commonly led them to support the conservative side, for balloting was not secret. As for the merchants, the partisanship was so bitter among them that if one

---

[2] Autobiography, 9-16; A. J. Weise, *History of the City of Troy*, 272, and his *Troy's One Hundred Years*, 310; John Lambert, *Travels*, II, 34-35; Commonplace Book, cited above, pp. 31-32; Mary Pattison to George Newell, Oct. 5, 1859, M.P.

of their number chanced to be Republican he was likely to be refused credit by the others.[3]

From the very beginning, Marcy made his friends chiefly among the local Republicans.[4] He also soon joined the Troy branch of the Tammany Society, then a national club for young men of the party. By the following autumn, he was so well thought of by the members of that order as to be asked to deliver the Columbus Day oration. This was an important annual event. Columbus was officially a sort of patron saint of the Tammany clubs, outranked in significance only by "Saint Tammany" himself. This early effusion of Marcy's, on October 12, 1809, was soon published by one of the two local Republican printers. In the same little volume, there was another literary product of his, *A Traditional Account of the Life of Tammany, an Indian Chief.*

Since these two outpourings were the only examples of Marcy's writing ever to appear in book form under his name alone, they cannot be passed by without notice. Yet they do not deserve very much. In each, the style was sophomoric: turgid, overly classical, and far-fetched in its epithets. One paragraph, from his criticism of the reaction of the Federalists to the embargo which the Republicans had imposed upon United States' commerce in the two preceding years, may perhaps be quoted, because it displays not only his style but also his strength of feeling toward the opposition:

. . . At the sight of this lowering cloud of adversity, the Demon of Toryism, as if regenerated by a MEDEAN process, started forth into vigorous life, raised the *horrid yell* of treason, even within the *walls of Congress,* made common cause with one of the trans-Atlantic powers, unfurled its *hostile banner,* congregated a band of *disappointed traitors, monarchists, aristocrats,* and *deluded Americans,* and assumed the terrific *name of Federalism.*

As for the life of "Saint" Tammany, that was pure fiction, of a particularly unconvincing sort, all the way through.[5] It would have been

---

[3] Autobiography, 11; Dixon Ryan Fox, *The Decline of Aristocracy in the Politics of New York, Columbia Univ. Studies in Hist., Economics and Public Law,* Vol. 86, pp. 37-40, 56; D. S. Alexander, *A Political History of the State of New York,* I, 8-9.

[4] Autobiography, 10.

[5] *An Oration on the Three Hundred and Eighteenth Anniversary of the Discovery of America, delivered before the Tammany Society, or Columbian Order, in the County of Rensselaer and the State of New-York. With a Traditional Account of the*

of better character if, as the bibliographer Sabin supposed, Marcy
had indeed borrowed its substance from a similar "life" by another
Tammany man of the period.

What brought Marcy more seriously to the attention of the Rensselaer Republicans than these frothy ebullitions was the Hubbard
affair, which occurred in the early months of 1811. At that time,
Marcy was finishing out his law training in the office of John Russell,
having left Mr. Bliss, his "worthy old master." The latter was too
much interested in the movement of Napoleon's armies across Europe
and was neglecting his clients. The incident came in connection with
the annual state elections, which were then held in the spring. It was
an off year, and the chief concern locally was in the choice of a state
senator, for which role Ruggles Hubbard, the county clerk, was a
candidate. A prominent member of the Tammany Society, Hubbard
had canvassed around busily among the voters and had won much
support, but Marcy was thoroughly against him. Marcy knew that
Hubbard was dishonest and otherwise unfit for the post and he was
not the only one who thought so. To prevent the nomination, he
wrote a violent piece of criticism of the man for the *Northern Budget,*
one of the two local Republican papers. By some accident, the article
was not printed until after the convention met, at which time Hubbard received the nomination. Then, regrettably, it did appear. This
was especially unfortunate, for the Republicans always found it hard
to carry Rensselaer and Marcy was very loyal to them.[6]

"Monitor," to use Marcy's *nom-de-plume,* expressed himself well.
As the first important illustration of his countless political articles
in the press of the state, the piece showed that when he pruned away
the "flowers of literature" somewhat he could write in a very clear
and forceful manner, although there was still a bit more pruning to be
done. He argued that the best candidates available would be those
not actively seeking office. Then, amidst several paragraphs flaying

Life of Tammany, an Indian Chief. (Published by request of the Society); Troy,
N.Y. Printed by Oliver Lyon, 1809. (71 pp. altogether; the Oration ends on p. 41.)
Marcy's life of Tammany was also published by the Phoenix Press, Providence, in
1810.

[6] Autobiography, 9-14; for a confirmatory view of Hubbard, see Jabez D. Hammond, *The History of Political Parties in the State of New-York,* I, 399n.; *Budget,*
Feb. 26, Mar. 19.

the characters of such persons as intrigue for their own advancement, he said:

Men who so ardently aspire to distinction, are generally destitute of principle. They attach themselves to a party, that they may enjoy the favors it has in its power to bestow: when its fortunes change, they change also, or are perhaps uniform because they are continually fed on the public bread. They address themselves to the vanities of the human heart; they flatter the proud, and practice upon the weakness of the foolish. . . . By assiduously courting the passions, and flattering the weakness of our nature, they may become agreeable companions of the board of conviviality, and convenient friends in the minor duties and domestic concerns of life, but can never be calculated on as those firm pillars of the fabric of government, which will support its massy dome under the shocks of external commotion and internal schism. . . .

He concluded by remarking that it was the duty of the good citizens and "it will be the employment of some" to expose imposture and hypocrisy.

Although the article did not mention Hubbard by name, the allusions were fully understood. They aroused extreme wrath in a large sector of the party. Colonel Albert Pawling, the leader of the county's Republicans, attacked Marcy hotly as probably the author and added that if he were Marcy's legal patron he would not shelter him under his roof a moment longer. Marcy admitted at once that he had written the offending screed. The upshot was that when he went to the office the next morning he found a note from Mr. Russell containing a certificate for his months of clerking there and saying that his assistance was no longer required.

The embryo lawyer stood by his guns, determined to make the best of a bad job. Fortunately he had the help in this of Oliver Lyon, the *Budget's* editor, who permitted him to continue his fire, so that a new "Monitor" appeared in the very next issue. In it, Marcy stated that he approved of the policies and measures of his party but insisted upon retaining his right to pass upon candidates for whom he was asked to vote. "Let it not be a reproach to any party," he went on, "that they have unworthy adherents; for even among the disciples of the Son of God, there was a *Judas Iscariot.*" As for Hubbard, he was merely an "itinerant politician" who rode around the county "gaining proselites by a profusion of promises which he never means to perform, and defeating the claims of those in whose favor the public

voice is decisive, by falsehood, misrepresentation and detraction. . . ."
Marcy kept up the fight in the next several issues, becoming the
paper's chief contributor. Hubbard received the support of the second
Republican paper, the *Farmers' Register,* but the Federalist *Troy
Gazette* found the division in the Republican ranks an opportunity too
good to miss and attacked the nominee joyously.

The results were varied. Hubbard was hurt sufficiently so that he
polled fewer votes than the other Republican candidates, but all of
them, including himself, were elected. Doubtless this was fortunate
for our protagonist. Another consequence, felt only momentarily, was
a rumor that Marcy was so embittered at being ousted by Russell that
he was changing parties and would enter the law office of John D.
Dickinson, a Federalist. This was true only to the extent that there
was rather a problem as to what other office he could go into. The
only other Republican lawyer was William McManus, a close friend
of Hubbard. But when Marcy applied to McManus, he was after
some hesitation allowed to enter. As for Mr. Russell, Marcy later
forgave him and sometimes employed him as counsel in his cases;
when Russell was in his last illness, he watched with him, the last
time only a night or two before he died. One other result was that
the fast friendships which Marcy made in the *imbroglio* led him to
decide to stay on in Troy permanently.[7] He was accordingly admitted
to the county bar. And on October 15—the year was 1811—the
Budget bore his card informing the public that he had taken office "in
Congress-street, next door east of the *County Clerk's Office,* where
he [would] attend to the business of an *Attorney at Law."*

The practice which Marcy now began was destined, however, to
be interrupted very shortly by exterior events. The war in Europe
between Napoleon and his adversaries, which had so engrossed Mr.
Bliss, had come to the point where the United States was involved.
The depredations of Britain upon American commerce, including
impressment, and the Indian disputes on the frontiers, allegedly pro-
voked by the British, to say nothing of a western demand for more
territory, were causing the western congressmen to push the country
into war with England. President Madison and the other southern
leaders, moreover, had come to accept the idea, to some degree for

[7] Autobiography, 13-16; *Budget,* Mar. 5; *Farmers' Register,* Apr. 21, 30, June 4;
Troy Gazette, Mar. 5.

purposes of party unity. The Federalists of the northern seaports, on the contrary, remained friendly to Britain, having close commercial ties with that country. They also respected the power of her navy. Despite the seizure of some of their ships, their business was paying handsomely; they had not the slightest intention of supporting the administration in such a conflict.

When war was finally declared upon Britain, in June of 1812, Marcy's home state of New York was at once caught in a crossfire between these conflicting policies. Most of her congressmen had voted against the declaration, but her Republican governor, Daniel D. Tompkins, and the upper house of the legislature were both in favor of war. The Federalist Party, which was just about synonymous with the peace party, was strengthened, on the other hand, just after the vote for hostilities, by the fact that De Witt Clinton, a New York Republican, ran against Madison for the presidency. This helped the Federalists to keep control of the assembly and thereby to thwart the war program. New York state was not so bad as New England, however, from the "War Hawks" point of view. The latter section was to lend President Madison virtually no aid whatsoever.

Marcy himself was a thorough backer of the Republican policy and was quite ready for war. He was only twenty-five and was an officer in the militia. He was in a company, moreover, which was highly Republican at that. Soon after reaching Troy, he had joined the Invincibles, one of the uniformed or select detachments, as most up-and-coming young men did; he had been promoted to ensign, the lowest of the commissioned ranks, the month before Congress voted for war. When the Invincibles and the other local Republican company, the Fusileers, were called into service, Marcy "cheerfully obeyed," he said.[8] Most of the other members apparently did the same. The government discreetly avoided calling up the Federalist Trojan Greens.

The Republican companies, which were both of the 155th regiment of light infantry, marched out of Troy on September 19, destined for the northern frontier. Marcy was not with them, however. He was in Sturbridge, preparing for a great event. On the 13th, he and Dolly Newell of Sturbridge had registered with the town

---

[8] Josiah Derrick to Marcy, June 15, 1853, M.P.; Autobiography, 24; *Military Minutes of the Council of Appointment of the State of New York,* II, 1361.

clerk their intention to be married. Dolly was two years younger than he was. They had attended the same district school, but she does not seem to have figured in his life until long after; she is not mentioned in his commonplace book for 1808. Her father was Captain Samuel Newell, who has been referred to already. He ran a rake-making business over at what is now called Globe Village, Southbridge, in the winter keeping several hands busy at this in the ell at the rear of his house and in the summer going out to peddle his rakes among the farmers of the area. The marriage was on September 27.[9]

By the latter part of October of that year, 1812, and probably sooner, Marcy was with his company at French Mills (now Fort Covington), west of Plattsburgh. This is not far from the St. Lawrence. Late that month and in November, he and his associates were involved in two engagements in which he won much repute.

In the first of these cases, the problem was one of ousting some Canadian forces which had been sent into the St. Regis Indian reservation, which straddled the frontier not far from French Mills. It was suspected that these men had been sent to bring the natives out of their neutrality and to inspire assaults upon the nearby settlements. In a surprise attack upon the Canadians, just before dawn on October 23, Ensign Marcy had the role of honor. In charge of a file of five men, he was sent to break into the building where most of the enemy were quartered and compel their surrender. His little autobiography describes the incident as follows:

I broke open the door myself and found in it 45 men with arms in their hands. They were what are called Canadian *Voyageurs* and had been in the service of the Hudson [sic] Bay Fur Co. They talked *French,* which I did not understand. When I first entered there was much confusion . . . and they seemed to be debating among themselves whether they should surrender or resist. I took the arms from the hands of those nearest to me, and finally all gave theirs up, some with great apparent unwillingness, and were taken away as prisoners.

This proved to be the only considerable body of Canadians present, and their capture ended the attack. The Indians played no part in the whole incident. In the building that Marcy entered there had been a

---

[9] "Births Marriages Deaths Intentions," vol. 1, p. 2, town hall; Ammidown, *op. cit.,* II, 323, and his "The Southbridge of our Ancestors," *Quinabaug Hist. Soc. Leaflets,* I, no. 3, p. 55. Members of the Newell family, who continue to occupy the old house, point out to visitors the back parlor in which Marcy allegedly did his courting.

British flag, the first one captured in the war. This was regarded as a great trophy by the young Republicans from Troy; they accorded it all the dignity which a captured regimental standard would have received. The *voyageurs,* moreover, were the first enemy prisoners of the war, excepting some in the Detroit sector who were later recaptured by the British. These achievements were naturally credited particularly to Marcy, whose bold conduct was much praised.[10] His prompt action and convincing demeanor, incidentally, had probably saved several lives.

A few weeks later the Invincibles and the Fusileers took part in a potentially more serious engagement, when General Dearborn in his timid and bungling style invaded Canada by the Lake Champlain route. There is no need to go into the chapter and verse of that dismal campaign, which after a century and a half can be dismissed as little more than comic opera. But it did serve to show Marcy as once again in the forefront of the fighting. He and his platoon were sent, as the first to cross, over a log bridge that spanned the little LaColle River, directly in front of the enemy breastworks. They expected to be shot down as soon as enough other Americans had crossed to make it worthwhile for the enemy to fire. "This was the most anxious moment of my life," he admitted. But the outcome was not what he expected. It was soon found out, happily enough, that the enemy had already given up its position there.[11]

After General Dearborn's debacle, the Invincibles and the Fusileers returned home, to be given the warmest of receptions by the local Republicans. A month later, on January 5, 1813, they were feted in a formal procession to Albany, where Marcy's "British colors" were presented to the state with much pomp.[12] Marcy himself, however, had not returned to private life. He had been brevetted to the rank of lieutenant and had been given the thankless job of serving on the courts martial for the trial of those men who had refused to take part in the campaign. Since a third of the American people considered the war unnecessary, this was a futile task and as a matter of

---

[10] The above is based upon Major Young's report, in H. A. Fay, *Collection of the Official Accounts,* 40-42; and Autobiography, 24-26. Young termed the flag a "stand of colors." The correct total of the prisoners was forty.

[11] Autobiography, 26-30.

[12] Weise, *History of the City of Troy,* 94.

fact the government soon decided that it was wiser not to inflict serious punishment.

Marcy saw no real fighting after the year 1812. His company was called up late in the summer of 1813, but it did not leave the vicinity. Meanwhile, he had accepted a second unpleasant assignment, that of principal assessor of the emergency United States direct tax upon property in his county[13]—a part-time job. Most of the property in the area was owned by Federalists.

Early in 1814 he took part, quite anonymously, in a newspaper controversy which aroused statewide attention, acting as the defender of the War Hawks against attacks made upon them by Solomon Southwick, the editor of the *Albany Register*. Marcy wrote four able articles in reply to Southwick, signed "Vindex" and published in the *Albany Argus*. These pieces are important for us in that they show his bitter feeling toward the national enemy and also toward the Federalists, who were still obstructing the war effort. In angry terms, reflecting not merely his own fiery attitude but also the increasingly warlike spirit among the people in general, he asked for "less delicacy" towards both. He also attacked Southwick hotly. He said he was not trying to compete with that editor for the "palm" in scurrility —any fool could do that, he explained—but he hit with relish at Southwick's connection with a political scandal of a few years before and also charged that the man was now trying to undermine American liberties. He declared that Southwick was "a wretch whose past conduct is an earnest of future aberrations . . . in speculation a *monarchist,* and in practice a *trimmer.*"[14]

In the summer that followed, the hostilities came to a climax. With the defeat of Napoleon by the European allies, the British were for the first time able to pay much attention to the United States and the whole character of the war in North America changed. Whereas hitherto the United States had been trying in vain to conquer Canada, Britain now made plans to invade New York state with a large army of veterans from Europe. A diversion was also arranged along the seaboard. Under these conditions the country became unitedly bel-

---

[13] Autobiography, 30.

[14] An example of Southwick's attacks is seen in the *Albany Register,* of January 4, 1814. Marcy's replies were printed on February 8, 18, March 11, 25. Autobiography, 16.

ligerent for the first time; Federalist companies, including the Trojan Greens, turned out with as ready a will as the Republicans. Marcy's unit, the Invincibles, saw service again, but no fighting. During September, when it was on its way to Plattsburgh, it was met by news of the defeat of the British squadron on Lake Champlain,[15] an event which caused the British commander in that area to order a withdrawal of his army. Although most of the Troy men were let out in November, Marcy was retained under arms until early in 1815,[16] when there came the happy tidings of the making of a treaty of peace with Britain.

Returning to civilian life, he now resumed his law practice. Republican lawyers seldom made large sums of money in Rensselaer County. Yet the connection with the Republicans was valuable to him, for his party continued to be regnant in state and nation. He was retained in his post as assessor of the federal tax for the brief period in which that levy endured and was also made a master in chancery and a deputy to the United States district attorney. There was also some revenue to be had, presumably, from the work on the *Northern Budget,* of which he was at times *de facto* editor.[17] The latter job could be done chiefly on weekends and on Monday nights after the steamboat brought up the news from New York City.[18] Visitors to the office would find him rather carelessly attired and often with his boots up on the table.[19] He continued to be very active in the militia, moreover, although not for the sake of any income. With the benefit of a series of vacancies which occurred and because of his popularity and his good war record, he rose very rapidly in rank. At the close of hostilities he still had the permanent listing of ensign, but by 1818 he had become a lieutenant colonel. When the Rensselaer County Military Association was formed, in 1820, he became its first president.[20]

When Troy became a city, in 1816, his rising stature in the community was signalized by his being made its first recorder. The choice

[15] *Public Papers of Daniel D. Tompkins,* III, 520, 521, 524, 579-581.
[16] Weise, *op. cit.,* 102; Autobiography, 30.
[17] Autobiography, 16.
[18] See the issue of April 10, 1809.
[19] Alexander, *op. cit.,* I, 293.
[20] *Military Minutes of the Council of Appointment,* II, 1569, 1663, 1799-1800, 1954; Weise, *op. cit.,* 122-123.

was that of the state council of appointment, which at the moment was under regular Republican control. Since it was then his firm principle to take no office that would not advance him in his profession, the post was very suitable. Although the recorder was vice mayor, he was, more significantly, a judge, exercising a jurisdiction much like that of the courts of common pleas in the counties.[21] For a man who had had to make his own way in the world and who was not yet quite thirty, Marcy had therefore done well. In that year a friend in New England wrote to ask him how he was getting along, enquiring, incidentally, if he sought to become a "climber of congress." Marcy replied that he was not a candidate for congress, for the very good reason that the Federalists had a large majority in the district. He added that his fees as recorder were worth about $500 annually. A year later he told his friend that the recordership was now producing $1200 and that he had now no *desire* to be a congressman. He listed his various posts and titles with considerable contentment.[22] As a matter of fact, his other posts gave him little or no income.

William L. Marcy had now completed his political apprenticeship. He had studied law, a step always so helpful to a statesman, while in his official roles he had served the public directly and undoubtedly very well. During the disillusioning years of the late conflict he had shown not only bravery—and enough of it to make him a hero—but also a firm patriotism. He had also studied party management, in the close school of Troy's Tammany Society. His contributions to the *Budget* and the *Argus* had become famous for their clear and hard-hitting style. When he had been attacked for them, he had shown the courage to stand fast even when criticized by the leaders of his own party, let alone by the Federalists. During these years, moreover, he had won a name in his section of New York as a thick-and-thin adherent of the Republican Party. Strong as was his previous purpose of using politics only as an adjunct to his profession of law, an inveterate interest in public business and the yearnings of an ambitious heart were to prove even more powerful. He was soon to be drawn into the vortex of state affairs.

---

[21] Autobiography, 19, 31.

[22] Marcy to John Bailey, July 8, 1816, Aug. 30, 1817, Washburn Papers, M.H.S. His various posts are given in the 1816 letter.

III. BUILDING THE REGENCY

"We are now witnessing a new political era,—and in our opinion it will be *much* worse or better than those which have preceded it." (Marcy in the *Northern Budget,* September 9, 1817)

WHEN Marcy had swung back into civilian life early in 1815, there had been a happy flush of patriotic sentiment on the faces of the American people. The humiliations of the recent war, the lack of economic strength which in part explained them, and the separatism and disloyalty which had been so obvious had all contributed to the birth of a deep longing for national unity and national strength. By the end of the war, moreover, the Federalist Party had widely come to be looked upon as disloyal and was thoroughly discredited almost everywhere outside the New England states. In New York it put up candidates only locally, having no hope of carrying the entire state. The Republican Party, by contrast, received a virtual monopoly of public support throughout the Union. In their desire to strengthen the country, the Republicans, paradoxically, now put into effect such old Federalist policies as founding a national bank and increasing the permanent armed forces and they even went so far as to establish the first protective tariff. With one party all-powerful and its measures for the time being endorsed by all, there thus ensued an "era of good feelings," which was to last for several years.

In New York state, the titular head of the Republican party was still Governor Tompkins, a man of great charm who was loved for his patriotic behavior during the war.[1] Behind him, however, there already loomed up a younger and far abler man, Martin Van Buren. The son of a tavern keeper of Kinderhook, Van Buren had entered the state senate in 1812 as the youngest member that it had ever had, but he had almost at once risen to be its leader. He was slight in stature and rather formal in his conduct and lacked the boldness or picturesqueness needed to arouse great popular enthusiasm for himself, yet he had a talent that amounted to genius in the arts of per-

---

[1] Hammond, I, 360-362; Alexander, *op. cit.,* I, 219.

suasion and conciliation. He had supported the war program un-
flinchingly[2] and he was to become known as a rather consistent democrat and liberal. The backers of Van Buren and Governor Tompkins,
the erstwhile war party, comprised the more radical, hotblooded and
generally less prosperous elements among the voters, and especially
the dirt farmers. The New York Tammany Society, the only branch
of its order to survive, was also a tower of strength.[3] In opposition to
the "Bucktails," as the members of the Tammany-Van Buren alliance
were coming to be called, there was also in the party a faction of conservatives, of whom the chief was Judge Ambrose Spencer, an ex-
Federalist.

As if to confound all the soothsayers, the most dynamic force in
the post-bellum years was supplied by the renegade Republican who
had headed the peace party in 1812 and who was therefore cordially
hated by such men as Marcy. This was DeWitt Clinton. So tall and
handsome that he was dubbed "the Magnus Apollo" (or "the
Magnus") and so vain that he was also derisively called "the great
man," Clinton had in his early days ridden into politics on the coat-
tails of his uncle, Governor George Clinton, rather than working up
the hard way. His desertion of the Republicans in 1812 had not
been the only instance of his unreliability as a party leader.[4] At the
close of the war, he had hardly any adherents left. Yet he was resourceful. He put himself at the head of the revived movement for a
canal to link the Hudson with the Great Lakes, for he saw that it
might be made a reality in these years of rising wealth and expanding
settlement. He helped to arrange meetings for the purpose at New
York City and elsewhere and to win the businessmen and many of
the politicians over to the scheme.[5] It was soon obvious that he was
once again a real danger to the regular party leadership.

---

[2] The best biography of Van Buren is still that of E. M. Shepard (*Martin Van
Buren*). On his personality, see James Gordon Bennett's ms. diary, 1831, N.Y.P.L.,
espec. June 22.

[3] Hammond, I, 396.

[4] Cf. the observations of Hammond, long a Clintonian, II, 267-277; also John
Bigelow, "DeWitt Clinton as a Politician," *Harper's New Monthly Magazine,* vol.
50, p. 571; Fox, in *D.A.B.*

[5] Noble E. Whitford, *History of the Canal System of the State of New York,
Supplement to the Annual Report of the State Engineer and Surveyor . . . 1905,*
I, 62-70.

From the beginning, Marcy viewed Clinton's threat of revival with deep distaste. In a letter to his friend John Bailey in 1816, he said:[6]

A number of political adventurers whose future hopes and fortune are dependent upon Clinton are determined to leave no means untried to reinstate him in the public confidence which he had so justly lost and to elevate him to the Chief Magistracy of this State. Clinton, I scarcely need tell you, is a man of talents but not as his partizans would make it believed, *"the formost [sic] man of all this World."* An inordinate ambition and a want of moral honesty in principles make him dangerous as a politician in proportion to the extent of his capacity. . . . I should be unjust to involve all the Friends of Clinton in the same indiscriminate censure but his most active supporters are really worthy [of] their patron. Among them are a Knot of Villains who a few years past carried bribery and corruption to such an extent as to controul the presses of the State and contaminate the purity of legislation. . . . What little I can contribute to avert the danger I shall most assuredly do and if in the contest I should be required to sacrifice and suffer I think I shall do it without repining. . . .

The Magnus went on, however, aided by a reconciliation with Judge Spencer. In 1817, by resort to the device of a state nominating convention, then a new scheme, he confounded his enemies by being put up for governor. Ostensibly in the race as a Republican, but with the support of the whole Federalist group, he triumphantly defeated the regular Republican nominee. Before he entered office steps were already being taken to dig the great canal which he had sponsored.

It was very possibly because of Marcy's fear of Clintonian rule in the state that he did not serve as a member of the bipartisan canal committee which was set up at Troy in 1816.[7] What brought him out in open opposition to Clinton, however, was the latter's appointment of many Federalists to office. To Marcy as to many other War Republicans, this was not only loathsome in itself but also alarming, because it confirmed their fear that he was deliberately breaking up their beloved party.[8]

The fruit of such feeling was that Marcy and like minded men throughout the state began to close their ranks, uniting around Van Buren, who was now the state attorney general. In this tentative coalition, Marcy was from just about the beginning one of the four

---

[6] July 8, 1816, Washburn Papers, M.H.S.
[7] He did not oppose the canal, however. Autobiography, 35, 42-45; Weise, *History of the City of Troy,* 105-106.
[8] Autobiography, 35-36.

or five chief persons.[9] It was his task to mobilize the forces in Rensselaer County; his allies there were not numerous, but they were very determined and they had the help of the *Northern Budget.* Another of the group was Roger Skinner, a state senator who was "one of the most active, ardent democrats in the whole country."[10] A fourth member was Benjamin Knower of Albany, the leading master hatmaker there and the president of the Mechanics' and Farmers' Bank. He is of particular interest because, after the death of Dolly Newell Marcy in 1821, he eventually became Marcy's father-in-law. A frank and generous man who often helped young workers get started in their own hat businesses, he was at this time still liberal in his views and was the political leader of the "mechanics" or master craftsmen at the capital.[11] These four were the most important members of the inner circle of what in time was to be christened the "Albany Regency."[12]

Following Clinton's election in 1817, an era of calm had ensued, in the state, like that in the nation, during which the only paper of any importance to criticize the governor was the *National Advocate.* This was the organ of the New York Tammany group. Even in 1817, however, in an article in the *Budget,* Marcy had coolly notified the state council of appointment that it must not build up a machine for Clinton. Then, early in 1818, he contributed a warm piece on the same subject to the *Albany Argus,* urging the War Republicans to rise and defend their party. The upshot was that Clinton arranged for the hiring of an unemployed journalist from New York City to attack him in the columns of the Troy *Farmers' Register;* and the issue was fully joined. Marcy soon, to use his own words, not only defended himself but "carried the war into the enemy's country."

Clintonians very logically thought of having Marcy removed from his post as recorder, which was a state office. The local Clintonian Republicans especially desired this. Under the leadership of Thomas Turner, a candidate for the assembly, and with the aid of the *Register,* a full blown plot was worked out to this effect, with a large number

[9] Cf. Thurlow Weed, *Autobiography,* 67-69.

[10] Silas Wright to Azariah Flagg, Dec. 20, 1827, F.P.

[11] Hammond, I, 562-563; obituary, quoted in Arthur B. Gregg, *Old Hellebergh,* 110.

[12] Samuel A. Talcott soon also became a member of the inner group, while General Erastus Root was a valuable ally at times.

of persons promised shares in the proceeds. Among other things, the *Register* would get the profitable printing of certain legal notices and Marcy would be replaced as recorder by one man and be deprived of promotion to the colonelcy of his regiment, which was vacant, by the elevation of another person. When the *Budget* publicized the various arrangements, however, it was clear that Marcy and his friends had most of the Republicans behind them. But when the election was held, in April of 1818, the Turner clique responded with special tickets which included some Federalist names. Marcy and his friends in turn brought out tickets which omitted Turner's. One result was the defeat of all of the Republican candidates.

A second result, two months after, was the removal of Marcy and his friends from their places. This was rather a blow to Marcy financially, among other things, and he tried for a federal district judgeship and even speculated about a judicial post in the talked of new territory of Florida, of which the United States had so far not even taken possession. More to the point, he and his faction now fought tooth and nail to win control of the party in the county. In a series of conventions early in 1819, they insisted that past loyalty to Republicanism—which would include a record of support for the war—be a test for all future nominations. And, when this failed, they organized conventions of their own. The elections of that spring saw another Federalist triumph, of course. But Marcy and his allies polled two thirds of the party vote and were clearly on their way to victory.[13]

At Albany, likewise, the Bucktails were fighting it out openly. The *Argus* was brought definitely onto their side and by the end of the legislative session the Regency men issued their own address to the voters, the contemporary equivalent of a party platform, which Marcy had framed. The elections did not go particularly well, however.[14]

Discouraged and even despairing, the Regency made a frantic effort to win aid from the Federalists, their old enemies, in the 1820

---

[13] Hammond, I, 467-472, and W. L. Mackenzie, *Butler and Hoyt*, 36-37; Autobiography, 35-39, and note on Hammond's remarks *re* his removal, filed in M.P. at end of 1818; on the Turner plot, *Budget*, Sept. 9, 1817, Apr. 14, 23, May 5, 12, 26, Oct. 27, Dec. 15, 1818; on a federal appointment, letters to J. Bailey, Mar. 4, Nov. 9, 1819, Washburn Coll., M.H.S.; on the conventions, *Budget*, Feb. 2-May 11, 1819.

[14] *Budget*, Mar. 9, 1819; Hammond, I, 477-486, 505.

legislature. Helped somewhat by Marcy, and very secretly, Van
Buren wrote a pamphlet urging the War Republicans to back Rufus
King for reëlection to the United States Senate. King was a Federalist, but he had gone along with the Madison administration during
much of the war. It was hoped that in turn some of his party would
coöperate with the Bucktails. When the matter first began to be
bruited about, incidentally, the *Northern Budget* expressed a doubt
that such a pamphlet existed and denied flatly, in any case, that
Marcy had any knowledge of such a writing! The Bucktails' desertion
of their old principles did no good, as it turned out.[15]

In spite of that, in the year 1820 the current of popular feeling
began to set strongly against Governor Clinton. Among other causes
of this were his patronage of erstwhile "blue-light" or pro-British
Federalists and his arrogance and conservatism. In the elections of
1820 the Bucktails won control of both houses of the legislature.
Early in 1821 Van Buren was elected to the United States senate.
Better than that, a friendly council of appointment was chosen,
headed by Roger Skinner. Under his partisan lead, the Regency
settled down to the task of "reforming" the state administration,
which proved to mean mostly the eliminating of Clintonians. The
council of appointment worked rigorously, supported by the clamor
of what at times seemed to be the whole population of the state, and
many officeholders were quickly ousted.

"But the removal which produced the greatest excitement," wrote
Judge Hammond, the historian of the era, "was that of Solomon Van
Rensselaer from the office of adjutant general," in whose place Marcy
was appointed. The shift was bewailed by many, for General Van
Rensselaer, although a Federalist, had commanded the courageous
but unsuccessful attack upon Queenstown in 1812, during which he
had been wounded. On the other hand, it was not the first time that
he had been removed. Nor was he aloof from politics himself, for
he had abetted Clinton in the latter's use of the militia as a field for
patronage in 1818 and 1819.[16]

As the furore over the expulsion of Van Rensselaer gradually died

---

[15] Van Buren, *Autobiography*, 100-101; Hammond, 515-517; *Budget*, Dec. 14,
1819.

[16] Hammond, I, 531, 561, 568; *Civil List . . . State of New York*, 1869 ed., 77;
cf. the *New York Evening Post*, June 22, 1819; Autobiography, 45.

down, moreover, the public came to realize that it had acquired a very able adjutant general. The post was only a part time one, but the hours which Marcy put in at it—in his law office at Troy[17]—were utilized very effectively, as was shown, for example, by the fact that he was prepared to make useful recommendations for militia reform immediately after coming into office.

The militia system was far from popular, because under it just about every able-bodied man was obliged to serve, providing his own musket and turning out—unpaid—for training on certain days each year. To the poor, this meant a loss of income. On the other hand, the training was so inadequate that muster days were a farce. While genuine reform would have to await federal action, which was long in coming, Marcy did the best he could to patch the system up for the time being. His changes were made in an act adopted on March 31, 1821, six weeks after he took up his duties. This provided that there should be a better enforcement of the rules as to attendance and equipment and an increase in the training given to the commissioned and non-commissioned officers. When the constitution adopted in this same year made some changes in the militia pattern, moreover, Marcy prepared a bill adapting the system to it. More original, however, was his arrangement in the new bill that courts martial might "mitigate or wholly relinquish" any penalty in the case of a man too poor to pay for the equipment which he was supposed to have. Enacted in 1823, the measure stood more or less unchanged for some years.[18]

The new state constitution just alluded to was drafted in 1821. In the first phases of the movement for it, Marcy and Van Buren, cautious politicians that they were, took no part. According to Marcy himself it was only in May or June of 1820 that he came to see the need for the change. He then undertook to persuade Van Buren to support it publicly. Van Buren at first continued to hesitate but was soon convinced of the step's desirability. On the Fourth of July, 1820, the Bucktail chief delivered a toast in favor of reform, "and," adds Marcy, "the party went seriously to work to bring it about." For

---

[17] See his official letter to Major General Edward F. Laight, from the "Adjutant General's Office, Troy," July 28, 1821, in the Ford Collection.

[18] *Autobiography*, 45-46. The second was the act of April 23, 1823.

some time it proved difficult to win over Rensselaer County, that stronghold of conservatism, but eventually some headway was made. Once started, both there and elsewhere, the movement was irresistible. By the Fourth of July, 1821, when Marcy gave a public toast to it at a dinner at Pierce's Tavern, at Troy, he could do so with the fullest confidence of its success.[19] He was not a delegate to the constitutional convention, but Van Buren was there and had things under control. The suffrage was made practically universal for white men, while the unpopular and inherently vicious council of appointment was done away with and a number of other worthwhile changes were made. It was a result highly creditable to the Regency. It also clinched the organization's hold upon the public favor. Clinton, who had opposed it, was entirely undone. "Appearances now justify a confident belief that Mr. Clinton is at the close of his political career," commented Marcy contentedly.[20]

The Regency now entered a seeming heyday. By the spring of 1823 they had men of their own choice in control of every branch of the state government. For Marcy, this naturally meant further promotion. His friends put him up for comptroller and carried his name through the party caucus by "a handsome Majority," despite a strong push at the outset by the backers of a rival; in the legislature, he received the full support of the party.[21] He had not sought the office,[22] for it was a full-time one and would mean giving up his profession. On the other hand, it was far too attractive to refuse. From a purely administrative point of view it was the most important post in the state government, while only the governor himself had more prestige and influence.

Our protagonist accordingly gave up his residence in Troy and his law practice there, terminating a partnership which he had had in the last few years with Jacob L. Lane. He was soon installed in the comptroller's quarters in the old brick State Hall on State Street, Albany, where most of the other high administrators were found. He acquired lodgings at Leverett Cruttenden's boarding house in

[19] There is no major article on the subject in the *Budget* prior to the first part of 1820; Autobiography, 48-50; *Budget,* July 10, 1821, Jan. 22, 1822.

[20] Marcy to John Bailey, Nov. 24, 1821, Washburn Papers.

[21] Skinner to Van Buren, Feb. 15, 1823, V.B.P.; Hammond, II, 114-115.

[22] Autobiography, 51.

nearby Park Place. Both of these buildings were near the capitol, i.e. well up on the hill, overlooking the Hudson.

As comptroller, Marcy's labors were to be onerous and exacting. In the words of the *Albany Argus,* the comptroller was "the one-man of the government," who needed a hundred eyes and a hundred hands. He not only paid all of the bills, he also audited them; he had full charge of state lands, he made tax sales, and he handled the invested funds of the state—to mention just a few of his duties. In addition he had a thousand tasks to perform in connection with the great canal. In the year when Marcy took over his work, the combined sloop lock and barge basin was just being constructed down on the riverfront at Albany for that enterprise, and it was not until 1825 that the whole route to Lake Erie was opened. Marcy was *ex officio* a member of the Canal Board and of the Commissioners of the Canal Fund, but as comptroller he would also know the merits and foibles of the various lockmasters on the canals, the reliability of the scales at the locks, and a great many other things. The historian of the comptrollership has stated that it was largely Marcy's careful scrutiny of the construction accounts of the canal which kept that project within its estimates.[23]

Besides effectiveness in day-to-day running of his office, Marcy also showed a capacity to innovate. In consultation with the canal commissioners, he worked out a new method of proving the canal tolls against the commissioners' accounts, a method considered so excellent that the *Argus* claimed that there was no better revenue-collecting system in the world.[24] A second achievement was the start of a policy of obtaining interest on idle state funds, which up to now had simply lain in the till. The moneys were deposited in various banks on call and earned a rate of interest established by competitive bidding. At first the earnings were low, but it proved possible to increase them as time went on.[25] He was also a general watchdog of the treasury, as against public demands for further expenditures, as became a longtime Jeffersonian. He consistently recommended against new internal improvements, such as "lateral" canals to connect the

---

[23] *Argus,* cited in J. D. Hammond's *Wright,* 113-115; J. A. Roberts, *A Century in the Comptroller's Office,* 5-34; cf. Wright to Flagg, Aug. 10, 1833, F.P.

[24] *Argus,* Dec. 25, 1830.

[25] *Argus,* Jan. 17, 1832.

back parts of the state with the Erie route or the project of a great toll
road to run westwards from the Hudson across the "southern tier" of
counties. He held that such plans were likely to prove uneconomic,
and they were not pursued during his incumbency.[26]

Marcy's hours in the comptroller's office were long, but they were
to some extent of a routine nature. Outside, in mealtime and evening
talks with lawmakers and officials and in the abundant correspondence of a Regency school politician, he continued to help run the
party. This was always a pleasure.

The most exciting political event for him in this era was the presidential campaign of 1824, in which there was a grand free-for-all
struggle for the control of the party, both nationally and in the state.
President Monroe had managed to please the different interests in the
all-powerful Republican group reasonably well, but there was little
harmony on the question of who should succeed him. His own choice
was William H. Crawford, his secretary of the treasury. There were,
however, four other Republicans who had strong backing, John
Quincy Adams, Henry Clay, Andrew Jackson, and John C. Calhoun.
These were all highly distinguished men. The administration was
able to get Crawford approved by a caucus of the Republicans in
congress, which was the traditional means of nomination. On the
other hand, each of the four rivals had already been proposed by
meetings or legislatures in different states. The upshot was a race
that was wide open.

To the Regency, the problem in New York seemed simple enough.
The organization was for Crawford. Since it had full control of the
legislature, which chose the electors, the entire vote of the state could
be cast for him. The backers of the other nominees, however, were
not to be beaten so easily. Led by the fertile-minded Clinton, they
came forward with the suggestion that the system be changed so that
the choice be given to the people themselves. The Regency resisted
the idea, knowing that there were many supporters of Adams and
Clay among the voters and fearing a resurrection of Clinton; they
failed to realize what a vast popular appeal the plan would have to
the public. The Clinton organization went ahead, however. It quickly
established a "People's Party," devoted to the popular choice of

---

[26] Roberts, *op. cit.*, 34; *Journal of the Assembly, 50th sess.*, 265-270.

electors, and in the balloting for the legislators in November of 1823 got droves of its men elected.[27]

As the senators and assemblymen arrived in Albany for the opening of the session in January, 1824, Marcy and his fellow officers at once went to work to win them to Crawford and the old system of choice. Marcy was doubtful of success, but he recognized that if they failed Clinton and the "People's Party" would triumph everywhere.[28] His rooms at Cruttenden's and the rooms there of Roger Skinner and Edwin Croswell, the state printer and one of the editors of the *Argus,* became a veritable hive of lobbying. From the capitol, a few steps away, and from their lodgings round about, wavering legislators were brought over and subjected to barrages of pleas; in the words of a legislator who was kept at Cruttenden's until far past midnight— then a very late hour—and finally put to bed in Croswell's room, the Regency were "good drill-masters."[29] Nor were Marcy and his friends entirely unsuccessful. Seventeen senators were persuaded to hold firm, forcing a compromise which put off action until November, i.e. until it was too late for the choice of electors by the ordinary voters. This in reality left the matter to the legislature. It was a Pyrrhic victory, however. Popular feeling became savagely hostile to the Regency, with the "infamous seventeen" being blacklisted in taverns and newspapers all over the state. To make matters worse, some of the Bucktails in the last heated hours of the session sponsored a bill which removed Clinton from the board of canal commissioners. This spiteful step produced public meetings everywhere to vindicate the Magnus and led indirectly to his being an irresistible candidate for governor.

Having sowed the wind, the Regency now reaped the whirlwind. In the 1824 elections, Clinton was indeed chosen governor, and three-fourths of the assembly was likewise lost. To cap it all, the firmness of the seventeen who had stood for a legislative choice of the electors did no good, for when the two houses met in joint session in November the Adams and Clay cohorts by clever maneuver were able to take nearly everything. Only the fact that the senate

[27] C. H. Rammelkamp, "The Campaign of 1824 in New York," *Annual Report of the Amer. Hist. Ass'n., 1904,* 182-184; Hammond, II, 130-132.

[28] To Van Buren, Dec. 14, 1823, Jan. 11, 1824, V.B.P.

[29] Weed, *op. cit.,* 131-133.

continued in Bucktail hands forestalled the removal of Marcy and his colleagues from their posts in the executive departments.[30]

As can be imagined, the Regency came out of the campaign in a very chastened spirit.[31] When Clinton returned to the governor's chair early in 1825 they kept an outward peace with him, to avoid stirring up opinion in his favor any further. In private, however, their feelings were not so bland. As Wright hopefully put it in 1825:[32]

. . . we may again *heave the Magnus down* and if we do and he does not get his *bottom scraped,* depend upon it I shall be ready to damn my friends. If that creature gets worried into life by us again I will quit politics.

Very quietly, they worked to win support in the legislature and also to get federal patronage. Clinton's behavior was identical with theirs. As it turned out, neither party was fully successful in winning support, so that the stalemate continued right up to Clinton's death in 1828. The one Regency gain was the recapture of the assembly. This permitted the re-election of Marcy and the other state officers.

In the interim, Marcy and his colleagues gradually swung over to the group supporting Andrew Jackson for the presidency, Crawford being ineligible because of ill health. The winner in 1824 had been John Quincy Adams, who had been elected by the house of representatives. The Regency had been cool towards Adams even at the start and, as his domestic policy had unfolded, had come to like him even less. They fought his plan for internal improvements at federal expense (New York having built its own chief "internal improvement," the great canal, at state expense), were against his doctrine of a high tariff, and were growing jealous of the great central bank at Philadelphia. In all these matters, in short, the Regency favored a moderate return to state rights and saw eye to eye with most of the Jackson men in other states. The Regency were also attracted by the great popularity of the Tennesseean as the principal hero of the last war.

In the formulation of Regency policy in these years, Marcy played a large role. He was the author, for example, of a famous editorial in the *Argus* urging a "non-committal" course towards President Adams,

---

[30] The legislature elected in 1824 provided for the popular choice of electors; Rammelkamp, *loc. cit.,* 188-201.

[31] Wright to Flagg, Jan. 28, [1825?], F.P.

[32] To Flagg, Nov. 20, 1825, *ibid.*

at a time when the president seemed to be winning favor with the Bucktails. The piece was generally laid at Van Buren's door and, much to the latter's annoyance, was a large factor in fixing his subsequent reputation for caution.[33] By the end of 1826, when the Regency was ready to take a more definite stand, Marcy was again the spokesman. He declared in the *Argus* on December 5 that:

The republicans of New-York, in their adversity, viewed the indifference of the general administration towards them, with dignified composure: in their day of better fortune they will not stoop to beg its friendship, or be betrayed into folly by its caresses.

In 1827 the Regency came out openly for Jackson.[34]

The early part of the following year, 1828, was one of the crucial ones in Marcy's career. He was widely considered for the nomination for governor. Since he had served with distinction in the state's number two post,[35] this was entirely proper, while the retirement of Mr. Knower from public life in 1824[36] and the death of Roger Skinner in the next year had left him the Regency's senior member after Van Buren and hence a particularly logical choice. It was expected that Jackson would be elected easily and that Van Buren would be his secretary of state. The sudden death of DeWitt Clinton in February of 1828, moreover, made the victory of the Regency candidate certain.

Unluckily for Marcy, Senator Van Buren decided that he ought to be the candidate himself. He had never been elected to office by the people of the state as a whole, yet he wanted to enter the Jackson administration with the prestige which a popular vote of that sort could give him, so as to have a really good chance to be Jackson's successor.[37] The party was anxious for the latter object to be attained and agreed to the proposal. Since the "Little Magician," as he was often called, would plan to quit the governorship in March of 1829, if Jackson were elected, Marcy might just as well have been put up for lieutenant governor and allowed to inherit the top position. But

[33] Marcy to Hammond, July 21, 1852, State Library.

[34] Hammond, II, 246-247, 259; the *Argus* article after the November election in 1827 was the public signal.

[35] Ebenezer Griffin to Flagg, July 30, 1828, F.P.; Wright to Van Buren, Dec. 7, 1823, V.B.P.; *Memoirs of John Quincy Adams,* C. F. Adams, ed., VII, 388, 404.

[36] Obituary, cited above.

[37] Cf. the letter of Lot Clark, a printer and businessman of Lockport, to Van Buren, April 10, 1828, which may have given him the idea, V.B.P.

this was not done, either. Instead, the relatively insignificant Enos T. Throop was given the second place.

While these decisions were being made, there occurred at Albany an agitation of the tariff issue which conceivably explained why Marcy was not nominated. A new schedule of duties was being drawn up at Washington, intended for political purposes but naturally of interest to many people everywhere. In New York state, for example, there was a strong desire, almost a craze, to establish factories. But what made the question of great interest to Marcy was the fact that Mr. Knower, now his father-in-law, had a direct concern in it. After leaving the treasurer's office, Mr. Knower had become more than simply a hatter and banker. He had become a speculator on a grand scale, dealing variously in wool, lands, water rights, and other things, but especially in wool. As such, he insisted that wool be dutied highly. He also used every political connection he had to get what he wanted, making himself one of the leaders of the protectionists in the city.[38]

Marcy himself was rather ill at the time. In December of 1827 and until late in January, 1828, he was coughing up blood off and on. While he kept at his desk, he was weak and irritable. He was thus the less able to resist the demands of his father-in-law.

It was apparently at Mr. Knower's urging that early in January he sent a most forcible letter to Silas Wright, the leader in the tariff-making. He minced no words:

I think the protection should be carried beyond a point at which any one manufactory *favorably situated and ably managed* can sustain itself, to a point where a *number* of manufactories equal to a supply to a considerable extent [of] the wants of the Community managed with *ordinary skill and abilities* can be sustained with *ordinary profits* of investment.

This was strong doctrine for a supposed state-rights leader, yet he followed it with more in the same vein. Wright was furiously angry. In a long reply to Marcy, he seems to have accused him of having a direct interest in Knower's affairs. The quarrel was later patched up, Marcy admitting that "I am no oracle" and Wright saying that he had himself been "imprudent" and was not hostile to Marcy.[39] As

---

[38] Cf. Flagg to Wright, Jan. 10, 1828, F.P. Some of his speculations will be mentioned in the next two chapters.

[39] Marcy to Van Buren, Jan. 29, 1828, V.B.P.; Wright to Flagg, Jan. 16, Feb. 8, 1828, F.P., quoting the above paragraph and speaking of his reply to Marcy.

for Mr. Knower, however, he persisted in his agitation, holding meetings of protectionists in his house and even getting up a long public petition. This was all very embarrassing.[40]

Despite his chagrin over these recent events, Marcy could take only pleasure in the results of the year's election. The sweeping triumph by Jackson and by Van Buren, who was chosen governor and who did become secretary of state soon after, meant that the Regency had finally won that unqualified leadership in state affairs for which they had so long been contending. These changes also were harbingers of a first-ranking position nationally. In the eyes of the public at large, moreover, the coming of Jackson meant a change in the direction of American government as a whole. Henceforth, the American system was to be one not only of government of and for the people, and more so than earlier, but also of government by them, and the Democratic Republicans or Jacksonians were to come into their own. If their enemies dubbed them "Democrats," a term which then implied vulgarity, the Jacksonians did not mind too much; they believed in popular rule and they had the power of the people behind them. Soon enough, in fact, they would assume the debated name deliberately and glory in it.

The Albany Regency, to the creation of which Marcy had given and was long to give so much, were well qualified to take the lead in this new age. Although dignified and formally polite in accordance with the best standards of the day, the members were of humble origin and knew the people's needs. If we include such additions to the inner circle as Benjamin F. Butler, John A. Dix, Azariah C. Flagg, and Silas Wright, it may be noted that three of the group as a whole, Van Buren, Butler, and Croswell, were all sons of tavern keepers, while Flagg had been a printer's apprentice and Wright, like Marcy, had done part-time teaching to help pay his way through college. Only Dix had had definite advantages as a child.[41] In contrast, the two other most famous American political organizations in the first half of the century, the Richmond and Essex juntos, which at one time or another ruled Virginia and Massachusetts, respectively, were aristocratic.

---

[40] Flagg to Wright, Mar. 13, 16, April 13, 1828, all in F.P.; petition in V.B.P., under March, 1828.

[41] See especially the sketches of these men in the *D.A.B.*

The Regency leaders, furthermore, were as a rule persons of exceptionally high character. Those of the 1830's were of particularly impressive strength, hardly to be outdone anywhere in any period. What better democrat and more frank and independent leader was there than Silas Wright, who came to the state senate in 1823 and in 1827 began a long career in Congress,[42] what more devoted democrat and public servant than Azariah Flagg, who had been editor of the *Plattsburg Republican* and like Wright had begun a career at Albany in 1823,[43] what more skillful editor than Edwin Croswell,[44] and what lawyer of greater integrity and professional competence than Benjamin F. Butler, Van Buren's law partner?[45] Even aside from Van Buren and Marcy, it was a veritable constellation of stars.

The party organization under which these Regency figures entered the new era was also an exceptionally strong one. For these were men who were willing to confer and coöperate with each other on a friendly and trustworthy basis. There was no Magnus Apollo among them.[46] After a decision had been reached, moreover, it was held to faithfully and every member would fight tooth and nail to carry it into effect.[47] A great reliance was placed upon caucuses, both in the legislature and elsewhere, and the fullest acceptance was obtained for their decisions.[48] There was also great pressure upon the members of the party to support duly nominated candidates in a public election. This was shown almost too well in a letter which Marcy sent to Flagg in 1825:[49]

An opposition to a candidate which is abstractly right may be politically wrong. We had better support a man that we believe to be unsound than

[42] The latest and best biography is John A. Garraty's *Silas Wright*.

[43] N. S. and L. C. S. Flagg, *Family Records of the Descendants of Gershom Flagg*, 48-49; Wright to Marcy, Dec. 18, 1835, M.P.

[44] J. W. Webb to a gentleman in Harrisburg, in *Argus*, Jan. 27, 1832; Hammond, II, 123.

[45] He should not be confused with the Benjamin F. Butler of Civil War notoriety. A. C. Flick, ed., *History of the State of New York*, VI, 54.

[46] Cf. Van Buren's role in the nomination of Rochester for governor in 1826, in his *Autobiography*, pp. 160-164.

[47] To give one example, Wright had been for Adams for president in 1824 and Flagg at first preferred a popular choice of electors, but these two men were the Regency leaders who in the senate and assembly, respectively, fought to block popular choice and elect Crawford. (Wright to Flagg, Dec. 20, 1827, F.P.; Fox, *op. cit.*, 283.)

[48] Hammond, II, 114.

[49] Oct. 20, 1825, in F.P.

to oppose him if by so doing we insure success to others equally unsound and at the same time hazard the election of political friends who are worthy of our confidence and whose success is necessary to the triumph of our cause. I sincerely lament your peculiar situation as to the senate nomination. I know you view a support of it as humiliating and I fear an opposition to it will be mischievous. I know . . . that the support of one improper candidate encourages others to prefer their claims and that the party who support men without principle suffer disrepute and injure their cause. . . . I do not wish to ask an unreasonable thing nor do I presume that I have better views than you have on this subject but I hope you will not oppose the nomination . . . more, that you will support it.

He had traveled a long way in the direction of partisanship since the Ruggles Hubbard affair of 1811!

On the subject of patronage, too, Marcy was a typical representative of the Regency attitude. In 1833 he was to write:[50]

. . . In bestowing the patronage entrusted to me I first look to the qualifications of the candidates; if they have these their political merits and the wishes of political friends are next to be regarded.

This was a fair statement of the matter and is understood correctly only if taken in its literal meaning. He and his coadjutors handled appointments customarily with great care and a good deal of wisdom. One branch of the patronage, the state printing contract, was used with particular success, in the support of the *Albany Argus,* the powerful party organ.

"I do not believe that a stronger political combination ever existed at any state capital, or even at the national capital," wrote Thurlow Weed, long the Regency's principal opponent, years later.[51] "They were men of great ability, great industry, indomitable courage, and strict personal integrity. Their influence and power for nearly twenty years was almost as potential in national as in state politics." And if, as Weed here implies, the Regency indeed constituted a "machine," it was none the less one which brought beneficial results. It came to perform the invaluable service of marshaling the democratic elements in the state into a single, well defined body. It also brought many important reforms.

That William L. Marcy was one of the Regency's principal fashioners was therefore a point very much to his credit. In the earliest period

---

[50] To W. J. McNeven, Oct. 14, M.P.
[51] *Op. cit.,* 103.

his most distinctive offering had been in his powerful newspaper articles, but by 1823 or 1824 there were several members who wrote well and his services were no longer needed so much in this way. At all times he was a careful, efficient, and hard-working public servant. His greatest contributions, however, were in his marked common sense and his rugged loyalty to Democratic Republicanism. By the spring of 1829, having completed six years as the comptroller of the state, he was ready for new duties and stood upon the threshold of a celebrated career.

*   *   *

During these years of exciting political developments, Marcy had lost his first wife, Dolly, and, as has been mentioned, had married a daughter of Benjamin Knower. Dolly had died in 1821, during his second month as adjutant general.[52] She had borne him two sons, William and Samuel, the latter on the preceding Fourth of July.[53] It may have been that Samuel's birth had weakened her so much that she had simply never recovered. In any event, she was ill for a long time. It was probably during this period, when she was at home with her parents at Southbridge, that he wrote her a long letter dated "November 24."[54] He started by saying that a severe cold in his lungs had made him ill for the past three weeks but that he was now well and wished that she were equally so. Household affairs were going smoothly, he remarked:

Sylva by direction of *my Steward George* [her youngest brother, who was with him] scalds the pickles and sweetmeats about once a fortnight. I hope you will hold yourself prepared to return to the husband you have abandoned [,] on the shortest notice. If there should be sleighing about the middle of Dec. I shall come after you; but if it is no do [sic] that I can come so as to return here by the last of December, I shall have to defer my journey until after the court at Albany which will terminate about the middle of January. After that time if the travelling will permit you may expect to see me at Southbridge.

"I have been expecting a letter from you for several days [he went on] but as yet have been disappointed. I do hope you will not deprive

---

[52] (According to the date given by Henry Hun, in "A Survey of the activity of the Albany Academy," typescript, vol. IV, p. 12, State Library.)

[53] Marcy, *Moses Marcy*, 10-12.

[54] Original in possession of Old Sturbridge Village, Sturbridge; photostat in M.P.

me of the satisfaction of a letter from you each week." After some
mention of relatives and friends, he concluded:

> "Do write me often.
> I subscribe myself your dear husband
> W. L. Marcy
> Dear Wife D. Newell"

For a long time after Dolly's death, the children stayed with their
grandparents at Southbridge. Marcy seems to have lived alone during
most of this era. His wife's brother, George W. Newell, had come
to make his home with them at Troy during his tenth year (perhaps
in 1816), but was now attending the academy at Dudley, Massachusetts. This was at Marcy's expense, for he had become to all
intents and purposes an adopted son. When he was home from the
academy on vacations and later when he had become a clerk in one
of the state offices, he was a great comfort to the adjutant general,
who was exceedingly fond of him. In fact, after his studies at Dudley
were over, Marcy put him through a program of supervised reading,
over the years, to complete his education. Intelligent, likeable, and
of the highest character, he was to be a valuable aide to Marcy upon
many occasions. While Marcy was comptroller, Newell rose to be
chief clerk of the canal department, a post of much importance and
which he filled with unusual ability. He was a zealous servant of the
public. Even in 1832, when John Jacob Astor offered him double his
state salary if he would take charge of the Astor affairs, he was not
lured away.[55]

Marcy's second marriage, to Cornelia Knower, did not come
until three years after Dolly's demise. Cornelia was Mr. Knower's
eldest daughter, a dark-haired and attractive girl of a rather retiring
disposition.[56] She was twenty or twenty-one, and he thirty-six, at the

---

[55] Newell to Marcy, various dates in 1821-1822, and account book of Newell,
1821-1822; also William Hancock to Marcy, Oct. 21, 1821, all in State Library. For
the adoption of Newell, see his statement of about 1832, *ibid.,* "From my tenth
year, and I am now 26 . . ."; for his age, the same and the manuscript genealogy
of the Newell family prepared and owned by Miss Chase of Sturbridge Center. The
papers of Harry C. Newell, Southbridge, contain a rough draft of one of George's
letters (of Sept. 1825) which indicates that he was at that time still a student at
the academy but during vacations was a clerk in the comptroller's office, of which
Marcy had by then taken charge. On the Astor post, cf. several letters, April,
May, 1832, N.P.
[56] Photograph and comment, in Virginia Clay-Clopton, *A Belle of the Fifties,*
p. 63.

time of their wedding in 1824. The ceremony took place at the residence of the Knowers in West Guilderland, in the spacious hall under the overhanging stairs.[57] When Marcy arrived for the occasion, walking up the short path under the canopy which had been erected, he came to marry more than Miss Cornelia, however. For while Dolly had represented a tie with the mechanics and yeomanry of Massachusetts, Cornelia represented something different. Despite her impeccable Regency background, she was affiliated through her father with the rising merchant capitalism of a new era. As has been pointed out in relation to the tariff crisis of 1828, moreover, Mr. Knower was fast becoming deeply conservative in his political views. Nor would this be the last occasion when he would interfere, out of his own passionate self-interest, in Marcy's political affairs. In the years to come, as Marcy unconsciously shrugged off some of his early Republicanism, the link with Mr. Knower, *via* Cornelia, was to be an important cause of that change.

---

[57] Gregg, *op. cit.,* 112-113; the building still stands.

IV. PUISNE JUSTICE

"Sir, if you will shut out your testimony from the court, by swearing your answer will implicate you in murder, you must do it; I cannot prevent it, but there is a God who will punish. . . ." (Marcy to a witness in the Masonic trials, June, 1830)

"MARCY was so situated that I must make him a judge or ruin him," wrote the imperturbable Martin Van Buren early in February, 1829. He referred to the fact that on January 15 he had sent to the legislature a nomination of his old ally as an associate justice of the state supreme court. He did not add, as he might have, that if he had not taken the gubernatorial nomination from Marcy the year before, there would have been no problem. But he did explain that a plan which the Regency had had to give his old seat in the United States senate to Marcy had gone awry, because of the machinations of a certain clique in the party. The circumstance was that the friends of Greene C. Bronson, a Utica lawyer, had entered into a shrewd arrangement with some of Governor Van Buren's own personal friends, by which one of the latter was to get the senate seat in return for support for Bronson. The clique's candidate for senator was the wealthy Charles E. Dudley, an amiable but weak man. When the Bronsonite plan was carried through, incidentally, it also brought the defeat of a second Regency stalwart, B. F. Butler, for the attorney generalship.[1]

It was a strange result for the Regency, now apparently at the height of their power. The truth was, however, that the Democrats (for such we may as well call them) had succeeded rather *too* well in the state elections of the year before, so that their majorities in the legislature were so large as to be embarrassing. With everyone a Democrat, the party tended to break up into factions, permitting men like those in the Utica set to take charge. In the long run, no very great harm was done and Bronson merely became one of the Re-

[1] Van Buren to Hoyt, Feb. 8, 1829, in Mackenzie, *Butler and Hoyt,* 44; *E. Post,* Jan. 17, 1829; Van Buren to Hoyt, Feb. 1, 1829, in Mackenzie, *Van Buren,* 206; Wright to Van Buren, Dec. 7, 1828, V.B.P.

gency's counsellors, if not always the most reliable of them. But for the moment the turn of events was not too happy.

On his own side, Marcy was disappointed. He probably had not wanted the senatorship too much, judging by his later feeling, but he could look upon the judgeship as only a second or third choice at best. One reason was that his long years away from his profession had left him very rusty. ("I was never a lawyer enough to hurt me," he remarked modestly in 1849.)[2] But what was far worse was having to give up politics and go into the virtual retirement, politically speaking, of the court, for Marcy by this time had politics in his blood. The salary as a judge would be smaller, too. On the other hand, it had come to be expected that he would not be put up for a third term as comptroller and other plans were being made for that post.[3] In view of his outspoken opposition to the lobbies for a state road through the "southern tier" and a canal up the Chenango Valley, moreover, very likely some of the Regency were definitely eager to get him out of there. In all probability, this opposition had counted against his nomination as governor in 1828, also. In any case, the judgeship came as a refuge.

When the die was cast and the state senate had confirmed his nomination, Marcy turned to his duties upon the bench with hardly a moment's delay. Startling as it is to tell, in the very next month he rendered opinions in a score of cases. He had always been a hard worker, but his new assignment at first called for even more than his usually onerous hours. This was because Chief Justice John Savage and Jacob Sutherland, the only other associate justice, were both rather unwell.[4] In these same weeks, Marcy's smaller salary and his need for frequent travel to attend the sessions at other cities caused him to move his family into Mr. Knower's house on State Street. This made it necessary for Newell, his brother-in-law, to find separate quarters.[5]

---

[2] Marcy to Buchanan, Dec. 10, 1849, B.P.

[3] There was a desire to make room for Wright, who had lost his election to congress through a technicality; R. H. Walworth to Flagg, Nov. 17, 1828, F.P., and Wright letter, above.

[4] J. L. Wendell, *Reports of Cases Argued and Determined in the Supreme Court*, II, 241-278.

[5] Newell's statement, about 1832, in N.P., with reference to his relations with Marcy; *Albany City Directory*, 1831-1832.

During the two years which Marcy was to pass upon the bench, he continued to work without ceasing. He produced over two hundred opinions. This large number of decisions was made necessary by the ease with which cases tried in the lower courts could be brought up to the highest court on appeal. Besides the regular sessions, however, which were held at Albany, New York, and Utica, there were also labors at the court of errors, which dealt with appeals in equity, and sessions of the supreme court at Albany (on first Tuesdays when there was no regular term) to consider points of procedure and cases not on the formal calendar.

Chancellor Kent's *Commentaries* and Benjamin F. Butler's revision of the statutes, "the first modern American code,"[6] were at this time giving the state's legal system a standing which other commonwealths might envy. Yet Marcy and his fellow justices seldom had time to do more than render a decision upon the merits of a case; this had to be done, it may be added, in the most simple and commonsense way possible. All the same, Marcy's opinions were written with that fine lucidity which was coming to be expected of him; they also reflected his strong mental faculties and his natural balance of judgement. His most scholarly opinion was in *Rogers* v. *Rogers,* involving a discrepancy between the devise and the *habendum* clauses in a will, but his ruling in *The People* v. *Stone* was more memorable.[7] In the latter case, which dealt with the right of a criminal court to grant a new trial in a perjury cause, he spoke eloquently of the fundamental human right that was at issue. He argued that to leave no avenue for redress other than through a pardon was unjust. He went on to say:

This mercy is but a miserable relief for the injury he has suffered. It may save his property from forfeiture, and himself from the ignominy of the gallows, but the foul blot remains on his reputation. Time does not obliterate it; the grave does not cover it; it is an inheritable curse that must and will be the portion of his posterity. It is mockery to tell a man who has been unjustly condemned that his redress is in a pardon.

What attracted far more attention than all of this regular work put together, however, was Marcy's role as a judge in the trial of some members of the Masonic order. A foul crime had been committed, allegedly by the Masons, and its perpetrators had not been

---

[6] Charles Warren, *A History of the American Bar,* 524-525.
[7] *Wendell,* III, 520-528, V, 39.

brought to justice. In 1826 a stonemason named William Morgan, of Batavia, New York, had been abducted and presumably murdered for threatening to reveal the secrets of Masonry, to which society he belonged. This had come after he had been refused admission to a new chapter which had been founded there. Seeking revenge, he had arranged to have all the mysteries of the fraternity published.

Partly because the order included most of the lawyers and politicians and a large number of the other people of prominence in the state,[8] he had run into serious opposition at once, and had, it was generally believed, come to a violent end of the sort just mentioned. In the process, he was believed to have been carried to Lewiston and then to Fort Niagara, where the Niagara River enters Lake Ontario. Here, he was locked up in the fort's old magazine. He was never heard from again. By general consent, it was the Masons who had done this; Eli Bruce, for example, the sheriff of Niagara County, had had charge of Morgan over a section of his enforced trip. Affairs were made far worse, however, by the indubitable efforts of members to bar the course of justice in the investigations which followed—strange as that sounds in the light of the order's record for good citizenship in the twentieth century. Within the westernmost, or eighth, judicial district, sheriffs time after time packed grand juries with fellow Masons, Masons refused to testify, and money was gathered among them to aid the members who were "sufferers." Where, even so, the processes of justice went on, those adjudged guilty were let off with sentences of only a month or so. The sense of popular outrage at these developments soon turned into a frenzy, of such force that the area became known as the "infected district."[9]

Nor were the efforts of the state to deal with the situation particularly fortunate. There were bungling and half-hearted action. By the people of the district, the latter was attributed to the fact that Governor Clinton, President Jackson, and many other prominent officials were themselves Masons. As a result, a separate political organization was set up, the Antimasonic Party, in opposition to the

---

[8] Weed, *op. cit.,* I, 215-216; Hammond, II, 237-238.

[9] Weed, *op. cit.,* 245-255; John B. McMaster, *History of the People of the United States,* V, 109-120; statement of Mr. Clarence O. Lewis, official historian of Niagara County, as to the site of his incarceration. Mr. Lewis, a Mason, is probably the leading living authority on the Morgan affair; Whitney R. Cross, *The Burned-over District,* is a general account of the area.

Regency, and the Regency returned that hostility. The antagonism came to a head in the spring of 1830, when Governor Throop refused to grant a pledge of *nolle prosequi* to Elisha Adams, a participant in the Morgan matter, to induce him to turn state's witness. This led to an angry exchange of letters between Throop and the special prosecutor who had been appointed to handle the affair. The latter was a political enemy of the governor; the letters were published, after which the legislature retaliated by reducing the prosecutor's salary and that worthy not unnaturally resigned. As might have been foreseen, there was a new outburst of wrath from the western counties.[10]

It was amidst these unpropitious circumstances that Governor Throop in May of 1830, in pursuance of a recent act of the legislature, chose Marcy to preside over a special criminal court which would be held for the purpose in the following month, in Niagara County.[11]

The appointment was one which no man who cherished political ambitions could desire, especially a Democrat, for the district was bitterly hostile to the Regency. A man of less courage than Marcy might well have feigned a diplomatic "illness" or might even have resigned from the bench rather than accept. To sit in trial at Lockport, the county seat of Niagara, indeed, presented an embarrassment to Marcy on another score. At that strategic point on the Erie Canal, where boats from Lake Erie descended by a series of five locks to the lower level that lay to the east, his father-in-law and three other prominent Regency figures had in the two preceding years acquired important interests. They had obtained rights to the highly valuable water power, had bought up an alleged 80,000 acres of land, and had organized a bank.[12] There was nothing illegitimate about these transactions, but there was naturally a suspicion of political favor in the securing of the bank's charter, which as usual called for a special act of the legislature. While comptroller, Marcy had written a friendly letter to the head of some opposing investors in the area,

[10] Hammond, II, 305; *Anti-Masonic Review,* II, 181-188; *Argus,* May 10, 11, 14, 20, 1830; *Courier & Enquirer,* June 16, 1830.

[11] *Argus,* May 20, 1830.

[12] *Albany Evening Journal,* May 6, 12, 25, Dec. 16, 1830; *Argus,* Jan. 8, 20 (including report of canal commissioners), 22, and Dec. 16, 20, 1831; Bennett, diary, N.Y.P.L., July 26-Aug. 14, 1831; Lot Clark to Flagg, Dec. 4, 1826, F.P.; Dix to Micah Sterling, Feb. 16, 1831, State Library.

urging him to make a peaceable settlement, and he had bought a small share of stock in the bank.[13] This hardly constituted a personal involvement, but Mr. Knower's presence among the major promoters was in itself rather compromising. As far as that went, one of the main reasons that the people of the whole western area had turned to an opposition party was the fact that the landlord group there was traditionally allied with the Regency.[14] When Justice Marcy accepted the appointment to the special court, therefore, he needed a double boldness.

Lack of space forbids a detailed discussion of the events of the crowded weeks which he spent at Lockport that June. Let it be said first, however, that despite the angry tensions of the courtroom and of the whole "infected district," he emerged from the affair with a greater reputation than he had when he took it up.

This was all the more remarkable because Judge Marcy himself acted in place of triers in the choice of jurors for the two cases which were dealt with and because he gave a ruling on jury service which was markedly favorable to the Masonic order. In an earlier case, that of Simeon B. Jewett, in the supreme court the autumn previously, he had said plainly that the exclusion of Masons from a grand jury was "improper and reprehensible." No objection, he held, could be raised to them if they were *"probi et legales homines,"* except the usual ones of relationship, proven bias, and so on. In this he was substantially in concurrence with the chief justice. Since the requirements for petit jurors were the same as those for grand jurors, it was obvious what his course would now be. Yet counsel for the state presented evidence that Masonic oaths called for the members to succor one another when given the hailing sign; they also brought witnesses who testified that, while upon taking the oath for the first degree there was an assurance that moral and civic obligations would not be interfered with, for later oaths this guarantee was left out. As judge, Marcy held, however, that these oaths were extra-judicial and applied only to acts which did not necessarily conflict with public law. This ruling made it possible for Masons or ex-Masons to protect

---

[13] For the letter, report of canal commrs., cited above; for the stock, *Assembly doc. 89, 1833,* pp. 9, 38.

[14] Cross, *op. cit.,* 116.

their fellows. In the second of the trials, that of Solomon C. Wright and Jeremiah Brown, the decision was afterwards alleged to have been the main reason for the acquittal of the defendants. In the first case, that of Ezekiel Jewett, on the other hand, the recalcitrance of Masonic witnesses was the chief cause.

If Marcy was wrong in admitting Masons as jurors, as he probably was, there was some justification for his action in the extreme scarcity in the "infected district" of people who were not either of that group or else violently hostile to it. In any event, he did partly make up for this step by his sternness in dealing with the Masonic witnesses. He held that each refusal by them to testify would be classed as a separate contempt of court, argued that a claim of possible self-incrimination could not be allowed on the mere basis of presumption, and passed out fines and jail sentences very liberally to those who would not comply. His charges to the jury were in both cases notable, also, for their candor and directness.[15]

In short, although there were no convictions, Marcy won much credit with the Antimasons. If not wholly persuaded that he had acted impartially—and of that it was difficult to speak certainly— they were sure that he had at least done much to call attention to the malpractices which had been indulged in. As the Antimasonic *Niagara Courier* of Lockport summed up:

Whatever objections we may have to this gentleman as a "Regency" politician—and however widely we may differ from him in opinion as to the nature of the masonic obligations, and the fitness of free-masons to sit on juries when members of the institution are parties to suits—we deem it required of us to state at this time, that so far as we are capable of judging, he has appeared to hold the balance of justice with an equal hand, thus far, in the abduction trials, and to have meted out the healthful provisions of the law, "without fear, favour or affection." We feel satisfied he has lost nothing with those whose opinions are worth caring for.

The journals of Albany and New York, of whichever party, also

---

[15] The complete report of the Jewett trial and an adequate coverage of the second case were printed in the *Niagara Courier* (Lockport), prepared by the editor, July 1, 15, 29, Aug. 5, 12, 19, 1830. For the Simeon B. Jewett case, Wendell, III, 316 ff. On the juror problem, *Journal*, July 20. On the role of a Masonic juror in the second case, see the letter to the editor, June 20, in *Journal*, July 3; also *Niagara Courier*, July 1. Mr. Lewis told the present writer that the witnesses' testimony as to subsequent oaths was incorrect.

praised his "inflexible and impartial conduct."[16] Although the ghost of William Morgan had not been laid—and would not be in the trials afterwards conducted by Judge Samuel Nelson[17]—Marcy had in general done rather well. He had, in fact, won the approval of the "infected district" as fully as any member of the Regency could be expected to. His two years upon the state supreme court, moreover, had increased his reputation in other respects, making more obvious his general ability and his talent in the despatch of business. The period had also widened his acquaintance among the influential classes of the Empire State.

---

[16] *Buffalo Patriot,* June 22, quoted in *Courier & Enquirer,* June 28; *Buffalo Republican,* June 26, in *Argus* of July 1; *Journal,* June 23, 28, July 1; *N.Y. American,* in *Argus* of July 3; *Journal of Commerce* (New York), June 25; *Anti-Masonic Almanac,* 30. See also *William H. Seward: An Autobiography,* 84.

[17] Nelson followed Marcy's precedent as to jurors; there were no convictions under him, incidentally, either, Weed, *op. cit.,* 285-295.

V. THE SENATE OF WEBSTER AND CLAY

"I do not ask you what the ambitious—what the office seeker
—what the popularity hunter will do. . . . My determination
is to do what to my best judgement appears to be right and
leave the consequences to the overruling providence of
God." (Marcy to Benjamin Knower, May 6, 1832[1])

AT THE start of 1831, without much warning, the Regency decided to send Marcy to the upper house of congress. The
trouble was that the affairs of the organization were in a crisis at
Washington. A gradually developing rift between the forces led by
Secretary of State Martin Van Buren and those led by Vice President
Calhoun had come to a head in the preceding year. It was now expected that the cabinet would break up and the supporters of the
Carolinian would be dismissed. The extreme state-rights stand which
the latter group had taken had turned the president against it and
had led him to look to Van Buren for counsel instead. But the
Calhounites were not ones to accept defeat calmly. They were already playing a heavy fire upon the Little Magician and more was to
be expected. Under the circumstances, it was natural for the Regency
to seek to have a stout supporter in the federal senate.[2]

To Marcy, the proposal that he go to the senate was not a very
welcome one, for he was all too well aware that he was awkward as
a public speaker. In addition, his intensive labors as comptroller and
judge had left him worn out and rather ill. On the other hand, he
was just as ready as ever to consider the wishes of his party. Beyond
that, moreover, he may have been tempted by the thought which
some of his friends had; this was that a period in the senate would
help to groom him, in the public eye, for governor—and the latter
post was definitely to his taste. Accordingly, he did not fight the
plan regarding the senate post. As a result, he was given it. This was
on February 1, 1831. He received overwhelming majorities in both
houses. When he was officially notified of this, he wrote a letter of

---

[1] M.P.
[2] N. S. Benton, *A History of Herkimer County*, 331.

thanks in which he said, and quite correctly, that if the duties proved too much for his talents he would at least have the consolation that he had not sought them. "I happened to know that this statement was strictly true," Judge Hammond assures us.[3]

Before the beginning of his new work, he was allowed ten months of rest and recuperation, for the new congress would not meet until early December. It was a blessed circumstance. During this interval, he made at least one visit to Saratoga Springs, but the highlight was his trip to the New England coast for about a month in July and August, of which he kept a record in a little journal. He made his headquarters for a part of the period at Wood's Hole on Cape Cod, no doubt hoping that its famous sea breezes would help to cure his old bronchial trouble.

At the start of his excursion it was his aim to do some serious reading, which might be of help in his debates in the senate. The selections which he had in mind and his comments on his reason for choosing each of them were in accord with the usual standards of formal public addresses of that day, which were customarily long and florid. Thus, before he left he had begun the *Federalist,* which, as he noted, could be useful for discussions of constitutional points. He was planning also to read Butler's *Hudibras* (as a model of trenchant satire), Pascal's letters (for their clarity in argument), La Bruyère (for his knowledge of human nature), and one or two other works. How much of this was done cannot be said, but the truth probably was that he went through these volumes in a rather relaxed way, if at all. He was a lover of serious writings as much as of *belles lettres;* in his listless mood of that summer, however, his taste presumably ran more to such things as Rousseau's *La Nouvelle Héloise,* a portion of which he read while sailing from New London to New Haven.[4] This was a novel.

Despite the month of relaxation, Marcy continued to feel in "impaired health" when he went to the national capital. Although he was no doubt very much rested, basically, by that time, it was only

---

[3] *Ibid.;* Marcy to P. M. Wetmore, June 21, 1839, M.P.; *Journal,* Jan. 15, 18, 1831; *Argus,* Feb. 12, 1831; Hammond, II, 347.

[4] The above account and the reference to Saratoga Springs are both from his "Journal of a trip to the sea-shore," M.P. See also his volume of notes on the *Federalist,* M.P.

with the excitement of the opening weeks of the new congress that he
began to feel better. This is shown by his statement on January 20,
that his condition had "been improving every day since I came to
this city." It was well that it had. As he remarked after the close of
the session:

The business of legislation was entirely new to me & I was so unfortunate
as to be placed on two of the most laborious committees raised in the body
to which I belonged. I represented one of the largest states in the union &
from the public stations I had held in it had become extensively known &
was freely applied to to transact business at the public offices and which
consumed much of my time. . . . Not infrequently I received fifteen or
twenty letters a day, replies to which . . . could not be dispensed with.
For months I did not retire to bed until midnight.

The fact was that his friends at the capitol expected great things of
him. Isaac Hill, for example, the hard-bitten Jacksonian senator from
New Hampshire, knew that Marcy could be a staunchly partisan ally
worth "at least half a dozen of those nominal friends who are so dignified in small matters that they do not know friends from enemies."
The outcome was that he was appointed to both the finance committee
and the judiciary committee and, great honor for a freshman senator,
was made chairman of the latter. He also served on one *ad hoc* committee, that on the reapportionment of seats in the house of representatives.[5]

As if this were not bad enough, the session into which he was now
plunged was to prove one of the most excitedly partisan and one of
the most fatiguing in the history of congress up to the mid-century
mark. Senator Thomas Hart Benton considered it the worst of them
all, likening it to a "siege" of seven long months against the party in
power, "fierce in the beginning and becoming more so from day to
day until the last hour of the last day of the exhausted session."[6] For
such an occasion, Marcy was to have need of all of the statecraft which
he had acquired in his ten years in Albany and of a great deal more
than any vacation gleanings from Pascal and Samuel Butler.

---

[5] Marcy to D. Cushman, Sept. 22, 1832, copy, M.P.; Dix to Marcy, Dec. 26, 1831,
and Marcy to Hammond, Jan. 20, [1832], H.S.P.A.; Hill to Flagg, Feb. 17, 1831,
F.P.; McLane to Van Buren, Dec. 6, 1831, V.B.P.; Ammidown, *op. cit.*, II, 548;
the *Register of Debates in Congress . . . First Session of the Twenty-Second Congress,* vol. VIII, part I, 503-509, gives his reply, as a member of the apportionment
committee, to Webster.
[6] Thomas Hart Benton, *Thirty Years' View,* I, 266.

The situation was that President Jackson's principal policies were crystallizing and were arousing bitter hostility. Already, Jackson had intimated his belief in the permanence and inviolability of the Union; this had done more than anything else to cause the break with Calhoun. He had also blocked the construction of internal improvements at federal expense. In this session, decisions were to come on the other two great economic issues, the United States bank and the protective tariff. In addition, the career of Martin Van Buren would be up for debate, for since Marcy's election the Little Magician had resigned from the cabinet in order to give the president his opportunity to remake that body. Van Buren had then taken an appointment as minister to England. He had gone to London and started upon his work there, but the senate still had to confirm the appointment. To make things worse, 1832 was an election year.

Of all the public problems dealt with, the question of a recharter for the great bank was the most momentous. In this particular session, indeed, there was told merely the opening chapter in a story which was to last for several years and which was to provide the very keynote of the political history of the decade. The Bank of the United States, located in Philadelphia, was rather like the Bank of England of that day; it was run for private profit but had large powers over the banking and currency of the nation.

Those in the know expected that the recharter bill would get through both houses, but it was also thought that Jackson might possibly veto it. One factor was that the president spoke for the West, which wanted a freer supply of capital for its development and regarded the great bank as an obstacle. Among Jackson's other sources of support were many small businessmen, who desired the maximum freedom for private enterprise, the working classes of the eastern cities, who were coming to distrust all banks, and the view of many Americans in general that to have a single great bank was undemocratic. As far as the Regency went, their opposition to the "monster" was in great part founded upon the fact that New York City was speedily becoming the focus of the banking capital of the nation. As such, the metropolis resented the favored role of Philadelphia, while the rest of the state—and most of the Democratic leaders—had much the same attitude, preferring a banking system under their own control.[7] Marcy shared in these special York-state motives. His father-in-law was a bank president, after all, while he himself had while comptroller had so many contacts with the state's banks that he understood their ways and their problems. In the present period (i.e. in 1831 and 1832), moreover, he subscribed to $3000 worth of stock, all told—not only in the Bank of Lockport but also in the Bank of Oswego.[8] Bank stock ownership prevailed, incidentally, with most of the other political leaders of the state, both National Republican and Democratic.[9] If the two major parties differed in their attitudes towards capitalism, it was largely that the Democrats wanted equal opportunity for all, whereas the National Republicans were more ready to confer special favor, *via* the big bank or the protective tariff.

Marcy's role in the senate on the bank recharter bill was one of persistent hostility. He and Thomas Hart Benton and the other Jackson leaders, however, found themselves unable either to block the recharter bill or to limit very greatly the privileges which it conferred.[10]

On the tariff question, by contrast, Marcy's position was that of the majority of congress. The existent law was the one engineered by Silas Wright in 1828, which was strongly protective and would have been even more so if Marcy had had his way. Now, however, Marcy and the Regency were very much concerned at an uprising of the South against the tariff, lest that section's strength of feeling should weaken the protective principle as a whole and should cause a more serious rift in the party than had yet occurred. Very likely Marcy was also influenced by Jackson's insistence upon partially meeting the South's demands. Marcy's final decision was along that line, that reasonable concessions must be made at once, in order to head off further trouble. When Mr. Knower wrote to press for high duties,

---

[7] The New York legislature early in 1832 adopted a resolution opposing recharter; S. R. Gammon, "The Presidential Campaign of 1832," *Johns Hopkins Studies in Hist. and Pol. Science,* XL, no. 1, 131.

[8] *Assembly doc. no. 89, 1833,* 9, 38; not all of this money would necessarily be called for.

[9] Bronson, Butler, Croswell, Register Porter, and Samuel Beardsley were on the same list, while Throop (Throop to Van Buren, Nov. 23, 1837, V.B.P.) and Wright (Garraty, *op. cit.,* 142) also acquired stocks.

[10] *Journal of the Senate . . . First Session of the Twenty-Second Congress,* 154; *Register of Debates,* 978, 1005-1010. R. C. H. Catterall, *The Second Bank of the United States,* 235-238.

giving as one of his reasons the fact that he had almost 50,000 lbs. of wool on hand and that the price of it might be affected by the rates set, Marcy was in no mood to conciliate him, although he was in fact against cutting the wool duty excessively.[11] In a letter to Mr. Knower on May 6, he pointed out very forcibly the feeling of the South and West against the high duties. He also argued that wool and woolens were now as low in price as before there was any protection of them at all, although the present tariff was high.[12] In the senate, accordingly, he took a stand against duties on non-competitive products, except luxuries; he favored competition by foreign goods in the American market, he said, but on terms which would give a reasonable encouragement to domestic goods. He therefore supported John Quincy Adams' bill, in the house, using all the influence he had with the New York members of that body, and backed the measure when it came to his own branch.[13]

The question that brought Marcy most prominently before the public, however, was the one destined to enshrine a phrase of his in volumes of "familiar quotations" ever after. This was the affair of the confirmation of Van Buren as minister to England, which in turn was linked with the patronage. It was thought that John C. Calhoun and his friends, with the aid of the National Republicans (the party of Clay and Adams), might try to block approval of the appointment, so as to humiliate Van Buren and put a check to his career permanently. Marcy and his associates, it may be remarked, doubted that the opposition would dare to take such a step. They thought, shrewdly, that it would link the Old Hero's name irrevocably with that of the minister-nominee, under circumstances that would excite public sympathy. Marcy believed that this, in turn, would produce a vice-presidential nomination for his old friend and thus designate him as Jackson's chosen successor.

Marcy was soon to be undeceived. When the subject of the appointment came up for extended consideration, on January 24 and 25, the scurrilous and vindictive attack launched upon the Little Magician

---

[11] Knower to Marcy, Mar. 28, 1832, M.P.; Marcy to Dix, May 1, [1832], Dix Papers, Columbia University.

[12] M.P.

[13] Speech of March 22, 1832, *Register of Debates,* 608-610; *ibid.,* 676, 1174-1192; McMaster, *op. cit.,* VI, 134-138; Marcy to D. Cushman, Sept. 22, 1832, copy, M.P.

made the opposition's purpose fully clear. Van Buren was charged, and rightly enough, with unsuitable language in the instructions on certain recent West Indian negotiations. He was also charged with having broken up the cabinet, and even with improper behavior with certain Washington women. In the debate which followed, Marcy confined himself, however, to replying to a fourth charge, the assertion by Henry Clay that the New Yorker was chiefly responsible for an "odious system of proscription" in federal office and that this in turn had been simply a nationalizing of the patronage practices of the Regency.[14]

The widespread adoption of office-mongering by the Jackson administration had of course been ground for a good deal of complaint by the National Republicans, even though the shift from Adams to Jackson had been essentially a change from one party to another. Although by no means the worst in American history, the removals had been considerable, more sweeping than when the Republicans had supplanted the Federalists in 1801.[15] In his first annual message, President Jackson had dignified the changes by describing them as part of a democratic process of rotation in office, which he considered a healthy one. In an age when most offices involved rather simple duties only, there was much truth in what he said. But, to his opponents, it was all simply a gloss to hide an ugly fact.

It was in reply to Clay's charges that Marcy discussed the system of patronage-mongering and voiced his celebrated axiom. He began by saying that he might well be conceded to speak with authority regarding the charge that a "pernicious system of party politics" had been nurtured in his own state and transferred to Washington. It was a charge strictly in keeping, he said, with the habit of some senators to speak of New York affairs with reproach. The fact was, he commented proudly, that the state's great political contests and its diversified interests inevitably aroused attention elsewhere. Then followed the curiously blunt assertion so often quoted:

It may be, sir, that the politicians of the United States are not so fastidious as some gentlemen are, as to disclosing the principles on which they act.

---

[14] Isaac Hill to Van Buren, Jan. 29-Feb. 12 (one letter), V.B.P.; T. H. Benton, *op. cit.,* I, 214-215; *Register of Debates,* 1310-1324.

[15] Carl Russell Fish, *The Civil Service and the Patronage,* 124-127; Shepard, *op. cit.,* 211-213. Leonard D. White, in *The Jacksonians,* 307-308, also points out that the extent of the removals by Jackson has been exaggerated.

They boldly preach what they practice. When they are contending for victory, they avow their intention of enjoying the fruits of it. If they are defeated, they expect to retire from office. If they are successful, they claim, as a matter of right, the advantages of success. They see nothing wrong in the rule, that to the victor belong the spoils of the enemy.

"But if there be any thing wrong in the policy which the Senator from Kentucky has so strongly reprobated," Marcy added, Clay must know that in New York state it was not confined to Van Buren's friends. On the contrary, it had been applied most sweepingly under a Clay partisan, and had been initiated long before Van Buren was old enough to have had a part in it. As for the Little Magician himself, Marcy ventured to say that he knew of no person who had "acted with, or advised to, more moderation."

There later ensued some debate between Marcy and Clay as to the extent of the removals practiced by Clay's adherents in both Kentucky and New York, after which Marcy observed rather coolly that there was an unfortunate gap between ideals and behavior:

He [Clay] advocates a course of conduct towards political opponents, characterised by great moderation and forbearance, and, what's more, he professes to have conformed his actions to his precepts. We all of us, I believe, admire these liberal sentiments, and feel disposed, in our abstract speculations, to adopt them as the rule of our conduct. The theory is, indeed, beautiful; but, sir, do we put them in practice when brought to the experiment?

He charged that Clay did not.[16]

Clay's allegation that the new federal attitude was the result of a New York influence was none too well founded, as Carl Russell Fish has pointed out. The removals by Jackson arose rather from a widespread desire among the masses for a role in the government, now that the "people's" man had finally been made president; it arose also out of the shift from National Republicans to Democrats. Patronage practices in New York, it is true, were more partisan and ruthless than in most of the other states, but it was hardly the fault of the Regency that they were. Spoils-mongering there went well back into colonial days, while the jealousies of the leading families and the irresponsibility of the council of appointment in the early federal period had made things worse.[17] Taking these conditions for granted,

---

[16] *Register of Debates,* 1325-1327, 1356-1358.
[17] Fish, *op. cit.,* 105-118, 86-88.

the Regency really acted with much restraint, the one exception having been with Skinner's council in 1821.

Marcy's own record, unquestionably, shows that his practice was better than what he preached to the senate. While comptroller, if we may take his own version of it, he made but one removal and that of a member of his own party, although the patronage was considerable and the incumbents were mostly of the opposing group. As governor, he also showed caution. And, if we look beyond the Regency epoch to his years as a federal cabinet officer, the story is likewise a favorable one. In the appointments under his own control in these later years he showed real moderation, as an historian of the department of state, for example, has testified. It was only in connection with offices mainly at the bestowal of the president but subject to Marcy's recommendation, as with the choice of men to be diplomats in 1853, that he is to be criticized.[18] His normal rule was that of his letter of 1832, that he first looked to a candidate's qualifications. For him, "to the victor belong the spoils" had a more personal, though none the less pregnant, meaning.

Marcy's famous dictum may well have been based upon some words used by James T. Austin, a Massachusetts politician, in a recent biography of Elbridge Gerry; Gerry had been governor of Massachusetts just after Marcy moved from that state to New York. In the second volume, which had come out only three years before, Austin asked: "But after all, what is the worth of a victory if the enemy are allowed to possess the spoils?" It would seem likely that Marcy had read the book, although he apparently did not acquire a copy of it. If such was the fact, it was none the less he who coined the apothegm.[19]

---

[18] Unsigned article in Marcy's hand, 1849, M.P., defending himself against the charge of being a spoilsman; for the war department era, see *House Exec. Doc. 56, 29th Cong., 1st Sess.,* pp. 4-18. The Indian agents, presidential appointees, were the officeholders most affected. The report covers March 5-Dec. 31, 1845. For Marcy as secretary of state, see G. H. Stuart, *The Department of State,* p. 119.

[19] *The Life of Elbridge Gerry,* vol. 2, p. 322; *Catalogue of the Libraries of the late Ex-Gov. Wm. L. Marcy, and Ex-Gov. Washington Hunt,* prepared for the auction in 1871. According to a note by Newell, "from hearsay" (at end of 1839, M.P.), Marcy did not deny his authorship. In the last months of his life, after Pierce had been succeeded by Buchanan, another Democrat, Marcy is said to have complained at the extensive removals being carried out. The person to whom he was talking replied that Marcy was after all the creator of the "spoils" doctrine. "True [,] replied the Governor [Marcy] but that is a very different matter from . . . plundering your own camp."

Commenting upon the debate in the senate, William Cullen
Bryant's independent Democratic newspaper, the New York *Evening
Post,* declared that Marcy's utterance "repelled with dignity" the attack which Clay had made upon New York. The conservatively Democratic *Courier & Enquirer,* also of New York, also lauded his "stubborn honesty" and "manly frankness."[20] Despite these and other
friendly remarks, however, it was difficult to escape the fact that the
speech had been in decidedly poor taste.[21] Candor was admirable. But
it would have been better simply to have left some of these things un-
said, if he believed in them. In any case, he could easily have omitted
the more quotable portions of his remarks before publication, without
committing any very grievous sin. It had been a secret session and
only after Van Buren's rejection had the senate decided to have the
speeches published, so that the reports printed were not the verbatim
ones of a stenographer but "sketches" submitted by the orators themselves at their convenience.[22] Instead, he let his words stand, thus con-
doning the rising use of office-mongering and sharing a part of the
blame for it, as Jackson's expression on "rotation" also had to do. As
far as concerned the defense of Van Buren, moreover, he had done
practically nothing.

None the less, the advancement of Van Buren proceeded gloriously.
When the matter of his confirmation was put to trial on the second
day of debate, the vote was by prearrangement tied, so that Vice-
President Calhoun could have the pleasure of casting the deciding
ballot against his enemy. "It will kill him, sir, kill him dead,"
chortled Calhoun. Marcy, however, was also delighted. He told Gideon
Welles that evening that the coalition had made a serious mistake.
"There would have been some difficulty in enlisting the popular feel-
ing in his [Van Buren's] favor, but the blow aimed at Van Buren [,]
Old Hickory will receive, and the two are and will be identified."
Next day, he wrote happily to London to inform Van Buren of it,

[20] Feb. 6, Mar. 7, 1832.

[21] *The Albany Evening Journal* (April 19) called it "shameless," while the *Journal
of Commerce* (New York) on Feb. 8 described the Democrats as "stall-fed recipi-
ents of governmental favor." Even the *Evening Post* eventually referred to the
famous phrase as "Governor Marcy's neatly turned but somewhat unlucky apothegm."
(May 2, 1837)

[22] *Register of Debates,* 1310; Hill's letter, cited above. Thus, the scurrilous remarks
about Van Buren were suppressed.

jokingly pretending to be transmitting evil news. He added that Van
Buren would be nominated for the vice-presidency whether he liked
it or not.[23] In the weeks which followed, Marcy was also very influential in securing a Regency decision in favor of that step and in
mobilizing support for it in other ways.

William L. Marcy's record on the issues treated in the first session
of the twenty-second congress was in general a praiseworthy one. He
had played a large role for a novice, whether in committees or in
discussion in the full chamber, to say nothing of his place in the
councils of his party. If he had conducted himself in a partisan
fashion upon the bank question, his behavior on the tariff issue was
admirable. On some minor topics that were taken up he also did well.
He was willing, for example, to see a moderate cut made in the price
of the public lands in the West. He also opposed the session's principal pork-barrel bill and took a statesmanlike position on the reapportionment of seats in the house of representatives. As to the pork-
barrel measure, which involved river and harbor improvements and
especially the elimination of a sandbar in the Hudson not far below
Albany, his negative vote was to cause him much embarrassment. In
view of the many wasteful items embraced in it, he was correct in
helping to vote it down. Yet his political opponents and the powerful river interests which had long advocated the removal of the bar
were to give him no peace for years.[24]

The most conspicuous feature of his seven months at Washington,
however, was his loyal and unyielding partisanship. His behavior on
every one of the issues mentioned above was in accord with Jackson's
policies, and in the case of the bank this was signally true, as likewise in connection with the promotion of Martin Van Buren. In his
utterance on the "spoils," moreover, he was blatantly, callously partisan, using terms more befitting the chief of a guerilla band than one of
the heads of the admirable Albany Regency. Even his own summa-
tion of the record was unfavorable. Most chiefly, he deplored his
ineptness in public speaking; as he was to tell a friend a few years
after, he could not commit a speech to memory and was not good at

---

[23] Van Buren, *op. cit.*, 532-533; T. H. Benton, *op. cit.*, 214-219; "Recollections of
Gov. Wm. L. Marcy," in box 3 of Papers Relating to Gideon Welles, compiled by
H. B. Learned, L.C.; to Van Buren, Jan. 26, 1832, V.B.P.

[24] J. S. Jenkins, *Lives of the Governors of the State of New York*, 569-570.

reading one, nor had he any gift for making extemporaneous re-marks.[25] This was a serious handicap, and particularly so in the senate of America's golden age of oratory, the senate of Webster and Clay and Calhoun.

Burdened at the outset by poor health and always by excessive labors, Marcy had in fact as early as January decided that the halls of congress were not for him. Since that time, quite ready to give up the more than four years which remained in his term, he had been striv-ing for the greener pastures of a new position.

---

[25] Letter to Wetmore, cited above.

VI. AN INTRIGUE WITH THE
COURIER & ENQUIRER

"For Governor. Subject to the decision of the Herkimer Convention. William L. Marcy" (*The Courier & Enquirer,* April 12, 1832)

EARLY in 1832, dissatisfied with the senate, Marcy entered into an intrigue with a New York editor for support for the governorship, which would be subject to an election that autumn.

Marcy had probably wanted the post for some time, as has been said. He had also been widely talked of for it in 1827 and 1828, and after his role in the Masonic trials had had quite warm support from many Democrats in the "infected district." One of them, Abijah Mann, a legislator, had begun to work openly for him.[1] One factor in this movement for him was that Enos T. Throop, the incumbent, had handled the Masonic difficulties poorly, as has been said. In addition, that "small light" was unpopular because he had opposed the building of a Chenango canal, which was getting to be an unsafe attitude to take; he had also been clumsy in handling the patronage and in disposing of other matters. In consequence, there was a widespread wish to replace him. By March 1, 1832, Van Buren was writing from London to ask if Jackson could find him a high federal job.[2] What was more, if we may go by a letter written to James Watson Webb, the editor with whom Marcy was now to conspire, Throop had pretty well disregarded Marcy and the other usual heads of the Regency, except for Edwin Croswell, the editor of the *Argus.* Aside from Croswell, he had relied for counsel chiefly upon his brother-in-law, who was the register in chancery, and Thomas W. Olcott of the Mechanics' and Farmers'.[3] Regardless of that, it is clear that Marcy had no high

---

[1] By 1832, the other leading prospective nominee was Chief Justice Savage. W. C. Bouck to Flagg, July 24, 1830, and G. C. Bronson to same, July 31, 1830, F. P.; Bennett's diary, N.Y.P.L., June 21, 28, July 1, Aug. 4, 6, 7, 1831.

[2] Hammond, II, 414-416; Van Buren to Jackson, "March 9?", 1832 (but probably about March 1), V.B.P.

[3] Webb to a gentleman in Harrisburg, cited already.

opinion of him and also that Croswell opposed putting Marcy in his place.

James Watson Webb, whose paper was the New York *Courier & Enquirer,* on his part detested Croswell. Probably his feelings towards Throop were colored by this. A man of violent passions who had on more than one occasion gotten involved in duels or other clashes with those he disliked,[4] Webb was jealous of the Albany editor because of the patronage which the latter had as state printer and the prestige which he enjoyed as the controller of the party's chief organ. Because Webb had begun to back the Bank of the United States, moreover, he had lost favor with the party. As a result, he now sought to rebuild his prestige, by taking a lead in party affairs himself.

The story of what followed was told later by James Gordon Bennett, who at this time was Webb's Washington correspondent. Bennett saw Marcy daily at the capital that winter, he stated, and on one of these occasions Marcy invited him for a stroll down Pennsylvania Avenue. Marcy had something "heavy, very heavy indeed," on his chest, Bennett learned. If we may trust his language in the affair, it was "after a great deal of backing and filling in the way of language and in a style something similar to that in which Caesar refused the crown in Shakespeare's play" that Marcy divulged his desire—to have the *Courier & Enquirer* bring him out. Bennett favored the plan and persuaded Webb to take it up. "In all this business," he said, "Senator Marcy wished to stand still between the two contending *cliques,* while I was to work the wires in Washington, and Mr. Webb was to fire off the big gun in New York."

Although Marcy publicly denied the truth of this account when it came out in Bennett's flamboyant *New York Herald* in 1845,[5] and although he plainly pretended to be embarrassed by the *Courier & Enquirer's* step and to be reluctant to be nominated at all,[6] the story

---

[4] C. H. Levermore, "The Rise of Metropolitan Journalism, 1800-1840," *Amer. Hist. Rev.,* VI, 453-454.

[5] This was on Sept. 26. His narrative was issued in rebuttal to statements by Webb on the subject in the *Courier & Enquirer* on Sept. 25, which in turn had resulted from the publication of W. L. Mackenzie's muck-raking *Butler & Hoyt* on Sept. 22. Marcy's denial, in a letter to a newspaper, is mentioned in S. D. W. Bloodgood to Marcy, Oct. 1, 1845, M.P. Much search has failed to locate it.

[6] Cf. Marcy to Hoyt, 1832, in *Butler & Hoyt,* 112; B. F. Butler to Mrs. Butler, Mar. 20, 1832, Butler Papers, Princeton.

seemingly is true. Bennett was too invariably hostile to Marcy throughout the rest of his life for us to believe otherwise; in 1855, for example, he told a mutual friend that Marcy had "made use of him" and then repudiated him.[7] After being elected governor, furthermore, Marcy attended a public dinner for Webb, although he seldom went out of town for such occasions and although Webb was in especially low repute by then.[8]

One part of the narrative, however, appears to be invalidated by known facts. This was Bennett's allegation that Marcy agreed to repay Webb for his support by supplying confidential Regency news for the columns of the latter's paper, so that it could checkmate the *Argus* on its own ground. This is not only too much to believe, in view of Marcy's generally very high reputation for integrity,[9] but is contradicted by the absence of any such material from Webb's paper in the months in question. More probably, Marcy's contribution was in the very proposing of the idea, plus certain details which would strengthen his candidacy. His willingness to recommend a Chenango canal was one of these last.

It was on January 27, 1832, that the *Courier & Enquirer* first acted. In an editorial, it asserted that "many of the republican members of the Legislature" were for Marcy and that there was no individual "more acceptable . . . [or] better qualified for the office." It added, however, that although he was the sort of man who would not refuse a summons to duty, he did not personally wish to be a candidate, not having had time as yet to master his role as senator. "In making these remarks we but express the wishes of Judge Marcy," the paper added. Three days after, it hoisted to its masthead the names of Jackson and Van Buren as candidates for president and vice president. The rejection of Van Buren as minister to England had occurred in the interim. While this first mention was in the nature of a trial balloon, on April 12 Webb's paper went further. It called openly for a nomination of Marcy as governor. It conceded that the January proposal had been made without his consent, but declared that he was now considered

---

[7] Statement of Henry Wikoff, who had talked to them both on the subject; *The Adventures of a Roving Diplomatist,* New York, 1857, 291-293.

[8] *Courier & Enquirer,* Sept. 25, 1845; diary, June 27, 1833, M.P.

[9] Cf. the resolutions of the Albany bar at the time of his death, which singled out especially for praise his "high unbending integrity"; *Journal,* July 9, 1857.

the only man who could preserve party solidarity. After some general praise, the editorial went on to say that he would "revive and cherish the great system of internal improvements" and "respect and foster the interests of the south western counties," which included the Chenango area. The paper also asserted that it had asked him if he was willing to run and had learned that he would make the necessary sacrifice of his senatorial seat if the party required him to. Other Democratic journals were asked to join in this move.

As has been said, Marcy did not admit that he wanted a gubernatorial nomination, particularly at the hands of the *Courier & Enquirer*. He did write a letter to Benjamin F. Butler, on April 22, in which he rather intimated that he had earlier said he would be willing to accept a nomination if made under the proper circumstances. Only a few persons, however, can have known of this.[10]

The reaction of New York state Democrats to the newspaper's move was at least rather mixed. At Lockport, Lot Clark acknowledged that "Doubtless it would be better for us if you were quickly seated in the gubernatorial chair," but feared that before Marcy got there much ill will would have been produced in certain sectors of the party. Clark also doubted whether Marcy could with dignity accept such an "Irish hoist" from Webb. Other persons, such as Flagg and Churchill C. Cambreleng, an influential New York City congressman, would only say that the problem could be handled best at the state convention and that perhaps the election would be an easy one after all, i.e. that there might be no great difficulty in re-electing Throop. As for Croswell, he wrote privately to Marcy that Throop ought to be retained; he even suggested suavely that Marcy write a letter to that effect to some person at Albany. In the *Argus,* he said merely that Webb was "raising some topic" to divert attention from the bank affair.[11] This was not being very courteous to Marcy.

As time went on, however, there was a slow development of support. Aside from approval of his record as a public servant, there was

---

[10] Butler Papers, Princeton. Cf. also Bennett's despatch to *Courier & Enquirer,* issue of Apr. 24, and Marcy to Dix, Apr. 27, Dix Coll., Columbia University.

[11] Clark to Marcy, April 10, M.P.; Cambreleng to Hoyt, Mar. 15, in Mackenzie, *Butler & Hoyt,* 101, and Flagg to Hoyt, Mar. 26, 1832, in Mackenzie, *Van Buren,* 173; Croswell to Marcy, April 9, 1832, M.P.; *Courier & Enquirer,* Feb. 16, quoting *Argus.*

the feeling that his comparative remoteness from state politics in the past three years would help him to be a leader of the whole party, aloof from the schism which had arisen between the Throopites and non-Throopites.[12] The Chenango canal interest, moreover, was much pleased. When, in April, moreover, Governor Throop declared that he would not run again, Marcy's stock rose greatly. Throop's declaration was soon offset, however, by the public knowledge of large loans which had been made to the *Courier & Enquirer* in the past year by Mr. Biddle's bank. This was a grave disclosure. The result was that Marcy now began to behave even more cautiously, backing water with might and main. By this time, on the other hand, a number of the leaders in the state had come to see that his nomination might be necessary. A delegation was therefore sent to Washington to get him to promise not to persist in declining, for the present. This he did.[13] Under this *modus operandi,* discussion continued all through the summer, with the elements that composed the normal majority of the party gradually swinging to him. Marcy endeavored to encourage that trend. On his way home from Washington at the end of the session he travelled through the critical Chenango country, ostensibly because of the cholera at New York City, and while there doubtless showed approval of the canal so much desired there; he was still outwardly against being nominated.[14] When Webb, after a long period of growing cool towards the party, finally come out for the opposition, lowering the Jackson-Van Buren-Marcy banner, the whole problem was clarified. This was on August 23. The Regency's lieutenants now did not hesitate to declare themselves openly for Marcy. When the convention met on September 19, therefore, there was hardly a contest.[15]

Marcy's conscience must have troubled him that summer, however, as he thought of his deception of his close associates. So, too, with his yielding of his old opposition to a Chenango canal, which project was now becoming a political inevitability.[16] It is revealing that the one

[12] Jenkins, *Life of Silas Wright,* 79.

[13] Marcy to Hoyt, June 3, in Mackenzie, *Butler & Hoyt,* 112.

[14] Hammond, II, 422; *Journal,* July 27; Dix to Flagg, Aug. 16, F.P.

[15] Cf. the *Evening Post,* Aug. 23; *Argus,* Sept. 21, in semi-weekly of 25th; on the first ballot, Marcy had 113 out of 119 votes.

[16] For its inevitability, Hammond, II, 422.

example of a gift or gifts by him to charity which was mentioned after his death was in behalf of the cholera sufferers at Albany at this
time. Very privately he made repeated donations through the minister
of the church which he attended.[17]

In the ensuing campaign, he and his fellow Democrats were confronted for the first time by a coalition of both of the conservative
groups in the state, the National Republicans and the Antimasons.
These two elements had already united for governor upon Francis
Granger, who was a wealthy young man of considerable charm but no
great ability. The address of the Democratic convention, written by
Silas Wright, made much of the diversity in the enemy ranks, calling
them "a compound of contradictions" and added adroitly that Granger "fits them all." It contrasted his "aristocratic family" and "im-
mense fortune" with the career of Marcy, who was described as "a
democrat without variableness or shadow of turning" and was lauded
as a self-made man.

The campaign was a hot one. Jackson had issued a flaming veto of
the bank recharter bill, shrewdly written to appeal to the sentiment of
the masses, and had thus provided the central issue. The opposition,
which regarded the bank as the keystone of the American economy,
was quick to take up the challenge and worked frantically to defeat
his re-election. The vice-presidential race of Van Buren also aroused
its ire.

The conservatives soon realized, however, that it would be difficult
to combat the popular appeal of the president or his veto and the al-
lure of Van Buren as a native son, and instead shifted much of their
fire to Marcy.[18] His utterance upon the "spoils" had made him a convenient target, while a minor and harmless indescretion or blunder of
his, when found out, was destined to make him an even better one.
Thurlow Weed, the editor of the *Albany Evening Journal* and the
bellwether of the enemy press, sounded the signal from the start, taking his own view of the "comfortable living" which the Democratic
platform had credited Marcy with earning for himself. Weed affected

---

[17] Sermon of Rev. B. T. Welch, reported in *Journal*, July 14, 1857.

[18] Cf. A. B. Johnson to Marcy, Nov. 10, 1832 (M.P.), on the "inveteracy" which
existed towards Marcy during the campaign and the "mode of warfare" waged
against him.

to relish Marcy's nomination hugely, arguing that it would offer an unerring test of the power of the Regency, that "club of political demagogues." In these years when he was fighting the Regency, his public comments upon them were unlike those which he was to make in his autobiography, fifty years after. As his paper said on September 21:

Marcy is a politician by trade. His sole reliance, for support, has ever been upon the "Spoils of Office." From the first moment that he set foot upon our pavement, his bread and his meat have been obtained from the Public Treasury. . . .

Later he asserted that since 1813 Marcy had drawn $38,000 from the public till. Another constant object of enemy salvoes was the aforementioned sandbar in the Hudson, the removal of which had been provided for in the bill which Marcy had voted against a few months earlier. His opponents joked that since vessels often went aground upon the bar the best solution would be to elect Granger governor and anchor Marcy there as a warning to shipping; the spot was dubbed "Marcy's Farm." As a sort of reply to the Democratic criticism of the central bank, Weed and company talked of Marcy's connection with Mr. Knower and thus with the Mechanics' and Farmers' Bank, which was described alarmingly as "the great financial engine of the Regency" and blown up into a fearsome bogey.[19]

The most effective single point of attack, however, materialized when Thurlow Weed dug up from the printed state records Marcy's account of his expenses while holding the special court for the Masonic trials. Marcy had been comptroller just before that time and as such had inveighed against officials who did not turn in their charges for expenses in a detailed form, since the lumping of items was frequently a cloak for fraud. As a judge, he had himself determined to hand in model accounts.[20] His claims for expenses had been reasonable, and they had been largely for travel, "Phillips' bill for board," and similar needs. He had also gone into detail on such items as "mem. book for expenses . . . $.25" and "baggage . . . 40." Then, unfortunately, had appeared that fatally vulnerable entry: "mending work done to pantaloons . . .50." Weed paraded this bill under the giant heading of "spoils," and added gleefully: "Here is the bill of a

---

[19] *Journal,* Sept. 20, 21, Oct. 24.
[20] Marcy to Hoyt, Oct. 16, in Mackenzie, *Butler & Hoyt,* 111,

man who lives on 'spoils,' and what a precious exhibition of meanness and rapacity, it is!" He made no mention of the well-known inadequacy of a judge's salary and in fact pretended that the compensation was princely.[21]

To Marcy's opponents, Weed's "hit" was utterly delightful. It was exactly the sort of thing which would catch the ear of the masses. They made the most of it, while the *Argus* and other Democratic sheets for a long time were stumped for effective replies. Marcy himself wrote to Jesse Hoyt at New York that his foes would "have their laugh," and added "I feared no danger for I knew no sin," but in truth he was disturbed. He supplied Hoyt with an account of his military exploits on the St. Regis in 1812 for publication in friendly newspapers, hoping that this would help. A much better retort was his sarcastic thrust at Weed over an expense account that the latter had himself once submitted. Weed had gone off to fetch Elisha Adams as a witness in the Morgan affair and for the purpose had gone to Auburn, Governor Throop's home. This was to get Throop to make out an official requisition upon the governor of Vermont, in which state Adams had taken refuge. He had afterwards billed New York state for the cost of the trip to Auburn. Marcy readily conceded the propriety of "transporting" Weed to the place, which was the location of the state prison, and said that it was cheap at the price![22]

The onslaught continued, however. One writer for the *Journal,* alluding to the "britches bill," called it perhaps unfair to urge this argument "*a posteriori*," but surmised that the damage to the breeches might have been caused by a fall over the rocks surrounding the mill sites which Knower and the others possessed at Lockport. After all, he asked mischievously, had the editor considered the economy of electing a governor whose clothes had *already* been mended at the public expense? At Rochester, an opposition town, a fifty-foot pole was erected in the main street to display to onlookers a huge pair of patched black trousers.[23] The Democrats, however, had on their side

---

[21] *Journal,* Oct. 11, citing "State of New York to William L. Marcy, Dr. to expenses holding special court at Lockport in June, 1830."

[22] *Argus,* Oct. 12, 13; Marcy to Hoyt, Oct. 16, cited above; Weed, *op. cit.,* 454-455.

[23] *Journal,* Oct. 13; H. B. Stanton, *Random Recollections,* 25.

not only Jackson and the veto but an enthusiastic and superbly organized party.

In the first important test of the campaign, the Albany charter election on September 25, the hostile coalition showed great power, although the Democrats protested that huge sums had been spent to procure this result. On October 1, Marcy wrote to Hoyt that they would probably lose the state:[24]

The U.S. Bank is in the field, and I cannot but fear the effect of 50 or 100 thousand dollars expended in conducting the election in such a city as New York. I have great confidence in the honesty of the people, but it will not withstand all temptations. The corruption of some leads to the deception of many. . . .

Though I speak so discouragingly of the result, I do not doubt, if money could be kept out of use, we should beat them. But it will not. Yet great efforts without money may save us.

I hope those efforts will be made in New York. . . .

He then added:

My advice is—don't Bet your money, but spend it, as far as you legally can, to promote the election. We are all determined to deserve success, and do not despair of getting it.

When the polls opened on November 5, there was still much pessimism, but the results proved to be heartening even from the first. The final count showed that Marcy won by about eleven thousand votes out of a total of some three hundred thousand. He ran somewhat behind Jackson. Significantly, however, he carried the southern tier of counties, including Chenango.[25]

In the following spring, according to an anecdote told years after by H. B. Stanton, Marcy was riding in a coach over a very rough road in western New York. When the vehicle hit a particularly bad spot, the driver cried: "Now ladies and gentlemen, hold on tight, for this is the very hole where Governor Marcy tore his breeches." The governor paid for the dinners at the next tavern![26]

But that was looking ahead. Meanwhile, in the weeks after his election, Marcy had begun to make the various arrangements that were

---

[24] F. P. Blair to Van Buren, Sept. 30, V.B.P.; *Journal*, Sept. 26; Marcy to Hoyt, Oct. 1, Mackenzie, *Butler & Hoyt*, 112-113.

[25] *Journal*, Nov. 7-20, *passim*.

[26] Stanton, *op. cit.*, 25.

called for prior to his inauguration, which would come on New Year's Day. He chose as his residence a house at number two Elk Street, "the street of the governors," facing across the park towards the capitol. It was one of a row built wall-to-wall, but was a roomy house, the hallway and parlors on the first floor being well adapted to receiving large numbers of people. On the front there was an iron balcony from which a governor could conveniently acknowledge the traditional Fourth of July serenades.[27] Marcy had no intention of living in a lavish style as New York's chief executive—in contrast to his successor, the spendthrift William H. Seward[28]—but he found his new rank costly enough as it was. By May 4, 1833, including various charges prior to his inauguration, he was to find that he had spent a full $5,000, which was $1,000 more than his entire salary for a year.[29]

Choosing personnel for his administration was no very great trouble, for his power of appointment was chiefly in connection with the militia. One choice only is worthy of comment, that of Horatio Seymour, a young lawyer of Utica, as his military secretary. It was the beginning of a notable political friendship.[30] As to the more important state officers, who were chosen by the legislature, Marcy had every reason to be well satisfied. Azariah Flagg, the new comptroller, and John A. Dix, who took the latter's old seat as secretary of state, were both very admirable men, able, zealous, and clean-handed to the last degree. Greene C. Bronson, the attorney general, and Edwin Croswell, the state printer, who were the other chief members of the group, were likewise persons of marked ability. "The Governor is fortunate in his counsellors and rich in the morality of his staff," conceded Gorham A. Worth, a New York City banker, who really belonged to the opposition.

The Regency, take them all in all, are not so d - - - - d profligate as the Whigs represent them. Flag [sic] is to be sure a radical in grain, but then he has sense, and I believe *some* principle. Dix belongs to the *clean shirt* party of the Democracy, and is quite a gentlemanly Loco Foco. Croswell is

---

[27] *City Directory*, 1833-1834. It is now the residence of Mrs. Charles E. McElroy. In the 1837-1838 and 1838-1839 directories, however, he was listed as at 81 and then 58 North Pearl Street.

[28] F. W. Seward, *Memoir of William H. Seward*, I, 381-382, 650.

[29] Diary, May 4, 1833, M.P.

[30] Horatio Seymour, *D.A.B.; Evening Post*, Jan. 8, 1833.

a plausible dog, and can tell a *thumper* with more art & address, & with a graver face than any one of the editorial corps of my acquaintance—He turns a compliment too devilish well, and for a sly touch under the ribs there is no one like him.

It was a just appraisal, if allowance was made for Worth's dislike of Jacksonian democracy. The party was also in extraordinarily good shape; Judge Hammond was to comment that perhaps none had ever been better organized.[31] With the United States steadily more prosperous and the sun of Jackson's popularity casting its rays upon the political scene, the auguries were for a successful administration.

---

[31] Worth to Marcy, Oct. 16, 1838, M.P. There had been no important changes in personnel by then; Hammond, II, 429-430.

VII. THE BANK WAR OF '34 AND
A QUIET INTERLUDE

"the Loan Law . . . without any step towards its execution,
has effectually dispelled alarm, restored confidence, and frustrated the efforts of the Bank of the United States. . . ." (the
State Democratic Platform, September, 1834[1])

ALTHOUGH the issue of banking—and its twin, the currency
question—was to run as a *leitmotif* through Marcy's years as
governor, the first great national question was the old issue of the
tariff, which came up in the very month he entered office, i.e. in
January, 1833. What happened on this foreshadowed rather boldly
his increasing conservatism.

The situation was that the much disputed tariff of the past year had
run into grave opposition in the South; the state of South Carolina
had in fact declared it null and void. President Jackson and the federal government as a whole, on the other hand, had determined to
resist such noncompliance. And Marcy, who had worked hard to get
the bill adopted, fully upheld the president. In his first annual message, of January 2, 1833, presumably written after consultation with
Van Buren, Marcy held that Carolina's course was "fatally repug-
nant" to the cherished purposes of the constitution; he added that
"substantial relief to every real grievance" should be given her, but
he said that the protective idea should not be given up. The legislature followed his lead, in resolutions which Van Buren himself
framed.

When the question of appeasing the South was debated in congress, however, Marcy used his influence to prevent any drastic
changes. "I went to Washington a friend of protection and I came
home a friend of protection," he had written a few months earlier.
In addition, he was doubtless influenced by the plight which his
father-in-law had fallen into, for Mr. Knower's dealings in wool had
brought the old gentleman to the very verge of bankruptcy. What

---

[1] *Argus*, Sept. 13.

was more, Mr. Knower was moving heaven and earth to prevent any reductions in the wool duties, lest the price in some way be affected. On January 24, for example, a great meeting was held at Albany for this purpose, called by him. Since Marcy in general was on his side in this tariff matter and since three of the other Regency chiefs, Flagg, Dix, and Butler, led a secession of most of the persons at the meeting and assembled them into a rival gathering which took a contrary course, the tension within the Regency can well be imagined. One sequel was a rather sharp exchange of letters between Marcy and Van Buren.

Apart from putting a strain on the Regency, Marcy's conservatism was also criticized because it helped the opponents of the Jackson administration to secure greater tariff cuts than the president and his party wanted. This in turn permitted South Carolina to win something of a victory. A by-product of the agitation at Albany was a new defeat for Butler, incidentally; Butler was seeking the United States senatorship, but found that his rival was aided by Knower and the other protectionists.[2] These were serious matters.

To return to the banking problems, the first fact to note is that during the summer of 1833 President Jackson decided that it was time to remove all federal moneys from the great bank. He considered that his reelection constituted a mandate to him to bring that institution to an end without delay. Marcy was not consulted in the affair. He was away at the time, but if he had been asked he would probably have suggested waiting until the president could broach the subject in his annual message, as Van Buren and Wright advised. Before all such proposals were turned in, however, and as early as August 12, Jackson had made up his mind to start the program quickly. On that same day, oddly enough, the Bank began its counter-policy, which was to curtail its credits drastically. Although it later averred that its intention was to increase its cash reserves, in the face of its forthcoming dissolution, the real plan was to create a general business depres-

---

[2] Charles Z. Lincoln, ed., *State of New York, Messages from the Governors,* Albany, 1909, vol. 3 (hereafter referred to as *Messages*), 420-421, 427-429; Marcy to D. Cushman, Sept. 22, 1832, copy, M.P.; Van Buren, *Autobiography,* 549-552, 562-563; Flagg to Wright, Jan. 24, Feb. 13, F.P.; *Argus,* Jan. 26; Wright to Van Buren, Jan. 29, Marcy to Van Buren, Feb. 13, V.B.P.; Hammond, II, 432-433.

sion, with the aim to force the government to stop the removals. The result was a desperate struggle between it and the administration. Pressure was exerted notably upon the state banks. By January, the shortage of credits was so serious that rates on loans were as high as three percent per month, which caused many firms to fail and led to some unemployment.

Although Marcy stated in his second annual message, of January, 1834, that the great bank could not really put the banks of the state to "a severe trial," affairs went from bad to worse.[3] For Mr. Knower, the crisis was soon reached. Just before this happened, however, namely on January 29, Marcy endorsed some notes for him, only to learn soon after that Mr. Knower had directed them to Biddle's bank for discount! This was too much for the governor, who wrote post haste to "Old Nick" Biddle that:

In the present aspect of political affairs connected as they are with the deposite question and the renewal of the Charter of the U.S. Bank I should have declined endorsing the notes or drafts, if I had known that they were to be presented to the U.S. Bank. I have been long opposed to that institution and never more so than at this time, and I could not therefore consistently with my ideas of propriety do any thing (while the present controversy concerning it is going on) which should look like asking a favor from it even for a friend.

He therefore asked Biddle to cancel his endorsements, adding out of justice to Mr. Knower that he did not "take this step from fear of pecuniary responsibility." As it turned out, the notes were returned without being discounted, because the bank had learned that Knower was totally unable to meet his cash obligations. Knower was reported to be so situated as to count upon paying his debts in full, in time, and even to expect "a handsome property" left over, but it was a distressing period for the governor. He felt embarrassed both personally and politically. On the first count, he had to cope with the old gentleman himself, who had fallen into a bad state of hypochondria, and to try, despite that, to get the latter's affairs in order. Secondly, of course, he was charged with letting his public policy be influenced by this; it was suggested, among other things, that he was likely to become a

---

[3] Wright to Van Buren, Aug. 28, Jackson Papers, L.C.; Van Buren to Jackson, Sept. 4, V.B.P.; Catterall, *op. cit.,* 314-325; *Messages,* 476.

bankrupt himself.[4] When he acted in the crisis, however, it was for other reasons than these.

As banking and credit affairs had deteriorated further, there had come demands from many businessmen and even from some of the more conservative members of Marcy's party that the Bank's charter be renewed. There was also a proposal from some interested persons in New York City that the state should itself give a charter to a great rival bank there, to take over the functions of Mr. Biddle's institution. But the sentiment of the Democracy, both in New York and across the country, was beginning to stiffen. There were loyalty meetings held in the principal cities. And, in the middle of February, when a merchant wrote a letter in criticism of Jackson's policy, Marcy hotly penned the following:

> I must question its [the letter's] soundness or your candour, if by saying that the distress of the money market is the consequence of the removal of the deposits you mean to be understood that it is the necessary consequence. . . . The bank is the sole cause of the distress and can in a single day remove it. It has now more funds than it uses . . . why therefore give it the government deposits to enable it to lock them also from the public. . . . Why not turn your indignation against that corrupt and tyrranical [sic] institution which perverts the power to destroy, which was given to it to aid & support. . . . You (I mean the national merchants) kiss the hand that chastizes you and ask the Government to overlook its enormous corruption and surrender the liberties of the country to an unfeeling monster & Tyrant.

By the end of the winter, Marcy and the other Democratic leaders had begun a definite counter-attack. In Pennsylvania, which had hitherto supported the Bank, Governor Wolf dealt it a crippling blow in a powerful message on February 26; soon after, most Pennsylvania Democrats arrayed themselves against it. The policy of New York's state administration was, first, to ease the situation for the country banks—by letting the Albany banks, with which the former dealt, have freer use of the canal fund deposits. Then, when the banks of the metropolis got into straits, Marcy came forward with the boldest plan of his career.

On March 24, Marcy sent to the legislature a terse and pointed message indicting the great bank for its work in creating the distress;

---

[4] To Biddle, Jan. 30, 1834, H.S.P.A.; *Argus,* Feb. 4, *E. Post,* Feb. 10, Nov. 1; Van Buren to G. A. Worth, Feb. 28, V.B.P.

he added that the New York banks had been particularly singled out for attack. He therefore asked for a state bond issue of four or five million dollars, to be loaned "if necessary" to the metropolitan banks. Clearly anticipating a charge that he was partial to the latter, he commented that the state banking commissioners had reported that the country banks were sound and he explained that the institutions at the metropolis would in any case have to bear the brunt of the attack; he noted that the measure would permit them to work for "the relief of the whole community." He went on to say that the state's banks should be allowed to increase their discounts.

This scheme, which in part represented a plan to head off a renewed drive for the establishment of a rival "monster" at New York,[5] at once met with hearty general approval. Van Buren praised it, while the Little Magician's son, "Prince John," privately paid Marcy the compliment of indulging in a little furtive speculation in the stock market, sure that business would soon recover. More to the point, the legislature authorized what Marcy wanted.

There were some doubts as to whether the act could ever give much relief, for it provided no scrip or legal tender and relied solely upon the possibility of selling the bonds for cash. As it happened, however, the Bank itself could also read the signs. Very soon after Marcy's message, its directors voted to put off any further contraction. This not only permitted the state banks to consolidate their positions but made it inevitable that the Philadelphia institution must in time yield. And this was what happened; in July, the directors voted to begin expanding loans once more. Meanwhile, business had begun to revive everywhere.[6]

If the message had also been written to ward off a defeat for the party in the spring election at New York, on the other hand, it was in that respect a failure. Throughout the three tumultuous days of polling, in fact, the opposition made Marcy's loan policy one of the chief targets; it was commonly termed a scheme to "mortgage" the state's credit, present and future, to the monied institutions. When the autumn came, however, the result was different if the methods were

---

[5] T. Suffern to Van Buren, Jan. 12, *ibid.;* Marcy to (?), Feb. 18, not sent, M.P.; Catterall, *op. cit.,* 339-340; *Argus,* Mar. 20; *Messages,* 483-492.

[6] *Journal,* Jan. 8, 1835; Van Buren to Marcy, Mar. 31, A.D., V.B.P.; John Van Buren to Hoyt, Mar. 22, *Butler & Hoyt,* 60; *Argus,* Apr. 1, 26; Catterall, *op. cit.,* 344, 348.

not. Although some dissatisfied Democrats and the old combination of the National Republicans and Antimasons coalesced to form the Whig Party, as also occurred elsewhere in the United States, and although Thurlow Weed again unearthed a useful campaign item, in the bank stock purchases of Marcy and other Regency heads in the bank distributions of 1831-1832,[7] Marcy won a sweeping victory. He carried even Albany and Rensselaer counties. He was aided in this by the small appeal of his opponent, for the Whigs put up William H. Seward, a young Auburn lawyer who had performed well in the state senate but was politically immature and not well known.

The question of chartering a central bank was now settled once and for all, which permitted Marcy and his associates to enter a period of profound quiet, politically. The people's love of Jackson, more than ever "the Old Hero," and the position of the Democracy as the savior of the nation from the "villain of Chestnut Street" set the party at the very flood tide of its strength. In this feeling Marcy of course shared. Even more helpful, while it lasted, was the boom prosperity which had enveloped the country at the close of the recent bank war. For the next two or three years, indeed, there were phenomenally flush times. In consequence, few people were inclined to criticize either the state or the federal governments. This political quiet was observable even in the presidential election year of 1836, when Marcy was nominated for a third time. As he wrote to Wetmore in July of that year: "I have never known a political calm at a period so near an important election." Nor did Jesse Buel, the Whig candidate, who edited an agricultural paper, do much to disturb things. Marcy was reelected by a margin of over 29,000 votes, the largest he ever enjoyed. What was also agreeable was that Van Buren was elected president. It was a splendid outcome. Yet, as Marcy had shown in his recent annual messages, the spirit of speculation had gone dangerously far, so that the prevalent prosperity was increasingly somewhat spurious. In addition, there was a growing rift in the party at New York City, because of deep seated discontent over the inflation and the often much depreciated bank money. There were to be difficulties ahead.

[7] *Assem. doc. no. 89, 1833, passim.* For more on the investments of the state's political leaders, see Ivor D. Spencer, "William L. Marcy Goes Conservative," *Miss. Valley Hist. Rev.*, Sept. 1944, 214-215.

VIII. THE PANIC OF 1837 SWEEPS OUT THE PARTY

"There is a terrible panic in the market. . . . All eyes are directed to Albany." (New York *Evening Post*, May 5, 11, 1837)

WITH the removal of the restraining hand of the Bank of the United States, the growing boom of the 1830's had little to check it. State banks enjoyed their very heyday. They were chartered more freely than ever and they issued paper money at a rising clip. Similarly, great projects of internal improvement, both public and private, trod their proud paths across the stage. The real estate business was likewise more active than previously, entire "lithographic cities" being created almost overnight. Factories also mushroomed up. Along with these booming developments in business as such, moreover, there was also a new trend in the way in which enterprise was to be organized. The fact was that promoters of every sort were asking that they be allowed to set up corporations, which had hitherto been reserved chiefly for banking and insurance. Since the charters needed for such firms could be had, as yet, only *via* special acts of legislatures, the pressure upon the members of such bodies, both at Albany and elsewhere, increased very greatly. After the session of 1836 at Albany, for example, Comptroller Flagg wrote sadly that "the corruption of a Senator . . . to the vision of a majority of the Senate, appeared to be a very harmless matter."

The greatest weakness of the time, however, was in that state banking which the Democrats had now so largely liberated. Provided that the men who desired to set up a bank could get a charter—from the legislature—they could at once enjoy great profits. There were generally no requirements as to specie reserves and there was little in the way of inspection by public officials. The promoters simply hired an engraver to make some attractive plates and then ran off thousands and thousands of paper dollars. This was all clear profit. In addition, there were the usual earnings to be had from lending. And here again there was ground for complaint, because the loans were made too extensively to the members of the inner circle and often for enterprises which were not in any sense liquid and which were hence more properly subjects for investment banking than for commercial banks. In New York, the only worthwhile state restrictions were those provided through the safety fund, which had been set up by a levy of a small sum from each bank to create a state reserve to back up the paper notes of any weak members of the system. While the state's banks were generally passably sound, neither they nor the safety fund system were strong enough for periods of crisis. Beyond this, the notes of banks in the western states also circulated; these were often quite unreliable and were always at a discount.

In the face of these problems, which were soon to produce political commotions fully as serious as the battle with Biddle, William L. Marcy was to take a moderately conservative stand. His conservatism was genuine and had many sources. He was growing older, reaching fifty in 1836, and in his more relaxed moments he often felt very tired, indeed aged. His judicious temperament and his years of experience with the Regency had made him politically cautious. His association with his father-in-law, moreover, had wedded him, *via* Cornelia, increasingly to the aspirations of the established bankers (the "monopolists," as critics called them) and of the speculators. Aside from this, there were his bank stock purchases—to say nothing of the far larger purchases of bank stocks made by some of his political associates. Marcy himself, by the way, was beginning to dabble in western real estate, also.

Beyond such ties of self-interest as these, Marcy was influenced indubitably by his personal friends. He had the counsel of some of the best liberals of the era, in Flagg and Dix of his own state cabinet and in Silas Wright and Churchill C. Cambreleng, both of whom were at Washington. Yet the truth is that he increasingly did not listen to these men. Instead, he turned more and more to a new friend. This was Prosper Montgomery Wetmore, who became his close companion and correspondent (more especially the latter) soon after the start of the governorship; Wetmore had been paymaster general of the militia, a rather nominal sort of office, under Governor Throop, and Marcy retained him in that post. Mainly, Wetmore was a businessman, a merchant in downtown New York, but it was the other sides of his life which appealed to Marcy especially. He was a poet of some considerable repute, a point which made him highly congenial to the governor, and was also a patron of the arts. His modest and affectionate nature was also very attractive. With him, Marcy could unbosom himself without restraint and could find relief from his pressing duties, for Wetmore always enjoyed and praised his comments upon literary and cultural matters and upon the passing scene in general.

In return, the many sided Wetmore, amateur politician as well as amateur of the arts, was increasingly Marcy's consultant upon public affairs. And Wetmore was hardly a liberal. A disliker of the mob, he was to be revolted at some of the scenes at Van Buren's inauguration. Instinctively, he preferred men of means, like himself; when he discussed a certain applicant for office, for instance, he condemned him not merely because he was "a pot house companion of our party rowdies" but also because he was "not worth five hundred dollars in the world." And his influence was to be important. As far as that went, Marcy's other personal friends of the era were also conservative. Congressman Albert Gallup, lawyer John P. Cushman, politician Abijah Mann, banker Gorham A. Worth, and Peter Wendell, his doctor—these were all conservatives, many of them deeply such. And if none of them had so much influence with Marcy as Wetmore did, they all pulled him in the same direction.[1]

With his outlook increasingly one of moderation, Marcy's approach to the reform of the state's banking system was a predictable one. He set his course squarely between the Scylla and Charybdis of wildcat inflation and of a violent, unreasoning opposition to the credit system. Far from opposing the existing system of a limited number of banks—limited by the difficulties of getting charters—he set himself to reform it. In his annual message of 1834 he laid down his program:

Our business transactions [he said] have been so long conducted by means of bank credits, and by the use of a paper currency, that this course has become firmly settled, and, if it were desirable, it would be scarcely possible, to change its direction.

Nonetheless, he reasoned, the granting of charters to one group and

---

[1] On Marcy's conservatism, see Ivor D. Spencer, cited above; on Wetmore, see Ivor D. Spencer, "William L. Marcy, 'an Educated Northern Democrat,'" *New York History,* Apr., 1941, 187-189, and Wetmore to Marcy, Mar. 19, Apr. 3, 1837, M.P.

not to another was unfair. Discussing a number of alternative cor-
rectives for this situation, he argued that the best solution was to appoint state commissioners to see to it that the shares of stock in a new
bank should be widely and rightly distributed. These should be persons who lived outside of the county where the new bank was to be
located; they should also be disqualified temporarily from any connection with it. More important, he asked for safeguards as to the number or capital of new banks created and as to the volume of notes
which they might issue. These steps were called for, he said, to protect the public against "seasons of great commercial revulsion and
general embarrassment."

"In the course of events, such seasons will come, and the increase of banks
may be one of the causes that will contribute to their recurrence; and when
they do come, it will certainly be the cause of aggravating the severity of
the public distress."

He asked therefore that the legislature be slow to grant new charters.
He also requested that, in the case of new banks, the charters limit the
note issue to amounts equal to the capital stock. Such a rule should
also be applied gradually to the older banks. A year later, he asked
that there also be limits on the creation of deposit credit.[2]

It was a good program; had it been accompanied by a strong specie-
reserve requirement, it might have worked fairly well. Unfortunately,
the legislature did not adopt it. Not only were the restrictions which
he advocated not written into the new charters, but scores of new
banks were created. Since bills for these latter had to have a two-thirds
majority of all elected members of both houses, anyway, Marcy could
do little to check them, for vetoes could have been overridden easily.
The only success he had was in securing commissioners to distribute
the new stocks.

What came instead of the moderate reforms which he had proposed were several radical changes, which did not originate with him.
The first great step was an attempt to outlaw bank notes of less than
five dollars. This was an idea not favored by Marcy at the outset but
sponsored by the Jackson administration and supported in New York
state for some time by men of both parties. The hope was that by
barring small notes a void would be created, which would attract

---

[2] *Messages,* 469-476, and (for 1835) 519.

specie from other states and from abroad, and that thereby the currency would acquire a sounder basis. The New York legislature pondered the idea in its 1834 session and then called upon Marcy to investigate the possibilities. In his annual message of 1835, Marcy gave the plan his full blessing, saying that it would relieve the laboring classes from payment in bills that were worth less than their face value and would stabilize the currency by lessening the contractions and expansions to which paper was liable. He emphasized, however, the need for carrying out the project gradually. It should be done by successive denominations, he pointed out, to avoid hardship for the people or the banks; he added that the notes of other states should be banned. The legislature responded with a suitable act, which applied the policy fully by September 1 of 1836.[3]

Meanwhile, some elements in the party were pressing a much more radical demand—the total abolition of the "monopoly" system—so that anyone would be free to set up a bank. The reason, of course, was in the undemocratic character of the practice of giving charters to some but not to others; there was also objection to the corruption which the older method sometimes entailed. During the year 1835, this plan was widely adopted among the Democratic leaders at New York. When the conservatives attempted to suppress it, at a meeting at Tammany Hall, by turning out the gas lights, the radicals were found prepared. They struck the new "loco-foco" (strike-anywhere) matches and lighted candles with which they had provided themselves. They thus added a new term to the state's already luxuriant political nomenclature. Besides favoring such "free banking," these "loco-focos" also hoped for an elimination of paper money entirely.

Although Marcy's program was far sounder, in view of the lack of a central bank and of specie requirements, the loco-foco ideas spread rapidly. By the end of the legislature of 1836, which had been unruly and at times corrupt, Marcy and his Regency associates had decided that they must go part of the way towards free banking. The plan was to allow financiers to engage freely in receiving deposits and discounting loans, while not granting the privilege of note issue. The *Argus* came out for this in May, a number of county conventions of the party followed suit, and in September the state convention did likewise.

[3] *Messages,* 516-519, 519n.; *Laws . . . 58th session,* ch. 46, pp. 37-38.

Meanwhile, the Whigs, in great part, had swung over to wholly free banking. These party commitments to an extent explained the fact that late in 1836 Marcy was converted to the discount and deposit program. But his shift had other factors behind it, also. For one thing, his health was poor. In addition, he recently had been obliged to take full charge, once again, of the disordered affairs of Mr. Knower, and had found it necessary to raise $120,000 to keep things afloat. Undoubtedly these circumstances contributed to his turning to what was essentially an inflationary line.[4]

In contrast to his annual message of 1836, which had contained a stern warning against the easy money trends of the day, Marcy in his 1837 message reasoned that credit had grown dangerously tight and called for a loosening of the restraints upon it. He was undoubtedly correct in his assumption as to the state of credit, for business had developed so fantastically that it had carried the banks and financiers to just about the breaking point. To those who knew, and Marcy was one of them, it was all too apparent that something would have to give way, if a serious economic setback was to be avoided; for one thing, the financial institutions, the very heart of the economy, might be ruined. But while Marcy was correct in his feeling of alarm, the measure which he now advocated as a corrective was ill-advised. For what he was suggesting was that more air be blown up into the bubble and the sides be stretched thinner. In contrast, President Jackson had in the past year demanded that all payments made at the public land offices be in gold, as a means of curbing the inflationary tendencies. Significantly, Marcy passed over the heads of Comptroller Flagg and the other rather agrarian advisers of his state cabinet and consulted instead the business-minded Jesse Hoyt of New York City. Hoyt may have written the substance of some of the document's passages.[5]

The banks chartered at the last session, Marcy pointed out, had had "no agency in preventing and very little in removing" the pressure upon the money market. It was upon this ground that he asked that the discount and deposit business be made free to all! He pointed out, as a sop to the cautious, that there was a distinction between such

[4] Flagg to Van Buren, May 27, 1836, V.B.P.; *Argus,* May 25, Sept. 16; Flagg to Hoyt, Oct. 3, *Butler & Hoyt,* 116; on the Whigs, cf. Beardsley to Van Buren, Apr. 17, V.B.P.; Marcy to Wetmore, Jan. 1, Mar. 19, 1837, M.P.
[5] Marcy to Hoyt, Nov. 24, 1836, *Butler & Hoyt,* 116.

"free trade in money" and the right to issue paper notes, which were merely "a fictitious representative of money." This approached soph-istry. As a further reassurance to the opponents of his plan, he reasoned, and correctly enough, that in so far as it cut the demand for new banks of issue it would lessen the likelihood of moneyed in-fluences upon the legislature. In fact, he asked that no new banks of issue be chartered. On the other hand, he called for a repeal of the punishments for lending at above the legal rates of interest, arguing that such practices were already being indulged in.

In essence, Marcy won out. The radical Democrats, who were satis-fied with his main recommendation if not with some of his arguments, and the Whigs joined hands to carry it through. The legislature also gave up the penal clause in the usury act.[6]

Before the latter step had been taken, however, the bubble had burst and, as Marcy had anticipated, a grave panic had resulted. The terms of his warning in 1836 were all too well borne out. In the words of the latter, there were "a mutual suspicion, and its concomi-tant evil, a pecuniary pressure . . . followed by . . . a derangement of [the] circulating medium; embarrassment in trade; and numerous bankruptcies." The causes of the panic were various, but many of them are somewhat apart from our story and must be omitted. Jack-son's specie circular had in itself helped, in a way, to precipitate the crisis. Let us notice only one other factor. This was that in the past year congress had voted that all surplus federal funds be distributed to the states, technically as loans but actually as gifts. The step had deprived the banks, which had up till then been holding the moneys, of some of their needed reserves, while at the same time encouraging freer expenditure elsewhere. In New York state, for example—and upon Marcy's recommendation—the federal surplus was distributed to the counties, which made loans to their citizens. This was of course in keeping with his last-minute policy of easing credits. But whatever the causes, it was indisputable that in May of 1837 there set in the worst revulsion the country had yet had.[7]

Governor Marcy did not need to be told that the crisis had arrived. For one thing, he was having a frightful time with Mr. Knower's business. He had been obliged to pledge some of his own resources to

---

[6] *Messages,* 625-632, and footnotes.
[7] *Messages,* 557-566, 623-624.

keep the latter solvent; what was more, he had even resorted to the new county loan commissioners, and borrowed a small portion of the federal surplus.

Apart from such personal concerns, moreover, he had as governor to confront the problem created by the state banks, which had stopped specie payments. According to the terms of their charters, the banks were at once faced with the legal penalty of winding up their businesses for good. Although some radicals, such as Cambreleng, could argue that such a deflationary step would be helpful, Marcy would have none of this. He insisted that they must be granted a period of grace, and he was supported in his view by the state banking commissioners and by the business community generally. Although his cabinet was divided on the issue, and frequently bitterly, he acted quickly. He requested that the legislature allow the banks a year of grace. Although that body was also divided on the issue, moreover, he won out. It was at this time, also, that specific limits were set to note issue, as he had long ago asked, even if the limits were too liberal to have any immediate effect.[8]

As to another relief measure which was demanded, a repeal of the ban upon small bills, Marcy held firmly against it. He had admitted in his annual message that other states had not adopted the measure sufficiently and that inferior bills from out of state were being used in New York. Yet he refused to yield. As a result, no such measure was passed at the regular session; and when there was a call for the summoning of a special session for the purpose, he declined to do so. It was probably his stern stand on this question which led Silas Wright to comment that "The Governor is sound and ardent and more bold than I have ever before known him." Wright went on to say that the strain of the times had worn Marcy's temper a bit thin, causing him occasionally to speak somewhat more critically than usual of those who did not cooperate.[9]

---

[8] To Van Buren, May 25, 1837, V.B.P.; to Bancroft, June 17, Bancroft Papers; Loan Comm'r's Office Book, Albany Co. Clerk's Office, vol. B, #80; *Journal*, May 22, 24; Marcy to Wetmore, May 14, 16, M.P.; Wright to Van Buren, May 13, V.B.P.; *Laws . . . 60th session*, 514-517.

[9] W. Trimble, "Diverging Tendencies in New York Democracy in the Period of the Locofocos," *Amer. Hist. Rev.*, Apr. 1919, 406; Wright to Van Buren, May 13, V.B.P.; for an earlier comment of his on Marcy's staunchness, see letters to same, Sept. 4, 1836, *ibid.*

The reception of the period of grace was rather mixed, but generally moderates of both parties praised it. The independent *Journal of Commerce* said, for example, that Marcy had gone "with good sense and good feelings, for those measures which the public good" demanded. As for Whig criticism, Marcy did not care very much. But the scathing comments which many of the radical Democrats were making did hurt his feelings. It was largely in reply to them that he wrote to President Van Buren; this was on May 25. Alluding to Mr. Knower's difficulties, he stated that "Whatever might have [been] my own condition I do not believe I should have taken a different view of the subject." He went on to say that:

For five years as a public man I have labored to reduce our system of credit, denounced its extention [sic], & fortold [sic] the consequences of its explosion, but when the much dreaded result happened . . . it was the duty of even those who had forewarned to do what they could to mitigate those evils.

He then told the president quite frankly that any attempt of the federal government—in its own affairs—to shift to specie only, a measure which the loco-focos were asking, would in his opinion be unsuccessful. He was opposed to it, he said, just as he had shown himself opposed to a repeal of the small-bills ban; what was needed, he insisted, was a mixed currency, of bills and hard money alike. None the less, he hinted that an issue of federal notes would be helpful in getting the country through its difficulties.[10]

As the summer wore on, Marcy watched eagerly for an improvement in business, but he found none. As far as the federal government was concerned, indeed, it was almost wholly without funds, for its deposits in various state banks had been frozen as hard as the Erie Canal in midwinter. One result was a growing acceptance of the very idea against which he had warned the president, that the government should divorce itself entirely from these banks and simply keep its money in its own vaults. After his letter of May 25, Marcy wrote no more on this to the White House, but his views did not change. He held that such a scheme would be the opposite of his program of relief for the business community, for it would work to reduce the

---

[10] *Journal of Commerce*, May 16; to Van Buren, May 25, V.B.P.

banks' normal operating funds. Some other people did not keep silent, however. United States Senator Nathan P. Tallmadge attacked the proposal in a letter to the *Argus,* and addresses in the same vein were gotten up at both New York and Albany. Although Marcy had no role in the getting up of these public papers, when he travelled to the western counties in August he was pleased to observe that there was not much radicalism there; it was found chiefly at the metropolis, he wrote privately.[11]

When a special session of congress was held, early in September, and President Van Buren came out flatly for the radical scheme, Marcy therefore received a rude shock. For the Little Magician's special message declared that the government ought to rely wholly upon specie, to be kept in an independent treasury. Marcy exploded with vexation. In a two-hour talk with Benjamin F. Butler, who upheld the administration, he "uttered more and more imprudent things." Feeling that the document "made mighty men of the Locofocos," he excitedly asked if he should be expected to proclaim a divorce between the *state* and the banks, and should ask the exclusive use of coin in *state* business. When Butler replied that this was not contemplated, Marcy asked "Who then shall shield us . . . from the wrath of the loco-focos?"—how could he as governor, he asked, defend the federal program and yet refuse to support its equivalent at home? He warned Butler—and also Croswell, who was present and tended very much to agree with Marcy—that if the issue were put to a popular vote in the coming election the party would not be able to carry ten counties. Subsequently he wrote to a friendly congressman that if Comptroller Flagg had duplicated the federal course and "come forth with flourish and parade with his orders for payment of [canal] tolls [,] auction and salt duties and other public dues to this State in specie," there would have been a "torrent of discontent among the entire mass of the people as broad & deep as the Gulph [sic] Stream." He saw no reason, he added, for different policies under the two jurisdictions. He went on to say that the state banks had not had a fair trial and that to abandon them now would greatly weaken them. There was, he felt, a Jacobinical spirit abroad: "The

[11] *Argus,* June 6; to Wetmore, Aug. 18, M.P.

cry is up against the banks," he said, "and they must be surrendered to the Hideous Monster of locofocoism," which would devour next the speculators, then *"unpatriotic merchants,"* and finally all business men who were in debt.

Later Marcy cooled down somewhat and became less panicky. He also kept his criticisms more to himself, for whatever else happened he wanted very sincerely to hold the party together. He wrote a letter to the president in which he said: "I confess that I shall be brought with great reluctance, if at all, to the immediate and full application of the doctrine of divorce and the exclusive use of a metallic currency in the fiscal affairs of this state." Later, however, he set this draft aside, and when he did send off a letter, several days after, omitted most of it, saying merely that the president was "doubtless prepared for some diversity of opinion" and that he hoped that it would be no greater than Van Buren had counted upon.[12]

In the next month or two the governor was harassed in spirit as he had seldom been in his life. His health had been poor through most of that winter and spring, and the burdens of his dealings with Mr. Knower on the one hand and of his public station on the other had been almost unbearable. During the autumn, his health was no better. He had "a locofocoism—[a] foulness," as he liked to put it, in his stomach, which caused him headaches; he also was for the time being blind in one eye, and had a constantly "simmering" noise in one ear which made him deaf on that side. In desperation, he gave up the use of snuff, but found that this did not help much. Later in the autumn he was to be ill with fever. As Wright commented, the visits of Marcy's physician, Dr. Wendell, that fretful conservative, probably did him more harm than good. Others remarked that he appeared to be growing old fast. During October, he managed to take a fort-night's vacation, or a little more, in his old home state, to see his mother and to get away from the pressures of his office, and he also visited George Bancroft, the writer and politician. He improved some-what. Politically, however, he was still deeply alarmed. He continued to tell his friends that the anti-bank movement was a dangerous one, and that any marriage between himself and loco-focoism would be

---

[12] To Wetmore, Sept. 9, to A. Gallup, Sept. 23, M.P.; to Van Buren, Sept. 13, ADS, H.S.P.A.; to Van Buren, Sept. 18, V.B.P.

only a forced one at best. On the other hand, he was too afraid of a split in the party to say such things in public.[13]

But if Marcy was on the whole discreet, the *Argus* was working in the conservative cause, while men of Tallmadge's stamp virtually left the party and made common cause with the Whigs. The outcome was that in county after county moderates of Marcy's sort were defeated in the competition for nominations to the legislative posts, with either hardened radicals or Tallmadge men chosen instead. This played into the hands of the Whigs. What with the continuance of poor times and the fact that the banks were unable to resume specie payment, together with a grave lack of small bills, the triumph of the Whigs was a certainty. Such proved to be the case. In the assembly, there were one hundred and one Whigs elected, to twenty-seven Democrats, while in the senate the party's majority was much reduced.[14]

It was an outcome, however, which resolved Marcy's problem for him. Since the Tallmadge conservatives had thrown the game to the Whigs and there had been few of his own middle-of-the-road group left, he was faced with a clear choice between Whiggery and radical Democracy. To a man of Marcy's party loyalty, this was hardly a choice at all. In consequence, he put any family considerations aside and rejoined the national leadership of his group. In this course he had the aid, very agreeably, of a conciliatory message from Van Buren, whose annual report to congress early in December contained much balm for the moderates.[15]

Marcy's own message, in January, 1838, was the product of some suggestions of his own friends, modified a bit by his "cabinet council." Justifying his demand for a period of grace for the state's banks, he asserted that the latter were using it in a proper manner and that at its end all of the reasonably sound ones would be back at par. His first real news, though, was a call for free banking, including the right to issue notes—except that there must now be a specie reserve requirement. What attracted much greater attention, however, was his state-

---

[13] To Wetmore, Sept. 26, Nov. 6, 9, Dec. 17, M.P.; to Bancroft, Oct. 3, 31, Bancroft Papers; Wright to Flagg, Sept. 29, F.P.; recollections of Marcy, autumn of 1837, by Gideon Welles, Papers Relating to Gideon Welles, L.C.

[14] Flagg, Nov. 5, 9, and Cambreleng, Nov. 9, to Van Buren, Hammond to Butler, Nov. 7, all in V.B.P.

[15] To Van Buren, Dec. 8, V.B.P.

ment on the independent treasury problem. This, which reflected the artistic hand of Prosper Wetmore, declared that it would be all right for the federal government to make its collections in "the legal currency [i.e. specie] or its equivalent"! and also *either* to discontinue using the banks as fiscal agents or to use them on the condition that the federal moneys would not be loaned out or be the subject of loans. While at times Marcy seems to have persuaded himself that he had thus discussed the independent treasury idea and rejected it in favor of something else, most people who read the message concluded that he had simply used a face-saving style for yielding to what Van Buren was demanding. The president was quick to write that the document was "altogether such as your friends can approve."[16]

Meanwhile, the session of 1838, one of the most excited the state had ever known, was getting under way. As it turned out, free banking went through rather easily, although it was long in the process. As finally passed, it had a provision that all bank notes be backed up by high-grade securities deposited with the state comptroller. This was a huge step forward and one which would be copied by the other states and later by the federal government. Also praiseworthy was the adoption of a legal specie reserve. The great storm of the first months of the session, however, was over small bills. Marcy had remained silent on the measure, seeking no change in the law, but as a matter of fact the public really needed such currency. As a result, the Whigs favored a complete abandonment of the small-bill measure, while the Democrats were divided, some wanting such a move and some merely a temporary issue. Marcy finally adopted the latter view. He found the going hard; "I have never know[n] so much difficulty in get[ting] our friends to act together," he complained. What transpired was a triumph for the radicals, but on such a basis that it would do the party little good. A measure was adopted which on its face permitted small bills at once—subject to gradual elimination over a period of two years—but with the proviso that such money, if issued by the state's banks, must be redeemable in specie at all times! This meant that notes would not be issued till after the resumption; it also would place the blame for the currency shortage on the party. It was for this reason that the Whig house, no doubt, approved of it.

[16] Marcy to Wetmore, Nov. 6, Dec. 31, Jan. 22, M.P.; *Messages,* 654-667.

During the session, Marcy watched anxiously for signs of a resumption by the banks. In April, finding that the metropolitan institutions were ready to do so and that the upstate banks would try to go along, he proposed a great state loan of six or eight million dollars to the former to back them up. The Whig assembly, under Seward's leadership, killed this, for purely political reasons, although, in business circles at least, Marcy had the credit for the proposal. What was more significant was that the resumption was completed anyway; this was on May 10. It came despite the fact that the western states and Mr. Biddle's bank, which was aligned with them, failed to resume.[17]

When the legislature adjourned, Marcy was able to comment that the Democrats parted in good feeling, and this was true enough, for the events of the session had done much to strengthen the party. Marcy had adopted free banking, to the approval of the more radical Democrats, while some of the latter, such as Flagg, had sanctioned his loan project. And, by the end of the session, Marcy had definitely adopted the subtreasury scheme. As for the unreconciled conservatives, the Tallmadge wing, they had left the party, but their going had helped to unify it. If the party was a tight one, again, however, the prospects for the autumn elections were still only fair.

Despite this fact and despite his accumulated weariness and recurrent illness, Marcy was ready to run again. What was more, the party needed him. There was some hostility to a renomination because of desires of certain groups for shares in the patronage, and the old Throop faction was more outspokenly critical than before; in the Ithaca district, moreover, the proponents of a new railroad were his enemies, while in the radical camp there were many who disliked him. On the other hand, there was no suitable rival candidate and there was no one else at all who could so well reconcile the divergent views in the organization. In consequence, the state convention renominated him quite easily.[18]

In the hot campaign which now took place, Marcy again ran

---

[17] *Laws . . . 61st session,* 245 ff.; *Messages,* 667n.; Wetmore to Marcy, Jan. 27, H.S.P.A.; Marcy to A. Gallup, Jan. 30, M.P.; *Messages,* 694-703; Flagg to Van Buren, Apr. 12, V.B.P. ("The Gov. has done his duty manfully," said Flagg of the message *re* a new loan.); Marcy to Wetmore, Apr. 12, 17, 19, M.P.; *E. Post,* Nov. 6, 1838; McMaster, *op. cit.,* VI, 419-420.
[18] To Wetmore, Mar. 6, M.P.; *Post,* Sept. 18.

against William H. Seward, his rival in 1834. Indeed, to many, it
was a contest between "Big Bill" Marcy, the tall and now rather
fleshy governor, who had opposed the use of small notes, and "Little
Bill" Seward, the slender and slight Whig who proclaimed his readiness to have them made available. This was a play upon words which
appealed to many. There was also the humorous charge of the
Courier & Enquirer on October 20 that Marcy's pardon of a former
counterfeiter proved his friendliness toward "irredeemable paper."
But, in the main, it was a grim battle. No quarter was asked and none
was given.

Besides the small bill question, which hurt the Democrats very
much, there were all the other discontents connected with the banking
system. Most serious, of course, was the continuance of the hard
times. While recognizing that many voters would swing to the
Whigs, Marcy had hopes that some traditional backers of that party
would aid him because of his support of the state's banks and of the
credit system. We find him instructing Wetmore, for example, on the
preparation of a letter to a New York City paper, with the aim of
winning over some of the Whig merchants.

As a matter of fact, Marcy was able to raise some money for campaign printing funds in such conservative circles, but the total was
not great nor were many voters won to his cause. On the other hand,
Senator Tallmadge and his faction, which came out for Seward, won
many conservative Democratic votes for the enemy; they also did their
best to weaken Marcy with the radicals by emphasizing how he had
at first been against the sub-treasury. Although Marcy did not fully
realize it at the time, moreover, the state banking interest entered the
campaign against the Democrats much more heartily than ever before.[19] For if loco-focoism had alarmed Marcy, it had quite terrified
the more conservative of the state's bankers.

Apart from the issue of finance, however, there were two other
special factors of importance in the 1838 election. One was the popular sympathy in the northern counties for the Canadian Rebellion.
Marcy lost ground on this, because, as will be discussed, he had made
efforts in the past year to keep the peace along that frontier. As to
the second, the abolition movement, which will be taken up shortly,

---

[19] To Wetmore, Oct. 19, Dec. 17, M.P.

he also suffered by his stand. During this campaign he and Seward were confronted with a questionnaire from the friends of the negroes. Did they favor the existing federal fugitive slave law, they were asked; did they approve of the property qualification for negro voters; and did they sanction the law which let slaves be brought into the state for a nine-month period without becoming free? Marcy decided not to answer unless Seward did, commenting that "it is surmised that the little man dare not. He is secretly with the abolitionists but is ashamed of the connection." While there was much to warrant Marcy's summary of Seward as a "little man"—his invariable term for him—he was wrong in supposing that Seward would not reply. Seward did answer, in a spirit of warm humanitarianism but without urging any direct steps of any sort. By contrast, Marcy simply upheld all of the existing provisions. His response was not such as to aid him with the rising antislavery set.[20]

Despite a good deal of optimism, based upon the enthusiasm of the party workers and clear signs that many would vote Democratic who had not done so before, Marcy learned in November that he was not to have a fourth term. He polled a larger vote than in any of his three former races. Yet the Whigs carried the state. Seward had 192,882 votes to Marcy's 182,461. It was a disappointing result, but far from a disgraceful one.

Taking the record *in toto,* Marcy had undoubtedly given New York sound guidance and leadership in the difficult financial and banking problems of the era. If his counsel on the tariff had caused the party some trouble, it was not inherently bad counsel, certainly. And as for the banking fracas, he had helped to defeat Mr. Biddle, had fought sturdily for hard money for every-day currency, and had seen a number of wise limitations imposed upon the state's banks. These included the backing of the note issue with bonds or mortgages deposited with the state government, the beginning of the requirement as to specie reserves, and limitations on the proportion of note and deposit credit. He had also, if reluctantly, adopted the principle of free banking and the independent treasury, in these matters deferring to the wishes of the party. Although the destruction of the "monster" bank was in the hindsight of history theoretically wrong,

---

[20] To Wetmore, Oct. 23; *Courier & Enquirer,* Oct. 26; *E. Post,* Oct. 29.

it must be admitted that once Biddle had tried to coerce the government there was no alternative but to put him down. Granted that, Marcy had in general handled the state banking problems very well and did not deserve the rebuke which the public had given him. As far as that went, if allowance is made for the usual fate of incumbents during major depressions, the small margin by which he had been defeated constituted almost a moral victory. On only one point, his advocacy of further inflation on the eve of the crash, did he deserve round criticism—and all the more so because self-interest was involved. To repeat, however, the record was a good one, all in all.

IX. LESSER PROBLEMS OF THE GOVERNORSHIP

"You know Gov. Marcy was of Troy, and was Vice President of our Lyceum. He has considerable taste for Natural Science, and possesses strong powers of mind. . . . Gov. Marcy will not be under the influence of party in the smallest possible degree in making the appointments [for the state geological survey.]" (Amos Eaton to John Torrey, March 26, 1836[1])

ALTHOUGH financial questions were dominant in Marcy's three terms and of critical weight in the decision of the voters in 1838 to replace him with William H. Seward, there were several other notable issues with which he dealt. Some of these, such as internal improvements, abolition, and the Canadian Rebellion, have been alluded to in passing already. Taken as a group, they cast much additional light upon his career, showing very nicely his intelligent approach to affairs, and revealing, too, his moderation or conservatism. It is only proper, therefore, to take them up in some detail.

In regard to his conservative approach to public questions, perhaps the most significant of these lesser issues was that of internal improvements. For here he aligned himself quite clearly with those elements in his party which were friendly to business and which did not object to a reasonable level of state expenditure to promote it. As has been hinted, the chief problem was that of opening up additional areas of the state by means of new transportation facilities. Somewhat regardless of the intrinsic merits of particular projects, it had become quite impossible to argue that any one section, such as that along the route of the Erie Canal, should have the benefit of state aid but that other areas should not.

Among the most pressing of these rivalries were those involving feeder or "lateral" canals to connect with the Erie. Marcy had in essence, of course, committed himself to such "laterals" prior to the election in 1832, in that he had indirectly endorsed the Chenango canal project. This route was an expensive one to consider, for it

---

[1] E. M. McAllister, *Amos Eaton,* 324.

meant a climb of fully seven hundred feet from the altitude of the great canal, at Utica, before descending to the Susquehanna Valley and Binghamton. In his opening message, in 1833, however, he did not boggle at the scheme. Far from that, he laid down a liberal rule which was meant to apply to all such cases.

If the revenue [of a new work] promises to be sufficient to keep it in repair when finished, to defray the expenses of superintendence and the collection of tolls, and to meet the claims for interest on the capital ex-pended, sound policy requires that it should be constructed. Even if a less favorable result should be anticipated for a few years, the question . . . may yet be very properly entertained. An improvement, opening an easy and cheap communication into the interior of any part of the State, would soon develop new resources in that section, increase the quantity of its productions, and expand its trade. . . .

These criteria typified the thought of the day.[2] And, indeed, there was no reason why a wealthy state, which was making large profits on the main canal, should not adopt such an attitude. Speaking then specifically of the Chenango route, Marcy conceded that some esti-mates ran very high, and that there were honest doubts whether the project would meet his terms. Yet he went on to say to the legislators that "It remains for you to decide upon these conflicting opinions . . . I commend this proposed work to your favorable notice. . . ." To the lawmakers, this was word enough.[3]

Having thus at the start shown himself a friend of the canal system, Marcy in his second annual message took up the problem of increas-ing the capacity of the Erie itself. He commented on New York state's good fortune in having "the most practicable route" from the seaboard to the Western lakes in her territory.

If our canals are to be what a wise management cannot fail to make them —the principal channels for this trade—we must calculate its extent, and make them adequate to this object. When our system of internal improve-ments was commenced, a great part of this fertile region was a wilderness, and scarcely a sail was spread, for the purposes of commerce, on the great western lakes.

He observed that Lake Erie was now "like a frequented track in the highway of commercial nations," its shipping having trebled in the past three years. There were twenty steamers and 128 sloops and

---

[2] Cf. *Amer. Quarterly Rev.,* Dec., 1830, p. 300; Whitford, *loc. cit.,* 679.
[3] *Messages,* 418-419, 419n.

schooners on the lake, he noted, and in the past year 100,000 passengers had gone to the West from Buffalo. "The western trade is a
noble prize," he said. He therefore recommended that a new set of
locks be added, to double the capacity of the canal at the critical
points, and that there be a widening and deepening of the channels.
The legislature complied, in this year and the year after, making provision among other things for increasing the original four-foot depth
to seven. Subsequently, Marcy also approved further lateral canals.
He also endorsed the request of the New York and Erie Railroad
Company for a large loan. This project was for a route across the
"southern tier" of counties and essentially took the place of the long
debated state highway in that area, which he had as comptroller opposed. In advocating it, Marcy stressed among other things that the
line "would be opened earlier in the spring and continued later in the
autumn" than would the Erie Canal. The legislature granted it
$3,000,000.[4]

Marcy was not successful, on the other hand, in persuading the
legislature to levy additional taxes to finance these works, although
he persistently asked that a general property tax be imposed for this
purpose. The lawmakers would not hear of it. In the face of the
excess revenues piling up from the great canal, they simply refused
to take such a step. Instead, they loaned some of these surplus canal
moneys (over and above those used for the canal's sinking fund) to
the general fund of the state. In spite of his failure to obtain tax
support for internal improvements, when the panic of 1837 came
Marcy boldly insisted that the state continue with the Erie enlargement and this was done. Money was borrowed for the purpose. In
summary, his record on transportation was an excellent one. Much
was accomplished, yet at the end of his term the general fund debt
had risen to only a bit over a million and one-third dollars. While the
lateral canals never paid for themselves, the canal network as a whole
did, and quite handsomely.[5] It was only when the Whigs came in,
with their profligate plans, that serious trouble developed.

Aside from internal improvements, there were countless other state
concerns, as such, to be dealt with. Marcy's most noteworthy achieve-

---

[4] *Messages,* 459-462, 465, 506-510, 550-553, and notes.
[5] *Messages,* 415, 503-505, 544, 549, 670-671, 707, and notes.

ment along such lines was in securing the use of the federal surplus of 1836-1837 for an endowment for the schools. Thus, while the money was loaned out, immediately, to private persons, the income from it served, for one thing, to double the annual grant to the public elementary schools. His administration also brought the establishment of school-district libraries, additional provision for teacher-training, a first state insane asylum, and the first separate prison for women criminals.[6]

Of much greater intrinsic interest, however, was Marcy's work in connection with the state's geological survey, which was begun in 1836. Although he did not initiate the movement for the survey and although it was John A. Dix, the distinguished secretary of state, who drew up the basic plans, the governor's role was a highly important one. Marcy picked the very best men available for its staff, entirely disregarding political considerations, with the result that not one of the four chief geologists was a New York state man and only one of the seven chief appointees as a whole was a Democrat! Since there was no provision for a single head for the staff, moreover, he himself did much to provide correlation between the different zones and phases of the project. Typically, also, he read extensively on the subject. The survey had many useful results. For Marcy, the most interesting one personally, no doubt, was that the highest peak in the Adirondacks, Tahawus, "the cloud-splitter," was renamed for him.[7]

While all of the above questions were at least in a degree nonpartisan, there was one problem which would be of a political character from the outset and become more so as the years passed. This was abolitionism. During the early 1830's, the question of abolishing slavery in the South had begun to be discussed in a more serious way throughout the North than had been the case earlier. In New York state this was largely the doing of certain evangelical preachers in the west as well as of some leading philanthropists at the metropolis. Their spirit was a reasonable one, even though their work was increasingly overshadowed by the pronouncements of extremists like

---

[6] *Messages,* 611-614; libraries, *ibid.,* 499n, 538, 651-652; teachers: 408, 454n, 538, 613-614, 650, 652-653; the asylum (at Utica), 452, 676; women's prison: 515.

[7] D. R. Fox, "The Rise of Scientific Interests in New York," in A. C. Flick, *Hist. of the State of New York,* IX, 108-112; Marcy diary, June 2-3, 8-10, M.P.; *Messages,* 638-644, 680-683; tribute of Lyell, *Travels in North America,* I, 13-14.

William Lloyd Garrison and Wendell Phillips at Boston. As the discussion went on, however, there were protests not merely from south of the Mason and Dixon line but also from merchants and manufacturers north of it, for the latter feared that business would be upset. Members of the two great national parties, and especially of the Democratic Party, also objected; if the agitation went very far, it would plainly tend to break up the parties and could imperil the union. In consequence, there was a rising resistance to the movement; this resistance came to a head in the summer and autumn of 1835. Among other things, there were race riots at New York and other conservative demonstrations elsewhere.

Now, Marcy and other Regency chieftains had long been acquainted with slavery and slaves, not merely through visits to the South but also by contacts with negroes still in bondage in New York itself. The state's plan of emancipation had been of the gradual kind and the last "class" of negroes had been freed in 1827. While Marcy was associated with the *Budget* at Troy in 1817, for example, it had carried an advertisement[8] for the sale of a nine-year old slave girl, and it is possible that "Silva," the servant mentioned in his letter to Dolly at about 1820, was a slave. As far as the Regency went, there was also the highly practical point that in the next year, 1836, Van Buren was expected to be the party's candidate for the presidency. But it is only fair to add that the Regency's heads, like virtually all other leaders in northern society, truly did not approve of this sudden and violent campaign of abuse directed at sister states.

One result was that Marcy and his associates determined to put their whole weight against the abolition talk. For this purpose, Marcy united with the rest of Albany officialdom and the other well known figures of the city in a great public meeting on September 4, 1835. He not only presided, but he doubtless also had a hand in the framing of the resolutions which were adopted. These condemned "the unwarrantable intermeddling" of the abolitionists in a question which was termed one properly to be decided by the southern states; they also hinted that New York was ready to use "all constitutional means" to restrain such disturbers of the public peace.[9]

---

[8] July 15, 1817.
[9] *Journal,* Sept. 5.

In his annual message of January 5, 1836, he went slightly beyond this. Ascribing the movement to "a few individuals . . . acting on mistaken motives of moral and religious duty, or some less justifiable principle," he noted how cautiously New York itself had acted on the problem, despite its relatively "trivial" scope there, and pointed out that those who stirred up the issue could hope for action by congress only if a constitutional amendment were passed, since at present slavery was purely a state matter. Yet such an amendment would be impossible, he reasoned, from the very fact that the anti-slavery leaders had already excited the South so much. What he feared was really the intention of the abolitionists, he avowed, to embark the state upon "a crusade against the slaveholding States," which would surely mean "the end of our confederacy." After this prophetic passage, he went on to say that the problem must be left to the southern whites. But if public opinion did *not* curb the abolitionists in New York, he added, there would come up the serious question of how far the states could, and should, provide "by their own laws, for the trial and punishment by their own judicatories, of residents within their limits, guilty of acts therein, which are calculated and intended to excite insurrection and rebellion in a sister State." Such a power was inherent in state sovereignty, he declared. This was in accord with a specific suggestion by Silas Wright, who, like Van Buren and Benjamin F. Butler, had been consulted in advance. All three had urged a strong statement. Marcy discreetly closed the subject, however, by referring to his refusal to extradite Robert G. Williams, a New York abolitionist, to Alabama in accordance with a request of the governor of that state.[10]

Applause greeted the message everywhere, and of course particularly in the South. W. C. Rives, the prominent Virginia senator, praised it unlimitedly, saying that "It will, I hope, do much good at the North by its operation on the Fanatics, as it has already done to the South by counteracting the Nullifiers." Silas Wright, admitting that he wrote "under some excitement," commented to Marcy that

---

[10] *Messages,* 570-584. In consulting these men, Marcy had admitted that for purposes of state politics alone, silence on the subject would be preferable, but he was anxious to serve the party. (To Van Buren, Nov. 22, Dec. 3, Van Buren to Marcy, undated draft, V.B.P.; Wright to Marcy, Dec. 18, M.P.; Marcy to Butler, Jan. 4, Butler Papers, Princeton.)

You will not believe that I design to flatter you, but I say in sober truth that, in my humble judgement, all the acts of your public life, prior to this message, will not have done you so much credit in the estimation of this whole country, and I fondly believe in the estimation of the Citizens of our own State, as this part of this message.

When Wright had shown the document to two Missourians, Congressman Linn and his wife, Mrs. Linn had exclaimed "God bless the man; that message ought to be printed in letters of gold and put into the hands of every man in the South"—after which she had rushed off with it to make a tour among her southern friends. George Bancroft, Marcy's friend in the state of Massachusetts, also praised it to the skies. What was more important was that the state legislature adopted resolutions voicing a "full and cordial concurrence" in it.[11]

Marcy's reading of the riot act, however, proved to be like King Canute's effort to stay the inrush of the ocean tide. It was in that same month that John Quincy Adams began his long fight over the right of petition and in the summer of the same year that Theodore Dwight Weld began the intensive preaching that was to make upstate New York the very heart and center of abolitionism. It would not be long before the New York *Evening Post,* perhaps the most admirable of all of the newspapers of the day, would cease to call abolition a "fanaticism." For Marcy, the declaration in his 1836 message was none the less to be among the most vital of his career. It represented, moreover, a commitment which he never wholly modified.

It was about a year after Marcy made this important pronouncement that there arose the ill-fated Canadian rebellion. This uprising never had much popular support in the areas in which it occurred, namely in parts of present Quebec and Ontario. Afterwards, however, a number of the leading participants fled to the Niagara and St. Lawrence frontiers of New York, where outbursts of approval followed, for many of the residents there warmly sympathized with what they had attempted. Marcy was at first inclined to play the affair down, writing to Sir Francis Bond Head, lieutenant-governor of Upper Canada, that since foreign affairs were the province of the federal government there was "very little" that the state could do. Later, indeed, the matter became more serious, for many unemployed

---

[11] Rives to Van Buren, Jan. 29, V.B.P.; Wright to Marcy, Jan. 10, H.S.P.A.; Bancroft to Marcy, Feb. 28, M.P.; *Messages,* 582n.

canal workers began to enlist in a "patriot" army recruited to invade
Canada, a son of the Van Rensselaer family became its commander-
in-chief, and the "patriots" moved over from Buffalo to Navy Island,
on the Canadian side of the Niagara River, and began to drill; the
rebels also seized large numbers of arms from state arsenals in nearby
areas. Then, on January 1, 1838, Marcy received sensational reports.
Canadian militia had crossed to the American side and seized and
burned a little American steamer, the *Caroline,* which had been ferry-
ing supplies to the rebels. Marcy was perturbed. He requested the
legislature, next day, to grant funds in case he should have to call out
the militia. Soon after, partly at the instigation of General Winfield
Scott, whom Van Buren was sending to the area, the governor went
there himself. Upon reaching the frontier, he found that there was
some hazard in any call which might be issued to the militia, since
they were so in sympathy with the rebels that they might do more to
aid the latter than to curb them, if mustered. None the less, he called
some units out. Together with Scott, he also toured the danger spots
to try to keep the peace. The two had talks with young Van Rensselaer
and eventually Marcy extracted a promise from him that the "patriot"
troops would soon be led outside of New York's jurisdiction. This
was not done, but on January 14 the "patriots" were evacuated from
Navy Island and all public arms were surrendered to the authorities.
It was only after Marcy had gone home that Van Rensselaer took his
followers, now fewer in number, to the St. Lawrence border, where,
in February, he made a brief and half-hearted sally across the line.[12]

Great excitement continued throughout the year, none the less. On
June 1, Marcy received tidings by express that a Canadian steamer
named the *Sir Robert Peel* had been boarded, robbed, and burned by
a guerrilla gang which included a few Americans. In alarm, he made
a flying trip to Watertown, where he decided to direct that two companies of militia, already called out by the local authorities, be kept
available on a "ready" basis. He also wrote to the secretary of war
that what were really needed were five hundred men well equipped

---

[12] Marcy to Head, Dec. 21, H.S.P.A.; *Messages,* 678-680; O. E. Tiffany, "The
Relations of the United States to the Canadian Rebellion . . .," *Pubs. of the Buffalo
Hist. Soc.,* VIII, 78, and *passim; Daily Buffalo Journal,* Jan. 5-18; C. V. R. Bonney,
A Legacy of Historical Gleanings, II, 84-92; M. Sterling to B. F. Butler, Feb. 23,
V.B.P.

with fast boats, because the malefactors were operating in the Thousand Islands, which was an ideal territory for the purpose. He posted a $500 reward for the capture of their leader, Walter Johnson. When he went over to the islands in person, however, he concluded that suppression would be extremely hard. Johnson, for instance, was said to be armed with "six pistols, a repeating rifle, a dirk and bowie knife" and to travel in a fast eight-oared rowboat; he took pains to notify the governor that he was engaged in honorable warfare against the Queen of England, under a commission from the rebel "government." Marcy's trip was perhaps useful in stirring the local authorities into action. In any event, the state militia, along with the royal marines across the frontier, did eventually force Johnson and his men to disperse. As for the *Peel* affair, American juries declined to convict the men who had taken part.[13]

Throughout the whole *imbroglio,* Marcy's course, like Van Buren's, was the patriotic one of trying to keep the frontier disturbances from going so far as to bring on a war between the two countries. In the long run, he and the president were successful. On the other hand, there is no doubt that this policy helped to defeat Marcy in 1838, as it would Van Buren in 1840.

Marcy's behavior in dealing with these diverse problems of the governorship is valuable in rounding out the picture of the man. It was obvious that he could yield to political necessity, which had in part been involved in both the Chenango canal and the abolition declaration. Yet on the whole he had clung to a broad and patriotic conception of his duty. In the geological survey, this had been particularly plain. At the same time, the survey had appealed to his scholarly bent, as had the various efforts to promote popular education. During the border troubles, moreover, he had served the best interests of the state and country without too much thought of the immediate political consequences. Finally, it may be said that again and again he had revealed his concept of a democratic regime in which progress was made steadily but without undue speed, and in which there were reforms to benefit the common people but with due regard for property rights and the advancement of enterprise. These

---

[13] To Secretary Poinsett, June 3, ADS, H.S.P.A.; to Wetmore, June 11, M.P.; Tiffany, *loc. cit.,* 89.

tendencies were characteristic of his middle-class background, as, in a very different way, was his stand against the abolitionist agitation. But, before concluding a study of Marcy in this section of his career, a brief glance at his personal life is in order.

*   *   *

Marcy's private moments were none too plentiful in his six years as governor, except in the relative calm between the adjournment of the legislature in the spring or early summer and the start of the autumn campaign. There was always a campaign for the legislature, if nothing more. Yet even these intervals were far from free from business. This is neatly shown in his diary for May 10, 1833, which seems to have been a fairly typical day. It began as follows:

> . . . Arose later than usual, about 6 o'clock [!] Read in the forenoon Hume's *Essay on Money,* pages, 13, 'multum in parvo'; before I had finished it 'Old Hayes,' the Rogue catcher, called on me to get two pardons —conversed with him about one hour. Another person called with him to get appointed measurer of grain in N.Y.—both applications deferred until my visit to N.Y.—Adjt. General called before they left, on official business; conversed with him until noon.

Before either of the above visits, Judge Woodworth had come in, to apologize for certain political acts in the past. A woman had also called, about a pardon for her son. After dinner, Marcy signed some commissions and then took a nap. During the rest of the afternoon he read about fifteen pages in an essay on the "search after truths," which he praised, and then had tea and made a call upon a man at the City Tavern. Also, at one time or another during the day, he had visits from an applicant for the office of notary and from a politician of Oswego County, with whom he discussed affairs in that place.[14] Although this entry does not show it, Marcy had a warm personality. He was gruff on the outside, but he had a twinkle in his eye, much of the time.

On the other hand, Marcy did his best to keep his private life from being encroached upon by his public business. His gruffness and an occasional coldness of manner were probably in part assumed in order that he might the better protect himself and his family from intrusion. At other times, he could ward off interference from the outside

---

[14] M.P.

in more politic ways. Once while he was governor, for instance, a woman of social-climbing propensities hinted all too unmistakably to Mrs. Marcy that she would be pleased to call upon her. As it happened, the second Mrs. Marcy, i.e. Cornelia, was of a retiring disposition and had not at all looked forward to being a governor's wife. Marcy, who was present, at once saved the situation by replying with an appropriate expression of his face that this would never do, because his wife had already heard too much of his old flirtations with the woman in question and would never consent. The stratagem worked well.[15]

In some ways, on the other hand, Cornelia Marcy was quite able to set the pattern of their life herself. She could be domineering, even, at times. This was notably true in connection with his snuff habit, which has been alluded to. Mrs. Marcy would confiscate any supplies of that item and then dispense them to him in small quantities; the upshot, however, was that Marcy commonly had Wetmore smuggle some up to him, as for example when coming up to the legislature. If Wetmore mailed the snuff, however, there could be trouble, for the "Madam" was occasionally known to interfere with the mails. Marcy was very fond of her, however.[16]

William and Samuel, his sons by Dolly Newell, felt differently about Cornelia, if we may generalize from a letter by young William to his Newell grandparents. "The Old Lady begins to open her jaws against us," he wrote in 1833, adding that he would be glad to get away from this "relentless stepmother."[17] While this letter may really be a better indication of the character of William, who was to be the black sheep of the family, than of his stepmother, both he and his brother left the nest at a fairly early date. In 1838, William became a teller at the Bank of Commerce in New York, while in the same year Samuel joined the navy as a midshipman and went off to sea. Samuel's decision was an unpleasant one to the governor.

Meanwhile, Cornelia had borne some children of her own. The

---

[15] Mary Pattison to Newell, Oct. 5, 1859, M.P.; E. Knower to same, Nov. 15, 1832, N.P.

[16] He commonly applied the snuff to his nose with his long forefinger and thumb, his head cast down as if he was in a deeply meditative mood; to Wetmore, Nov. 26, 1835, M.P.; M. B. Field, *Memories of Many Men,* 168.

[17] Sept. 28, N.P., State Library.

first, a girl, died at an early age, but a son, Edmund, named for Mrs.
Marcy's brother, was born in 1831 or 1832; a second daughter,
named for Cornelia herself, was born about 1834.

To mention the above, however, is only to begin to discuss the
family. There were also the many "in-laws," notably George Newell
and the Knowers. Marcy seems to have been very affectionate toward
the whole Knower progeny and to have really enjoyed those periods
when the two families were crowded together under one roof—as in
a "hive," to use Newell's expression. The only unfortunate side of
this family connection was his relation to Knower himself, who by
1836 was definitely in his dotage, but the subject of their relations
has been mentioned already. Although Marcy sometimes wrote to
Wetmore, by the way, of his troubles in untangling Knower's financial affairs, he loyally avoided any complaint of him on the score of
political embarrassment. For Marcy was a good husband; he was also
an affectionate, if at times stern, father.

Despite his preoccupation with his household, his four children,
and his in-laws, to say nothing of his many duties as governor, Marcy
always found some time for reading. This was his favorite pastime
throughout his life. The size of his library is not known, but it was
large enough so that when, after his death, it was acquired by Washington Hunt and mingled with the latter's collection, the two together
were in the neighborhood of three thousand volumes. His reading
was not systematic, however. He preferred to dip into several books
in the course of a single day, even when callers did not interrupt him,
and into ones on wholly unrelated subjects at that. Thus, in May of
1833, he was reading Moore's Lord Byron, the Duke of Sully's
Memoires (in French), the *Wealth of Nations,* the life of a preacher
(on a Sunday), Lord Bacon, Herschel's Discourse on Natural Philosophy, Justice Story on the federal constitution, Sir Thomas Browne's
Religio Medici, Hume's *Essay on Money* (as mentioned before), and
a sermon on "Modern Infidelity." A month later he was delving into
Bossuet's *Histoire Universelle,* a life of Burke, and Droz's *Economie
Politique;* at other times he was to be found reading works by such
varied men as Hallam, Coleridge, Lord Bulwer, and John Jay.[18] Over

----

[18] Diaries, 1833, 1835, M.P.; *Catalogue of the Libraries of the late Ex-Gov. Wm.
L. Marcy, and Ex-Gov. Washington Hunt* (notice of sale, L.C.).

the course of a week or so, he usually finished the books, in their turn, if they were new to him, but he did not always do so. He liked to browse. As the above titles show, his preferences were for statecraft, economics, and literature, with something of a religious type commonly on Sundays.

The excellence of Marcy's written messages was, of course, a direct result of this wide reading, as well as of his years of part-time newspaper writing. He wrote in an easy and lucid manner, with a detached, philosophical spirit, and in a most persuasive tone. Even his firmest opponents admitted that his communications were "intelligent, comprehensive, and dignified," while Judge Hammond felt that Marcy had no superior in the state as a political writer. The only fault with the messages was their length, which was in part to be explained by the need to present a very great variety of topics.

Marcy's broad culture was also seen, and most agreeably, in the charm of his private conversation. Here, his sly and often mischievous humor also asserted itself to the full, making him a delightful companion.[19] He also liked to play at cards, especially whist, but since his youthful years at Troy he had entirely given up playing for money.

Marcy was, incidentally, not only a large man, but also, all other things being equal, a strong one. When at home in Southbridge to visit his mother, he loved to ramble over the hills on foot to visit his many relatives. On one occasion, he took Cornelia with him to see the site of the old Marcy mills on the Quinabaug. Wanting to cross the river, he is said to have remarked that "I'm not going around by the bridge. I believe I'd like to go over just as I did when a boy, and I'll carry you across." He thereupon took off his shoes and stockings, rolled up his trousers, and carried her across, to the applause of the workers who were watching from the windows of the factories nearby.[20] Southbridge was much changed, from the period of his boyhood.

Marcy's conservatism and also his disposition to accommodate his views to the desires of his beloved party were well displayed in a

---

[19] F. Byrdsall to Buchanan, Dec. 1, 1851, B.P.; G.T. Strong, *Diary*, II, 335.
[20] Recollections of [Prof. Cutting of Univ. of Rochester], *Journal*, July 28, Aug. 28, 1857; Ammidown, "Southbridge," *loc. cit.*, 42.

letter which he wrote two months after leaving office. It was written in reply to an invitation to a proposed public dinner for him, to be given by some of his political friends at New York City. He declined the honor, but commented interestingly and at length upon the political battles of the past decade. In the course of these contests, he asserted, " 'the great principles of Democratic liberty' have been more discussed, brought out into bolder relief, and better appreciated by all classes of our citizens . . . than at any previous period in our history. With whatever secret disfavour these principles may be regarded by a portion of the people, the approval of them by a large majority has been so decided, that the question of their soundness or *the policy of making them the basis of conducting the administration of the government, has not been put directly in issue. . . ."* Later in the letter he commented that much was yet to be done to secure to the people "the full benefit" of the American system of government, but that their support had to be won for each step which was taken. *"As a public man I felt bound to keep steadily in view the distinction between what was desirable and what was attainable. . . . Though I have regulated my own steps by the general movement on these subjects, I have endeavoured to accelerate it in the direction which my judgment approved."*[21] If this was the statement of a moderate, it was also the testimony of a political realist and a practising one, as the passages which have been italicized make very clear.

In this same year, also, he wrote the brief autobiographical sketch which has been so much cited in the first chapters of this work. From the vantage point of this composition, he was moved to comment that he had "occupied a greater number of offices of the higher grade in the State than any other individual." This had happened, he asserted, although he had commonly not sought the places he had received.

Repeating the remark that he had early decided not to take any office not advancing himself in his profession of law, he went on to imply very strongly that he regretted that he had not held to this rule. Officeholding, he said, should have been simply an "incident" in his legal career.

A dependence upon official patronage for the means of obtaining a livelihood [sic] is of all others, the most uncertain; the most successful

---

[21] To John Targee, etc., Feb. 25, 1839, Ford Coll.

realize both in fame and profit less than they expected and others are more severely disappointed. By far the greater part of those who in this manner have been turned away from the steady pursuit of their professions, have had cause, in looking back upon their course, to regard the acquisition of an office as an adverse event, though, at the time it happened, they esteemed it an instance of good fortune.

There are many circumstances of annoyance and danger in the situation of an office holder which are not taken into account by those who wish to be invested with that character, as the means of comfortable support. A man's mind must be peculiarly well balanced, if it is not occasionally disturbed with anxiety when he reflects that his expectations of advantage depend upon his retaining his office, and this depends again upon the success of his party, and the continued favor of his political friends. A sense of insecurity, which results from such a situation, must be a source of constant inquietude. . . .

Office holders as a body are exposed to some malign influences that do not assail men in other situations, and the instances are not a few in which they have yielded to a temptation which has led them into a strange obliquity of conduct. Office long enjoyed, or the hope of it too long and ardently indulged, has a tendency to beget selfishness, which may be, and often is, of so rank a growth that it obtains the mastery of integrity, and a political career commenced in honesty has, in consequence thereof, terminated in apostacy and disgrace.

While he did not particularly imply that he had felt the pull of such "malign influences" himself, as an officeholder, it is not to be doubted that he had felt them. There had been some surrender of integrity, unquestionably, in his last half-dozen years. This was true despite his generally praiseworthy record. In his subsequent career, however, such sacrifices, while by no means predominant, would be more readily apparent.

X. A WHIG INTERVAL

"The sum total of my losses on account of Banks is nearly
$20,000, & it is high time I should be an anti Bank man.
Well this is the condition of human life and it is useless to
repine." (Marcy to Wetmore, August 29, 1841[1])

IN THE months following his defeat, Marcy made the most of the
leisure which he had craved so long. He was deeply fatigued after
his long years in office and his health, which had been particularly
bad perhaps in that anguished autumn of 1837, had recovered only
slightly since then. It was accordingly a great happiness to settle down
to a calm and relaxed routine, with plenty of opportunity for that
favorite pastime of reading. Early in this new period he moved his
residence. He and his family had lived at two different addresses on
North Pearl Street in the latter years of his governorship, but now, in
March, he and John Knower and Benjamin Knower, Jr., rented a
house at 4 Academy Park and the combined families moved into it.
This was the famous "three-walled house" which Croswell had sold
to the state for a governor's abode but which the Marcys had not
occupied and which Seward now disdained. That Marcy chose to live
in it showed his indifference to politics, for it had been the target of
many Whig jokes in the late campaign; it had no wall of its own on
one side, using the wall of the house against which it was built.
Soon Marcy was helping "Madame" move to it, trudging a bit self-
consciously through the streets, "loaded with rubbish like a broad
shouldered porter." But then, he had the shoulders. By early May, he
was spending most of his time at a farm which he had bought near
Troy two years earlier. He gardened all day long and did not bother
even to read the *Argus*. Since Mrs. Marcy preferred to stay in Albany
much of the time, he was alone a good deal. He amused himself at
times by composing imaginary conversations with the great writers
of the past, which he later recorded in long screeds to Wetmore. He
remained at the farm most of the summer.[2]

---

[1] M.P.

[2] To Wetmore, Mar. 22, 31, May 5, June 5, M.P.; Van Deusen, *Thurlow Weed*,
100-101; to Samuel, May 21, Aug. 21, M.P.; to Wetmore, Apr. 23, 1837, *ibid.*

On only two occasions did he depart from his nonpolitical course. The first was in composing a clever little satire on the new Whig administration. He described Seward, its head, and other state officers, as being put through a drill by Thurlow Weed, the party boss, whom he had beating a drum to set the pace for their steps and making, thereby, "more noise than music." Seward, meanwhile, was "making a painful effort to keep regular pace," so that he not merely trod exactly in his drummer's footsteps but even imitated the motions of the latter's arms. In fact, he looked like Weed, except that he carried his head higher and seemed, for so slight a man, "much more expanded with conscious self-importance." The sketch was published in the *Argus* and was later to come out in the form of a lithograph, based on a drawing by an artist named J. E. Freeman. Marcy's name was not divulged, however. In July, Marcy wrote the address of welcome for President Van Buren, who paid a visit to Albany.[3]

For years, Marcy had been buoyed up by hopes of accumulating a sufficient personal fortune to give him financial independence. Like other Albany men, he was on the spot when lands were put up for sale by the state for unpaid taxes.[4] He had made a number of purchases of such "wild" lands, often in conjunction with Mr. Knower, who had for some time been going into real estate on a large scale. Some of his wife's money may have been used for this and for other investments, as were a part of the savings of George Newell and of Samuel Marcy, or "Mr. Midshipman Easy," as Marcy called him.[5] During the irredeemable-paper interval in 1837-1838, he made several large purchases of lands from Mr. Knower, on credit, probably partly as a means of meeting the demands of his father-in-law's creditors. These included a half interest in the valuable water rights and lands at Lockport, plus a whole batch of lands in several counties in that area, for a total commitment of at least $52,000. The most valuable of these properties were the water rights and a flour mill and cotton mill associated with them; in these, Washington Hunt was his equal

---

[3] *Argus,* April, 1839, *passim;* Weed, *op. cit.,* 64-70; *Argus,* July 27, 1839.
[4] "The exactions of Albanians, who buy up lands for taxes has produced more prejudice against your city than all other causes." (W. Hunt to T. W. Olcott, Apr. 14, 1846, in possession of Douglas W. Olcott, Rensselaer, N.Y.)
[5] Cf. Newell's "Settlement with Marcy," May 1, 1833, and Marcy's note of indebtedness to him, Feb. 7, 1850, M.P. Also Marcy to Samuel, Feb. 28, May 11, *ibid.*

partner. Marcy also had some lesser holdings in the Troy and Albany region and in Michigan, and stock in several corporations.

During the year 1840, however, Marcy found to his dismay that his hopes were chimerical. Even in January, when one of his bigger corporate investments took a turn for the worse, he confided gloomily to Wetmore that "These times I fear will compel me to abandon my plan of retirement." As the spring ran its course, his fears were realized, for several of his corporate ventures proved very disappointing. Then, to cap it all, the cotton mill burned down. Since neither he nor Hunt had the capital to rebuild it, the valuable site lay idle for years. Before this time, i.e. during the summer of 1839, Mr. Knower had died. Even with the Knower estate, Marcy found it possible to salvage very little for the present; although in November of 1837 he had counted upon saving over $100,000 for the several heirs, including his wife, it appears that in the long run less than that amount was obtained, and that in a very long run indeed. In short, any plans of retirement based upon independent means were gone, for years to come. This was an important circumstance, for if he had had an independent position, his political career might just possibly have been different, in one way or another, in the latter part of his life.[6]

Anticipating this result, Marcy had already begun to cast about for employment. At first it seemed that this might well be by an arrangement which Newell suggested. Newell, who had been ousted from the canal department by the Whigs, was preparing to open a law firm. In January, 1840, he suggested that Marcy join him, "not exactly as a partner on the record . . . [but as] a chamber counsellor; . . . the business [as Marcy put it] in some sort [to] be under my supervision." Feeling out of touch with the technical side of the law, and too indolent to brush up, Marcy apparently also felt that it would be humiliating to step down into ordinary practice.

By this arrangement I should, they think, avoid the hazard of growing rusty—find as proper employment for my mind as in any other occupation, and not incur the risque which would attend a return to my old profes-

[6] Cf. Deeds, vol. 19, p. 449 and p. 452, also Mortgages, vol. 16, p. 655, Niagara Co. Clerk's Office; W. Pool, ed., *Landmarks of Niagara County,* 108-112; Deeds, vol. 47, p. 375, Erie Co. Clerk's Office. Marcy's statement to Wetmore (July 31, 1837, M.P.) that he had bought Lockport property to the amount of $90,000, however, may have been a slip of the pen. See also to Wetmore, Jan. 27, May 18, June 8, 14, Sept. 11, to Newell, Sept. 11, M.P. To Wetmore, Nov. 25, 1837, *re* Knower estate, *ibid.*

sion—I should be so situated that I could change my position any day—
& should not be subjected to a severe drudgery.

The project was interrupted, however, by a different assignment. At
the personal solicitation of the chancellor of the state, Marcy early
in February, 1840, became receiver of the bankrupt City Bank of
Buffalo.[7] This task required his full-time services for some months.

Marcy was sworn in as receiver amid strong objections from the
Whigs, who even considered adopting a law which would permit his
removal. One of their worries was that the state government had kept
large funds in the bank, despite its increasingly bad reputation in the
past year, and they feared that Marcy would publicize this. As Marcy
wrote sagely to Wetmore, "they know they cannot escape censure but
hope to blind the eyes of their friends by raising a smoke about my
taking this business in hand. They do not like to have me situated for
most of the coming year in their stronghold . . . I do not [he added]
intend to do them any good," but he went on to say that with himself as well as with the chancellor it was essentially a business matter.

As it turned out, the work proved onerous and involved, although
Marcy from the beginning had the skillful aid of Newell. The bank
was typical of many of those chartered in the 1830's. It had lacked
sufficient backing, had invested hugely in lands, and had made its
loans chiefly to its own directors. After Marcy had examined its affairs
for several weeks, as a matter of fact, he commented that the stock
was entirely worthless and that the state's safety fund, moreover,
would have to be charged some $200,000 to make good the circulat-
ing notes. As for the assets involved, these were typical of investments in general in the whole western area, where one had to rob
Peter to pay Paul and found that Peter's assets were tied up anyway.
Long before Marcy could untangle the concern's affairs—or get very
far in the chamber counselling idea, for which he rented offices at
Albany—he was drawn off to another assignment. As a result, he left
the bank business in Newell's hands. This was reasonably satisfactory,
for by the late 1830's his protégé had become one of the most trusted
financial officers in the state. Afterwards, in 1841, Newell was formally made the receiver himself.[8] This was far better.

---

[7] To Wetmore, Jan. 27, Feb. 4, 1840; diary, July 23, 1843, *ibid.*

[8] S. Croswell to Newell, Mar. 12, N.P.; Marcy to Wetmore, Feb. 4, 14, Mar. 17,
1840, to Newell, Mar. 30, 1840, M.P.; assignment by Marcy of the bank's stocks
and rights to Newell as receiver, Apr. 17, 1841, N.P.

Marcy's new post, which would occupy him from July 23, 1840, through most of April, 1842, was as one of two American commissioners appointed to settle the claims of United States citizens upon Mexico, under a convention which had been signed in 1839. Altogether, there were claims amounting to quite a few million dollars. These had arisen from the arbitrary seizure or destruction of American property during various uprisings and from the occasional arrest and even murder of Americans in that infant republic. Mexico herself was to name two commissioners. In disputed cases, however, the decision was to be made by an arbiter appointed by the king of Prussia.[9]

When Marcy arrived in Washington, late in July, he found only the other American commissioner, John Rowan of Kentucky, present. After the two Mexican spokesmen appeared, three weeks later, there were further delays. For one thing, Marcy and his colleague were touchy on the subject of the method of swearing in the commissioners, fearing that if it were not handled rightly Mexico might later use it as a pretext for invalidating the entire arbitration. Subsequently, there was also a long disagreement as to the procedure to be used in handling the claims. Marcy and Rowan wanted to settle the business with as little protocol as possible, in the spirit of mutual confidence and easy cooperation. This was on the whole not achieved. Instead, there was usually an almost entire disagreement as to the amounts to be granted, followed by long written presentations—one of the American arguments ran to one hundred and thirty pages in length—to the umpire, and the latter had to make the decision. In one case, for instance, the amount originally claimed was $121,000, the American commissioners cut it to about $26,000, the Mexicans were quite unready to yield even that, and von Roenne, the umpire, decided upon about $10,000.

By the legal deadline on February 25, 1842, cases to the pretended value of $6,648,812 had been passed upon, with awards of $2,026,139. Unfortunately, another alleged $5,201,776 worth, in all, remained undecided, although about one third of these, in terms of value, had reached the umpire's hands. To a great extent, the trouble

---

[9] Diary, July 23, 1843, M.P.; C. C. Kohl, *Claims as a Cause of the Mexican War*, 32; D. Hunter Miller, *Treaties and Other International Acts*, IV, 189-197.

had been in the delay of the claimants in presenting their cases. Unquestionably, however, much of a useful sort had been accomplished.[10] For one thing, the awards which had been obtained were reasonably liberal. That Mexico paid only a few installments and then stopped, so that the claimants had to wait until the United States had fought a war with her before receiving full payment, is beside the point.

Throughout the work, Marcy had undoubtedly been the mainstay of the operations, for the Mexican representatives were of low caliber, Judge Rowan was old, ill, and feeble, and Henry M. Brackenridge, who replaced him and was in some ways admirably suited to the task, served only six months.

During his period of service on the commission, Marcy commonly kept bachelor quarters, since Mrs. Marcy came from Albany only in cool weather and even then was often kept in the North by illness in her family. Marcy lived quietly in his leisure hours, doing much reading and often playing cards at the home of the James Larneds, who were relatives of his. His lodgings were at Mrs. Brereton's, as before. When he could get to Albany himself, he had the pleasure of living at 132 State Street in the former Knower residence, which had now been remodelled in very handsome manner to house the two families. Its parlors had been redone in a "chaste and beautiful" style on the Doric order, while the house as a whole had been modernized to include every convenience. Of the Marcys, there were present the commissioner and his wife and their young children, Edmund and Cornelia. Samuel, now a "passed midshipman"—a rank in which he was to lie becalmed for over a decade in all—was home only rarely. As for William, the older of the sons by Dolly, he had not made a great success of his life and had become rather estranged from the rest of the family.[11]

During the whole Whig interlude, which ran until 1845, Marcy paid relatively little attention to politics, even when at Washington.

---

[10] J. B. Moore, *History and Digest of the International Arbitrations. . .*, II, 1220-1238; Kohl, *op. cit.*, 33-34, 37; Hunter Miller, *op. cit.*, IV, 204-205; Rives, *The U.S. and Mexico*, I, 431; to Wetmore, Dec. 16, 1841, Jan. 16, Mar. 2, Apr. 19, 1842, to Newell, Feb. 26, 1842, M.P.; J. H. Smith, *The War with Mexico*, I, 80.

[11] To William, Feb. 8, 1841, diary, Aug. 6, 1843, Gilmer to Marcy, Oct. 18, 1841, M.P.; J. Burke to Marcy, Jan. 15, 1841, State Library.

He seems to have had no interest in a renomination to the governor-ship. Certainly he was not proposed for it. His own choice for the role, by June of 1840, was William C. Bouck, a popular canal com-missioner, and Bouck was the man put up. But the campaign that year was also a presidential one, and very famous.

As ever, the Whig party was divided and weak. It was divided in that it embraced both the National Republicans of Clay and Webster and the extreme state-rights Democrats of Calhoun, a combination illogical enough to ruin any party; it was also weak simply because most voters were usually Democrats. Yet there was still the great depres-sion. In addition, the Whigs had heavy financial backing and were possessed of some clever leaders. This party nominated William Henry Harrison, a popular nonentity who had many years before been identified with the growth of the Northwest Territory and who had once fought a major Indian battle; with him was run, for the vice-presidency, John Tyler, a Calhounite! As for the Democrats, they put up Van Buren again.

There followed an extraordinary electoral race, in which the Whigs made much of Harrison's life in a log cabin and his alleged liking for hard cider. Their campaign was a masterpiece of misrepresenta-tion and general buncombe, but they won by a landslide. It seems that the voters were simply too blindly angry at the bad times to care much who they voted for, if he was not a Democrat. While the strug-gle was at its height,[12] Marcy put his own affairs aside and stayed at Albany, hoping in vain that his efforts would help to produce Van Buren's reelection.

Little as he expected of the new administration, Marcy was of course surprised by what did happen. For the new president died a month after his inauguration, so that Tyler, the state-rights Democrat, became president. Then, when Henry Clay and the Whig majority in congress sought to push through a whole program of the old National Republican type, including a national bank and a higher tariff, Tyler vetoed several of its more significant features. Marcy was present at Washington during this crisis between congress and president, and had some influence in shaping Tyler's veto of the bank charter bill.[13]

---

[12] To Newell, Oct. 13, 16, to Wetmore, Nov. 6, M.P.
[13] To Wetmore, Aug. 18, 1841, *ibid*.

On the whole, however, like everyone else, he looked chiefly to the time when Tyler should be replaced, in so far as public policy was concerned.

On the other hand, Marcy did actively try to win an appointment from Tyler for himself, namely as a judge of the federal supreme court. This was especially true after December, 1843, when Justice Thompson, a New York state man, died, because it was expected that a fellow New Yorker would be named to take his seat. But for two factors, Marcy might well have received this post. The first was that in September, 1843, he presided over the state Democratic convention, which endorsed Van Buren for a renomination. Secondly, Marcy's chief friend and contact in the Tyler government, Secretary of the Navy Gilmer, was killed in an explosion on the warship *Princeton* in the following year. The upshot was that Reuben H. Walworth, the state's chancellor, was offered the seat. Then, after the senate failed to confirm him, he was replaced by Samuel Nelson.[14] Even before this time, however, Marcy had given up the idea.

As for a high New York state office, this was most improbable, for Marcy was the leader of the conservative wing of the party there, which meant that he favored reasonably liberal credit, the extension of the state's system of internal improvements, and a moderately protective tariff; in short, he spoke for the Democrats in the industrial and mercantile community, while the radicals were more representative of the agrarian interests. Such conservatives were in the minority. It was this conservatism, it is true, which had made his somewhat diffident approaches to the Tyler administration rather natural. At the same time, although he was personally friendly to Van Buren, he knew that the latter would never endorse him for a really significant post. The gulf between the two wings of the party was considerable, and Van Buren blamed that gulf to a great degree upon Marcy, particularly because of the independent treasury disagreement of 1837.[15]

Under the circumstances, Marcy was looking around for a private position at the same time that he was trying for the court appointment. He wanted a secure post which would carry him to an age

[14] J. D. Stevenson to Marcy, Feb. 9, 16, Mar. 3, Marcy to Wetmore, Feb. 16, M.P. Wright repeatedly backed Marcy for the post.
[15] Cf. how unready Van Buren was to discuss affairs with him during his New York visit in 1839 (Marcy to Wetmore, Sept. 1, 1839, M.P.).

proper for retirement. Accordingly, when an old friend, Stephen Allen of the New York Life and Trust Company, asked him if he would care to be the president of that business, he was more than receptive. As early as May of 1843 he declared that he was ready to accept, if all of the directors wanted him and if the salary of the post were restored to its old level of $5,000. As it happened, the directors made one difficult proviso. They demanded that an old mortgage which he and Washington Hunt had given on their Lockport properties first be cleared up. The trouble was that this pledge, to the sum of $50,000, had been made to the North American Banking and Trust Company, which had afterwards been proved to be a fraudulent concern, and that Marcy and his associate had therefore refused to honor their commitment to the full. He and Hunt were willing to compromise, and British investors who were the successors to the North American concern were finally ready to take $30,000 in settlement, in a manner typical of the reduction of debts which took place in the 1840's. But whereas Marcy was able to meet his half of this, Hunt was not. The outcome was a continuance of negotiations, which went on through nearly all of 1844.

With the collapse of his supreme court design, Marcy was fully ready to go into the Life and Trust position, if the embarrassing mortgage issue could be cleared up. In a letter which he wrote to one of the leaders of the company, on October 30, 1844, he stated candidly and significantly that he would accept, if no considerable number of the directors opposed him, and would not look to any change in employment so long as he was wanted there.[16] Nearly fifty-eight years of age, he was ready to renounce politics and public affairs for good. As it happened, however, something quite different was in store for him.

---

[16] Allen to Marcy, May 23, 30, 1843, Marcy to Allen, May 28, June 1, Marcy to Judge Vanderpoel, June 18, Butler to Marcy, Sept. 15, Marcy to Wetmore, Dec. 8, 13, Jan. 25, 27, 1844, A. Mann to Marcy, Sept. 10, 1844, Marcy to D. S. Kennedy, Oct. 30, all in M.P.

XI. POLITICS REGAINED

"Gov. Marcy abjures Van Burenism, and will probably get
in, if New York has a place at all. . . ." (Horace Greeley,
February 25, 1845[1])

ALTHOUGH in 1844 and even early in 1845 Marcy had been
ready to give up his chances of returning to public life, after
that time his views suddenly changed. Abruptly, the whole kaleido-
scope of affairs shifted and the parts took on a very different pattern,
far more pleasing to his eye. He was chosen to the highest office
which he had yet held, and his friends began to whisper that he might
yet become president. This strange climacteric in his career was because the Democratic party had undergone a decided shift to the
right, to conservatism. This in turn meant that Marcy's faction in
New York had suddenly become the one favored by the national
leadership, so that the remaining dozen years of his life would have
an importance considerably greater than the many which had already
been unrolled and far greater indeed than he could have anticipated.

Before the swing of the party nationally is considered, however, it
is needful to take a look at what had been going on in New York
state, with particular reference to the developing schism in the party.
Although Van Buren, the ex-president, was inclined to blame this
division upon Marcy, fairer-minded and better-informed men recognized that it was not wholly of his doing. Basically, it arose out of
deepseated differences as to state policy, as well as out of the desire
of the younger leaders in the party to seize power for themselves.

One salient fact was that during the administration (1839-1842)
of that "little man," William H. Seward, the Whigs had spent so
freely in support of canals and railroads as to weaken the credit of
the state. This result was in part, indeed, brought on by wretched
business conditions. Then, in 1842, the Democrats, who controlled
the legislature, had forced through a drastic stop to the Whig measures. All state expenditures had been ended, the canal revenues had

---

[1] *Tribune*, Feb. 26.

been pledged to a reduction of the state's debt, and a general property tax had at long last been applied. The men who had done all this were the radical members of the party, persons like Michael Hoffman and Azariah Flagg, approximately the same group as that which had long been affiliated with Van Buren. On the other hand, Marcy and the rest of the conservatives opposed this "stop and tax" approach. They held that what was needed was merely moderation, reasoning that the state's credit was inherently sound. They affected to call the radicals "Barnburners," on the ground that they were like a farmer who would burn down his barn to get rid of the rats.

On top of these differences as to finance, however, there was also an unhappy disagreement over who should do the state printing. In the session of 1843, Flagg and a number of the other Van Burenites at Albany supported a move to give it to H. H. Van Dyck, one of Croswell's partners in the *Argus,* instead of restoring it to Croswell himself. One reason for this was that for years Croswell had been rather lukewarm in his liberalism and had failed to back the party very effectively. In the ensuing melee, Governor William C. Bouck, who had just begun his term, favored Croswell. So, too, did Marcy, although he was not on hand. He was pleased to learn, late in January, 1843, that Croswell had triumphed over his rivals.

Marcy's chief desire in all of this was to hold the party together; if anything, he took a position between the factions.[2] One consideration was that he had no thought of running for state office again himself. Yet he could not help being involved in the growing squabble and he was steadily pulled to the side of Bouck, whose nomination he had favored. When the latter had come to Albany as governor-elect, he had consulted Marcy on his inaugural message; later, he had asked for or been offered suggestions on other occasions. Sad to relate, however, Bouck was not a highly effective leader, either as the chief executive or as the head of the Democratic Party. In spite of this, Marcy and the other conservatives felt obliged to support him; his views and theirs were somewhat the same[3] and he had twice been nominated by the party. On the other hand, the radicals not only con-

---

[2] H. D. A. Donovan, *The Barnburners,* 18-25, 36-41; Marcy to Wetmore, Jan. 15, 1843, M.P.; diary, Sept. 12, 1843, M.P.

[3] Bouck to Marcy, Nov. 30, 1842, M.P.; Marcy to Van Buren, Dec. 10, V.B.P.; Donovan, *op. cit.,* 25-27.

sidered Bouck's financial policies unsound but feared that he would be a drag upon the organization in the presidential campaign of 1844. In that year, they wanted above all else to make Little Van president again. This undeniable fact and the varied personal ambitions which were tied to it did not prevent them, however, from calling the conservatives "Hunkers" and alleging that the latter's only concern was a "hunkering" for office, which was hardly a fair comment. For, while the leaders on the radical side, who were generally younger, were possessed of a good share of idealism, it was partly their wish to replace men of the older generation, such as Croswell, which inspired them. If the Hunkers yearned to stay in, the Barnburners were eager to "reform" the state administration by ousting them.

As said already, Marcy was by no means unfriendly to Van Buren. The latter had had him as his guest at the White House and at a summer retreat in Georgetown in the months prior to the campaign of 1840, and Marcy had done what he could to prevent his old associate's defeat. Later, it had been at Van Buren's suggestion that he had helped Bouck with the latter's first message. And, in January of 1843 and after, Van Buren invited him to come to his estate at Kinderhook. Marcy was much too shrewd, however, not to know that Van Buren no longer really approved of him and that such invitations came chiefly on the eve of a national convention or election, when there was a need for the conservatives' votes. In fact, when he answered Van Buren's invitation, in January, 1843, it was to twit him for sending his regards to "Mrs. Knower" (there being no Mrs. Knower) and not to Mrs. Marcy, and to allude to Van Buren's estate as "Lindenwald, (so I think you call it)."[4]

When the delegates were chosen to the state convention which would select the deputation to the national convention at Baltimore, Marcy happened to be in New York City. Before he returned to Albany, he was distressed to learn that he had been chosen one of the delegates to this state gathering; his distress was because his selection had been made in opposition to the candidacy of Flagg himself, through no act of his own. Having been given such an assignment,

---

[4] To Wetmore, July 28, Aug. 21, 28, Sept. 11, 1840, M.P.; J. Burke to Newell, Jan. 2, 1841, N.P.; Van Buren letter, cited above; Van Buren to Marcy, Jan. 13, July 28, Dec. 6, 1843, and Marcy to Wetmore, Dec. 8, 13, 1843, M.P. Also Marcy to Van Buren, Jan. 27, 1843, V.B.P.

however, he went into it whole-heartedly. He was at Syracuse, the place of assembly, three days ahead of time.

As things turned out, Marcy's faction proved to have the lead and he was chosen to preside. For this role, he defeated the Barnburners' choice, Samuel Young, by a two-thirds vote, but probably many of the radicals had backed him as a conciliatory gesture. Surprisingly enough, however, some maneuverings by certain of Marcy's own supposed friends had the result of keeping him from being chosen as a delegate to Baltimore. This did not distress him, actually. "Upon the whole I was rather pleased," he was to write later, but he was sorry that he had not been able to subdue the factionalism which had been so prevalent. The convention had whole-heartedly supported Van Buren's renomination, however.[5]

Early in December, 1843, incidentally, Marcy finally spent the much talked of weekend at Lindenwald, which seems to have passed pleasantly enough. And, two months after, Van Buren even asked him to take on the task of writing his campaign biography. This Marcy dodged, however, and the job finally went to Bancroft.[6]

As it turned out, Bancroft's biography was not published until many years after, because Van Buren failed to win the nomination. The reason was that before the Baltimore convention he was asked if he favored annexing Texas, a question of great interest to southern Democrats. In a letter of March 20, Marcy himself advised Van Buren to speak out on the subject, arguing that abolition was gaining ground rapidly in New England; he apparently believed that it would be unwise to offend its adherents by going for Texas. Van Buren did decide to oppose the move. His reply, published in April, reasoned that it would bring about war with Mexico and would put the United States in a bad light because Mexico had a claim to the territory. Behind this doubtless lay such a political motive as Marcy seems to have had. Marcy's only comment on Van Buren's stand, afterwards, and on that of Henry Clay, who was soon to be the Whig nominee and who had much the same view, was to tell Wetmore that Van Buren's was the more statesmanlike of the two, but that both would tend to "abate the annexation fever to a considerable extent." Seemingly, he had no understanding of the way in which Van Buren's Texas letter would backfire.[7]

It was a fact, though, that the letter ruined Van Buren's chances. The latter's opponents included not only the annexationists, but also his ancient enemies, the Calhounites, plus those who were backing Lewis Cass of Michigan for the presidency. This coalition was able to get the two-thirds rule readopted, which prevented Van Buren's being chosen. Nor was Cass put up. Instead, the party nominated James K. Polk of Tennessee, a compromise figure acceptable both to the pro-Texas faction and to the Van Burenites. Though classed as a dark horse, he was a man of considerable talent. He had been governor of his state and speaker of the national house of representatives.

Before the convention was over, incidentally, Marcy was given a few votes for the vice-presidency, by some of Cass's supporters. He was one of seven persons honored by being so considered. This brings up the charge which had sometimes been made in the preceding three years, that he had been intriguing for advancement with various southerners, including Tyler and some of the friends of Cass. An examination of all relevant documents for the period, however, fails to support the charge. While he had tried for a court seat, through Tyler, he had more than once let it be known to Tyler or the latter's intimates that in 1844 he would be on the Democratic side and that Tyler could hope for nothing from him. Nor is there evidence of an intrigue with Cass, although there were one or two rumors to that effect. The fact was rather that he was simply a conservative Democrat. He was not only not of the Van Buren wing of the party, in person; he was also in his views more akin to Cass or (at least on annexation) to Polk, than to the ex-president. On the other hand, he had plainly supported Van Buren in the latter's drive for a third chance at the White House.[8]

Like the Barnburners, Marcy accepted the Polk nomination in good

[7] James C. N. Paul, *Rift in the Democracy*, 115-123; to Van Buren, Mar. 20, V.B.P.; to Wetmore, May 2, 1844, M.P.

[8] *Journal*, June 1 (from Balto. *Patriot*); on the charge, see Wright to Van Buren, Jan. 29, 1842, V.B.P., Marcy to Dr. N. Niles, Apr. 18, 1842, M.P.; Throop to Van Buren, Sept. 27, 1842, V.B.P., Marcy to Van Buren, Dec. 1, 1843, V.B.P.; for the rebuttal, see Marcy to Wetmore, Sept. 17, Oct. 19, Nov. 21, 1841, M.P.

part once it was made. More than that, he shortly wrote the nominee a long letter describing the political situation in New York and telling him that he could count upon the support of all the elements of the party there. Polk replied in a prompt and friendly manner that he would welcome further information and comments during the campaign. Marcy sent such comments at least once. He also wrote a brief introduction for a campaign volume on the lives of Polk and Dallas. No doubt he wanted the party's new leader to remember that he and the Hunkers existed.[9]

During the discussion of gubernatorial candidates, Marcy consistently urged that Bouck be run again. In reference to the talk that Silas Wright should be put up instead, he argued that such a move would line up Bouck's friends against Wright and increase the schism that prevailed. He added that the step would also raise the old charge of Regency dictation. In spite of this, he said further that:

I yield to no man in personal regard or in admiration for Mr. Wright. I think him the most perfect specimen of a democrat in the nation, and one of its ablest statesmen; The hopes of our cause and country rest more upon him than any man in it. Yet I would not have him used as a candidate for Gov. on the coming election and will do all that in me lies to prevent it.

None the less, various Barnburners throughout the state did talk up Wright's name very vigorously, and many moderates hoped that his popularity and good sense would help to reunite the party. Consequently, the movement for him grew overwhelming and he in time was given the nomination.

Since Marcy had opposed this, he wrote to Wright to explain why. He said frankly that he could not congratulate him upon the nomination and that he had tried to prevent it, although he promised his full support for his election. The basic trouble was in the disunity in the party, he argued, which would make a governor's task impossible, even for Wright. The very act of putting the latter up, he said, had been essentially a campaign against the incumbent, Governor Bouck, and those who had suggested that Bouck be put aside would want to have places in the new administration, which would greatly increase the factionalism. As for himself, he said, he had not been

---

[9] Diary, July 5, Polk to Marcy, July 9, M.P.; Marcy to Polk, Sept. 11, P.P., 1 ser.

really a prime mover in Bouck's nomination and had had little to do with his appointments. But since Bouck had asked his advice and to a considerable extent followed it, he could not condemn him unless he had erred "grossly" in other particulars. He denied that Bouck's administration had done this. The incorruptible Wright responded frankly that he regretted the nomination of himself as much as Marcy did, or more, and that he almost wished for defeat in order to escape the troubles which victory would bring. He lamented, also, he pointed out, the unhappy position which he had had in the United States senate in the past year, in which he had found every one of Van Buren's foes urging him for the presidency, at one time or another, in order to whittle Van Buren down. Now, he implied, he was sad to have become a stalking horse for the enemies of Bouck.[10]

Marcy kept his promise and worked to have Wright elected.[11] He and his fellow Hunkers, of course, did very genuinely respect Wright, as did every one else; they also realized that he had not sought, himself, to take Bouck's place. The difficulty, really, was to secure the triumph of Polk, who had had no personal following in the state and whose annexationist views were none too popular there. Such proved to be the case, for Wright ran ahead of Polk, but both were successful. Polk's narrow margin of 5500 votes in the state gave him the presidency.

Before the ballots were fully counted, Prosper Wetmore wrote to ask if Marcy had not made a mistake in committing himself to the New York Life and Trust Company. Marcy replied by summarizing his position with extreme candor.

Albany 10th Nov. 44.

My dear Genl.

Though we are not clearly out of the woods it is not presumptuous to talk as if we were so. I for[e] saw you would be surprised to learn that steps have been taken with my consent to bring me into [the] NYL & T. Co. but I am at liberty to decline and shall use that liberty if I see a reasonable chance of public employment. I was so situated that I must say something to the application which has been made to me before I could know

---

[10] To Hammond, June 1, 1851, M.P.; J. D .Perkins to Polk, June 3, 1845, P.P., 2 ser.; Marcy to Wetmore, July 20, 1844, M.P.; to Wright, Sept. 7, draft, and Wright to Marcy, Sept. 13, M.P.

[11] Marcy to Flagg, Oct. 11, F.P.

what were my prospects in another quarter, and should they prove to be better than I have or do now anticipate I can arrest the measure on foot in Wl. St. . . . I certainly much prefer public life to private station but have I well founded hopes that I can be indulged in this preference? . . . As to the [United States Supreme Court] Judgeship, I regard it as beyond my reach. If Walworth remains before the senate he will be confirmed— of this I have no doubt. Is there a probability that he will be withdrawn? Not the least in my judgement.

The next place partial friends would assign to me, would be the senate. In truth I have no great desire to go there but if I had, could I get there? Who are the candidates for that situation. [He then listed six or eight.] . . . In this squabble my chances would be but slight.

We come now to the cabinet. The first question to be settled is will the old one [Tyler's] be broken up. Doubtful. I think not wholly. It is probable that a New Yorker may sooner or later be introduced into it. Wright can go there if he wishes but he will not[,] but who will go there will depend in a great measure upon the opinion of Mr. W. and Mr. V.B. My own judgt is that the unbiassed opinion of W. would favor me. I think otherwise as to Mr. V.B. The whole *barn burning* interest would be in the field against me. They want office and would see [in] me in that position an obstacle. . . . I think you will agree with me that [my chances] are not very good.

I do not much doubt but that if I should decline the NY offer and turn office seeker I could ultimately get something worth having but probably not the first or highest object of my wishes—I should in all human probability experience a series of mortifying disappointments.

I confess I do not rightly understand my own position[.] I am almost certain that it is not so strong a one as my friends suppose and it may be a little better than I imagine. [He went on to say that if Silas Wright were there, he would have a talk with him.] I might and may converse with Mr. Flagg, who I think is better disposed towards me than any of his peculiar associates. . . .

It was an admirable description of his prospects and even more of his attitude. There were only two flaws in it and both of them minor. The first was that Walworth's name *was* withdrawn, for the judgeship; on the other hand, it went to Nelson, as has been stated. As to a senate seat, Marcy was wrong in thinking that he had no chance, for in the next few months Bouck and Wright each offered him one, in turn. When the offers came, however, he declined them.[12]

What Marcy really wanted was a seat in the Polk cabinet or some other high administrative office. Above all, he had his eyes fixed upon the post of secretary of the treasury. This was one for which he was

[12] Wetmore to Marcy, Nov. 8, Marcy to Wetmore, Nov. 10, 1844, June 8, 1852, M.P.

especially well qualified, after his long dealings with financial problems in his dozen years as comptroller and governor. He also must have been conscious of the great importance of the patronage which the role carried. Probably he confided this intent to some of his more intimate friends as early as November, but some of his Washington adherents seem to have begun to urge the idea without being prompted. On the other hand, Marcy was conscious that some men considered him "a by-gone politician," as a Whig sheet had put it, and he knew, as the above letter shows, that the Barnburners would warmly oppose him. However that might be, he carefully avoided any appearance of seeking an appointment. After the election, he took pains not to write any more letters to Polk. He also exercised great discretion in conversation and in writing to other men.

On November 18, Marcy wrote to Wetmore that he would not go to New York City to consult with the insurance company's heads until after he had had a chance to have his talk with Wright. It apparently was not much later than this that Wright came to Albany. Marcy asked him if he would mind conversing about the subject, to which the governor-elect answered that he had no hesitation. In the discussion which followed, Wright said that he would not support him for secretary of state, preferring Butler or some one else. As for the treasury department, on the contrary, he would take Marcy above anyone else in the state and—Marcy thought he remembered later—anyone else in the whole country. He said that he assumed that the lesser cabinet places did not interest Marcy, and he added that if he was consulted he would himself recommend "Mr. Flagg or some such man." "To this I replied," Marcy recorded years later, "that I had thought of no other place but the Treasury & did not believe I could make up my mind to take any other." He declared, moreover, that Wright promised to give him early notice of any news regarding Polk's intentions.

It was good, of course, that the hero of the Barnburners backed him for the place he especially wanted. Yet there were other people who would have a say. According to Marcy's account, Wright took a train to Kinderhook immediately after their interview, to consult with Van Buren about various matters. When he returned, Marcy realized that the Little Magician had rather altered the governor-elect's views.

"I thought Mr. W's manner was somewhat changed & less frank & cordial than on the former occasion . . . & [I concluded] that I could not expect any efficient support from him." Among other things, he learned that Van Buren favored his being a United States senator and seemingly not much else. Since Van Buren must have known how little liking Marcy had for a senate seat, he probably simply wanted his one-time associate disregarded. Van Buren was ready enough to have him muster the conservatives in his behalf or to have him perform so onerous a job as writing a campaign biography, but when the real test came, he wanted one of his own coterie to get whatever important billet was offered. Marcy was pretty well aware of this. He was rather shocked, none the less, to find that Wright had changed his tune also. When he learned that Flagg, Colonel Young, and "Prince John" Van Buren had been at Kinderhook at the same time that Wright had, however, he realized that he was confronted with a group decision.[13]

As for the senate seats, there were to be two available. When Marcy declined to accept one of them, they were divided according to plan between the Hunkers and the Barnburners, with Daniel S. Dickinson, the erstwhile lieutenant-governor, being chosen for the former group and Dix for the Barnburners.

Meantime, early in that month, James K. Polk sent Van Buren a missive asking for advice in the formation of his cabinet. He explained that he had offered Wright the treasury department but that the latter had begged off—yet that it seemed proper that New York should have either that position or the state department. Even so, he wanted suggestions as to the lesser posts. When Van Buren replied, it was to urge Butler for state and Flagg and Cambreleng for treasury. He added coolly that he would not speak of other New Yorkers, not wishing to disparage them. His letter was probably partly founded on one from Wright of the day before, along rather similar lines. At this moment, Marcy, on his part, was none too cheerful. He would gladly have settled for the supreme court, which was not cleared up until February 12. He also was half inclined to believe a

---

[13] Cf. Marcy to Polk, Nov. 20, 1848, AD, M.P.; John B. O'Connor to Polk, July 21, 1845, P.P., 1 ser.; Marcy to Wetmore, Nov. 18, 1844, to Hammond, June 1, 1851, M.P.

rumor that Calhoun, Tyler's secretary of state, would be kept on by Polk, in which case, he thought, all Democrats would do well to keep out, anyhow.[14]

When Polk arrived in Washington on February 13, he had still made no decisions as to his cabinet. On the 17th, however, he offered the state department to Senator James Buchanan of Pennsylvania, and Buchanan soon accepted. On the same day, Polk also chose his old friend Cave Johnson of Tennessee as postmaster general. Furthermore, he had Robert J. Walker of Mississippi, one of the leaders in the stop-Van Buren movement of the year before and a speculator in Texan scrip, in mind for one of the places—and he was also thinking of Marcy himself.[15]

Certain it is that as early as January, 1845, Polk's law partner and confidant, A. V. Brown, had been asking some New York congressmen if Marcy would not do for the cabinet and Flagg for the customs house. The latter post was the biggest federal plum below the level of the cabinet and the foreign ministries. Marcy may well have been his real preference among New Yorkers from the beginning, for he knew him, and Marcy opposed neither annexation—now, at least—nor a reduced tariff; these points were expected to be the cardinal policies of the new government. As for Van Buren's followers, they were mostly against the former measure, although Butler was not. Marcy's friends, moreover, were urging him actively. Petitions were sent to Polk in his behalf, signed by nineteen legislators and eleven congressmen, but the chief workers in his interest were Bouck, Edwin Croswell, and Senator Dickinson. The ex-governor wrote to Polk on February 18 that no Barnburner should be selected, because of the Texas issue; he asked that Polk consult with Dickinson, who was New York's best advocate of that cause. On this same day, Croswell wrote of Marcy as follows:

I know of no one whose appointment w'd be more in accordance with the public wish and expectation. To experience in financial affairs, and to familiarity with all the public questions of the day, he unite[s] enlarged and liberal views. . . . While he w'd be acceptable to the North, he w'd

---

[14] Polk to Van Buren, Jan. 4, Van Buren to Polk, Jan. 18, AD, Wright to Van Buren, Jan. 17, V.B.P.; Marcy to Wetmore, Jan. 10, M.P.

[15] H. B. Learned, "The Sequence of Appointments to Polk's Original Cabinet," *Amer. Hist. Rev.*, XXX, 76-83.

be scarcely less so to the South; for on all occasions he has sustained the broad democratic policy which upholds the Compromises and the Constitution, regardless of the clamors of fanatics or the designs of politicians.

In a letter to Senator Dickinson, shortly after, Marcy stated his entire readiness to back up the aims of the new administration.[16]

I beg you would not give yourself one uneasy thought. Were I not prepared to support what are known to be its prominent measures and to support them too in good faith & from a conviction that they are wise & the good of the country requires them to be carried out I should not permit myself to occupy for a single moment the position of a candidate for a cabinet office—or any other important office.

He had definitely changed his view, then, on the political desirability of annexing Texas.

Polk deliberated for some time. On Friday evening, February 21, he talked with both of the New York senators. It may have been at this time that Dix threatened him by predicting that if Marcy was appointed the Democratic majority in the state would be broken up. This was rather uncalled for; certainly it would be true only if the Barnburners made it so. On the 22nd, in any case, Polk wrote to Van Buren that he could not give either the state department or the treasury to a New Yorker and that he was considering George Bancroft for the latter; he explained that this was partly due to pressure from the South and West for a southerner for secretary of the treasury. Although he did not say so, he intended Robert J. Walker for the latter. He added that the only place left for New York was the war department. For this billet, he said, he presumed that Flagg and Cambreleng would not do. "*Gov. Marcy* has been strongly recommended, [he said, anent this seat] and Mr. Butler has been spoken of, but I have doubts from you whether the latter would accept."

Later that day, Dix and Dickinson had called again upon Polk. The two had discussed New Yorkers available for the place in question and had finally agreed that Judge Jacob Sutherland would be acceptable to both factions. Polk had not considered Sutherland satisfactory. As he explained to Van Buren, he was ignorant of the man's views and yet knew that he lacked much of a reputation nationally. He went on to say that if either Butler or Marcy would do, in the eyes of Van

[16] S. Stetson to Flagg, Jan. 25, F.P.; P.P., 2 ser., Feb. *passim*.; Bouck to Polk, Feb. 18, Croswell to Polk, Feb. 18, Marcy to Dickinson, Feb. 24, all in P.P., 1 ser.

Buren and his friends, he'd be satisfied. "I know them *personally*.—
They have both public character,—would be satisfactory to the public
out of N. York—, and give strength to the administration. . . . With
either—I know I would have an able and safe man." But before this
letter even reached Kinderhook, he felt obliged to act and proffered
the vacant place to Butler. The latter at once declined, although admitting that he would have accepted the state department or the
treasury.[17] As soon as Polk received this answer, he wrote to Marcy,
offering him the post. This was on March 1.

In his letter to Marcy, Polk explained his desire that the state be
represented in the war department. He was confident that Marcy's
opinions and views would fit with his own. "Your general political
principles I know, are such as meet with my full approbation." He
remarked that his views were those of the Baltimore platform of
1844. This last had called for tariff reduction and had been against
federal expenditures for internal improvements and a recharter of a
central bank. All these had become party commitments in 1840 or
earlier. The chief new feature of the 1844 platform had been its demand for "the reoccupation of Oregon and the reannexation of
Texas." While apologizing for his haste, Polk asked Marcy to reply
as early as possible and requested that he be in the capital by March
5, if he could. If necessary, he could return to Albany later to clear
up any private affairs. In a letter which he wrote to Van Buren at
the same time to explain his decision, he commented that Marcy
"possesse [d] undoubted talents and business habits," subjoining the
remark that Flagg, whom he had considered also, was unknown in the
country at large.[18]

Marcy's friends at the capital were quick to urge him to accept.
Samuel Nelson, the new associate justice, wrote that very afternoon
that "if you are tendered the *War* Department you must not hesitate
a moment in accepting it—. . . . This is the fixed advice of your friends
here." Senator Dickinson was even more pressing; he wrote breath-
lessly that "Polk is a prince & has done the best he could & it has been
full of difficulty and I have pledged you to stand it & you *must* for we
have been to the *death*." There were also those like Washington

---

[17] S. T. Van Buren to M. Van Buren, Mar. 2, Polk to same, Feb. 22, V.B.P.
[18] Polk to Marcy, Mar. 1, M.P., and to Van Buren, Mar. 1, V.B.P.

Hunt, who was now a Whig congressman, who were quick to reason that the war department would very likely soon be one of great importance. "I have expected no good from this administration," Hunt wrote, "but if you come into the Cabinet, my apprehensions of mischief will be much allayed."

On the same day, Sunday, March 2, that Hunt penned this, Marcy himself wrote to Wetmore that he would obviously not be given a cabinet seat. "I shall draw a blank," he said. He had accordingly written to Stephen Allen that he would take the New York Life and Trust offer. Luckily, Allen knew that Marcy might still have a suitable political post and would prefer it; he had replied in a kindly spirit that the subject could be deferred for another week. Thus, when Marcy received Polk's letter, on March 3, he was free to comply. His thought of accepting nothing less than the treasury was quickly brushed aside. He took the steamer for New York City that very night and, next morning, breakfasted with Wetmore and Croswell. He reached Washington early Wednesday morning.[19]

---

[19] Nelson to Marcy, Mar. 1, Dickinson, ditto, Hunt, Mar. 2, Marcy to Wetmore, Mar. 2, 4, Allen to Marcy, Mar. 3, M.P. Marcy to Polk, Mar. 3, P.P. ,1 ser.; *Journal*, Mar. 4, *Tribune*, Mar. 6.

XII. SECRETARY OF WAR

"I have officially acted on the hypothesis that our peace [with Mexico] may be temporarily disturbed without however believing it will be." (Marcy to Wetmore, July 6, 1845[1])

THOSE Whigs who had affected during the 1844 campaign not to know who James K. Polk was, were destined to get a better idea as the months of his administration unrolled. He was a man of decided views and great determination. Although of a rather narrow cast of mind and somewhat suspicious and lacking in personal warmth—despite his southern courtliness[2]—he was to prove one of the strongest presidents in the whole "middle period." As for his aims, they may be described as fivefold. One of them, it is true, the annexation of Texas, had in the main been met by Tyler and congress just before inauguration day. By a joint resolution, congress had voted its approval and Tyler had followed this up by dispatching a messenger to tell the United States *chargé* there to begin negotiations with Texan leaders. Polk's other aims, however, were ambitious enough for any man. They were the revision of the tariff, to put it on a merely revenue basis, the revival of the independent treasury, and, in the foreign field, the settlement of the Oregon issue and the securing of Upper California. All but the last of these had been foreshadowed in the party's platform in 1844, to which Polk had asked Marcy to adhere. It was a bold program.

As a further move to insure his success, Polk asked all of the future cabinet officers to endorse a circular letter regarding the internal conduct of the administration. Polk was letting it be known that he did not wish a second term,[3] thus inadvertently divesting himself of much of his control over the party. On the other hand, he desired his administration to be neutral as to the question of a successor to himself; he thus asked his aides to promise to resign at once if they

---

[1] M.P.

[2] Mrs. S. M. Maury, *The Statesmen of America in 1846*, 4-5.

[3] Cf. *Herald*, Mar. 11.

ever became candidates for the presidency themselves. Marcy and the other department heads were all quick to pledge this.[4] It was none the less true that Marcy and James Buchanan, the new secretary of state, and Robert J. Walker, the new secretary of the treasury, were all popularly thought of as candidates.

For himself, Marcy probably had no mental reservations in giving Polk the asked-for promise. While his appointment had revived his political interest and no doubt given him an occasional thought of the presidency, he does not seem to have used the Polk period for electioneering. Generally, indeed, it was not typical of him to do so —with the one exception of the *Courier & Enquirer* intrigue while he was senator. In addition, he was as usual inclined to think of himself as rather old.[5] What was more serious, he was all too well aware of the angry feelings which the members of the Van Buren-Wright wing of the party entertained towards him once he had accepted the new post. As he wrote sadly to Newell on April 6:

When I got here I was perfectly astounded at the violent unjust and cruel warfare which had been waged against my political character—at the men who had been the active participators in it and the free use of the . . . names and of great names too which had been invoked. . . .

He recognized that some of the bitterness was on account of the over-zealous activity of certain men, like John D. Stevenson, who had pressed for his appointment and in doing so had sometimes been none too scrupulous in their methods.[6] But there was little which he could do about that. It was plain that the old Bouck-versus-Wright rift had been replaced by a more serious cleavage between himself and Wright. This was regrettable.

Of the other members of the cabinet, the one who would intrigue really actively for advancement was to be Buchanan. This "timid but able bachelor of many friendships,"[7] whose career was to be intertwined with Marcy's during the rest of the latter's life, had already loomed upon the horizon as a presidential aspirant. He had accumulated a tidy fortune at law,[8] which gave him an enviable financial

[4] Polk's circular, Mar. 4, James Buchanan, *Works*, VI, 110-111. Marcy to Polk, Mar. 5, P.P., 1 ser.
[5] See Seward's comment, below.
[6] To Newell, Apr. 6, 1845, to Wetmore, Nov. 18, 1844, M.P.
[7] James Schouler, *History of the United States*, IV, 499.
[8] T. Jenkins to wife, "Jan. 1845," State Library.

independence. Yet, as Polk's careful diary was to record, he could shilly-shally most unpredictably, and always with an eye to the main chance. Marcy rather respected him,[9] however, and there grew up between them, eventually, something close to friendship. As for the second man in the cabinet, Robert J. Walker, the secretary of the treasury, he was the spearhead of the southern wing of the party, the low tariff and annexationist group. He also had great ability, while his key role in the advancement of Polk and also of the Texas issue and the important part which he would play in the framing of the tariff of 1846 were to mark him as the most influential of Polk's subordinates. Only the passage of years would show how basically unreliable he was. The other department heads were John Young Mason, of Virginia, the intelligent and amiable attorney general; Bancroft, Marcy's old friend, who became secretary of the navy; and Polk's personal ally and adviser on the patronage, Cave Johnson of Tennessee, the postmaster general. In Marcy, Walker, Buchanan, and Bancroft, the president had four aides of striking if varied ability.

Despite Polk's large desires, the first concern of the new government had to be with the further parcelling out of the loaves and fishes. There was no gainsaying the popular demand on that score. Since the days of Marcy's "spoils" dictum and Jackson's pronouncement on rotation, there had developed a surprising boldness on the part of the office seekers. One New York City man, for example, not only avowed that he was eager for "a chance at the 'public crib' " but asked the president himself, to whom he was writing, to "hurry up the cakes"! Another man, by the way, won credit with Polk by letting him assume that a missing arm had been lost in fighting for his country, after which Polk began to look to the man's interest—only to find later that the arm had been lost in firing a salute for Harrison in 1840! By and large, however, the administration made good appointments. On the other hand, it paid too little attention to conciliating the principal factions of the party and was to be almost wholly unsuccessful with the Van Burenites.[10]

The ousting of Francis Preston Blair from the public printing,

---

[9] To Wetmore, July 8, 24, 1841, M.P.

[10] John Hartwell to Polk, June 11, 1846, P.P., 2 ser.; auto. draft, by Polk, unsigned, Sept. 6, 1845, *ibid.*; N. A. Graebner, "James K. Polk, A Study in Federal Patronage," *Miss. Vall. Hist. Rev.,* vol. 38, pp. 613-632.

which came because Polk regarded the man as hostile, was not a step to please the Barnburners. Marcy also regretted it,[11] for Blair was one of the truest of the old Jacksonians. Yet he and the famous *Globe* were supplanted by Thomas Ritchie and the *Union,* with John P. Heiss as the business manager. Significantly, these men were to take a strongly pro-southern line, although Polk himself generally thought as a nationalist. In New York state, worst of all, the Barnburners were disgruntled. Early or late, Van Buren himself and Flagg, Cambreleng, and Dix all declined appointments at Polk's hand, considering what was offered to be beneath their deserts and suspecting the motives involved. Butler did become district attorney and Michael Hoffman naval officer, but the latter was an old friend of Polk. The Barnburners also argued that the richest plum of all, the collectorship at New York, had been promised to one of their number; when it went to Cornelius W. Lawrence, whom Marcy backed,[12] they felt cheated. On his part, Marcy was increasingly driven into the position of sustaining his own friends—not that this took much driving. This meant opposing the Van Burenites, and the gulf between the two schools grew wider. It is possible that if he had gone to Albany and Kinderhook shortly after he entered office and had had long and frank talks with Wright and especially Van Buren, sincerely offering to deal with them on a highly liberal basis and to give their counsels a careful hearing, a rift might have been averted and the history of the next few years might have been very different. But Marcy cannot be blamed for failing to foresee what did happen. He also knew very well how uncompromising the Van Burenites were; as it was, he in time complained that the Barnburners received more than their share of the offices.[13] Among his own adherents, Wetmore became naval agent, Bouck assistant treasurer, Albert Gallup the collector at Albany, and Stevenson, later, a colonel. But the end result was that neither he nor the Van Burenites were placated or gained in strength.

As for Marcy's own department, that was not used as a field of patronage. While the administration in general removed about half

---

[11] J. L. O'Sullivan to Van Buren, April 5, V.B.P.; E. I. McCormac, *James K. Polk,* 300-302.

[12] Dix to Butler, June 16, Butler Papers, Princeton; Marcy to Seymour, June 15, S.P.

[13] To Newell, Feb. 26, 1846, M.P.

of the Indian agents by the end of 1845, Marcy was careful to see to it that the war department proper went largely untouched. This soon quieted the fears of his Whig clerks, who had been deeply alarmed at the news of his appointment. By the end of 1845, in fact, he had in most of the offices made no changes at all. "I am altogether the most moderate man in the concern," he wrote.[14] This was particularly wise at the outset, when he was studying his new role.

Marcy was not wholly unprepared for his new tasks, of course, after his service in the War of 1812 and his experience as adjutant general of his state. He also knew personally several of the higher officers. He had become well acquainted with Scott, the commanding general, in Canadian Rebellion days—"I like him very well," he had written; among the others, he was well acquainted at least with General Wool, an old Troy man, and with General Worth, who had once been in business in Albany.[15] It was also true that the army in those days was far from a complex affair. The staffs were small. The secretary's own force, for example, had just nine clerks, two messengers, and a handyman, while the offices of the adjutant general, the quartermaster general, and so on, were even smaller. These offices were in the Northwest Executive Building, where the historic State, War, and Navy Building would later rise.

All told, the army itself numbered only fourteen regiments, and this was the entire army. There were no quartermaster corps, engineer troops, signal corps, or intelligence section, although the United States did have small staffs of quartermaster and engineer officers. In short, it was an army of only the bare essentials. The eight regiments of infantry were still armed with flintlock muskets, General Scott considering the latter to be on the whole the most reliable weapons. The four regiments of artillery were primarily equipped with heavy guns for coastal defense, and that was what their men were trained for; fortunately, however, each regiment had one company of "light" or field artillery, admirably trained. These four little companies of

---

[14] Report of personnel, with dates of appt., Jan. 7, 1846, *HED56*, 29th cong., 1st sess., p. 1-23; *Union*, Apr. 27, 1849; to Wetmore, July 23, 1845, M.P.; A. Campbell, Jr., to Marcy, Dec. 19, 1850, M.P.

[15] To Wetmore, Mar. 18, 1838, M.P.; Wool and Marcy had both studied law in John Russell's office at Troy (John Ellis Wool, *D.A.B.*); Worth to Capt. Chas. Weyler, Jan. 17, 1848, P.P., 2 ser.

mobile artillery were the best feature in the army. There were also two regiments of dragoons, i.e. cavalry. If the army lacked trimmings, however, it lacked volume even more. It had recently been cut drastically, in an ill-timed move for economy on the very eve of the age of "manifest destiny." The infantry companies were authorized to have only forty-two enlisted men, instead of the conventional hundred, while the artillery and dragoons had fared only a little better. In all, the maximum enlisted strength was only 7,883, and because of various circumstances the actual enrollment was usually about one thousand less. There were also one or two other defects. In the middle ranks of the officer corps there were serious gaps. What was equally bad was that few of the officers had ever commanded a unit larger than a company, let alone a division or corps, for the troops were widely scattered around the frontiers.[16] On the whole, however, it was a fairly good little army.

In spite of this comparative simplicity on the part of the military structure, Marcy moved slowly in his new duties. He felt his way in. He left the army staff more or less unchanged, just as he had done with the clerks, although it was heavily Whig in character. In fact, when a point of law made Polk require the dismissal of Major Samuel Cooper from the adjutant general's office, Marcy succeeded in having the law changed and that able officer returned to his post.[17] Marcy's time was very much absorbed, however, in general patronage and other political questions. In addition, many of his hours were used up in the handling of certain nonmilitary problems which were within his purview. These included pensions, the leasing out of mineral lands, and the making of Indian treaties.

Although Marcy was thus involved in a number of minor matters, his role as secretary of war was a serious one, for the United States' foreign relations were increasingly such that a major conflict might arise. In the first place, Mexico did not at all accept the idea of the United States' having Texas. As soon as Tyler had signed the joint

---

[16] Report of Secretary William Wilkins, Nov. 30, 1844, *HED2*, 28th cong., 2nd sess., 111-120; Report of Scott, Nov. 20, 1845, *HED2*, 29th cong., 1st sess., 209; J. H. Smith, *The War with Mexico*, I, 139-140, 450; O. L. Spaulding, *The United States Army in War and Peace*, 182.

[17] C. Johnson to Polk, May 23, 1846, P.P., 2 ser.; J. R. Poinsett to G. Kemble, June 26, 1846, *Calendar of the Poinsett Papers*, 204; *Journal*, July 28, 1857.

resolution to that effect, her minister had quit the country, severing relations; indeed, she had already announced that annexation would definitely mean war. In the months that followed, moreover, that weak but deluded country had taken one step after another to prepare itself for a contest. The result was that when President Jones of Texas publicly came out for union with the United States, Marcy had the task of ordering those units of the army which had already been assembled on the Texas-Louisiana border to make preparations to move in, and, if need be, defend Texas. As a matter of fact, Tyler had already seen to it that quite a large force was near by; it was commanded by General Zachary Taylor. Besides this, however, there was also a prospect of trouble as to where the boundary of Texas and Mexico would be, there was the president's desire for Upper California, and there were the claims of American citizens upon Mexico. On the last score, little of the money awarded to American nationals by Marcy and the other claims commissioners in 1841-1842 had ever been paid, to say nothing of other claims.

Over and above these difficulties south of the border, however—if there was a border—there was the grave Oregon issue. In his inaugural address, Polk had declared that the American title to "the country of the Oregon" was "unquestionable," although he had avoided saying how far north he would expect the claim to run. In brief, there was a possibility of serious trouble with Britain, too.

Marcy spent the month of June on a combination of inspection trip and vacation in New York state. During his absence, there were rumors that a great Mexican army had reached the Rio Grande. General Taylor was accordingly told to prepare his troops for embarkation to the western frontier of Texas; what was more, he was notified that his final aim would be to camp on or near the Rio Grande, which Texas claimed as her limit. This meant that Polk had already decided to occupy the almost wholly uninhabited land west of the Nueces River, which was nearly certain to be a bone of contention with Mexico. Marcy's own orders to Taylor, on July 30, while somewhat vague, were clear on that point: Taylor was to move at least part of his force west of the Nueces. All the same, Marcy did not expect war. Writing to Wetmore in this month, he commented that the process of annexation was going ahead well; he added that he had "at no time felt that war . . . was probable"; the most he looked for, he said, was a brief interruption of peace, a passing incident.[18]

On the whole, this was a satisfactory summer for him. The heat was intense, but it bothered him only slightly; he was helped by a shower bath which he had Wetmore send him and which he installed at his lodgings. These presumably were at Mrs. Latimer's, "on the President's square," where he and his wife had lodged during the spring and where the Bancrofts lived; it was a congenial household. "I am very industrious," he wrote to Samuel; "I go often to my office before breakfast & almost always after dinner. I am getting up quite a reputation for industry."[19]

As the autumn came on, Marcy increasingly did see that the army was not adequate for the emergencies which might arise. For one thing, although over half of its strength had been massed in or near Texas, this had not been enough to provide the fullest security in that area, so that in August Marcy had been directed to authorize Taylor to accept volunteers from nearby states. By contrast, however, the Indian frontier was only thinly covered. What was almost as bad was that there was only one regiment of some four hundred men on the whole northern boundary, and many coastal points, such as Boston and the mouth of the Potomac, had no men at all—although the affairs with Britain were nearing a showdown.[20]

In the matter of Oregon, President Polk had in July ordered Buchanan to renew the old offer of the 49th parallel to Britain as a compromise boundary. Marcy had supported this step. As it turned out, the British envoy rejected the move without even consulting London. It was not until October that the administration succeeded in mapping out a new course. This plan was that if the British minister made inquiries as to the chance for a modification of the 49th parallel project, Buchanan was to reply that the United States would consider such proposition as that country might make. The other part of it was a decision to assert publicly a title to the whole of Oregon and to ask the senate to authorize the giving of the twelve-months'

---

[18] Bancroft to Taylor, June 15, *HED60*, 30th cong., 1st sess. (hereafter referred to as *HED60*), 81-82; Marcy to Taylor, *ibid.,* 82-83; to Wetmore, July 6, M.P.

[19] To Wetmore, July 23, Aug. 1, to Samuel, May 13, July 27, M.P.

[20] Proposals of Scott *re* defense, Dec. 24, P.P., 2 ser.; Marcy's annual report, Nov. 29, *HED2*, 29th cong., 1st sess., 193.

notice needed to set the joint occupation aside. Congress would furthermore be asked to extend the jurisdiction of American laws to American citizens there, as Britain had done for her subjects, and to provide for a chain of forts to guard settlers going thither through the Indian country. These points were written out in Polk's annual message, which was later given the date of December 2. It was "a strong document—decisive—not spunky—I believe," as Marcy put it. He had approved of it when it was discussed in the cabinet, as with the previous step. Characteristically, he had not thought these questions out in advance and had been slow, therefore, to express opinions on them; on the other hand, having reasoned the policy through, he was ready to stand by it. The American people, incidentally, also endorsed it.[21]

It was against this background that Marcy prepared his first annual report, which he submitted on November 29. He urged that the army be increased substantially. His first proposal, which he evidently thought would be the more acceptable to congress, was that every company be raised to an authorized strength of eighty men. He indicated, though, that he considered that the creation of entire new regiments would be better, since this would make subsequent enlargement easy. Since he urged the building of the talked-of posts on the Oregon trail, moreover, he said that an extra regiment would be needed there anyhow; he also asked for the creation of an engineer company, as his predecessor had done, and for an improvement of the coastal defenses. This report, which was in general akin to one which Scott had recently made, was well received by such newspapers as considered the subject important enough to mention. By and large, the country saw little need for military preparation.[22]

With the coming of the session, which opened a few days after, Marcy anticipated a gruelling and laborious time. He laid in extra snuff to carry him through. On the other hand, he and Mrs. Marcy were ready to take a full part in the social season, which began simultaneously. He had found a suitable house on G Street, in the block west of 17th, just around the corner from his office. Since then, Mrs. Marcy had furnished the place lavishly. Referring to the movement

---

[21] *P.D.* (Polk's *Diary*, M. M. Quaife, ed.) I, 1-5, 73; to Wetmore, Nov. 28, M.P.
[22] Scott's and Marcy's annual reports, Nov. 20, 29, cited above; *Argus*, Dec. 12; to Wetmore, Dec. 14, M.P.

by the Barnburners in New York to cut the state's debt, Marcy wrote to Wetmore a trifle ruefully that she was certainly of the *"debt-contracting"* but not of the debt-reducing party.[23] Actually, however, he liked more and more to live well.

The Marcys appropriately gave their first big dinner party to members of the military world, including the house military committee. "My room restricts me to 14 persons," he told Wetmore, but it is apparent that he usually planned upon using the full capacity. This first occasion was a convivial one. "The fellows must have been a set of hypocrites if they were not well pleased—for they gave every indication that they were. The Whig part of them professed great confidence in the war minister and promised to vote for any & all appropriations the dept. would ask, but the second *sober* thought may modify their opinions." A congressman from upstate New York who dined with the Marcys a fortnight later was impressed with the finger bowls, the two handsome six-branched candelabras, the several china baskets of fruit, the handsome centerpiece of artificial flowers, and especially with the fact that each place had a decanter of wine and four different wine glasses by it. It was a full dinner, from soup through fish, duck, pickled salmon, broiled ham, and "about half a dozen dishes more," to the cake, "gell," and ice cream. A week after, William H. Seward, who had paid a New Year's call and been kindly received, was also a dinner guest. This was chiefly an affair for the diplomats, but Marcy entertained the company with reminiscences of old passages at arms in state politics. "It was a pleasant party for me," wrote this old rival. He added the telling comment, by the way, that "He [Marcy] lives in the past already, and evidently feels that he is descending the ladder on which he mounted so rapidly, so high"; Seward should have passed this on to Van Buren, for it went far to refute the belief that Marcy was out for the presidency. By contrast, it may be noted that Buchanan, who certainly had ambitions, gave a party the night after at Carusi's parlors to which he invited thirteen hundred people. All in all, this was a season of much gayety and frolic.[24]

[23] To Wetmore, Oct. 23, Nov. 16, to Samuel, Aug. 31, M.P.; *Washington Directory. . . ,* 1846.
[24] To Wetmore, Dec. 21, Jan. 18, M.P.; *op. cit.,* 771, 774, 780-782; T. Jenkins to wife, Jan. 10, State Library.

It was also a time of growing anxiety over the British and Mexican involvements. Even before word came from London of Britain's reaction to Polk's message, the news from that quarter was aleady alarming, for it told of warlike preparations. The administration became somewhat aroused, but Marcy himself did not believe that fighting would come. As he wrote to Wetmore on December 21:

Could a treaty be made for the 49. parallel and yielding the cap of Van-Couver's Island it would be ratified by a very strong vote in the Senate —I do not think there would be ten votes agt. it.

The message will create an outbreak of feeling in England, but it will be temporary—the position of the Oregon question is critical but war may and I still believe will be avoided—

This conclusion was doubtless based upon a knowledge that Polk was ready to compromise, for just two days after that Polk again told the cabinet that if Britain offered the 49th parallel, the United States would accept it. This was on the condition that the leading senators would also accept the idea in advance. Later, also, the United States minister at London was authorized to disclose this to the British government. In the letter quoted above, however, Marcy shrewdly added that "this state of things" would help to get the desired appropriations through. Since the members of the military committees of congress were now more impressed with the need for defence, he was able to have a number of satisfactory conferences, especially with Senator Benton and Congressman Haralson, the respective chairmen, and to make a fair amount of headway. By December 29, he was submitting requests for an authorization of 50,000 volunteers. The latter were preferred to militia, he said. He also asked for speedy grants of money, at least of small amounts to begin with, for fortifications, ordinance, and several other things.[25]

In the new year, moreover, the administration moved towards a sterner attitude as to Mexico. On January 13, Marcy ordered Taylor— again, really—to move up to the Rio Grande. Furthermore, John Slidell, who had been sent to Mexico in November to seek a general settlement—trading off all American claims for a Rio Grande boundary and offering $25,000,000 for New Mexico and Upper California —was on January 20 directed to act in such a manner that if his

---

[25] To Wetmore, Dec. 21, M.P.; McCormac, 582, 584; proposals of Scott, Dec. 24, and Marcy to Benton, Dec. 29, P.P., 2 ser.

mission failed the blame would clearly be Mexico's! By January 28, Buchanan was voicing the administration attitude when he said, in words which would be heard again, that if Slidell was not received by the Mexican government, "the cup of forebearance [would] then have been exhausted." The United States could then take the matter of redress for the injuries to its citizens "into [its] hands." Marcy put the matter less strongly. In a private letter, he said that it would be a major indignity, which could "not be passed without notice," but he revealed that what action would be taken had not yet been decided.

By February 17, however, Marcy was supporting Polk in cabinet discussion as to giving Mexico an ultimatum.[26] On April 7, the problem was made easier to discuss, in that Mexico had acted conclusively. Slidell had been rejected—technically because sent as a "minister," not a "commissioner"—but actually because close relations with the United States were not wanted. The cabinet decided, however, to await his return before taking measures. It was hoped that the Oregon issue might by then be nearly out of the way.[27]

Meantime, congress had been loth to give the money for the army and fortifications. The reasons lay in a rather greater interest in that body in who was to succeed Polk, plus inertia, parsimony, and, on the Whig side, a fear of increased Democratic patronage. The house had approved Marcy's plan for eighty enlisted men and the senate a bill for a regiment of mounted riflemen for the Oregon route, but neither bill had been passed by the other house. Congress likewise had hesitated for a long while to give the one year's notice to Britain.

Marcy was disgusted. He said on March 9 that congress was "behaving strangely." Had it granted the military increase and the notice, thus evincing a desire "to maintain our just right," he said, a settlement could perhaps have been had already. The one favorable turn had been that the possibility of a real war, and with Britain at that, had cooled the hot blood of the 54°40' men, i.e. those who insisted

---

[26] James Buchanan, *Works*, VI, 294-306, 361-365; *P.D.*, I, 91-94; Marcy to Wetmore, Feb. 1, M.P.; *P.D.*, I, 233-234.

[27] It may be that Polk, as charged, styled Slidell a "minister" deliberately, to provoke Mexican resentment, although Marcy's letter (just cited) said he was sent "on an express agreement that a minister [sic] would be received"; there is some ground for doubt as to what the Spanish word meant, but if the Mexicans had wanted to negotiate, they would have disregarded the title used. *P.D.*, I, 322, 327, 354, 363; McCormac, 401.

upon getting all of Oregon; even Senator Allen of Ohio, one of their chiefs, was affected. They were now willing to take the 49° line, if offered by Britain, and were even ready to have the responsibility for such a decision passed to the senate, as the administration planned, before a treaty was actually drawn up. As for the army bills, Polk and Marcy hesitated to raise a clamor for their adoption, lest there be a charge of war mongering; they and the cabinet as a whole had too long hoped for expansion by peaceful means, or, at worst, *via* a short and easy war. Finally, however, on March 24, a message was sent to congress asking haste in the passage of the bills and pointing to Britain's plans to enlarge her forces and alluding to Mexico's failure to receive Mr. Slidell.[28]

As to Oregon, congress did finally approve the notice of termination. This was on April 23. Early in June, when it was expected that Britain would respond with a suitable offer, Marcy was one of those ready to submit it to the senate for advance approval, as before, although Buchanan thought otherwise. The latter, after a long period of excessive caution, was now out for 54°40'.[29] When the British proposal did come, on June 6, it was dealt with as Polk and Marcy sought. The London government, with some qualifications, had yielded the 49th parallel. The senate agreed to this, with only twelve votes in the negative, or just two more than Marcy had predicted. This was on June 12.

The administration had, therefore, with Marcy's cordial backing and along the lines which his common sense much approved, disposed of the difficult Oregon issue. It had not yet succeeded, by the bye, in getting the tariff revised in accordance with Polk's wishes or in having the independent treasury restored, but these steps would follow during the summer. Before the tariff was adopted, Marcy would use his influence strongly in its behalf in the house. As for the subtreasury, he was also for that, although against the specie clause contained in the original bill.[30] This latter would have had a deflationary effect.

As to the Mexican affair, however, a peaceable solution had not

[28] *Congressional Globe,* 29th cong., 1st sess., Jan. 8 (senate, p. 162), Mar. 25 (house, p. 552); to Wetmore, Mar. 9, M.P.; *P.D.,* I, 133-136, 139, 147.
[29] *P.D.,* I, 447-448, 453.
[30] *P.D.,* I, 85, II, 10-11; W. Hunt to T. W. Olcott, Apr. 22, Olcott Papers.

been won. Indeed, as early as the last week in April, the president and his cabinet, including Marcy, had decided to give up trying for one. They had concluded instead to refer the whole matter of peace or war to congress. The expectation, or at least the hope, was for a short and successful military campaign in northern Mexico, or perhaps just the occupation of the desired territory. That the army enlargement had not gone through was considered embarrassing, but nothing more than that. In brief, the month of May, 1846, saw war in the offing. In the decisions which had led to this state of affairs, undoubtedly, Marcy was following the lead of the president and of the majority of the cabinet. As he was to write years later, he, himself, "abhorred" the "robber doctrine."

XIII. HOSTILITIES WITH MEXICO

"The cup of forebearance had been exhausted even before
the recent information from the frontier of the [Rio
Grande] Del Norte. But now . . . Mexico has . . . invaded
our territory and shed American blood upon the American
soil." (Polk's message to congress, May 11, 1846)

SATURDAY, May 9, 1846, was a day of a remarkable coincidence. At a cabinet meeting during the afternoon, Marcy and
the president and nearly all of the rest of the cabinet had agreed that
the United States' affairs with Mexico had come to such a pass that
the only proper step to take was to seek war. As far as the causes for
this drastic decision went, Marcy's reasoning seems to have been
much like that of the others. He knew personally of the history of
the unpaid claims of American citizens upon that country and agreed
with the occupation of the disputed area by Taylor's army. He also
approved of the plans to acquire further territory in the southwest.
And now he was ready to support the president in this decisive step,
even though there was news that American forces had begun a blockade of the Rio Grande, a move which might in itself cause war. At
about six that evening, however, news reached the war department
that the Mexican army had crossed the river in force and that sixty-
three United States officers and men had been killed or captured. The
adjutant general took the despatches to Polk first, but Marcy soon
heard and was down the avenue and into the White House before
the president had finished reading them. It was decided that a cabinet
meeting should be held at once. Then, when the members came together, a unanimous decision was reached, that war should be recognized as in existence. Even George Bancroft, whose New England
conscience was fresher from the font than Marcy's, no longer de-
murred. The opinion was that Congress should be asked on Monday
to take "vigorous & prompt" measures.[1]

---

[1] *P.D.* I, 8-10, 380 (receipt of Taylor's letter of 15th), 384-387; Taylor to Adjt.
Gen., Apr. 15, *HED60*, 138-139; Marcy to Wetmore, June 13, M.P.

In the writing of the presidential message which was prepared that weekend, with its allegations that war existed "upon the American soil" and "notwithstanding all our efforts to avoid it," Marcy took no part. He was ill much of the time. He approved, of course, of the document's request for "a large body of volunteers" for six or twelve months' service.

Events proved that the public was disposed to respond favorably, and with speed at that. The general idea, as a matter of fact, was that victory could be won quickly and the aims of the United States soon met. Marcy shared in this view. He also did his best to hurry the congressional leaders along, although they needed little hurrying. By the day after the message went in, both houses had voted for war, and a day later the calling of fifty thousand volunteers was sanctioned, on the basis of twelve months' terms. At the same time, the authorized strength of the companies of the regular army was raised to one hundred enlisted men each. Later in the week, the regiment of mounted riflemen and the company of engineers were also authorized. In short, Marcy's recommendations of the past winter had finally been adopted.

Marcy was not too happy, however. He was rather alarmed lest Taylor's small army be crushed, as capital gossips were already beginning to predict, for it had been reported as cut off, and he feared public censure. As it turned out, the news when it came was of a cheering variety. This was on May 23.

In two pitched battles, at Palo Alto and the Resaca de la Palma, the army had defeated an enemy of double its size and driven it headlong across the river. The result was that all was now heedless optimism rather than carping and foreboding; the mercurial public now talked in large terms of Taylor's probably being well on the way to Mexico City.[2]

The conflict which had started, however, was to be no light matter and would need careful planning. In view of this, it is sad to relate that the preparation of wise plans was not to be the administration's strong point. In the first place, the decision to use volunteers was bad. Volunteer troops were undisciplined, they neglected sanitation, they

[2] Marcy to Wetmore, July 6, 1845, May 10, 28, 1846, M.P.; *P.D.* I, 387-395, 422; C. M. Wilcox, *History of the Mexican War*, 73-74.

wasted their food and equipment, they were likely to break under enemy fire, and—to sum it up in George G. Meade's phrase—they "die[d] like sheep," whether in camp or in combat.[3] On the other hand, the political leaders of all parties were thoroughly committed to a preference for their use, holding to the old ideal of a citizen soldiery which sprang patriotically to arms at the sound of the tocsin. They also liked the patronage opportunities which were presented.

But the use of volunteers was not to be the only error. No one at Washington had made specific plans for the campaigns which would bring victory. Not only was there no War Plans unit in the war department, but all that Scott and Polk had done was to interview certain persons familiar with Mexico, by way of getting a more accurate general idea of the country. As for Marcy, he seems to have been building up his information from books, as usual. He termed Señora Calderon de la Barca's *Life in Mexico* one of the best.[4] Once the war started, moreover, he was beleaguered by men who wanted volunteer commissions, to say nothing of a thousand other problems of detail.

On the late evening of May 14, however, Marcy and the president and Scott held a conference which lasted until midnight and which produced a basic plan of operations. This called for moves to seize and hold the northern states of Mexico, including not only California and the huge state of New Mexico (as it then was), all of which Polk wished to acquire, but also other extensive areas which might be traded back to the enemy in return for a treaty of peace. It was also determined, at Scott's insistence, that twenty thousand volunteers would be called out; these men would come from the southern and midwestern states. In the cabinet, two days later, this general outline was elaborated. It was decided that small armies should proceed upon Santa Fé and Chihuahua, while the main army, much enlarged, should occupy the lower Rio Grande Valley and the adjacent interior. As to the troops, it was determined that the remainder of the fifty thousand volunteers authorized should also be mustered, to be held in reserve for any need which might arise.

---

[3] Meade, *Life and Letters,* I, 162-163; Scott to Marcy, Jan. 16, 1847, in Smith, *op. cit.,* II, 512-513.

[4] C. W. Elliott, *Winfield Scott,* 424; to Wetmore, May 3, M.P.

The three leaders then proceeded as rapidly as possible to work out these plans in detail. For Marcy, for one, it was a period of excessive labor. He had to consult continually with the two congressional military committees, attend the frequent cabinet meetings, keep an eye on the work of the general staff, and, above all, interview a host of applicants for the volunteer commands.[5]

It was soon also decided, as an outgrowth of the above plans, that Colonel S. W. Kearny, who headed the Santa Fé movement, should, if events warranted it, proceed to California with much of his force. Later, moreover, it was also directed that the volunteer regiment being recruited in New York should be sent to California likewise, going by sea around Cape Horn; its members would go out with the understanding that they would be dismissed there at the end of their service and remain in that country as a means of hastening its Americanization. For the command of this important unit, incidentally, Marcy soon secured the designation of John D. Stevenson, which showed that he had not wholly disapproved of how that worthy had lobbied for his appointment to the war department. This step, similar to ones taken with several of the regiments forming elsewhere, was essentially outside of the law, since the officers were supposed to be chosen by whatever process the states' own laws provided. Governor Wright accepted Stevenson's nomination, although reluctantly.[6]

As for the main enterprise, in the lower Rio Grande basin, it was to be put into Scott's hands. Since Scott was not only the ranking commander but highly able, this seemed inevitable, and it is a pleasure to record, as Scott was to do afterwards, that Marcy favored his choice from the start. This was a very delicate matter, however, for the doughty general was a candidate for the Whig presidential nomination and had come to be viewed, indeed, as the likely choice.[7] In the administration's eyes, naturally, there was no overwhelming eagerness to give him a command which would add military laurels to his presidential appeal. Yet the decision, at first, was in his favor.

It soon transpired, however, that Scott counted upon a long period of preparation before leaving for the front; he even spoke of not

---

[5] *P.D.* I, 400-404; W. Hunt to T. W. Olcott, May 20, Olcott Papers.
[6] Cf. Marcy to Wetmore, July 12, M.P.
[7] Scott, *Memoirs*, II, 398; Seward, *op. cit.*, 771-772.

departing until September 1. He argued that the volunteers would not be ready much sooner than that and that in any case it would be well to wait until the summertime fever season had left the Mexican lowlands. Essentially, he was right in all of this. The men really would need some training before engaging the enemy, while the problems of logistics would call for much time, also. On the other hand, Marcy and Polk did not adequately understand these facts. Certainly Polk did not. He termed Scott much too "scientific and visionary" an officer and demanded that Marcy spur him to quick action. In talking with Scott, Marcy did his tactful best, giving as his reasons the restiveness of the public and of the volunteers themselves and pointing out that certain volunteers who had been summoned would have gone home by September. This was on May 20. Unfortunately, Scott misunderstood the motive involved. He knew that Marcy had gone to the capitol the day before to ask the enactment of a provision for volunteer generals and he suspected, although wrongly, that there was a plot to supersede him. There was none at this time. Scott told Marcy, however, that he was sure that this was the plan. Then, next day, he wrote a letter to Marcy in which he said that the preparations which he was making for the army were very much needed. He went on to allude to the "impatience" felt, "perhaps in high quarters," and said boldly that it might be better if he *were* replaced:

My explicit meaning is—that I do not desire to place myself in the most perilous of all positions:—*a fire upon my rear, from Washington, and the fire, in front, from the Mexicans.*

President Polk brooded over this insulting and rather politically flavored letter for four days and at last decided that Scott should be removed. Whether Marcy favored this drastic step, cannot be said surely, but he presumably did not; on the other hand, he undoubtedly sensed that Polk would take it regardless of what he himself advised in the matter. In any event, when he wrote Scott the necessary letter of removal he said flatly that that officer's imputation of "ill-will" on the part of the administration made it unwise to give him the field command. He and the president both disregarded a newer letter from the general in which Scott continued to adopt a truculent tone but said that he would be ready to leave the capital in a few days. On the day after Marcy wrote, a final epistle came from that officer which began with the very quotable statement that he had received Marcy's letter just "as [he] sat down to take a hasty plate of soup" the evening before. The letter charged mistakenly that it had been Marcy himself who had used the four days "to reflect and to convict" him, and said that the charge of impatience and "pre-condemnation" was not meant to be aimed at Polk but rather—he said explicitly—at Marcy and at certain friends of the administration in congress. After this particularly *ad hominem* comment, he went on to say that he had felt for some days that Marcy had let himself be influenced against him by these lawmakers. Because of that fact, he supposed, Marcy had not made "the just and easy explanations" in his behalf which he could have, to the president. A further letter followed on each side, including an appeal by Scott for reinstatement.

When the senate asked for the correspondence between Marcy and his subordinate—this was on June 5—it was at once released. The result was a strong reaction in Marcy's favor. As the *Herald* said, Scott had put himself in the role of "a small politician seeking office." What was more, the "hasty plate of soup" clause was made the target of a limitless variety of jokes which pretty well brought Scott's presidential boom to an end.[8] In reality, however, the administration had not done particularly well, either, for it had deprived itself and the country of the services of its ablest officer, so far as concerned the field of battle.

In consequence, General Zachary Taylor was given the command. He was ordered "to prosecute the war with vigor, in the manner [he] deem[ed] most effective." Although the government was not at the moment sure as to the best objective, it soon suggested to him that this might be Monterey, the nearest sizeable enemy city. By early July, in any case, Taylor had himself decided to move in that direction; he started a slow transfer of his men to Camargo, a Mexican village a hundred miles or so up the Rio Grande. Both before this time and during his movement, incidentally, as he afterwards alleged, he was held up by a need for horses and wagons and for river steamers, neither he nor the department having shown the foresight to arrange for these things. Actually, this meant that the fault was in

---

[8] *P.D.* I, 401, 407-408, 415-428, 451; Scott to Marcy, May 21, 25, 27, Marcy to Scott, May 25, 26, *SED378*, 29th cong., 1st sess., 4-17; *Herald*, June 12, July 13.

no inconsiderable degree his own, for under the American system of military command a general in the field is given much freedom of operation and is expected to show initiative in his use of it.[9] In spite of his difficulties, he had nearly 15,000 men at Camargo by the end of August.

It was an uncertain summer in Washington, for much of the popular fever for war had vanished, in spite of the utter absence of a conclusive victory. Under these circumstances, the president cast about for short cuts to success and turned up a number of possibilities. In great part, these were the ideas of Senator Thomas Hart Benton. One was to detach some of the Mexican states from their central government by treating them in a kindly manner and encouraging secession. Orders to that effect were sent to Taylor. Since the northern states of Mexico were commonly disaffected and rebellious, this seemed plausible. As a second step, Polk let Santa Anna pass through the blockade into Mexico. This was done because that notorious Mexican leader, who was then in exile in Havana, promised that if he was allowed to return to Mexico he would soon regain power and would sell the United States the land it wanted. And, finally, Polk asked congress for $2,000,000 to be used for a quick cash payment to any Mexican regime willing to negotiate. Although Marcy had no especial role in the maturing of these plans, he made no objection to them. In other words, he shared the ignorance and optimism of the president and his senatorial adviser. He was ready enough to order Taylor to comply with the secession idea and he did not object to the $2,000,000 scheme. His hope for a short war and for the easy securing of what was desired was well shown in a letter which he wrote to Prosper Wetmore on June 13, the day after the senate's approval of the terms as to Oregon:

I hope the Mex. war will be short. When Mexico hears of the adjustment of the Oregon difficulty she will concent to treat. Must we not have a slice of Upper California (including the harbors of Monterey and San Francisco) to satisfy the claims of our citizens and the government claim for the expenses of the war? I am not avaricious or grasping but it appears to me our *forty two* line must be moved south to 34 or 36N. Lattitude [sic].

---

[9] As to transport, see Taylor to Adjt. Gen., Sept. 1, Jesup to Marcy, Dec. 5, *HED60*, 557-561; *P.D.* II, 118-119; Smith, *op. cit.*, I, 209, 482.

Such talk of 34° or 36° put him with the moderates in the cabinet.[10] This letter shows, moreover, that he did not understand any better than Polk the tenacious pride of the Mexican people, nor the fact that no government there could yield territory and stay in power, nor the truth that for the American forces to occupy some of the poor and thinly peopled border states meant little to the rest of Mexico. All of these hopes for victory by indirection proved delusions, however. There were no secessions, the congress for months refused to grant money for negotiation, and Santa Anna returned to his country only to become the very heart and soul of resistance to the invasion.

During this period, the United States also had made a proposal to the leaders as yet in power in Mexico, to the effect that a peaceful settlement be made. But when word arrived on September 19 that this was refused, the administration turned to the tasks of war with an added earnestness. At a special cabinet meeting which was held the very next day, it was pretty well concluded to press along with an already planned advance upon Tampico and the other key towns of the Gulf-coast state of Tamaulipas. What was more, in view of Taylor's lack of display of initiative in planning or marching, his observable blunders (as in his failure to build pontoons while on the eastern shore of the Rio Grande), and, perhaps, the talk which had already risen of making him president, it was decided that he should continue his advance upon Monterey. The Tampico move, however, was to be given to another commander. Marcy and Polk agreed that this officer should be Robert Patterson, one of the abler volunteer soldiers and a confirmed Democrat. At the same time, every effort was made to speed the departure of the California regiment, which was still at New York.[11] This unit had been held up by Wright's delay in formally giving Stevenson his colonelcy, by a fracas which arose out of an attempt by the latter—or his son-in-law—to profiteer in supplying the men's uniforms, and also by transport troubles. It was not until September 25 that Marcy finally received a telegram from Wetmore that the unit had sailed, by which time he had lost so much sleep over it that he had become ill with fever, for this expedi-

---

[10] *P.D.* II, 16-17, 50-51, I, 495-497; Marcy to Taylor, July 9, *HED60*, 155-158; Smith, *op. cit.*, I, 201-203; to Wetmore, M.P.
[11] *P.D.* II, 144-149.

tion was peculiarly his own and Polk was frantic with impatience concerning it. It may be added, as a family footnote, that Marcy's two older sons had departed with it, William as a commissary officer and Samuel in some naval capacity.[12]

It was therefore a relief to learn, by October 11, of good news from Taylor: "Old Rough and Ready" had taken Monterey. The report was unfortunately tempered by tidings of the clumsy and costly style in which that officer had used his forces and word of armistice which he had felt obliged to grant to the enemy, which had allowed them to march out with their arms and without being paroled. Marcy and the president wisely concluded, however, not to censure Taylor; he was simply told to end the armistice, in a despatch which was generous in tone but confined its praise to "the troops under [his] command."[13] Later that month, all the same, he was ordered not to advance beyond the vicinity in which he lay.

Before the news of Monterey came, the October elections, which many states held, had taken place. These had brought results disadvantageous to the administration. Yet in the elections in November, i.e. after this favorable war news, and, in fact, after the public had learned that American forces had overrun both New Mexico and California, the results were likewise bad. The truth was, unfortunately, that while the American people had been ready for a quick and easy triumph of a total sort, they felt little enmity towards Mexico and were wholly unprepared in their minds for a major war south of the border.[14]

As Marcy well saw, however, there was no satisfactory answer but to fight on. When he put his estimates for the next year before the cabinet on November 7, therefore, he called for funds which would allow for a regular army of 15,000 men (which had not yet been attained) and also for a new force of 25,000 twelve months' volunteers. This budget at once alarmed Polk and some of the other cabinet members, not only because of the turn of the elections but also because the treasury was finding it difficult to borrow money. It was

---

[12] Marcy to Wetmore, June 28, July 4, 12, 26, Aug. 1, 8, 23, Sept. 6, 27, M.P.; *Tribune*, Sept. 23, 24, 28; to Samuel, Aug. 23, M.P.
[13] *P.D.* II, 181-185; to Wetmore, Oct. 16, M.P., to Taylor, Oct. 13, *HED60*, 355.
[14] Smith, *op. cit.*, II, 269.

finally suggested by Buchanan that while the 15,000 regulars be granted, the large new force of twelve months' troops have substituted for it 10,000 additional regulars to be recruited for the duration only. Marcy quickly accepted this plan. He also became its chief backer. At the cabinet session on the 14th, for example, Buchanan was now cool towards it, as were some other members, but Marcy held firm. Fortunately, Polk agreed with Marcy. It may be commented, in passing, that Marcy's annual report defended the work of the volunteers in the recent campaigns but argued that for combat in a distant foreign land regulars were what were needed. He accordingly asked for bounties to encourage their enlistment.[15]

If there was not too much agreement on the size of the forces, however, there was even less as to where they should fight. For months there had been talk of taking Vera Cruz, the chief enemy seaport, which was the port for the capital region; it had been learned that an army could be landed near that place without first capturing the fort which guarded it. Marcy was willing to take up this idea. On the other hand, he did not at all approve of going on from there to take Mexico City, which was some two hundred miles inland and in the rich and populous heart of the country. He said as late as January 2, 1847, to quote Polk's diary, that he "had no confidence in the success of [such] an expedition." This was to be the thought, incidentally, of that great military expert, the duke of Wellington, after Scott (who was soon to be restored to command) had entered the central valley of Mexico; Wellington was to remark that "Scott is lost." In other words, Marcy thought of the expedition on Vera Cruz as comparable to that on Tampico in its extension of the control of the Mexican coast, or perhaps he simply preferred taking one step at a time. President Polk, however, said vigorously that he would himself insist on going through to the capital, *if that was necessary.*[16]

On the other hand, if we may trust Marcy's statement of years after, Marcy did early and persistently urge that General Scott be given the command of the new campaign; he said that he won Polk over to this and then won the cabinet in general.[17] Very likely he was

---

[15] *P.D.* II, 220-221, 232-235; for his report, *HED4*, 29th cong., 2nd sess., 46-60.
[16] Smith, *op. cit.* I, 349-351, II, 89; *P.D.* II, 301.
[17] Professor Cutting's reminiscence, *Journal*, July 28, 1857.

strongly persuaded of this need for Scott when he read the several
long and detailed memoranda which that officer drew up in October
and November as to the Vera Cruz landing. While Marcy saw increasingly in Scott the one officer of sufficient ability, experience, and
vision to carry out such an operation, the president, on his part, was
beginning to think of appointing none other than Senator Benton
for this task. The circumstances were that Benton was now one of
the few chief backers of full scale war, including the attack upon
Mexico City, and that he had done much to shape Polk's thinking
along these lines; if the senator were given the job, moreover, that
decision would help to win the support of the Van Buren wing of
the party, which was decidedly lukewarm thus far. Benton had himself suggested the scheme to Polk on November 10, explaining that
"a man of talents and resources as well as a military man" was needed
and divulging rather quickly that he thought himself to be exactly
the right person. He thought also that congress should create a new
and higher rank, that of lieutenant general, for the purpose. These
points were brought up in the cabinet on that same day, but were
not warmly received. In the cabinet conclave of a week later, it is
clear, Marcy was one of those advocating Scott for the assignment.
Polk was unhappy and non-committal, however, and really wanted
Benton. But on the next day he called Marcy in and received firm
counsel:

He [Marcy] said he had had great anxiety and trouble about it, but upon
full reflection, although he would do so reluctantly, he thought we would
be compelled to take Gen'l Scott.

He and the president talked further, but Polk was still not convinced.
Later, however, with Polk's approval, Marcy went to see Benton and
obtained the latter's assent to the plan, which caused Polk to yield
(although later in the day he none the less told Benton privately that
he would still give him the assignment if a bill could be secured for a
lieutenant-generalcy). Aided by Secretary of the Navy Mason, Marcy
kept up the pressure upon Polk in behalf of Scott; at his and Mason's
suggestion Scott was next day called in to the White House for an
interview and given the command. He left almost tearful with happiness.[18] He was, however, still cautious enough to leave town quickly.

---

[18] Scott to Marcy, Oct. 27, Nov. 12, 16, 21, *HED60*, 1268-1275.

This was on May 24, the very day after Marcy wrote his instructions.

Marcy's orders to Scott gave a very large latitude to that officer as to the methods and even the ultimate objectives of his campaign. This was probably because the administration lacked sufficient knowledge of the problems he would meet to attempt to hold him to a specific pattern. In some respects, as Robert S. Henry has pointed out, Marcy showed a better grasp of the realities of warfare in Mexico than Scott himself did. For instance, he had raised a doubt as to Taylor's ability to cross the barren wastes beyond Monterey and Saltillo as a means of attaining the capital, whereas Scott had considered this feasible. Even so, Scott was directed merely as follows:

to repair to Mexico, to take command of the forces there assembled; and particularly to organize and set on foot, an expedition to operate on the gulf coast, if, on arriving at the theatre of action, you shall deem it to be practicable. It is not proposed to control your operations by definite and positive instructions. . . . The work is before you. . . . The objects which it is desirable to obtain have been indicated, and it is hoped that you will have the requisite force to accomplish them.
    Of this you must be the judge. . . .

Even in later orders, there was no disposition to be precise. Those of March 13, for instance, said merely "If you should move into the interior. . . ." This was the first allusion to the Mexico City project in Scott's written instructions![19]

Although Polk did not tell Scott of it, he none the less went ahead with the lieutenant-generalcy scheme. On December 11, he had Marcy broach the plan to Senator Cass, who was a loyal supporter of the administration, and persuade him to comply with it. Cass promised to do so. At the same time, he and many members of both houses of congress warned that such a bill could not pass, which proved to be the case. It should be added that Marcy may have opposed the plan, secretly, in his talks with the congressional leaders, as Benton later charged.[20] More probably, he simply supported the plan in a perfunctory way, with an obvious lack of enthusiasm, and the lawmakers drew their own conclusions.

---

[19] Marcy to Scott, Nov. 23, Mar. 13, *HED60*, 836-837, 903-905; Robert S. Henry, *The Story of the Mexican War*, 80-81, citing Marcy to Taylor of June 8. The writer is indebted also to Mr. Henry for an interpretation of the instructions to Scott on May 23 and March 13.
[20] *P.D.* II, 271-276, 297, 334n., 418-420.

To some slight extent because of this *demarche,* but more chiefly because of a general coolness towards the war as a whole, congress delayed until February 10 its passage of a bill for the ten regiments of duration regulars. This left Marcy badly worried. He had anticipated a difficult time personally during the session and had told Wetmore that he was glad that he had a thick skin, but he felt that the ten regiments bill was the key to the whole future of the war. "If that . . . fails we shall be in a beautiful situation," he said. When it went through, along with his request for bounties, he was, of course, busier than ever. The selection of officers for the ten regiments, in particular, was a trying problem; this was partly because of the fact that regular army officers shunned the posts, fearing that they would be left without billets after the war, when the units were disbanded.[21]

From this point on, the problem was simply to try to get enough men, supplies, and transport for Scott's undertaking—if that could be called simple. After all, the plans for the move were on an unprecedented scale, quite unlike those in any previous war, for this was to be the United States' first great combined operation of naval and military power and, in fact, the country's first overseas campaign. Scott had said, for instance, that the government would need one hundred and forty surf boats, capable of putting ashore near Vera Cruz a force of five thousand men in the first minutes. He had planned, moreover, for a huge convoy of not less than fifty good-sized vessels, carrying siege guns, shells and rockets, supplies of every sort, wagons, horses for the dragoons and artillery, and an army that would total fourteen thousand men even at the outset.[22] Among other things, he had also asked for eighty to one hundred thousand ten-inch shells. Yet all of this was to be done by a nation only modestly industrialized and was to be carried out in a few months, over a distance of some two thousand miles, entirely by water in its later stages, and in a period when the American railway network was in its infancy and the telegraph system had not yet connected the capital with the Gulf.

Marcy was wary as to the ability to carry all this out. He endorsed Scott's memorandum as to ordnance, for example, with the words "comply with the above as far as practicable." But he also did his best

---

[21] To Wetmore, Dec. 5, Jan. 6, Feb. 18, M.P.; *P.D.* II, 379, 383.
[22] Memo. of Nov. 16, *HED60,* 1273-1274.

to give Scott what he asked. For one thing, he made every effort to spur on the somewhat old and lethargic bureau chiefs. In general he was successful. As for the especially vital quartermaster work, the heart of the problem, he was fortunate in having the aid of the able and experienced Thomas S. Jesup, the quartermaster general. He wisely gave Jesup a pretty free hand, although he did fret at him occasionally, once telling Wetmore that he wished he had him as quartermaster instead. Jesup and a small staff soon went to New Orleans and then to the mouth of the Rio Grande, where they were for weeks in direct contact with Scott, who approved of their work. Jesup was also willing to spend freely in order to avoid loss of time, which was a proper policy.[23]

Even so, there were embarrassing delays. It took nearly all of the furnaces of the country which were willing to take contracts, to make the ordnance; these furnaces, moreover, were generally in regions far from the points of departure for the front. As for the surf boats, they proved to cost about $950 each, whereas Scott had spoken of $200. Then, when the shipments were ready, they were held up by ice on the rivers, and, later, on the Gulf, by further bad weather. In time, however, some fifty-three vessels of all types sailed from Atlantic ports and one hundred and sixty-three from the Gulf. Marcy worked to the limit of his large capacity—or rather beyond it—in his efforts to supervise all these things, and so wore himself out that he was repeatedly ill. Yet he could take satisfaction when he received Scott's report of February 28, which complained of the slowness of the material to arrive but said none the less that "this army is *in heart;* and . . . I shall go forward."[24]

Before word came of Scott's arrival at Vera Cruz, there were tidings on March 20 that General Taylor was confronted by a vast Mexican force under Santa Anna. Two days later, the news from that area was so alarming that Marcy was concerned lest even the troops back on the Rio Grande be lost. He persuaded Polk, therefore, that all

---

[23] Marcy to Scott, Apr. 21, 1848, *ibid.*, 1239; to Wetmore, Nov. 14, Dec. 25, 1846, M.P.; Thomas S. Jesup, *D.A.B.*; Jesup to Marcy, Apr. 17, 1848, *HED60*, 1253-1255; *P.D.* III, 119 (etc.); Jesup to Sanders, July 5, 1846, *HED60*, 554; Scott to Marcy, Jan. 26, 1847; *ibid.*, 865-866.

[24] Marcy to Scott and Jesup to Marcy, cited just above; Scott to Marcy, Feb. 28, 1847, *ibid.*, 896-898; *P.D.* II, 431, III, 24.

units of whatever size of the ten regiments being raised should be
diverted to Taylor; soon after, when it was known that that officer's
communications had been cut by an "overpowering force," there was
anger as well as alarm, for he had been ordered by both Marcy and
Scott to stay near Monterey, which was a strong point.

On April 1, however, came word of a great, bloody, and hard-
fought battle, the most notable of the war, in which Taylor had
triumphed although outnumbered three or four to one. On the same
day that this news came, it was learned that Scott had effected his
dangerous landing near Vera Cruz, and that with surprising ease; the
reinforcements for Taylor were at once ordered rerouted thither. And
by April 12, when Marcy knew that Vera Cruz had been taken with
little or no bloodshed, he had written warm congratulations to both
commanders. He did express regrets to Taylor that the Buena Vista
victory had been "at so great a price . . . ," but his letter was sincere
in its praise. This did not prevent him from seeing, all the same, that
Taylor had fought himself into a presidential candidate.[25]

Still, there was no prospect of peace. There seemed no alternative but to go on to Mexico City. As a matter of fact, Scott had already begun that move. This was despite a very serious lack of transport and although his army, already smaller than he had asked,
would in May and June lose thousands of its twelve-months' volunteers. Now Marcy and Polk counted on his holding these volunteers
until the dates when their terms ran out, but even so they were
tardy in calling out additional ones and did not decide upon that
until April 14. As a result, it was with great dismay that they learned
six weeks later that the volunteers in Mexico had been let go in advance of their dates. What was not understood in Washington was
the excessive eagerness of the men to return home and the fact that
they became more or less mutinous at any hint that they would not
be sent back to the United States soon so as to be mustered out in
their homeland on the days of expiration. While Scott could hardly
have decided differently, the news was a shock to his superiors. As a
result, the army was left much too small, hardly large enough to defend itself, so that Scott merely moved on to Puebla and encamped

---

[25] *P.D.* II, 433-436, 451-452, 465; Marcy to Scott, April 12, May 20, and Taylor,
Apr. 3, *HED60*, 907, 953, 1117-1118; to Bancroft, Apr. 28, 1847, M.P.

to await reinforcements. He even decided that he lacked the strength to keep the road to Vera Cruz open. Upon hearing of this last, Marcy was very alarmed. "His forces is to[o] small—and he is scarsely in a sucourable [sic] position," he wrote hastily to Wetmore on July 16; "the abandonment of his line renders it difficult & dangerous to pass on the reinforcements to him—and the retaining [of] them at Vera Cruz is very bad." In this last, he meant to allude to the fever problem in the lowlands, which was a matter of life and death. He wrote to Scott on July 19 that since May 24 a total of five thousand new men had reached Vera Cruz and nineteen hundred others were believed to have done so. He noted that he had just ordered Taylor also to send on all possible troops to that point. Essentially, he was faced with the same kind of problem of extreme distances and slow transport which would harass the high command at Washington in the second world war. Yet he also had the trouble, not known later, of waiting even for months before he had accurate tidings of the situation at the front. Newspaper reports came frequently enough, but the more reliable statements given in the official despatches were desperately slow to come; on October 22, for example, Marcy had received no official despatches from Scott since that of June 4.[26]

With his great labors and the new anxiety as to the safety of Scott's army, Marcy was by the middle of August, 1847, so careworn, so nearly broken down, that he was obliged to take a long period of rest. Fortunately he had the competent Mason to turn his duties over to. He left for the north on August 18, still so feeble that he at first doubted the wisdom of having departed. As he traveled, however, the fever which had dogged him wore off and he began to recover his strength. He was back at Washington on September 18.[27]

In the interim, on September 9, Mason had written to tell him the glad news that Scott had won several battles outside of Mexico City. Scott had left Puebla early in August, with an army built up to

[26] *P.D.* II, 475, III, 123-124; Smith, *op. cit.*, II, 63-64; Marcy to Scott, May 31, July 19, Oct. 22, to Taylor, July 15, *HED60*, 960-963, 1002-1004, 1009-1010; 1193-1194.

[27] *P.D.* II, 91, 125, 176; Marcy to A. Campbell, Aug. 20, 22, M.P.; Elliott, *op. cit.*, 419-420.

eleven thousand effectives—to say nothing of some thousands who were not in fighting shape. After these new engagements, the exhaustion of the army and its lack of reserves plus an offer by Santa Anna to negotiate had led Scott to arrange an armistice. Although Marcy was not aware of all of the reasons, he refrained from chiding Scott for the step. Then, when the official accounts finally came in, he praised him warmly, alluding specifically to his "signal ability." This was only proper, of course. By that time, moreover, news had come, on October 20, of the spectacular conquest of Mexico City. Marcy naturally lauded Scott for this, also.[28]

Before peace could be made, however, there broke out a regrettable squabble between the general-in-chief and the administration, which did much to take the shine off these victories. What was worse was that this was not the only such *imbroglio*. In the first months of the war there had been an exchange of critical letters with General Edmund P. Gaines over that officer's call of thousands of volunteers for terms of service not provided by law or too short to be useful. This had led to a good deal of public criticism of Marcy. Marcy had tried to answer, anonymously, by spending a Sunday or two writing articles in his own defense, for the newspapers.[29] Later, there had been a letter from Taylor, that petulant commander, who was now thoroughly alert to his chances of being president. Deeply jealous of Scott, particularly since the latter had taken some of his troops, he had written to Gaines to reveal all of the plans for the Vera Cruz move. Since his letter was published and since it also had in it many complaints against the government, Marcy had been obliged to write a long reply. This was in January, 1847.[30] Then, in the autumn of 1847, had come a burst of trouble over a dispute as to the command of the forces in California. This led to a court martial of John C. Fremont, which was particularly embarrassing because Fremont was Benton's son-in-law. Marcy had upheld the call for a court martial. When the court gave its decision, which was that Fremont should be dismissed from the army, he insisted that the sentence be imposed, lest military custom be wholly disregarded, but

---

[28] To Scott, Nov. 19, M.P.
[29] To Taylor, June 26, Aug. 3, 1846, *HED60*, 307-309, 316-317; to Wetmore, Aug. 20, M.P.
[30] To Taylor, Jan. 27, 1847, *HED60*, 391-392. This was an able document.

he was willing to have the man pardoned; he won Mason and then Cave Johnson over to his view, and finally Polk.[31]

The Scott affair, which was more serious than these others, came up on and after December 29, 1847. On that date, Marcy learned that Scott had ordered the arrest of Generals Gideon Pillow and William Jenkins Worth and of a Colonel Duncan, because they had allegedly taken part in the preparation of newspaper stories which had glorified Pillow's role in one of the battles and discounted Scott's contribution. Scott might have disposed of the matter more simply, but he chose instead to make it into a bone of contention with the government. This happened all the more easily because Pillow was Polk's personal friend. Since counter-charges had been made against Scott by Worth, Polk was for removing the *former* from command until the expected trials could be held. He also wanted to try the two participants in the United States.

Marcy hesitated to agree to any of this. His chief explanation to Polk was that a trial, either in the field or at home, would be highly awkward, but he was presumably thinking also of how the whole affair would look to the public. He did agree quite soon to the temporary replacement of Scott, but he said that the trials must be kept in Mexico, for the reason that half of the officers in the army there would have to testify. Since others in the cabinet also advised that the trials be in Mexico, Polk finally consented, but it was arranged that the place be some Mexican city where few of the American troops were quartered. Throughout the many discussions of the affair, furthermore, Marcy tried over and over again to have Taylor be the officer to replace Scott, as against Polk's insistence upon William O. Butler, who was a volunteer and a Democrat. Polk was determined, however, and finally had his way, telling Marcy that he would take the entire responsibility in the matter. By January 13, Marcy had the necessary orders ready, removing Scott and directing him to attend a court of enquiry; this was a preliminary step which had been decided upon as less drastic than a court martial; he was then to come to the capital. As it turned out, Worth and Scott were persuaded to withdraw the charges against each other and Scott those against Duncan. This left only the Pillow business, which was

[31] *P.D.* III, 176-177, 180-181, 204-205, 228-230, 327-328, 336-340.

dragged out in a long series of sessions in Mexico and later in the United States and led to that officer's eventual reprimand.[32]

Of more interest for Marcy, however, was the counter-attack which Scott directed against the administration, but in name against him alone, in a powerful letter of February 24.[33] The proud general sarcastically described Marcy's orders to him of January 13 as "elaborate, subtle, and profound." As to Marcy's upholding the right of officers to appeal to the department against their superiors, he called it "a professional dissertation, with the rare merit of teaching principles, until now, wholly unknown to military codes and treatises, and of course to all mere soldiers, however great their experience in the field." But these were largely only words. More to the point, he made a long catalogue of complaints of non-support of his campaign, of what he called "some of the neglects, disappointments, injuries and rebukes" inflicted after he had left Washington. He charged that he had been allowed only four days' preparation there, alluded to the lieutenant-generalcy scheme, complained that he had been promised fifteen large transports from the Atlantic which had not been sent and that only half of the surf boats and siege cannon had come in time and that he had been censured for removing a Colonel Harney for violating orders, referred to his shortage of transport for the interior, said he had been rebuked for paroling prisoners taken at Cerro Gordo (on the way to Puebla), and alleged that the diversion of men to Taylor had left him so short of troops that, while at Vera Cruz,

like Cortez, finding myself isolated and abandoned, and again like him, always afraid that the next ship or messenger might recall or farther cripple me, I resolved . . . to render my little army *"a self-sustaining machine"* . . .

Marcy took a long while in preparing his reply to this broadside; his answer was dated April 1.[34] He stated that Scott was clearly trying to attack the president through him, since the articles of war banned disrespect for the commander-in-chief; it was a "device" which did more credit to Scott's ingenuity than to his soldierly character, Marcy

---

[32] *P.D.* III, 266-294, 426-427; to Scott, Jan. 13, *HED60*, 1040-1043; R. S. Ripley, *The War with Mexico*, II, 627-630.

[33] *HED60*, 1218-1227.

[34] *Ibid.*, 1227-1251.

said. He added that Scott plainly meant to imply that he had been given the Mexican command in order to ruin him. Such a charge, that the government had plotted the failure of its own plans, was too preposterous to need proof, said Marcy; he went on none the less to say that it was desirable for other reasons to reply to some of the specific charges. As to Scott's early departure, he cited the latter's own draft of a memorandum of November 23, which alluded to the fact that preparations were advanced enough to let him go, and pointed out that, after leaving, Scott had spent twenty-six days in getting to New Orleans. As to Colonel Harney, Scott saw the wrongness of his own act and himself reversed it, Marcy commented. What Marcy was not able to say in a public despatch was that he himself had held up the writing of a rebuke to Scott on this score until after Polk had threatened to write it himself, as Polk's own diary reveals.[35] In the matter of the Cerro Gordo prisoners, Marcy added, the official comment had been that Scott's policy had been "liberal and kind" and no rebuke had been given; a different practice had simply been ordered for the future, but Scott had shown "a diseased sensitiveness" in the whole affair.

Regarding the more important problems of men and transport, Marcy said anent the fifteen big Atlantic transports that to obtain vessels in the Gulf was cheaper; that Scott was demonstrably wrong as to the length of the alleged delay, at best; that Scott had been on hand at New Orleans and the Rio Grande during the critical period and Jesup had been serving under him—and so well that Scott had expressed his satisfaction at what he had done; and that Scott had specifically approved of Jesup's plan to obtain the vessels in the Gulf. As to the diversion of the men to Taylor, he pointed out that Scott, while Taylor's superior and nearer to the scene than Marcy was, had failed for forty-one days after hearing of the Buena Vista victory to take any step to order the men sent on to him, and had acted very indecisively even then. He closed with a personal note:

In conclusion, I may be permitted to say that, as one of the President's advisers, I had a *full share* in the responsibility of the act which assigned you to the command of our armies in Mexico. I felt interested even more than naturally appertained to my official position that success and glory

---

[35] *P.D.* II, 384-386.

should signalize your operations. . . . I never had a feeling that did not harmonize with a full and fair discharge of this duty. *I know it has been faithfully performed.* . . . From you I expected bare justice, but have been disappointed. . . . To your fame I have endeavored to be just. . . . In respect to your errors and your faults, though I could not be blind, I regret that you have not permitted me to be silent.

The correspondence was asked for by congress, and reached the press on April 30. It was at once a powerful political item, the Whig press endeavoring to keep Marcy's portion of it out of the public eye and the Democrats trying to feature it. As Marcy said himself, his reply reduced Scott's availability as a candidate. George Newell's comment was that if he were Scott he'd be as afraid of Marcy "as I would of a South Sea islander just after lent." On May 6, in fact, Marcy wrote that the documents had been important in the decision of the Whigs, just made at the capital, that Taylor, not Scott, should be the party's candidate for the presidency.[36]

Long before that time, if peace had not been made with the Whigs, it had with Mexico. In April, 1847, one Nicholas P. Trist had been sent to join Scott's army, empowered to make an armistice if he could secure what was wanted. This included the Rio Grande frontier, New Mexico, Upper and Lower California, and the right of transit across the isthmus of Tehuántepec in southern Mexico. For all this, the United States was willing to pay $30,000,000. Marcy had approved of these aims, as had just about all of the cabinet. Trouble had arisen, however, between Trist and Scott, who feared meddling in his military operations, and in October Trist had been recalled. During the discussion of their squabble, Polk had wanted to remove Scott also, but Marcy had checked that.[37]

By January 15, 1848, word came from Trist, who had stayed with the army despite the despatch summoning him home, that he had none the less begun negotiations; his message was insulting in its tone. The administration was at once very angry. It was at first argued by some that he should be ordered out of the country, but this was not done; in place of that, the cabinet on January 25 debated what to do if he sent home a treaty which contained the desired terms. Secretary Buchanan held that such a pact should be rejected. Marcy was

---

[36] To Wetmore, Apr. 30, to New[ell], May 6, Newell to Marcy, May 3, M.P.
[37] *P.D.* II, 472-473; III, 77; to Scott, Oct. 6, *H.ED60*, 1006-1009.

not present, being ill abed, but afterwards Polk and Mason went to his house to find out what his views were. Marcy agreed that a letter could be sent to General Butler, to tell him to send Trist packing for home, but he also "expressed the decided opinion that if a Treaty was made and ratified by Mexico upon the terms of our ultimatum in April last, that [Polk] ought not to reject it, but should send it to the Senate for ratification." After a further consultation with Marcy, next day, Polk determined to do as he advised. Marcy was not cheerful about the prospects, however. He wrote to Wetmore two days after that he saw no hope for either peace or a fight to the finish.

> We are approaching the end of our money means—our forces can at best be kept where they are as to numerical strength—& Congress are at a standstill, and, if perchance they should move, will probably go in the wrong direction. They will do more to prolong the war, [however], than can be expected of the Mexican Congress towards making a peace. . . .

This last was the factor which made him favor accepting a peace on the terms mentioned above, if Trist had secured one. He at last understood, as did Trist and Scott if not all of the administration, that the United States would be lucky if it found any government in Mexico ready and able to cede what was asked, and that the more likely prospect was that no treaty could be had at all. Indeed, in his annual report of December 2 he had spoken of the probable need for occupying the country for a long period before a pact could be won. In consequence, he had asked for ten added regiments of "duration" regulars.[38]

Despite his gloom, a treaty of the sort hoped for did arrive. This was on the evening of February 19. The chief alterations in the terms were that the United States did not get Lower California and paid only $15,000,000. At a cabinet meeting on the following evening, Marcy was present although still not very well and was one of the majority advising acceptance. He conceded that the action of Trist in negotiating without authorization was very annoying and expressed an "insuperable objection" to the tenth article, which dealt with land grants already made in the areas acquired. All the same, he "gave a clear & decided opinion" favoring submittal of the pact to the senate.

---

[38] *P.D.* III, 300-301, 314-317; to Wetmore, Jan. 28, M.P.; report of Dec. 2, *HED8*, 30th cong., 1st sess., 60-62.

From the notes on the meeting, dictated by Polk to his private secretary two days later, it is apparent that Marcy was the chief advocate of acceptance, aside from Polk himself. Polk decided to follow
this course; he did urge dropping Article X, however. The senate
complied. Marcy and Polk had thus headed off a growing movement
to annex much more of Mexico, or even all of it. By June 10, sure
that Mexico would ratify the altered terms, Marcy could write voicing
his hearty pleasure in this. He added that "I have at times feared that
I should not serve to the end of the war. . . ."[39]

The remainder of the conflict, while long and tedious, may be
passed over quickly. There was the work of bringing the forces home,
of selling surplus war supplies—at sad sacrifices in price—and of
demobilization. The last was no easy or pleasant matter. It meant
reducing officers to lower ranks, for one thing, a sort of patronage
problem in reverse. Nor was it a very happy period for Marcy personally. His mother had died in the spring, without his being able
to attend her bedside: "Though in some measure [I was] prepared
for the event," he told his brother Jedediah, "when it came it called
up a thousand endearing recollections of early life; and excited deep
sorrow." He added dourly that he felt "perhaps more sensibly than
at any time before" that his own part in life was "nearly finished."
This reflected his own weariness, of course. "I long for repose," he
said a week after. By autumn, however, as his official duties lessened
and there was time for an occasional round of whist—"my summum
bonum"—he felt better.[40]

*   *   *

Such was the Mexican War episode in William L. Marcy's life.
On the whole, it was not the most creditable chapter in his career,
although this was not entirely his own fault. Like the president, he
had shown a considerable want of understanding of the psychology
and the circumstances of Mexican life. Out of this had come a failure
to see the need for thoroughly drastic measures of war. Despite his
sensible doubts as to the possibility of a direct advance upon Mexico

[39] During the interval, it may be noted, Polk had vindictively concluded to order
Trist out of Mexico none the less. Marcy had opposed this as well as he could.
When he had at last obeyed the president's wishes, it had been after Polk had
promised to give him written instructions to do so. *P.D.* III, 345-347; notes of J.
Knox Walker, P.P., 1 ser., Feb. 22.
[40] To Wetmore, Aug. 20, Oct. 4, to Jedediah, May 7, to Samuel, May 14, M.P.

City from Monterey, he had even on the very verge of Scott's departure for the big campaign opposed the idea of an assault inland from Vera Cruz upon the central valley of Mexico.

On the other hand, he had tried manfully, in case after case, to uphold General Taylor and especially General Scott, when Polk had attempted to indulge in various petty and vindictive acts towards those two Whigs. This had been true particularly in regard to the integrity of command. The Harney case is an instance. What was more, he did the best he could as to supplies and transport. Over such matters, as also—and even more—in the politically pressing problem of appointments, he quite literally wore himself out. In the eyes of certain friendly critics, at least, Marcy was more than a competent administrator, nay, exceptional. Years later, it would ,be claimed that if he had headed the British war office in the Crimean conflict of 1853-1856, the history of that bootless campaign against the Russians would have been very different. There was much truth in this. Marcy also showed great fairness in making appointments. His selections of officers for brevets, in the summer of 1846, for example, struck George G. Meade, an unfriendly observer, as "most remarkably just." Similarly, he helped a number of Whigs to secure commissions.[41] As for his pamphleteering, that was a chapter by itself, really. It was done with a mild and even benign air and yet so competently that it left his Whig opponents, particularly Scott, quite crushed. But this was rather apart from the main narrative of events.

All in all, Marcy was an indefatigable public servant and generally a wise one, while secretary of war. His advice on the making of the peace, moreover, had been impeccable. And if, in the reliance upon volunteers, the acceptance of short terms for them, and the segregation of the regular officers with the regular army, he, like Polk, had erred, so too would Abraham Lincoln a decade and a half later, despite his experience as a congressman during this struggle. If it had not been Marcy's most creditable chapter, it certainly had been a worthwhile one.

---

[41] C. A. Davis to Marcy, Feb. 12, 1855, M.P.; Meade, *Life and Letters*, I, 128-129; J. H. Van Alen to Marcy, March 24, 1847, M.P.

XIV. THE REVOLT OF THE BARNBURNERS

"The Barnburners . . . seem determined on mischief—They are a pretty set of Pol. Knaves—If they cannot be everything they are determined that no democrat shall be anything." (Marcy to Wetmore, June 10, 1848[1])

IT WILL be recalled that Marcy's 1836 gubernatorial message had said that if necessary a state could provide by law for the trial of agitators who were upsetting the domestic peace of sister states. This had meant the abolitionists. In 1846, however, during the Mexican war, the slavery issue had arisen again. When President Polk sent the message to congress in August, 1846, which asked for an authorization of $2,000,000 for a quick cash payment if the Mexican government should be ready to deal with the United States, a house bill for the purpose had a significant rider attached to it. This was to the effect that slavery should be barred forever in all lands to be acquired. This northern move, led by Congressman Wilmot of Pennsylvania, threw the fat of sectionalism into the fire. For one thing, it aroused talk in the South of secession. It was also to have an enormous influence upon Marcy's career, for it would widen irrevocably the rift between his wing of the party in New York state and the opposition group. As a matter of fact, the manner and terms of the annexation of Texas had already contributed to a widening of that gap, as had the war with Mexico.

On the whole, the fault for the split, if any person's, was chiefly Wright's. While governor, he committed two serious errors. In the first place, he backed the stop-and-tax program wholeheartedly, despite the hostility of Marcy's friends to it, and called for a constitutional amendment to make it lasting. When Marcy read of this, in the governor's first message, in 1845, he at once commented that Wright could not win over the conservatives, and when writing to him he expressed his disapproval of that stand. Secondly, Wright

---

[1] M.P.

utterly refused to dispose of the patronage in such a way as to bring the party fully under his control, or, better, in such a way as to reject extremists of both factions. He acted as if office-mongering was something beneath him. It was probably this as much as anything else which led Marcy to comment later that "Wright seemed to me not to be himself from the moment he entered the governor's chair." Over and above these things, however, Wright allowed the Whigs to play off one Democratic faction against another; and when the Whigs by this means put through a call, along stop-and-tax lines, for a constitutional convention, Wright endorsed it.[2] Throughout this year, Marcy does not seem to have called upon his friends to back the governor's measures. He held to his position that they were unwise.

In the legislature of 1846, the radicals, somewhat strengthened, made a new attack upon Croswell. They tried to give the state printing to Cassidy, the editor of the *Atlas*. Marcy did not approve of this. He hotly supported his old ally, fearful lest radicalism be made completely official if Cassidy came in. When Croswell won out, by offering to do the printing for nothing, Marcy rejoiced that "the central domination at Albany is shaken." It was not surprising, therefore, that he was charged with trying to "kill Wright off." He wrote to Newell to deny this charge; it was "utterly unfounded," he said, pointing out, as has been remarked, that Wright's friends had been treated better in the patronage than had the Hunkers. He cited a great number of examples of the favor shown to the Barnburners. None the less, he did express a hope not long after that there would be no renomination of Wright, although he did not urge anyone else for the post. However, Wright was put up again.[3]

The prospects for the state campaign were none too good. As Marcy said prior to the state convention: "I fear [we] shall be obliged to fall quite down [i.e., be defeated] before we can get up & stand firm upon our legs again." This seemed all too likely. Apart from the unpopularity of the war, there were such state issues as the anti-rent trouble in the Hudson Valley, the stop-and-tax measures, and,

[2] To Bancroft, Jan. 4, 1845, Bancroft Papers; to Wright, Jan. 10, M.P.; to Bancroft, Apr. 28, 1847, M.P.; Garraty, *op. cit.*, 334-339, 355-356; H. D. A. Donovan, *The Barnburners*, 60-70.

[3] Garraty, *op. cit.*, 362-363; to Wetmore, Jan. 29, Feb. 1, 14, Mar. 9, May 9, to Newell, Feb. 26, M.P.; *E. Post*, Oct. 8.

very importantly, the personal antagonisms which had arisen. One reflection of the latter feature was that all persons who were seeking appointments at Washington felt obliged to identify themselves with either Marcy or Wright, since there was a sort of quota system in effect. This caused many such persons to take the added step of abusing the other side, thus making the trouble worse.[4] As Polk's diary shows, Marcy and Dix, the Washington leaders of the rival factions, were uncompromising themselves, frequently, in their patronage claims.[5]

During the campaign, Marcy again told Wetmore in effect that perhaps only a defeat could cure things.

> I support the nomination.—The degree of zeal exertions & means which I would apply to the election would if I were in N.Y. be a matter of consideration—Things will not get right till we are whipped—but when & under what circumstances the whipping shall take place is a question of grave importance—

He doubtless meant this only as a private comment, not an incitement to action. But if he was cool towards Wright, as this shows, many men of less reason and party loyalty, lower down in the ranks, were definitely hostile.

Realizing all this, Polk made a last minute effort at reconciliation. In September, he had both Buchanan and Bancroft visit the state. They let it be understood that the president wanted to be Wright's friend, that he had no plans as to who should be nominated in 1848, and that his choice of Marcy for the cabinet had been the result of circumstances rather than a desire to throw off the tie with the Van Buren group; they also encouraged Wright to open an exchange of letters with Polk, which was done.[6]

By the start of November, following a defeat for the party in Pennsylvania, Marcy was looking at the campaign with his more customary attitude, and doubtless his friends were beginning to, also. In fact, a conscious effort was being made in general to reunite the party. Marcy wrote that a reelection of the governor was essential,

---

[4] To Wetmore, Aug. 30, J. T. Hudson to Marcy, Mar. 22, 1846, M.P.
[5] *P.D.*, II, 399-405.
[6] To Wetmore, Oct. 5, M.P.; Buchanan to Polk, Sept. 5, copy, Polk Papers, N.Y.P.L.; Bancroft to Polk, Oct. 1, P.P., 1 ser.; Wright to Polk, Oct. 18, copy, Polk Papers, N.Y.P.L.

and he expressed his gratification at the harmony movement. "I rejoice to see that the work . . . has been begun in some hitherto distracted counties." When the ballots were counted, however, it was learned that Wright had been resoundingly defeated. Worst of all, this outcome had been caused to some degree by the defection of thousands of Hunkers. The news was a shock to Marcy, who had not quite understood what was going on. He called the tidings "a chilling blast."[7]

By this time, too, the Wilmot Proviso had been brought forward, which brings us to the subject of Marcy's views on slavery and its role in the federal territories. The fact was that William L. Marcy was just as convinced as the abolitionists were that slavery was evil—and for the same reasons, namely out of religious convictions.[8] Where he differed from them was in his recognition that the United States was huge and diverse and that the constitution had recognized this intentionally by leaving to the states the control of their domestic institutions. His views in this matter were well shown in a discussion which he had during the Polk era with Gideon Welles and Secretary John Y. Mason. Mason, a Virginian, was about to discharge an abolitionist clerk, while Welles had interceded in behalf of the man and had called Marcy in to help. The issue particularly brought up was if it was immoral to aid a slave to escape. As quoted by Welles in his recollections of Marcy,[9] Marcy "said very emphatically":

Mason you are entirely wrong, W——s views are correct. I concur with him most fully. Politically I can fight your battles so long as you make the constitution your fortress. But if you go to the bible [sic] or make it a question of ethics you must not expect me or any respectable number in the free states to be with you. The institution is one that I cannot indorse, but if you in Virginia, or in any other state choose to have it, I as a New Yorker cannot interfere to prevent it or abolish it where it

---

[7] To Wetmore, Nov. 1, 5, M.P.

[8] He was not a church member, although he attended Baptist churches regularly throughout his life and read the Bible and books of sermons extensively; he found no one of the established theologies just what he wanted. Cf. his diary of July 22, 1849, M.P. The pastor of the church which he attended at Albany, the Reverend B. T. Welch, divulged after Marcy's death (*Journal*, July 14, 1857) that Marcy had declined to join the church formally because of what he considered "palpable defects in [his] character"; he added that he had had long talks with Marcy, however, on religious subjects, and was convinced that he was a good Christian.

[9] "Recollections of Gov. Wm. L. Marcy," Papers Relating to Gideon Welles, L.C.

exists. That is a question that belongs to yourselves. On you is the responsibility [he added], and you must not ask me to share in that responsibility
for I will not take it. . . .

Mason then charged that the northern states had changed their views.
Marcy replied that this was not true—although clearly he was now
more tolerant as to the agitators than he had been in 1836. He went
on to say that "but the truth is . . . Mason, you have." He added that
the South was riding the slavery hobby to a regrettable extreme. This
was all too true, for since 1830 that section had turned away from
the doctrines of the Declaration of Independence and had begun to
argue publicly that slavery was a positive good.

As to slavery in the territories, Marcy upheld the principles of the
Missouri Compromise of 1820 and its geographical line separating
slavery and freedom; in a party which was national, as the Democratic
party was, some such compromise was of course vital. When the
Wilmot Proviso came up, therefore, he was horrified, as was the administration as a whole. He wrote to his son Samuel that

. . . a very ugly question has been started in Congress which will have
an unfavorable influence on the war. . . . The question is an exceedingly
embarrassing one and should not have been started at this time—Let us
first get the territory, & then settle . . . that question.

He supported the older plan, i.e. the Missouri line, as did the rest
of the cabinet. By contrast, the entire New York delegation, with the
exception of Senator Dickinson and one congressman, went for the
Proviso; this was partly because of instructions on that score from
the legislature, which had been adopted overwhelmingly. As it
turned out, the senate blocked the move and the house finally receded from it.

Just how active Marcy was in pressing congressmen to hew to the
administration line on the Proviso and other territorial measures
cannot be said, aside from some lobbying which he undertook to do
for the California statehood bill early in 1849. The government's
line was none too clear, however, because Polk long hesitated to
come out for an extension of 36°30'. In cabinet discussion, Marcy
consistently upheld the principle of 1820. The one exception came
on the last night of his term, when he agreed to the president's signing a bill which would have indirectly kept in force the old Mexican

ban on slavery in California and New Mexico. By this time, in any
case, a plan quite different from the extension of 36°30′ was being
advocated by the Democratic congressional leaders. This was to let
the settlers in a territory themselves decide for or against negro
bondage—a scheme which in time would be named "popular sovereignty."[10]

As the campaign of 1848 shaped up, it was adequately apparent
that the administration was not popular enough for any one in it to
make a good candidate. Buchanan appeared interested, but found the
signs unfavorable, while Marcy had long before made it known that
he did not seek a nomination. Marcy had a considerable number of
supporters, certainly, and his reply to Scott had won him a good deal
of favorable publicity. On the other hand, Wright's defeat had
focused attention upon the party split in New York, pointing up
the fact that Marcy could not very well carry his own state, if nominated; this deprived him of his greatest potential asset. It is not surprising, therefore, that he did not even consider himself a possibility
and instead accepted Polk's choice of Lewis Cass for that role. Cass
was a conservative Democrat who had supported the government
loyally during the war and who stood for popular sovereignty,
which the administration was now willing to accept. It may be noted
that when Polk drafted a letter for use at the convention, to ward off
any suggestion of his own name, Marcy was the first man he consulted over it. As this and other consultations prove, Marcy had by
this time emerged in Polk's eyes as an especially wise and helpful
counsellor.[11]

Before the national convention was held, it was certain that there
would be two rival delegations from New York, for the factionalism
there had intensified. Silas Wright had unexpectedly passed away in
August, 1847, but this had not helped the situation. Lacking his
disinterested leadership, his wing of the party had become more

---

[10] To Samuel, Jan. 11, 1847, M.P.; *P.D.* II, 287, 304-309, 335, III, 501-503, IV,
24, 61-62, 70-71, 364-365; F. B. Woodford, *Lewis Cass*, 251; Donovan, *op. cit.*,
84-86. On the other hand, Marcy endorsed Polk's plan to offer Spain up to
$100,000,000 for Cuba, a slave area.

[11] J. Y. Mason, Sept. 9, 1847, G. A. Worth, May, 1848, G. R. McFarlane, May 8,
1848, letter of N.Y. merchants, Sept. 28, 1848, *re* a dinner in his honor, all to Marcy,
M.P.; *P.D.* III, 335, 452-456; Woodford, cited above.

truly a faction, more Van Burenish, than before; at the same time, much of the loss anent his death was turned against Polk and Marcy, who were publicly charged with having killed him by their supposed enmity. In the 1847 campaign for a new legislature, the radicals had not put up a separate ticket. But they had held a convention of their own and had passed resolutions against slavery in the territories, which the Hunkers had declined to do. In the voting, moreover, the Barnburners had not supported the state ticket, which had been beaten. It was hardly a surprise, then, that they and the Hunkers had acted separately in the choice of delegates to Baltimore, for the Hunkers were ready to go for Cass, while the Barnburners' freesoil views led them to talk of Benton or Dix.

When the convention met, late in May, there was some talk of requiring the Barnburners to agree to support whomever was nominated, but this they were not ready to do, for they feared that Cass would be the man. What was done instead was to offer both delegations half of the vote to which New York was entitled. Both refused, however, so that the state went unrepresented. The outcome was that Cass was chosen, on a platform which was silent as to slavery in the territories.[12]

Following the disagreement at Baltimore, the Barnburners proceeded to establish a third party, which had considerable backing all over the North. They named their organization the Freesoil Party and put up Martin Van Buren himself for the presidency; their platform demanded not only a ban upon slavery in the territories but also free homesteads for bona fide settlers. For their own gubernatorial candidate, incidentally, the Barnburners chose Senator Dix, although he had opposed all of the earlier steps in this disruption of the Democracy.

In the eyes of the administration, which was horrified by this event, the chief question was whether to remove the federal officials who had countenanced it. One trouble was that the list was exceedingly long and was headed by some men of real note, such as Benjamin F. Butler. Marcy invariably urged that the culprits be ousted. Indeed, he

---

[12] Flagg to Dix, Aug. 31, 1847, Dix Papers, Col. U.; *Herald*, Oct. 3-6; Donovan, *op. cit.*, 91-103.

had sought, in vain, to have a beginning made along that line even before the Baltimore Convention. It was not until about September 1 that Polk yielded. He had hesitated to act, lest there be a charge that the Freesoilers were being martyred because of their principles—i.e. lest the step should do more harm than good. Events were to prove that the removals had precisely that effect.[13]

In the ensuing campaign, Marcy did what he could to help the Cass forces. He had the month of September off from his duties at Washington and spent it mostly in his own state, but he was tired and not too well and avoided people much of the time. If the chances in the state were very poor, there was a fairly good prospect nationally, of course. After he was back at Washington, he continued to do what he could to help. He contributed freely to the party funds, he went over to Annapolis for a day or two to encourage the leaders there; and not long after he used his influence to persuade Dickinson to stump the counties on both sides of the New York-Pennsylvania line. "Great efforts are to be made to put Pennsylvania *right side up*," he wrote on October 22. At the same time, he was not ready to do anything improper to aid the ticket. He declined to interfere with army officers who were thought to be working for Taylor, since their political activity was hard to establish clearly. He also refused to hold up the sailing of Colonel Riley's regiment for New York until after the election. "To do so would be going further than my political conscience would approve," he explained.[14]

Personally, he felt a marked equanimity of mind as to the decision, whatever it might be. He did not expect to continue in office and he did not want to; among other things, his private affairs needed attention. His attitude was well revealed in a letter to Wetmore on November 5, on the eve of the national poll:

It would be not a little strange that an administration which has been more than usually successful in its measures should be overturned—yet such things have been and may be again. When persons have done all the work they were engaged to do—it is common to dismiss them though the work has been admirably well done. We have not husbanded the job,

[13] *Ibid.*, 104-108; *P.D.* IV, 9-11; to Wetmore, Apr. 25, M.P.
[14] *P.D.* IV, 116, 135; D. B. Taylor to Polk, Sept. 28, Walker to Polk, Sept. 21, P.P., 2 ser.; Marcy to Wetmore, Sept. 8, Oct. 11, 22, 29, Nov. 1, M.P.; to Dickinson, Oct. 25, N.Y.H.S.

and left some substantial part of it unfinished—so that the usefulness of our future services would be more apparent.

This was a fair statement, of course. The government had succeeded in reaching its specified goals to an extent which few others have ever done: tariff, subtreasury, Texas, Oregon, New Mexico, California— few terms have been so productive. There had been a momentous by-product, a tragic and wholly deplorable incidental result, it is true, in the raising of the sectional issue. But, to return to Marcy's reflections of November 5, he said that it was the thought that his party would lose which really hurt. He had been attached to "the democratic cause" from his youth, he said; his attachment, moreover, had been "most abundantly rewarded." "I cannot endure the idea of reverses to it—without deep sorrow. . . ."[15]

His fears were to be borne out. Taylor won by a narrow margin, carrying Pennsylvania as well as New York, while Martin Van Buren obtained about ten percent of the total popular vote.

And so the Polk administration came to an end. General Taylor arrived at the capital, giving Marcy a surprisingly friendly greeting when they met: "It was kind & cordial in appearance & I believe in reality," Marcy told Wetmore. This was perhaps at Polk's big dinner for the president-elect on March 1, which the Marcys attended. On March 5, "Old Rough and Ready" was inaugurated. Then, that night, the Marcys were among those who escorted Polk, white-haired and careworn from his incessant toil, to his steamer for his trip south. Subsequently, they sold their furniture and turned over their house, which they had rented, to Colonel Walker, Polk's private secretary. Then, near the end of the month, they wended their way north, contented to be returning to "the good old dutch [sic] city of Albany."[16]

---

[15] To Wetmore, November 5, M.P.

[16] To Wetmore, Mar. 9, 1849, M.P.; *P.D.* IV, 358-359, 374-378; diary, Mar. 12 ff., M.P.

XV. MARCY PRESIDES AT THE PARTY REUNION

> "The game was an exceedingly difficult one to play—it combined the characteristics of *Brag* & *Whist,* to the *former* of which I can make no pretension." (Marcy to Wetmore, September 16, 1849[1])

FOR THE first two or three months after his return to Albany, Marcy was wholly satisfied to rest and recuperate, partly because he had been ill again in February. A regime of repose, in his handsome house on State Street, seemed utterly delightful. Once the pressure was removed, indeed, he felt old. "For me politically—there is no future, and it is well that I feel no aspirations," he wrote in April. Looking through some of his past letters, of which he burned huge quantities in these months, he was distressed to find that of sixty or seventy of his former legal associates, perhaps not a dozen were left. "But my turn must soon come," he added lugubriously.

He spent most of his time in reading. This was especially so after May 10, when he sprained his ankle severely in getting off a canal packet at Lockport, on the second day of a projected trip to the West; the mishap caused him to be laid up for many weeks. In June, his quiet was agreeably broken, however, by the return of his son Samuel after three years in the Pacific and the simultaneous arrival home from school of Mistress Cornelia and the advent of three of the Knower tribe. It was a happy reunion. Samuel, a lively young man, could tell interesting tales of the South Seas, although inclined to discount Melville's picture of the Marquesas as given in his book *Typee;* he had met few "Fayaways," he said, but he conceded that the author had described the islands well.

By the coming of summer, Marcy was beginning to think actively of the need to enlarge his income. He did not see quite the right solution, however. He was too hopelessly rusty at law to care to go back to it, or, so far as that went, to accept Governor Fish's proposal that

---

[1] M.P. Marcy did not italicize the word "former." "Brag" was somewhat like poker.

he be the Democratic member of the commission to revise the state code. He also declined Aaron Leggett's request that he take up the argument of the latter's claim against Mexico. He was deeply prejudiced against claims agents and their business. He did debate writing a life of Polk, of whose death, in June, he learned with great distress. Yet he felt that in praising Polk's achievements he would seem to be lauding his own and, more to the point, he was always too lazy to write unless he had to. More seriously, he considered taking charge of the great properties of the Van Rensselaer family, which had been the very focus of the anti-rent "wars" of the last few years.[2] That he even debated this, was proof of how completely out of politics he considered himself.

By mid-summer, however, Marcy was active again, part-time, at his old love. For months, a grass roots movement had been proceeding for a reunification of the Democratic Party. This was desired especially among the rank and file, who were less committed personally to one side or the other than the leaders were, and the work began quietly in various counties. Then, when the legislature was about to break up, the Hunker and Barnburner members both issued addresses to the people, of a conciliatory type, calling for reunion. Marcy had some hand in the Hunker letter. He also largely wrote the address of the Hunker state central committee of May 15. The latter called upon all Democrats, of both wings, to cooperate in choosing delegates to the regular (or conservative) state convention, to be held at Syracuse on September 5, but it also advanced some principles as the basis for the union. These were that the party did not favor slavery and was against its extension, but that congress had no power to interfere with it in the states where it existed; further, that congress lacked power either to impose it upon a territory or to bar it. Marcy found that this declaration was well received among the party leaders. He foresaw many difficulties, but in conversations at Albany and in letters which he wrote he did what he could to promote the movement. Undoubtedly he also backed the suggestion of the state committee, on

---

[2] To Jas. Larned, Apr. 4, N.Y.H.S.; to Berret, Apr. 14; to A. Campbell, Jr., May 28; to Wetmore, Apr. 16, 24, May 11, Sept. 28; W. P. Van Rensselaer to Marcy, June 20; Leggett to Marcy, Mar. 27, Apr. 4; diary, June 6-18; Samuel to Newell, Feb. 9; all in M.P.

June 20, that each side choose delegates to meet at Rome to consult; the two groups would meet separately but would negotiate with each other. The Barnburner committee also endorsed this plan.[3]

Although Marcy was persuaded to serve as a delegate to Rome and to Syracuse, he was none too cheerful as to the result. From Wetmore, for example, he was regularly informed of the deep conservatism of the leaders at the metropolis, where freesoilism scarcely had a hold at all. He wrote cautiously to Wetmore that he could not see how such efforts at union could be avoided, "yet I do not expect, & never did, that any good will come of it." Perhaps he was emphasizing his caution deliberately, for New York City's benefit. He went on to say, none the less, that the Barnburners would never budge from their views on slavery and its spread and that the trouble was, really, that the Hunkers in essence agreed with them but could not say so lest they divorce themselves from the party nationally. This left them at a disadvantage psychologically. Here, of course, he was also speaking for himself. He added that he could not, however, accept the view of the state committee, that congress did not have the power to bar slavery in the territories. "There are too many precedents against it," he explained.

Besides Wetmore, there were also many other men who warned of the dangers of yielding too much. Samuel Beardsley wrote from Utica, for example, to ask that the party restate its position as a national organization which did not interfere with state lines or institutions and which was opposed to sectional blocs; on the other hand, he was willing to state that there was no intention of interfering with the views of individual party members.[4] Generally, however, both branches of the Democrats accepted the idea of going to Rome.

Marcy reached Rome just in time for the gathering and was at once in the thick of things. When the Hunkers met in their appointed place, at the Presbyterian Church, he was chosen chairman by acclamation, the applause being "tumultuous." In his usual, awkward manner, he made a short speech, but it was one very pertinent in its con-

---

[3] To Wetmore, Apr. 16, May 31, Sept. 16, M.P.; *Argus*, May 17, 1849; diary, June 14; *Atlas*, June 23, July 3.

[4] To Wetmore, July 23, Wetmore to Marcy, July 24, Beardsley to Marcy, July 30, M.P.

tents. After asking indulgence if he should reveal any lack of parlia-
mentary skill, he said that:

I am certain that the democratic party, our constituents, look with un-
common anxiety to the proceedings of this convention—and it is my
sincere hope that we may not disappoint their expectations. I presume
every gentleman here is as well acquainted with the object of the assembling
of this convention, as I am myself. . . . I do not however understand
that we have come here to revise the principles of the democratic party,
in order to abandon any heretofore adopted, or to incorporate any new
ones. (Applause.)

He declined to refer to the causes of the recent dissensions: "I do
not propose to look back . . . ," he said. He alluded, however, to the
situation four years earlier, when one Democrat (Wright) had been
governor and another (Polk) president:

These men, both—though not far advanced in life—have descended to
the tomb, and have left behind them honorable memories—(Here Gov.
Marcy's voice fell with emotion, and the reporter could not catch more.)
Our object, gentlemen, . . . should be . . . to unite all men who believe
in the principles of the democratic party; and I am satisfied that we shall
conduct our proceedings in such a spirit as will conduce to this end. . . .
(Applause, long and loud, at his conclusion.)

Reporters said that he looked tired and that his eyesight was bad, so
that when there were statements to present he gave them to a clerk to
read out. Yet it is plain that he was the leader in the Hunker
gathering.

In the negotiations which followed with the Barnburner convention, which was meeting at the same time in the Baptist Church, the
method of procedure was by conference committees. Throughout the
ensuing discussions, Marcy and his friends did their best to achieve a
union. They finally adopted the resolution of Levi S. Chatfield, one of
their own number, which represented the most that they were willing
to concede. This said that "we are opposed to the extension of slavery
to the free territory of the United States; but we do not regard the
slavery question in any form of its agitation, or any opinion in relation thereto as a test of political faith, or as a rule of party action."
It also alluded to the power of congress over slavery in the territories
as a "controverted question." In general, this was going a long way,
further than Walworth or Beardsley or Dickinson, all of whom were
present, were willing to yield. The Barnburners would not accept the

Chatfield statement, however. The result was that the twin convention broke up on the 17th, the Hunkers with "three cheers for Marcy."[5]

Later, back at Albany, Marcy wrote to Wetmore that he was glad that the convention had made no greater sacrifice to the Barnburners. "I never had more apprehensions of a miscarriage in my life. . . ." This was an allusion to the fact that at the end it had been all that the Hunker leaders could do to prevent a secession of many of their delegates who wanted to move over to the freesoilers. In a letter to one of the radicals, on the other hand, Marcy explained that he could not go for the Wilmot Proviso because it would neither unite the Democrats of the state nor permit the survival of their party in the nation. A further point, he said shrewdly, was the following:

But suppose—*what I do not believe will ever take place while our bond of union holds us together* there should grow out of the Slavery agitation a great sectional party in the free states [,] what would be the order of merit—who would have just claims to be at its head? The Whigs could claim and would have the power to hold the first place. . . .

He went on to say, with great force, that there was really no danger of the introduction of slavery into any of the present territories, that all of them were free. "In my judgment [he added] the ill advised agitation has retarded the progress of emancipation" in the South. This letter, dated August 27, also contained a statement that he had no further political ambitions. This was no doubt true, but when he wrote to Mrs. Marcy on September 3, just before leaving for Syracuse, and said that he had been "*swamped* in politics," he seemingly relished saying so. Not office, but at least useful, influential political activity, had returned to him.[6]

At Syracuse, the Hunkers adopted a resolution calling upon the Barnburners to accept the Chatfield statement. They also nominated a full ticket of state officers. But of some of those named on the ticket, it was stated officially that they could be set aside if the radicals chose to put others in their places; in this way, a joint ticket could be composed. Marcy probably had a large hand in all of this, although in the end he had not been a delegate. At the state fair, which met in the

---

[5] *Atlas*, Aug. 16-21; *Argus*, Aug. 17 (his speech), 30; *Herald*, Aug. 16-19.
[6] To Wetmore, Aug. 24; to (?), Aug. 27 (italics added), published in the *Argus* in a different version on Aug. 31; to Mrs. Marcy, Sept. 3, M.P.

same place the following week, he was by contrast a figure of much interest. His heavy walking stick, a memento of the Mexican conflict, was also given a great deal of attention by the fair-goers. It was of wood from the flagstaff of the national palace at Mexico City and had other parts which were souvenirs of the war, while its ferrule was made of some of the first newly discovered California gold to be seen in the East. Marcy would comment jokingly that the ivory on its head, moreover, was from the "elephant" which so many of the volunteers had gone to Mexico to see. (Once having "seen the elephant," i.e. the country, according to the popular saying, they had wanted to go home!) "The Gov. is full of life & anecdote,—he seems to have a dozen campaigns in him yet," said the New York *Herald's* reporter knowingly.[7] Plainly, Marcy was excited by it all.

In their convention at Utica, the radicals accepted the arrangement as to a joint ticket, but not the Chatfield resolution. This may have been one reason why Marcy declined to serve as the president of the joint convention, which was held at Syracuse on September 14, for he probably could guess that too many of the Hunkers were ready to go over to the Barnburner stand and that reunion could be achieved, really, only on the basis of accepting it. He was present, however. And the outcome proved to be of the sort indicated, for the Hunkers gave in. Together with the radicals, they accepted a statement to the effect that congress not only had full power over slavery in the territories but ought to exert it on all occasions when attempts were made to introduce that institution. The only sop for the Hunkers was a clause which read that "but as the constitutional power is questioned, we are willing to tolerate the free exercise of individual opinion upon that question, among members of the democratic family who are willing to rally under one standard, and support the ticket nominated by the recent State Conventions." Marcy's readiness to accept this platform was doubtless because he knew that it expressed what the great majority of the party in the state believed. He could see well enough, of course, that this was not a "national" program and that the Barnburners could rejoin the party in the country at large, on it, only so long as the slavery question was kept down. At the moment, furthermore, the chances of doing that were not too good. In other words,

---

[7] *Atlas*, Sept. 6; *Herald*, Sept. 6, 16, 17; to Campbell, Sept. 19, M.P.

the party reunion would be a weak one. With Dickinson and Croswell and many other conservatives, moreover, there was only the most grudging acceptance. At New York City, the stronghold of "national" views on slavery, the party's general committee denounced the union and all of its works. Under the circumstances, it was not surprising that the Whigs scored an easy victory in the state, that autumn.[8]

Shortly before congress opened, Marcy received a letter on the sectional issue from Thomas Ritchie, the Virginia editor, which caused him to write a long and interesting reply. In relation to slavery, Marcy admitted, the North had been "mischievous" and the South "unwise." He hoped that each would mend its ways. Yet the indication which Ritchie seems to have given in his letter, that the South would oppose the admission of California with a free-state constitution which that territory was intending to submit, "somewhat disturbs my quiet nature," Marcy wrote. This would "be a fatal error" on the South's part, he warned.

It will evince a design to introduce slavery into that State against the expressed wish of the people. If the South become propagandist of slavery, they [sic] will put themselves where no northern man can cooperate with them. They have now, I lament to say, too few sustainers in the North. . . . They will fail in the attempt and, I fear provoke further agitating measures from the North. I need not tell you how fatal such a step would be to the friends of the South in the free states.

As for southern talk of secession, he added, that would be viewed as "idle bravado." "I think I told you," he said further, "that all my hopes of seeing things right in relation to the slavery question depended on the success of General Cass. He was weakened in the North because he held and openly avowed sentiments favorable to the rights of the South." All the same, said Marcy angrily, five of the southern states had gone for Taylor, a man whose position in the South was "more than equivocal" as to these rights and who was approved in the North because he was hostile to them.[9]

In spite of such warnings, the South did try to block the entry of California as a free state, none the less, causing a great crisis. This was

---

[8] Dickinson to Marcy, Sept. 23, M.P.; Croswell to Seymour, Oct. 20, S.P.; speech of Hughes, in *Atlas*, Feb. 13, 1854; *Atlas*, Sept. 13, 15; *Herald*, Sept. 17.

[9] To Ritchie, Nov. 29, *John P. Branch Historical Papers of Randolph-Macon College*, III, 405-409.

solved only because a series of compromise measures was put through, with the support of the abler leaders of congress. These were men of Marcy's generation, whose fathers had fought in the Revolution and who had themselves, many of them, fought for the Union in the War of 1812.

Marcy favored the compromise and similarly the spirit of reason which produced it. He warmly praised a speech which Senator Dickinson made in its advocacy. When some law business, to which he was beginning to turn, took him to Washington late in February, incidentally, he was able to attend some of the notable debates on the subject. On May 13, after he had returned to Albany, he bespoke his approval of the policy of mutual accommodation in a public letter on the occasion of the anniversary dinner of the Tammany Society. Pointing out that the Union was indeed in danger, he went on to say that "It is the solemn duty of all to come forth in its defense." Similarly, he wrote to Wetmore on May 20 that he did not fear secession in case the compromise failed. What he did worry about was "a bad state of things."

The bonds of affection will be weakened; the idea of disunion will become familiar to the mind of both sections & in calculating the value of the union both will be led to cheapen it.[10]

This was a remarkably apt description of what did in time take place. For the moment, however, such troubles were avoided. California became a free state, while Utah and New Mexico were organized as territories without any declaration as to slave or free states; this latter implied something like squatter sovereignty. The slave trade was banned in the District of Columbia. And a more stringent fugitive slave law, which contained many objectionable features, was adopted.

In view of Marcy's understanding of the seriousness of the crisis, it is remarkable that he declined to endorse the specific measures of the settlement in a public letter, as he was asked to. Nor did he use his influence in any active way to get it through, other than in such casual private letters as the one to Wetmore which has just been referred to. Just possibly, he was afraid that to do so would not sit well with his new Barnburner allies, whom he perhaps wished to cajole a bit further along the road to party union. More probably, however, it was

---

[10] Dickinson to Marcy, Jan. 29, 1850, Marcy to John Knower, Mar. 27, to Wetmore. Apr. 8, May 20, M.P.; *Herald,* May 15.

that old, selfish laziness as to public questions which characterized him when he was not in office or seeking it. This was one of his serious faults. On the other hand, when a public dinner was given to Dickinson at New York, Marcy sent a letter to the meeting praising him for his backing of the settlement. Also, when Marcy was at Boston that December, he sat on the platform of the great public meeting which endorsed the measures and was much moved at the clear signs of the popular will shown there.[11] On the whole, though, Marcy's attitude was a slothful one, that year.

In the following winter, the great question in Marcy's career was his alleged role in the defeat of Senator Dickinson for reelection. The fact was that the senator later blamed him for his failure. To furnish the answer at once, Marcy was not guilty. He was not wholly Dickinson's friend, it is true, because Dickinson had not backed the party reunion after its first stages. At the same time, as a letter from Isaac Butts of Rochester, dated June 25, 1850, shows us, Marcy was then firmly supporting Dickinson. Remember, too, Marcy's letter to the New York dinner for Dickinson, which was written that same month. Dickinson made matters difficult, however, by continuing to be outspokenly critical of the Barnburners. When the state convention met, accordingly, an official call for his reelection was blocked. In the local electoral arrangements of that autumn, moreover, the radicals worked hard to prevent the nomination of legislative candidates who would be for him and in the elections themselves they were ready to vote for Whigs, if anything, rather than see his backers win. The upshot was that the Democratic ticket had only a partial success and that the assembly became Whig; the senate was already Whig. After the poll, Dickinson's surviving friends in the legislature made matters worse, if anything, by issuing an address to him in which they spoke of the likelihood that he would not be chosen to return to Washington but looked to his "renewed elevation" at some future time. Dickinson replied in a public letter by saying that it was the character of the reunion which had led to his adherents' defeat. He added that he was "proud to enjoy . . . the hostility of all recusants." After this, cer-

---

[11] Sen. Foote to Marcy, requesting a statement, May 28, 1850, and Marcy's note on *verso*; draft of letter to Dickinson dinner, June 17, Campbell to Marcy, Dec. 19, M.P.; Marcy to Buchanan, Dec. 19, B.P.

tainly, there was no hope of his choice. Instead, a Whig was chosen. While Marcy later insisted that he "sincerely" wanted Dickinson's reelection "and did all [he] could" to secure it,[12] and while this was apparently correct, Dickinson never forgave him.

Marcy was at Washington during this period, from January 8, 1851, through April. He was working on two claims, despite his hostility to such employment, and also on some law cases. After a full-blown round of hospitality on the highest level, in January, he lived very quietly. He told Wetmore that he had "lodgings that nobody can find if they make the attempt. Even my letters wander about this spacious city three or four days before they come to me."[13] After he returned to Albany, his life was still a quiet one. As in 1844, he considered his political career at an end, and so did most other people. His principal problem was to make enough of an income to support his family, hence the spasmodic work at the legal cases. As for his investments, they were in better shape than before, because business was reviving everywhere. For one thing, the stock which he owned in the Michigan Southern Railway seemed promising. But he did not have a sufficient nest egg to live wholly in retirement. He was now sixty-five years old. Events were to show, none the less, as the *Herald* reporter had said in 1849, that he still had some campaigns in him.

---

[12] Butts to Marcy, June 25, 1850, Marcy to Campbell, Mar. 25, 1852, M.P.; address to legislators and Dickinson's reply, *Argus*, Jan. 24, 1851; Marcy to Buchanan, Sept. 20, Nov. 10, 1850, B.P.

[13] Diary, Jan. 1-June 30; to Wetmore, Feb. 15, M.P.

XVI. FAVORITE SON

"You labour under one of Mr. Webster's difficulties, that
you are almost universally conceded to be the ablest man
among the candidates. . . ." (John V. L. Pruyn to Marcy,
May 31, 1852[1])

IN THE first half of 1851, Marcy began to be talked of very prominently as a potential nominee for the presidency. This was
chiefly because he had been the principal figure associated with the
party reunion, which had made him the heir to the good feelings
which that event had produced. Amusingly enough, it was his old
enemies, the Barnburners, who were his main advocates. This was
because these men knew that they could not possibly put up one of
their own number, lest they revive the schism of 1848. With him, on
the other hand, they would expect to win the support of the main
body of the Hunkers. It is only fair to add, however, that the proposal was also made on account of the high opinion in which he was
held personally. As State Senator H. B. Stanton, General John A.
Thomas, the former commandant of cadets at West Point, and Fitzwilliam Byrdsall, the old Workingmen's Party leader, all put it, they
especially admired his "intellect." Some, in fact, considered him the
ablest man available in either party in the entire country. Congressman
Timothy Jenkins of Oneida County, for instance, called him "incom-
parably the most competent man" there was; John V. L. Pruyn, the
distinguished Albany lawyer, and Simeon B. Jewett, the Barnburner
leader, made comments of the same sort. It is not improper to add
that two twentieth-century scholars who have studied the period
closely, namely Roy F. Nichols and Allan Nevins, have in general
agreed.[2] In addition, the charm of his conversation won him friends.
In Byrdsall's opinion,

---

[1] M.P.
[2] S. M. Shaw, Jan. 15, 1851, Thomas, May 5, 1851, Pruyn (quoted above),
Jewett, July 4, 1851, all to Marcy, M.P.; T. Jenkins to sons, Jan. 26, 1852, State
Library; Byrdsall to Buchanan, Dec. 1, 1851, B.P.; Roy F. Nichols, *The Democratic
Machine*, 93; Allan Nevins, *Ordeal of the Union*, II, 15.

He has enough of the witchery of mischievous fun and tact to make him racy as a politician and delightful as an acquaintance. He is as piqueantly [sic] mischievous as Mephistopheles himself. . . . I both admire and like him.

Among Marcy's warmest backers, incidentally, were several of those men who had had years of close association with him in the war department. These included Archibald Campbell, Jr., and John D. McPherson, among the leading civilian employees, and some of the general staff, such as General Towson and Colonel Samuel Cooper. Since it was now expected that Winfield Scott would be the Whig nominee, the interest of army officers in the matter was a very keen one. While such men were normally all Whigs, they generally sided with Marcy against Scott. Unquestionably, this was partly out of mere dislike for Scott's vanity. One officer, for example, was in the habit of reciting parts of Marcy's reply to Scott (of 1848) to groups of his brother officers; he was reported to do it "with great unction" and no doubt he also did it with a great deal of relish. Another officer was said to "always read it when he was a little depressed in spirits." On the other hand, the liking of the officers corps also reflected a solid esteem for his disinterested work as secretary and his readiness to uphold the professional officers as against Polk's interference.[3]

Notwithstanding all this, Marcy was none too enthusiastic at the idea of running.[4] His wife probably did not approve, either. "The subject was not a favorite one when I was last at home," wrote Samuel Marcy early in 1852. Even so, several friends began to talk of the scheme and to write letters about it, and scattered newspaper items to that effect also began to appear. Marcy's own view, and a correct one, was that some "new" man would be most likely to win the presidency, because of the divided state of the two great parties, although he recognized that the Whigs were far too divided altogether to have much chance. As for the Democrats, he wrote to Archibald Campbell that Cass's popularity was on the wane, that Buchanan had little in New York, and that Sam Houston, whom some of the ex-freesoilers

[3] A. Campbell to Marcy, May 30, 1848 (and many other letters), M.P.; [John D. McPherson] in "'General Grant's Political Myth," quoted in Smith, *op. cit.*, I, 475; S. Cooper to Marcy, May 10, 1851, Campbell to Marcy, Feb. 4, June 7, 1852, M.P.
[4] Shaw letter, cited above.

liked, was not spoken of at all generally. As for Dickinson, whose friends were busy, Marcy held that he could not rally too many of the state's Hunkers even, let alone the radicals.

In this letter, which he wrote on May 28, 1851, Marcy added that "The section which opposed Cass would be equally opposed to him [Dickinson]; but many of them say—some of the most active & influential among them—that they will go for a candidate who can carry the state of N. Y.—and mention a person of your particular acquaintance as standing in that position." He went on as follows: "I do not put much faith in the sincerity of the declaration nor do I believe it is as extensive as it is represented to be, though there is more of that talk & probably more of that feeling than I had expected." While he was at Buffalo that June, he found some support for himself; on the other hand, in August, when he travelled a good deal to the fashionable summer resorts in the mid-state area, he felt no wiser than before. Apparently he was trying, that month, by talking of the chances of the various other candidates, to tell what people thought of himself. A letter which he wrote to Wetmore during this time is particularly interesting. He remarked that he was in "a balancing state" as to candidates—"and if you have any desire to have me go for your candidate (I presume you have one) you can easily get me to go along with you—provided he is *qualified* and *wants* the station."[5] Since this was to a very old and close friend, it had a touch of coyness about it.

It was also a sign of rising ambition, perhaps only half conscious as yet, that Marcy took a great interest in the plans being made for the coming state convention at Syracuse. It was not expected that this body would declare for a presidential prospect. But its platform for the approaching state election was sure to have a national bearing, notably in its remarks on the Compromise; it would be influential in shaping the opinion of the country and, in view of the New York Democracy's checkered history in recent years, would have a great influence upon the fortunes of any potential nominee from the state. It is therefore significant that Marcy demanded from the beginning a clear support of the Compromise. Apparently he reasoned that quite enough had

[5] Samuel to Newell, Mar. 5, 1852, N.P.; Marcy to Campbell, May 28; diary, June 9; to Wetmore, Aug. 22, to Campbell, Aug. 25, M.P.

been done to win the Barnburners and that now the tugging must be in the other direction. He was also against a "mum" policy, he declared.

Marcy's views were especially well shown in two long letters which he sent to Judge Fine, an influential Barnburner. He wanted an endorsement of the fugitive slave law, he said, although he would waive this if in any other way the platform could be made national. The South was entitled to have the constitution upheld in every detail, he argued, even in the return of fugitives; furthermore, the recent law on that subject had been the South's chief gain in the Compromise and it was less objected to in the North than it had been, he believed, and had "worked fairly well." In view of some instances of violations of the law in the past year, such as the cases of Shadrach and Sims at Boston, this might have been debated, but Marcy, of course, meant to allude to its general acceptance. He reasoned further that if there was fault in some of its provisions, the state ought none the less to voice its approval of having *some* such law. On the whole, he pointed out, the North had gained more from the Compromise than the South had; he therefore asked for an explicit endorsement, in general terms at least, without excepting the fugitive act. "My sole object is the success of the party to which I have always been attached. I owe it my devotion and services as long as I live."[6] In short, he was talking like a candidate.

By and large, the state convention did well. It endorsed the Compromise and declared that the Constitution must be upheld in every feature; it also promised that the party would back whomever was the national nominee. As before, a state ticket was chosen which embraced both Hunkers and Barnburners. A more important result of the gathering, however, for Marcy, was the crystallization of opinion among the delegates that he was the man who should be urged upon the Baltimore convention as the best one to put up. He was not present. Nor was any resolution adopted on this. Yet Simeon Jewett wrote to him afterwards that if such a step had been proposed, as the only business of the gathering, it would have found the members much more harmonious than they were.

---

[6] To Shaw, Sept. 7, S.P.; to Fine, Aug. 16, 27, 1851, in *Herald* of June 1, 1852.

With some of the Barnburners, it is true, the support given to Marcy would have been only nominal. John Van Buren, for example, wrote to a friend on September 13, the day after the convention ended, that he and his friends were for Marcy simply in order to get rid of the district system of choosing delegates; they were willing to send delegates who would be for him on the first ballot, but only if there was little danger of his being nominated. Van Buren himself was for William O. Butler, one of Polk's volunteer generals, who owned slaves but was opposed to the spread of slavery. Quite a number of the old Benton-Barnburner wing, by the way, wanted Butler. On the other hand, many other freesoilers, including Azariah Flagg and John Bigelow, were genuinely for Marcy all the way. Marcy understood these diverse motives rather well and his reaction was a mixture of both scepticism and acceptance. "I fear the Greeks when they bear gifts," he wrote to Wetmore later. He acknowledged that many of the Barnburners had turned to him simply because they had to have a "national," i.e. a non-sectional man, and they thought that by going for him they could reduce the danger of having finally to take up Cass—or Dickinson. This was "certainly . . . not very flattering" to himself, he said, yet he preferred to think this rather than to accept the other view, namely, that the Barnburners would go along with him merely until they had secured delegates. In any event, the combination of radicals and of his own faction, the moderate Hunkers, was an exceedingly powerful one, including in all probability at least eighty percent of the party.[7]

On September 25, when the party held its customary meeting at Albany to endorse the action of the state convention, the affair was arranged in advance to be a love feast between the two elements. It was also a demonstration of support for Marcy. The temporary chairman, Peter Cagger, who had once, as the *Herald* put it, been "the most vindictive of the barnburners," called Marcy to the chair amidst very hearty cheers. Marcy made a speech on party unity, in his always brief style, which was welcomed "with great approbation and much cheering." Even the *Herald's* correspondent was caught up in the

---

[7] *Herald*, Sept. 11-14, 18; Jewett to Marcy, Sept. 28, M.P. John Van Buren to F. P. Blair, Blair-Lee Collection, Princeton; *Democratic Machine*, 84; Wetmore to Marcy, Sept. 26, Marcy to same, Sept. 28, M.P.

enthusiasm: "And why not bring his name before the National Conv.," that reporter asked?

If the democracy of N.Y. unite upon him, he will receive the support of all the states north of Pa., & perhaps that state also unless they were quarrelling there between Cass & Buchanan. No man can doubt Marcy's ability, his patriotism, and his qualifications for the Presidency. He possesses a firmness of purpose more resembling Gen. Jackson's than any man living, and wields a pen that no man dares to encounter. . . . We believe he is [at] this moment the strongest man on the Democratic side in the U.S. and, as he has never been known to figure or lay any pipe for the Pres., he will come up as the spontaneous candidate of his party. . . .

From this moment, Marcy's name was of course given much attention both locally and outside of the state. Archibald Campbell, who had been in Albany when the plans were being made for the meeting, said that he found when he returned to Washington that "the Marcy Stock in politics had taken quite a rise . . . now your name is heard quite as often as Douglas's," and—he added—even more so. This was very natural. For Marcy was the choice, it seemed, of New York, the state with the biggest number of electoral votes. At home, moreover, considerations of state pride were on his side. Thus, it was not long before even Bennett's usually hostile paper carried an editorial in his behalf. This was an event of more moment than the screed of an occasional reporter.[8]

During the campaign of that autumn, Marcy labored earnestly in the party's interest. For one thing, he wrote a number of letters to key men in the western cities in the state, where there was discontent because of Whig promises as to canals. Then, when the *Argus*, like a few other conservative sheets, failed to back up the freesoil names on the ticket, he warned his old friend Croswell to be careful. When he was at New York, in October, furthermore, he used his best influence to encourage and harmonize the workers there; he was rather successful. It turned out that the elections were not wholly satisfactory, however. Some of the "ultra Hunkers," i.e. those who had not accepted the union, sabotaged the Barnburner nominees on the general ticket and one of them was beaten. Otherwise, though, the outcome was promising, quite the best since the radical revolt. Aside from the welfare of the party, the event meant, as General Thomas intimated in a letter

---

[8] *Herald*, Sept. 26, Oct. 2, 4; Campbell to Marcy, Oct. 11, M.P.

from New York, a good prospect for the Marcy candidacy. This was reflected in the Washington *Union*, for instance, which more than once praised Marcy; that influential paper called him the man "to whose judicious & patriotic counsel and advice this most important result [the party triumph in New York] must be mainly attributed."[9]

If Marcy had any doubts about Hunker support in the state, these seemed to be removed by an interview which he had in New York the week after the balloting. Daniel Sickles and Augustus E. Schell, two of the "ultra" or unreconciled Hunkers, called to see him. They told him, in part, something which he already knew, that the adherents of Stephen A. Douglas were making much headway in their drive for delegates. Marcy was already alarmed at this, as were his callers. He despised the claims agents and other "cormorants" which hovered about Douglas and he feared that the influence of the steamship lines would be used heavily in that connection. When his callers, therefore, proposed that he let his name be used to check Douglas, he was quite sympathetic. He also took the proposal at its face value; in short, he believed that these men really meant to push him for the presidency, although he knew that they really preferred Cass. This was all the more credible because of statements which he had had independently from some others there, including Croswell and Congressman Hart, to the effect that the Cass party had greatly declined.

Later, Marcy was to find to his dismay that such "ultras" claimed to have wanted him merely to use his general prestige against Douglas, while urging Cass for the nomination; also, that when they said "Cass" they seemed to mean "Dickinson." But that became clear only weeks after.[10]

From about this time forward, Marcy worked openly and directly for the nomination. One step was to build an informal organization, which he did with considerable success. At Albany, he and his friends on the spot could handle things. Upstate, generally, he had Horatio Seymour, his warm personal friend of twenty years' standing, who had been the party's selection for governor the year before and who

---

[9] H. K. Smith and A. Bronson to Marcy, Oct. 15, 17, H. Seymour to Marcy, Oct. 20, Nov. 11, 1851, M.P.; Marcy to Seymour, May 4, 1852, S.P.; Marcy to Shaw, Oct. 28, 1851, M.P., L.C.; Thomas to Marcy, Nov. 6, M.P.; *Union*, Nov. 11.

[10] Marcy to [Beardsley?], Dec. 10, D. Wager to Marcy, n.d., M.P.

was popular if not highly forceful. Seymour had been for Cass, but was won over. There was also John Stryker of the Michigan Southern Railroad, at whose imposing house Marcy had stayed during the Rome convention. He was definitely a man of action. At "the metropolis," Marcy had his bosom friend Wetmore, plus Lorenzo Shepard, a potent Tammany sachem, and, above all, the ardent and gentlemanly Thomas. The latter was now practicing law. Then, at Washington, there were the erudite Charles Eames, of the *Union* staff, who helped when he could; the affectionate Campbell, to move in military circles; and, soon, Congressman William W. Snow of Oneonta. In addition, Marcy brought his old whist crony, Colonel James G. Berret, into action. Berret was a claims agent, but of the better sort, and would later be the mayor of Washington.[11] In the South, Marcy operated chiefly through General Thomas and Thomas's brother, who were native Tennesseans; the latter still lived in Tennessee. In the West, Stryker was active, his business interests taking him often to Michigan and Indiana, where he had a number of friends. If this was a "machine" in the sense of an organized political coterie, in the unfavorable meanings of that term it was not. It was made up quite entirely of volunteers, all of whom were also men of high caliber. In addition, there seems to have been no fund-raising whatsoever; at the Baltimore convention, for example, there would be no reports in the press of any marked disbursements for the care and feeding of delegates.

In the matter of delegates from New York state itself, Marcy had a very difficult decision to make. Should there be a state convention to choose them? Or should the delegates be chosen by the congressional districts, which would allow the ultras a chance to win several seats? If the former were used, Marcy's coalition would be able to dominate it easily and could therefore give the ultras little or no share. The trouble with this was that the ultras violently opposed it; they threatened that if it were used they would boycott such a convention, organize one of their own, and send a rival delegation to Baltimore. In view of the course of some of them in the election just held, this seemed entirely possible. Another circumstance was that Marcy still

<hr/>

[11] To Seymour, Dec. 12, S.P.; *Herald*, Aug. 16, 1849; Charles Eames, *D.A.B.*; Eames to Marcy, Sept. 20, 1854, M.P.; William W. Snow, *Biog. Dir. of Amer. Cong.*; Marian Gouverneur, *As I Remember*, 367-368; to Berret, Nov. 21, M.P.

had some hope of weaning a few of them over to his own side, by treating them fairly. He regarded Croswell and Beardsley as prospects. After all, these men had once been his close associates. When they told him, moreover, that a state convention might play into the hands of the Barnburners, who in turn might not be loyal to him in the national meeting, he knew that this was entirely possible. He also was hurt to find, as he did at the Sickles interview, that the ultras doubted the purity of his motives and suspected him of having gone farther over to the radicals than he actually had. In consequence, although Thomas repeatedly stressed the need for a state convention and held that, if it were announced for a distant date, the minority would be forced by public opinion to agree to it, and although Marcy was warned that the ultras were out to wreck him, he began to weaken. By November 25, when the state central committee met at New York to take the matter up, he had decided to yield. This caused the committee to approve the district system—by a vote of nine to seven. "I had to yield to district elections or do worse," he wrote afterwards. Optimistically, he added that "I shall carry nearly all of them." Some other persons were less cheerful. Jewett wrote that he knew "better than yourself, the deep seated determination entertained by a few men to defeat the *United action* of the *democracy* of this State and *consequently* . . . yourself. The latter is regarded, with as much relish of soul as the destruction of the party—"[12]

In the ensuing campaign for the selection of the delegates, Marcy utilized every contact which he had. He wrote letters to influential persons all over the state, making lists for the purpose, and, indeed, if he did not know them, sent form letters; he asked for their support if they were not for Cass. If the suggestion of one John S. Weed was followed, that a certain figure in Saratoga County would "take soft-corn pretty well" and should be addressed as "an old & familiar acquaintance," the arts of flattery were also used. In New York City, he tried hard to win Croswell's support, or at least to neutralize him, but failed. Croswell was in the steamship group and stayed with Cass. As for John Law, the principal "steam power" man, he continued to work for Douglas; Marcy had tried to see him, at one time, but gave up

[12] To Seymour, Nov. 20, S.P.; to Stryker, Sept. 30, to Berret, Nov. 30, Thomas to Marcy, Oct. 31, M.P.; F. Byrdsall to Marcy, Dec. 1, B.P.

the quest. Yet when Douglas announced that he would defer to Marcy, as the favorite of the state, and abandon New York, apparently being convinced that he was only making enemies, the result was if anything to favor Cass, not Marcy.[13] Marcy did correspond at length with Samuel Beardsley, another Cass figure, but in vain. As for Dickinson himself, Marcy was to write that

I had a long conversation with him [at Albany in January] & endeavored to get him to disclose the grounds of his dissatisfaction. . . . His main & only specific ground . . . was the part I took in the movement for the union of the two sections of the party. . . . He alledged [sic] that that movement prevented his reelection to the senate and went so far as to charge that it had for its object hostility to him.

Marcy ended by being convinced that Dickinson was "ashamed to disclose his real motives," which he thought centered in a wish to be president himself. Before this time, incidentally, Thurlow Weed had played a role in the drama. Convinced that no Whig would win, he preferred his friend Marcy among the Democrats. Before leaving for a European trip, late in November, he had obtained a promise from two of the state's politicians that they would see Dickinson in his behalf. Apparently they afterwards decided that it was useless, for they postponed the step and then gave it up. The trouble was that the Dickinson movement was not only beyond reconciliation but also rather powerful. On the other hand, Marcy's friends were active at Washington. They probably accomplished a good deal, by getting congressmen to write to their constituents. Snow and Jenkins both played a part in this, as also did Berret.[14]

When the polls were taken, in mid-January, it was clear that Marcy had not succeeded as well as he had hoped. He had taken only 22 out of 33 districts, about half of the 22 being Hunkers and half Barnburners. The opposition of the Dickinsonians had been "insidious," he wrote, occasionally "under the mask of friendship." In some cases, men who were for him had actually been put up by his enemies but

[13] "Friends in & out of the State to whom I can write," filed under date of Nov. 21; to Campbell, Nov. 10, Weed to Marcy, Dec. 22, Marcy to E. W. Lewis, Dec. 30, to Wetmore, Nov. 26, 29, Wetmore to Marcy, Nov. 28, Thomas to Marcy, Dec. 29, Marcy to Berret, Jan. 2, M.P.

[14] Beardsley-Marcy correspondence, partly never posted, Dec. 9-17, M.P.; Weed, *op. cit.*, 197-198; Weed to Marcy, Feb. 1, Berret to Marcy, Dec. 5, Marcy to Berret, Dec. 14, M.P.

with instructions for "Cass," while in other districts Cass instructions had been secured on the supposed understanding that they would be for the first ballot only; there had also been some influence made by the letting to George Law of a reportedly corrupt canal contract at Rochester. Marcy affected to receive the news in a calm style, but it was the calm of "a chill winter evening." He was hurt at the several instances of betrayal which had transpired. When those selected met on April 7 to choose the delegates at large, however, he was able to insist that both be from his own faction. These were Seymour and St. John B. L. Skinner. One reason for this, naturally, was that if the Barnburners had had a share the Cass men might logically have claimed the other. As a matter of fact, though, there had been an effort by the Cass camp to conspire with some of the radicals, with an eye to taking both of the choices from Marcy; the plan was to select Beardsley and John Van Buren. This was evidence of the desperation of the Dickinsonians.[15]

In his search for national support, in this period, Marcy moved along much the same lines, although he had to rely more fully upon his associates than he did at home. His plan was to win friends in all camps, while making enemies in none. With his large block of firmly committed delegates, he would stand quietly through the successive ballots until the various aspirants who had been in the race all along should fail. It seemed likely that this would happen, in view of the customary two-thirds rule. In the matter of the rule itself, that probably would be readopted as a means of killing off Cass. As for Douglas, he was widely distrusted and had little chance. The chief threat was Buchanan, yet even he would find the going hard, for he had been in the field before and had many enemies. In regard to the other candidates, aside from Marcy, they seemed in general to be poorly qualified.

One of the chief problems of Marcy's agents was to convince all and sundry that he could carry New York state and could be surer to do so than any other candidate. Marcy's friends had no doubt of this whatsoever. That is to say, they had no doubts unless Dickinson and

---

[15] To Berret, Jan. 12, Feb. 4, to Campbell, Jan. 16; Tilden to C. H. Peaslee, Jan. 15, 1853, Tilden Papers, N.Y.P.L.; Marcy to Berret, Apr. 11, M.P.

company were ready to carry their enmity so far as to work for the defeat of a national ticket containing Marcy's name.

In New England, Cass was expected to be the overwhelming choice at the outset, but Marcy was hopeful of a good many adherents later on. He received favorable expressions meantime from Charles G. Greene, one of the chief Boston leaders, and from Caleb Cushing, a sometime Whig of Massachusetts who had raised a regiment for the conquest of Mexico. As for Pennsylvania, some overtures were made by his Washington spokesman to Senator-elect Brodhead, the anti-Buchanan leader, but the results were slight. On his own part, Buchanan himself did make some tentative approaches to Marcy, but these were declined. Marcy knew that the Pennsylvanian was not very popular in New York and was hence hesitant as to being able to transfer his strength to him. He also considered that his own chances were best if he avoided any "entangling alliances." In the South, on the contrary, prospects were good. Marcy's record in the Polk administration appealed to that section; besides that, there were his strongly anti-abolitionist roles in the Albany meeting of 1835 and in his gubernatorial message of 1836. The Thomas brothers secured newspaper articles in his behalf in two Nashville papers, while Cave Johnson, his old cabinet colleague, was of course friendly, although he would be committed to Buchanan at the start. Later, Thomas's brother visited the Mississippi state convention. He found there the answer which was general throughout the South, a readiness to take Marcy—plus at least some doubt as to his ability to carry his own state. There was also considerable second-choice support in Alabama, in Louisiana (chiefly in the outlying parishes), and in Georgia. In the middle west, too, there was much backing of this variety.[16]

During the national contest for delegates, the great Kossuth craze burst upon the country. This distinguished man, the head of the late Hungarian rebellion, arrived in the United States on December 6, hoping to raise funds or to get direct help for a second revolt. He was

---

[16] *Democratic Machine*, 47; Greene to Marcy, Dec. 2, Thomas to Marcy, Mar. 25, Berret to Marcy, Dec. 20, Marcy to Campbell, Nov. 10, Thomas to Marcy, Oct. 27, Dec. 9, Feb. 9, Apr. 1, Johnson to Marcy, Dec. 5, Jan. 14, D. Salomon to Marcy, May 10; W. Robertson to Marcy, Mar. 19, 1853; W. J. Brown to Stryker, Feb. 6, Stryker to Marcy, Dec. 3, M.P.

at once the man of the hour. Although his cause appealed mainly to some of the younger and more excitable leaders in America, all of the presidential possibilities felt obliged to express their sympathy. Marcy was no exception. He headed the call for a meeting by the citizens of Albany, and at this gathering praised the Hungarian as "one of the most remarkable men of the age." At the same time, he adroitly shrugged off any idea of intervention in Europe—unlike Webster and most others. He asserted that Kossuth came to the United States not only to tell of the wrongs done to his native land but also to represent the principle "of non-intervention, and that we [should] declare to the world that every people have a right to regulate their own affairs." To underline his point, he even mentioned the Monroe Doctrine. As he wrote to Wetmore on December 23, "I think I avoided *snags*."[17]

After the districts in the state had spoken, the national Marcy movement gained considerable power, for the technique used had allowed a very free demonstration of popular support. This made Marcy "quite hopeful." On the other hand, the Dickinson forces also rallied. Assured of a loud collective voice at Baltimore, they trusted that after Cass had failed the latter's supporters would swing to their own leader. In order to head off Marcy, they affected to believe that he had sold out to the freesoilers. In addition, they spread doubts as to his ability to carry the state. They made a particular effort to spread such ideas in Virginia, where Dickinson had some admirers. Dickinson was reported to have alleged, incidentally, that Marcy had no more chance of being president than he (Dickinson) had of being archbishop of Canterbury! In addition, Dickinson's brother-in-law, Congressman Birdsall, and Samuel Beardsley were very active at the capital, while the *Journal of Commerce* was busy in that interest at New York. "It is now clear," wrote Seymour, "that Dickinson's game is to be a desperate one."

Marcy was much worried at all this. To counter his rival's letters to the Old Dominion, he wrote a long letter to John Y. Mason, his old associate, and was pleased to have a favorable response to it, although Mason was for Buchanan. He also wrote an able letter to Campbell, who passed it on to Senator Hunter, Henry A. Wise, and others, all

---

[17] Thomas to Marcy, Dec. 19, Marcy to Wetmore, Dec. 23, M.P.; *Union*, Dec. 23.

of whom approved of it heartily. When Virginia's convention was held, it was mainly for Buchanan, but it greeted Marcy's name very warmly when there was mention made of it. This was in April. At about this time, also, John A. Thomas returned from the cotton belt in a quite optimistic mood. Late in April, moreover, when Seymour went to Washington, he had rather satisfactory talks with the Virginia senators and with Senator Atchison and other leaders. These men were all state-rights people, as were most of Marcy's supporters in the South. Duff Green, who was working for Marcy, too, was of course of this stamp. As for the last-minute Dickinsonian allegations, Marcy's friends met them by telling of Dickinson's conspiracy with Prince John in the attempt to secure the delegates at large and Marcy wrote an article for a New York paper to counteract the *Journal of Commerce*. It was clear, none the less, that the rival New York faction had done Marcy much harm and would continue to do so at Baltimore.[18]

In the last weeks of May, Marcy made his final preparations. When questioned by a Richmond editor as to his stand on the Compromise, as were all of the candidates, he replied that "if in an official station" he would use all of the power he had to see that its provisions were not disturbed, in whole or in part. He spent much time with the delegates, both at Albany, and, late the final week, at New York. He designated the two delegates at large and the Albany delegate, Erastus Corning, as his official agents at the convention. More particularly, on Saturday, the 29th, he directed Seymour, the chief of these spokesmen, to keep in touch with Cushing and Henry A. Wise. "They are very important men and their course will probably be very controlling in the convention. I hope you will establish very confidential relations with them." He added that he counted upon some of the Cass faction nationally for aid, when the latter's boom had ended. On that day, incidentally, his letters of the summer before to Judge Fine were published in the *Journal of Commerce*, without his knowledge. Although at first alarmed lest Fine and other Barnburners would think that he had divulged this private correspondence, he soon saw that the

---

[18] Eames to Marcy, Jan. 15, Snow to Marcy, Mar. 25, M.P.; Dickinson letter, in *Union*, Feb. 20; Campbell to Marcy, Mar. 23, Apr. 13, 24, May 3, 24, Mason to Marcy, Apr. 22, Marcy to Campbell, Apr. 27, Berret to Marcy, Apr. 30, Green to Marcy, May 21, Seymour to Marcy, Apr. 26, May 2, all M.P.; *Journal of Commerce*, May 7, 8, 19; Thomas to Marcy, May 21, M.P.

publication was on the whole much to his advantage, because while the Barnburners would know already that these were his sentiments and could not be much offended, there would be a clear gain in the South at such convincing proof of his conservatism. That night, he returned to Albany to await events. Next morning, he was in his customary seat at the Pearl Street Baptist Church. On the following day, the day before the convention opened, he penned an answer to a recent letter from Buchanan—in his usual, joking style—saying that he had not dared to take Mrs. Marcy with him to New York, because she was so strongly for his rival. He avoided any hint that he wanted a union of their forces, although this was undoubtedly why Buchanan had written.[19]

During the convention, Marcy received some personal letters from his adherents there, but he had to rely mostly upon the telegraphic reports and the longer accounts sent to the papers by mail, which came out a day after the wired despatches did. His adherents had established themselves in the Eutaw House. They were making much use of the Judge Fine letters, which had been copied into the Baltimore *Sun* and had also been run off in extra copies by the hundred. "Your friends are in high spirits & working like beavers," wrote Thomas.[20]

When the balloting finally began, on the morning of Thursday, June 3, Cass fell far short of the 197 needed to nominate, having only 116. Buchanan had 93, Marcy 27, including three from New England, Douglas 21, and, among the scattered votes, there was one for Dickinson. Although sixteen more ballots were taken that day, there proved to be no clear trends. Cass did weaken, but Buchanan merely held firm and the rise which Douglas experienced was only moderate. The Cass team very early asked for help from Marcy, but this was at once declined. Next day there were sixteen more polls. In their course, Cass at one time fell to 29, holding only Michigan, Ohio, and his New York coterie. Douglas rose to 80, with gains in all sections. Buchanan, however, shot up to 104. At this crisis in his move-

[19] To Robert G. Scott, May 25, in *Herald*, May 30; for the New York trip, cf. *Herald*, May 27, *Journal*, May 31; to Seymour, Skinner, and Corning, May 24, to Seymour [May 29?], S.P.
[20] Thomas to Marcy, May 31, June 2, M.P.

ment, Cave Johnson begged Thomas to bring New York to his side, promising Marcy help in turn if Buchanan failed. Thomas declined. This was for the same reasons that Marcy had had himself in not turning to Buchanan, plus the special factor that Buchanan seemed now to have run up as high as he could. Thomas also argued that if the bulk of the New York delegates were released they would in many cases go to Douglas or some other person and not to Buchanan anyway. On the other hand, it might have been impossible to recall such a diverse coalition of Barnburners and Hunkers to Marcy later. This event left the Pennsylvania contingent lastingly resentful. By the end of that day, incidentally, their man had dropped to 72. In turn Douglas had risen to 92. This had caused such a panic among the conservatives, however, that there had been a sudden sweep back to Cass.

During this day, Marcy had had only one opportunity. If he had been able on the 23rd ballot to secure Virginia, which was wavering, he might have begun a major advance, for Michigan seemed ready to follow the Old Dominion. In the net, at the end of this (the second) day, June 4, his position was unchanged. Among the delegates in general, however, the time for decisions was looming up, for there was excessive weariness and a fear that the convention might end without a nomination.

In this emergency, the Buchanan men sought for a way out. During the night, the Pennsylvanians met with the five southern delegations which were on "Old Buck's" side. It was determined that his own state and Georgia and Alabama should hold fast to him, so as to keep his movement alive; his friends in Virginia, North Carolina, and Mississippi, however, were to try their second choices. This meant seeing how Butler, Marcy, Dickinson, and a particularly dark horse, Franklin Pierce of New Hampshire, would run. Afterwards, when all such attempts failed, if they did, the especial adherents of these men would perhaps be ready, in their turn, to go for Buchanan. As for Butler, it may be explained that he had come out in favor of the Compromise and had lost his northern support, so his managers decided that his candidacy should wait until all of the northern men had been tried. Pierce, on his part, had been carefully groomed as a final resort. He had been inconspicuous for years and was highly "available," despite his role as a general in the Mexican War; he was conservative on

slavery. Both Marcy and Dickinson might be expected to do better
than he did, at the outset. Yet, in Marcy's case, there was a good deal
of rancor among "Old Buck's" friends because of the refusal to cooperate in the Pennsylvanian's movement during the past day.

Next morning, the issue was tested. On the first trial (the 34th
ballot), Marcy rose to 33, but Virginia came out for Daniel S. Dickinson. This put Dickinson in a quandary: he had based his campaign
on the support of Cass to the end, yet had been accused by Marcy's
friends of being a real candidate himself and, now, his chance had
come before Cass had been given up. The result was that he declined
this support, in a speech full of alleged nobility of purpose but which
the Marcy men met with quietly ironic smiles. Virginia accordingly
quit him on the next poll. This state's next preference might well
have been Marcy, and her delegates debated at length; unfortunately,
however, the two leaders to whom Marcy had chiefly looked, Cushing
and Wise, were split; although Wise was for Marcy, Cushing, himself
a Massachusetts man, helped to swing the state to Pierce.

On the other hand, on this same 35th ballot, North Carolina and
Mississippi did come out for Marcy. In particular, Jacob Thompson of Mississippi spoke of the determination to try Marcy, as a
northern man who would be an acceptable alternative to Buchanan,
and there was much applause in the hall. The shift of these states put
Marcy ahead of the Pennsylvanian. Then, on the 36th, Alabama
came over, and Marcy passed Douglas. The parade continued: Georgia
joined him, then Connecticut, most of Massachusetts, New Jersey, and
finally Tennessee, until, several ballots later, i.e. on the 46th, Marcy
had 98 and was the leader, ahead even of Cass. During this time, the
New York delegation withdrew to consult, Marcy's friends asking
that the unit rule be accepted, but the Dickinsonians refused. Seymour
did not press the issue. Had he done so, a few of the Cass men might
have been ready to comply, but the balance would probably have
resisted. Even so, when Marcy came to 98, Hamlin of Maine told
Thomas that if the movement could hold together for another ballot,
i.e. the 47th, and if Virginia would quit Pierce, Maine would come
over. Thomas then went to see Governor Porter of the Pennsylvania
delegation and sought to get him to swing Virginia over. Porter flatly
refused. Instead, he and the other Buchanan man urged Virginia to

hold on to Pierce. This was the state's decision—by a margin of one vote! According to Campbell, the balance was held by John S. Barbour, who was Marcy's enemy because of an adverse decision which he had given in a pension case while secretary of war. On such hair lines is history often decided!

Nor could the Marcyites hold on to what they did have. Although the Pierce cause had been marking time on the recent ballots, on the last (the 46th) Kentucky had swung to him. Now, on the 47th, Maryland and four Massachusetts delegates shifted to Pierce, while on the 48th he won added New England supporters. Even so, Virginia nearly came in for Marcy, who was 89 to Pierce's 55, but Barbour was resolute and in addition was able to divulge that on the next poll North Carolina and Georgia would also go for Pierce. This was Marcy's final ruination. On the 49th, in consequence, the convention fell apart, with the Pierce bandwagon first starting to roll and then racing irresistibly. As the delegations were polled, from Maine down through Virginia, there was no change, but, from North Carolina on, the wheels were turning fast. State after state deserted Marcy. Before the poll was finished, Seymour transferred New York to Pierce, to be followed by Dickinson and the Buchanan leaders, who did the same for their contingents. That afternoon, William R. King of Alabama was nominated for the second office. As for the platform, which was now finally put through, it was for state rights and an adherence to the Compromise.

Throughout the crisis, Marcy had been much too cool headed to have really strong hopes of success and he accepted the result in good spirits. His first thought was to console his affectionate friend Campbell. He sat down at once and wrote as follows:

I have this moment heard of the nomination of Pierce and, strange as you may think it, I really rejoice at it. Though towards the close of the ballotings I run [sic] up I did not for a moment take the slightest hope that I could go through. Pierce is a fine fellow,—a good friend of mine as I flatter myself, and what is perhaps of more importance, more sure of carrying this state than any other of the candidates save one, & probably more popular in other states than that one. I beg you will make up your mind that *all is for the best.*

It was a short letter. Soon after, he may have walked up State Street to see the bonfires and listen to the two hundred guns which his fellow Democrats were firing to salute the nomination of "Frank" Pierce.

Next day, he wrote to Colonel Berret, also. He explained that while he personally had some regrets, he knew his friends' regrets were greater than his. For one thing, he said kindly, "I have more just cause to be proud of my supporters in & out of the convention than they have to be proud of their candidate." He also wrote to Buchanan, asserting that if his adherents had been released they could not have gone unitedly for anyone. To solace his rival, he quoted a passage from the *Edinburgh Review*, to the effect that in a republic men must make themselves into dwarfs before they could enter public life. This rather fitted in with Marcy's statement as to Pierce's modest merits, in a letter to Wetmore on the 8th. He commented that he was better pleased with the nomination than some he had feared. He went on, however, to say that

Genl. P. has no freesoil leanings—rather stiff the other way—he is a man of noble impulses—hardly fitted for the drudgery of such an office—not fond of or trained to continuous efforts but he has fine talents and occasionally breaks out in bursts of splendour—His administrative capacity—the real touchstone—is to be tried & I think he will not be found wanting.

To speak thus of the nominee, at a moment when Democrats were moving heaven and earth to laud him, was almost to damn him with faint praise.

As a matter of fact, Marcy's backers thoroughly needed the consolation he was sending them. Colonel Berret wrote despairingly: "I am not in a Condition to write, but I need consolation and must appeal to you for it. Your friends fought the battle gallantly and died like men." Similarly Jewett felt ill when it was over, not to speak of the fact that "the malice of others made [him] dam[d] mad." He and the other Barnburners had, incidentally, been thoroughly loyal throughout. As for John Stryker, his reaction was more exclusively an angry one. He went through Albany without stopping to see Marcy; only when at New York did he write to give his pointed comments on the whole business. In his judgment, the nomination had been lost three times. First, because of Marcy's "magnanimity" in agreeing to district choice of delegates. Secondly, by not winning Virginia on that twenty-third ballot. Thirdly, by losing the decision at the end in that state's delegation, by the one vote margin. He also implied a criticism of Seymour on the score of ineptness and weakness. Yet, as he said, Marcy's friends had acted in good faith throughout. "We have left you with your escutcheon untarnished," he added.

Marcy's own chief addition to this review of the affair, aside from a possible dissent on the matter of district choice, was to lament that Croswell had not stood by him. He believed that Croswell could have swung affairs to him. Of Croswell, and of Dickinson, he commented in the already cited letter to Wetmore that "Looking the state over there are not . . . two men whom I have more faithfully served than D. & C." As for Dickinson alone, he recalled how he had declined a senate seat at the hands of both Bouck and Wright, which had permitted Dickinson to obtain that post; he added that he had helped him get oriented in his early days at the capital and that even in the winter before last, there, they had had "most friendly" relations. "As to C's course I am unwilling to say what I think," he concluded bitterly. According to Wetmore, incidentally, Croswell's behavior had been brought on by pressure from Law and Charlick. The latter was one of the New York City delegates.[21]

In any event, Marcy took a full and vigorous part in the Albany ratification meeting, on June 11; he also expressed himself explicitly in a letter of endorsement to the comparable meeting at New York. During the pre-campaign and campaign months, moreover, he was very busy. He helped win renominations for Seymour as governor and for Church (a Barnburner) as lieutenant-governor, although Dickinson and Van Buren, that oddly assorted pair, plotted to put it aside. He also had a direct part in helping Pierce, through an old letter refuting an allegation that the nominee had tried to arrange for making profits out of his men's pay and allowances, before accepting his commission in 1847, and through another letter answering a charge that Pierce had been cowardly in the field. To help defeat Scott, whom

---

[21] The above account is from the *Argus*, June 3-8, *Democratic Machine*, 129-146, and the following: Campbell to Marcy, June 7, Marcy to Campbell, June 5, M.P.; *Herald*, June 6; to Berret, June 6, M.P.; to Buchanan, June 6, B.P.; to Wetmore, June 8, Berret to Marcy, June 7, M.P.; Jewett to Newell, June 23, N.P.; Stryker to Marcy, June 7, M.P.

the demoralized Whig Party had nominated, Marcy's reply to Scott was duly republished. Marcy also spent a good deal of time at New York, furthermore, organizing the party, and took pains to talk "plainly" to Croswell about the need to back the ticket. This last had all too little effect. Marcy was sure, however, that Pierce would win; it was a "fixed fact," he said. When the returns were in, this proved to be the case. Pierce and Seymour both carried the state handily, while in the country at large Pierce won nearly everywhere. With the Whig party torn to shreds by the sectional troubles, indeed, a long era of Democratic rule seemed to be at hand.[22]

And so Marcy had played out the role of favorite son—the favorite, indeed, of the most populous state. Although he had been hesitant at first at taking it on, when convinced that he had the backing of New York he had done so quite wholehartedly. A large group of devoted friends, moreover, had done their best to secure the prize for him. When he had failed, it had been by the merest hair's breadth and because of the malice of the Dickinson faction. And when a lesser man had been given the nomination, he had accorded him the most devoted support. It had been a year which had added much to his stature as a leader.

---

[22] *Argus*, June 11, 12; letters *re* Pierce in *Union*, Aug. 21, and as cited in *Democratic Machine*, 155; *Providence Journal*, Aug. 26, clipping, M.P.

XVII. A WINTER IN GEORGIA AND FLORIDA

"I know that you care very little on your own account to
enter again in the turmoils of office. . . ." (Campbell to
Marcy, October 16, 1852[1])

AT ABOUT the time of the Baltimore convention, Marcy learned
with a shock that his son Edmund, the older of his children by
Cornelia, was consumptive. The indications were too convincing to
deny. He wrote to his friend Wetmore that "I fear my dear Son . . .
is destined to an early grave. . . . He has been for the last fortnight
under the care of Dr. Gray, and has considerably improved, but not so
much so as to disburden my mind of cruel apprehensions—We must
submit [he went on,] to the dealings of Providence with us, and console ourselves, if we can, that all is for the best. . . ." His son was
slightly better in the summer, it is true, and in October profited from
a cruise with Samuel on the practice ship *Preble.* Well before that date,
however, Marcy had decided to take him to a warm climate for the
winter.[2]

Ever since the convention, there had been talk that Marcy might be
made Pierce's secretary of state. Many persons, surely, considered him
the best man for the post; after the death of Daniel Webster, in
October, many held that he was the best person in the whole country
for it. As a matter of fact, Webster himself had spoken of Marcy while
on his deathbed, although not specifically for any one office, citing his
"integrity, devotion to the Union; fidelity to principle; and administrative capacity" and had called him "one on whom the country could
depend in any emergency."

Although Marcy sometimes voiced a reluctance to take any office in
the new administration, he was, however, increasingly interested in
the idea, especially if it be for the top post. His friends, furthermore,
were as eager as ever for his advancement. On the other hand, the

---

[1] M.P.
[2] To Wetmore, June 19, Samuel to Marcy, June 27, Oct. 31, Marcy to Campbell,
Sept. 8, M.P.

grave factional differences in the state of New York would surely make it difficult for Pierce to make any selection at all there. The Barnburners, for instance, wanted one of their own men chosen for whatever post the state was offered; they argued that since they had in the past year backed Marcy for president and Seymour for governor, it was time for the coalition to give them preferment. The man whom they wanted was Dix. As for the Hards, they worked energetically, as always, for the advancement of Dickinson. At times, not hopeful of this, they spoke of Charles O'Conor of New York, but actually they had little chance of winning, for Pierce knew that they were intransigent and during the campaign had let them understand that they must toe the line or else take the consequences. On the other hand, Pierce was definitely friendly towards Marcy. Late in October Marcy had an opportunity to converse with him, for he was one of the delegation sent by the Albany bar to attend Webster's funeral and was able to meet Pierce in Boston; the two had an hour's talk. "It was very satisfactory," Marcy said afterwards. It seems that nothing was said about the cabinet, but that Pierce displayed a high estimation of Marcy's value as an adviser.[3]

When Marcy was at the metropolis just after the election, making arrangements for the trip south, he talked with Dix and with Azariah Flagg. He was at once impressed with the strong push which these men and the other Barnburners were making to get Dix in. It was perhaps as a reaction to this that he wrote to Pierce on the 7th, suggesting that the latter and his family accompany him on his tour. This would have been beneficial to Mrs. Pierce, who was not strong, but Pierce declined. At the same time, he asked Marcy to come to see him before setting out. "I desire very much to see you—I am sure I need the benefit of your wise counsel in a full & free conversation—"

When they met, the president-elect none the less stated frankly that he considered that it would be better not to appoint him, in view of the cleavage in the party in New York. He doubtless said also, however, what he told Augustus Schell and some other Hards during the train ride from Concord to Boston that day, namely that Marcy was at

[3] Bancroft, Oct. 18, Thomas, Sept. 24, Campbell, Oct. 14, Nov. 1, S. D. Bradford (quoting Webster), Nov. 29, Jewett, Oct. 19, M.P.; Marcy to N. G. Upham, Nov. 3, Amer. Phil. Society; Pruyn Journal, Oct. 27-29, State Library; Marcy to Seymour, Oct. 31, S.P.

least to have the right to say who should *not* be in the cabinet. This
was a bitter pill for the Dickinsonians, surely. If Pierce did repeat this,
Marcy probably said that he did not oppose the choosing of Dix but
that he preferred a Union Hunker, i.e. one of his own group. Perhaps
he also hinted at the violent reaction to be expected from southerners
if a Barnburner was picked. In any case, when he was back in New
York, two days later, he wrote to Seymour to ask that the latter and
Erastus Corning go to see Pierce also; he suggested, furthermore, that
Seymour talk things over with Dix and Flagg. "All sorts of intrigue
are on foot in this City," he added. This was not an overstatement![4]

It was on that same day that Marcy and his son left on the steamer
for Savannah. They had a quick passage, taking only sixty-four hours.
The first day out was very rough, with "something like a snow squall,"
and Marcy spent the first half of the trip in his berth. "I was not very
sick," he wrote to Wetmore, "but should have been if I had not placed
myself in a horizontal position." Lying thus, he spent his time thinking about Pierce's task of cabinet-making and concluded that the president-elect had an unenviable job. He found himself, at least, unable to
hitch together a satisfactory team. As for New York, he reasoned that
Dickinson would be urged strongly, would fail, and that the Dickinsonians would then back Dix, so as to prevent *"another's"* being
selected. He was interested in the latter's chances, and asked Wetmore
to collect newspaper items on the subject and give them each Saturday
to the captains of the steamship line.[5]

For the next several weeks, Marcy and his son travelled in South
Carolina, Georgia, and the Jacksonville district of Florida. Then,
towards the end of January, Marcy decided that it might be well for
them to go to Nassau, in the Bahamas; at just about the end of the
month they went up to Savannah to take a steamer to that quarter.
Although Edmund had not been markedly better, Marcy had been
grateful for the journey as offering a chance to become more intimately
acquainted with his son, for whom he was developing an increasingly
strong feeling of attachment and respect. This only made him all the

---

[4] To Bancroft, Nov. 6, 10, Bancroft Papers; to Pruyn, Nov. 19, in clipping, *Knickerbocker Press*, Mar. 9, 1913, possession of Mrs. Chas. Hamlin, Albany. Pierce to
Marcy, Nov. 9, M.P.; Claude M. Fuess, *The Life of Caleb Cushing*, II, 128;
F. Byrdsall to Buchanan, Nov. 24, B.P.; Thomas to Marcy, Nov. 20, M.P.
[5] To Wetmore, Nov. 16, M.P.

sadder, however, because he was convinced that at best his son would not live for many years.[6]

Meantime, he was keeping an eye on the prospects regarding the cabinet—and becoming less cheerful on that score also every day. The fact was that Franklin Pierce had decided soon after the election to make up a cabinet in which "southern rights" elements—the principal groups in the South—should be represented in one of the two chief positions, i.e. in the state department or the treasury. This would be offset by having a freesoiler in the other one. In other words, his plan would be to have representation in his administration for all of the various groups which had supported him at the polls, and the two chief posts would go to the most widely variant of them all! Since Pierce wanted not only a freesoiler but someone close to the Van Buren-Benton coterie, moreover, for one of these two, Dix was a logical choice. Not long after the balloting, in fact, Pierce seems to have more or less promised him the state department. As for the southern rights group, he finally hit upon Senator Hunter of Virginia. With his usual sapience in such matters, Marcy had concluded before he left that this was to be approximately the answer, and surely as to Dix; he had, as his Wetmore letter shows, decided that the pressure of the Hards against himself would aid Dix. When Seymour and Corning went to Concord, late in November, however, they tried to persuade Pierce to come out definitely for Marcy; if this were done, they held, Seymour would be strengthened as governor and faction-alism in general in the state would be reduced. Pierce did not comply. Pruyn wrote to Marcy to intimate that Pierce had told his two visitors just about the same things he had told Marcy.[7]

As it turned out, when the idea of a choice of Dix was broached to the state-rights leaders, there were the expected cries of protest, which led Pierce to give up the idea and to swing to Marcy once again. When Pruyn went to see him on January 19, for example, he came away convinced that such was the decision; Pierce had spoken guard-edly, but had asked for Marcy's address in the South. Since Senator

[6] To Berret, Dec. 7; Campbell to Marcy, Dec. 10, Marcy to Samuel, Dec. 14, to J. Knower, Dec. 15, 1852, to Wetmore, Aug. 27, 1853, M.P.
[7] Roy F. Nichols, *Franklin Pierce*, 220-223, *Democratic Machine*, 172-177; Pruyn, Nov. 23, Seymour, Dec. 1, to Marcy, M.P.

Hunter had meanwhile declined to take an office, moreover, Pierce had begun to turn to Jefferson Davis, whom he had, in fact, considered earlier. By February he was urging Davis to be in Washington as soon as possible, although without revealing why. It may be noted, incidentally, that Pierce had paid little attention to the Cass men for the top positions and had disregarded Douglas and his faction; as for Buchanan, he had thrown him a sop, in the choice of Campbell, an adherent of his, for postmaster general. At about the time he urged Jefferson Davis to get to the capital early, Pierce directed his private secretary to write to Marcy in much the same vein. The secretary wrote the letter on February 6, as follows:

Dear Sir.

It is deemed exceedingly desirable, upon grounds that will be explained to you hereafter, that you be in Washington on the 18th or 20th of this month—by the last date at farthest. You will please regard this as confidential, in the highest and strictest sense, both before and after your arrival at the seat of Government.

With high regard,
very respectfully yours,

Sidney Webster

P.S. Should you be able to be at Washington as proposed, please to telegraph to Col. C. G. Greene of Boston Ms. thus—"Will be there by the — day of February." *and sign no signature.*

S.W.

In this furtive manner did Pierce try to safeguard himself from additional pressure.[8]

Meanwhile, Marcy had become rather tired of the whole business of cabinet-making. The papers which had been sent to him had arrived very late and the letters had not given a full view of how things were; all in all, he was usually a week or two behind on the news. While a statement of the Concord *Patriot* in December, that members of the Polk cabinet would not be barred, was commonly interpreted to mean that Marcy would go in, Marcy himself was sceptical. He went on supposing that Hard pressure would help the appointment of Dix. Then, after Hunter was rumored to have declined a place and because of the encouragement which Pierce's delay had given to factionalism, Marcy had quite lost his enthusiasm for office. He merely said "it is best to quietly await the issue." When he reached Savannah, he did telegraph

---

[8] Pruyn Journal, Jan. 18-19, State Library; Webster to Marcy, M.P.

to Seymour to ask if there was any reason for not making the projected trip to Nassau. Seymour wired back that it would be better to
remain within reach, but Marcy was not impressed, merely dubious.
He decided, however, to send Edmund off on the steamer alone and to
start a slow trip toward Washington, so that he would be available if
called upon yet avoid reaching the capital until Pierce had made up
his mind. He wrote to Colonel Berret to this effect on February 8:

I confess to you that I should like to find myself there just after the
curtain rises and as the new actors have made or rather are making their
debuts before the anxious & expectant audience. I sometimes give myself
up to reverie & visions—I fancy myself with you and some other good
fellows. . . . Our little sequestered company will be philosophically cool
& discriminately just—we will praise the actors if we can; condemn them if
we must—In one sentiment we shall cordially unite, i.e. they were unwise
to engage in such a corps. . .

Perhaps his mood altered, next day, when he received Pruyn's optimistic letter of the 4th, but he replied that Pruyn was "more hopeful"
than he was. He continued on his way northwards.[9]

---

[9] To Berret, Jan. 15, 24, Feb. 8, Pruyn to Marcy, Feb. 4, M.P.; to Pruyn, Jan. 19,
Feb. 9, in *Knickerbocker Press*, possession of Mrs. Hamlin.

XVIII. SECRETARY OF STATE

"It is . . . certain that he went into the Department without
much knowledge of its appropriate duties. But he is a
strongminded and clearheaded man; and, although slow in
his perceptions, is sound in his judgment. He may, and I
trust will, succeed; but yet he has much to learn." (James
Buchanan on Marcy, June 25, 1853[1])

IT WAS at Richmond, on his leisurely trip northwards, that Marcy
was on February 17 overtaken by the letter which Franklin Pierce's
private secretary had written on the 6th. Marcy was stopping at the
home of Judge John Y. Mason, his old colleague, intending to be at
Washington at about the start of the new administration so as to be
able to look after the interests of his friends, but loth, as has been
said, to be there before the decisions as to the cabinet were made.

Marcy arrived in Washington early Sunday morning, February 20,
and put up at Willard's Hotel, where Pierce planned to stay. Next
morning he visited the senate chamber. Although accompanied by
James C. Dobbin, James Guthrie, and Robert McClelland, all of whom
also expected to be in the new cabinet, he was at once the center of
attraction.[2] This was not merely because it was by now pretty well
granted that he would be the secretary of state or "premier" of the
organization. It was also a tribute to his eminence in public life. In
this interlude between the passing of the giants of the old era—Clay,
Webster, and Calhoun—and the coming of the ranting sectionalists
of the later 1850's, he had few peers. He also looked the part. Broad
shouldered and still exceeding six feet in height and two hundred
pounds in weight, his face particularly forceful after the fining down
of recent years, the hair on his craggy brows a pale grey but that on
top of his head still black and abundant, he was an impressive figure.[3]

[1] Buchanan's memorandum of how he was appointed to London, in G. T. Curtis,
Life of James Buchanan, II, 76-83.
[2] Sidney Webster to Marcy, Feb. 6, Marcy to Wetmore, Feb. 9, to Berret, Feb. 8,
14, to Edmund, Feb. 10, to Samuel, Feb. 25, M.P.; *Times* correspondent, in *Journal* of
Feb. 21; *Herald* correspondent, *ibid.*, Feb. 22.
[3] Recollections of Gen. John G. Walker, as told to John Bassett Moore, 1891,
Moore Papers; engraving, facing p. 12, in John Livingston, *Portraits and Memoirs
of Eminent Americans now Living* (1854).

In his long conference with Pierce, next day,[4] Marcy presumably learned exactly who the rest of the cabinet officers would be. Guthrie and Dobbin were to take charge of the treasury and the navy, respectively. Both were southerners but of a pro-union sort and were to prove good friends and commonly allies of Marcy throughout the administration. The same could also be said of Robert McClelland, who had left the governorship of Michigan to become secretary of the interior; he supported the Compromise of 1850, but, because he had once favored the Wilmot Proviso, his appointment was to be unpopular with the South. These three men, and also James Campbell of Philadelphia, the new postmaster-general, did not any of them have large political influence, however. The two remaining members, Caleb Cushing and Jefferson Davis, were to be far more important.

Cushing, who had nearly been given the state department and who was to be attorney general instead, was a New Englander as erudite as George Bancroft or Edward Everett. He suffered, however, from a lack of balance of judgment and was looked upon rather doubtfully because of his earlier enrollment in the Whig party. Since the Mexican War, in which he had been a brigadier general, he had taken an increasingly southern view of territorial problems. He was energetic and coldly ambitious and, as Marcy no doubt realized from the start, he would be Marcy's chief rival in the cabinet. It was also disturbing that Jefferson Davis was to be the secretary of war. He had opposed the Compromise and since Calhoun's death had been the very leader of the southern state-rights group.[5] In other words, the president had truly held to his plan to give representation to all who had supported him, by including Compromise men as well as extremists, both north and south. What was more, the violently pro-southern group had in Cushing and Davis, in that order, two very aggressive spokesmen. It was a cabinet which satisfied nobody.[6] But Marcy was inclined to be tolerant, for he was very happy at returning to public life.

In his conversation on February 22 with Pierce, Marcy also dis-

---

[4] *Tribune*, in *Journal* of Feb. 23.

[5] Caleb Cushing, *D.A.B.*; Nichols, 247-250; on Cushing, see also Fuess, *op. cit.*, II, 131, 136, 146, and F. P. Blair to Martin Van Buren, Nov. 27, V.B.P.

[6] *Journal*, Mar. 8; D. D. Barnard to Fish, May 23, Fish Papers; Benton's opinion (*Journal*, Mar. 4, citing *Tribune* correspondent); August Belmont to Buchanan, Mar. 5, B.P.; *Herald*, Feb. 25.

cussed, no doubt, the coming inaugural address. In general, this proved to be a conservative document.[7] It was strong on economy and on the constitution and the preservation of the Compromise. It also breathed the spirit of the Monroe Doctrine, spoke of the rights of American citizens abroad, and urged the expansion of commerce overseas. Perhaps one thing only was alarming. In the recent campaign, the party had talked much of acquiring Cuba; this had been especially so in the South, but the thought appealed to nationalists in all sections. In the inaugural address, Pierce had accordingly inserted the comment that his regime would "not be controlled by any timid forebodings of evil from expansion." This might well have been a matter for some concern, in the light of the sectional troubles which the last acquisitions had caused. Marcy did not oppose expansion as such, however.[8] He doubtless also reasoned that as the president's chief adviser he should be able to prevent serious trouble; it should be remembered, also, that he was not one to cross bridges before he came to them. There is no question, incidentally, but that he had a genuine liking for the new president.[9] Pierce was a man of considerable charm and quite a bit of talent. His weaknesses were in judgment and firmness of decision.

Marcy's concern, if anything, was more as to his own adequacy for dealing with foreign affairs. Aside from the hopes for expansion, there was already in being a grave dispute as to the right of American vessels to take fish on the coasts of the British North American provinces, there was grave disagreement between the United States and Great Britain over the meaning of a pact which Secretary Clayton had made with that power concerning Central America, and there were various Mexican problems. The Central American treaty, for one thing, had been violently criticized by the Democrats during the late campaign. Marcy was aware, on the other hand, of his lack of experience in handling such affairs. He had never been abroad and although he read widely it had seldom been in connection with foreign relations. He could write teasingly to Buchanan on the day after the inauguration that "It is now gen-

[7] *Mess. and Pap.*, 197-203.
[8] Cf. his letter to L. B. Shepard, Apr. 15, 1855, M.P.
[9] Mary Pattison to Newell, Oct. 5, 1859, M.P.; John Law to Pierce, July 9, 1857, Pierce Papers.

erally believed here—and I believe it myself" that he was to be in the cabinet, but he also said:[10]

I hope to have a frank and free intercourse with you—I will go further. I hope to have—what I know I shall much need—the aid on some emergencies of your greater experience and better knowledge.

Strolling out on the North Road with his friend Charles Eames of the *Union,* at about this time, he frankly admitted to feeling oppressed by the heavy load he had taken on.[11]

It is only fair to add that the public had fewer qualms. As was pointed out in the press, few Americans had had more practice in dealing with public affairs in general or had demonstrated larger talents as administrators. In addition, the choice was very gratifying to all conservatives. As Cornelius W. Lawrence, an old friend, said in New York, the entire commercial and financial world was pleased. Or, as William C. Rives, the Whig minister to France, commented, Marcy had the qualities most particularly needed: "experience of affairs, large views, & sober & well-poised judgment." In Marcy's own state, not only the more conservative Whigs and his own faction, the soft Hunkers, were satisfied. The Barnburners were, reasonably so, too. Only the Hards were unhappy.[12] Elsewhere, the opposition lay with the southern "fire-eaters," such as those who had backed the several filibustering moves made against Cuba in the last few years. Allied with these men and largely the same in personnel was the group known as "Young America." This latter cherished the idea of overthrowing the monarchies of Europe and setting up republics in their place, with at least covert aid from the United States government. Both detested Marcy as the very worst of "old fogies."[13]

Part of the burden which Marcy had taken on was in connection with the condition of affairs at his department, which was then in a two-story Georgian building at Fifteenth Street and Pennsylvania,[14]

---

[10] March 5, B.P.

[11] Eames to Marcy, Dec. 8, 1856, M.P.

[12] Concord (N.H.) *Patriot,* in *Union,* Mar. 8; G. Davis to Marcy, Mar. 23, Rives to Marcy, Mar. 31, S. B. Jewett to Marcy, Mar. 14, M.P.; Barnard letter, cited above.

[13] Cf. the *Union* article, Jan. 15, 1854, as to the filibustering and Young American view of Marcy when appointed.

[14] U. S. Dept. of State, *History of the Department of State,* 1901, p. 10.

in other words very near the White House. The trouble was that for a period of "manifest destiny," his agency was woefully under-staffed. It was true that a recent act had provided for an assistant secretary, but aside from that functionary there were only a chief clerk and some fourteen lesser ones in the whole department.[15] What was more, the department had been allowed to get sadly behind in its work under the aged and ill Daniel Webster, and Edward Everett had been in too briefly to be able to straighten things out.[16] And if there was reassurance in the fact that the top-ranking clerks were able and experienced,[17] it was unfortunately also true that William Hunter, the chief clerk, was dangerously ill.[18]

Under these circumstances, Marcy's initial effort was to find a competent man as assistant secretary. He turned first to William Beach Lawrence, a Rhode Islander who was an expert on international law and had had diplomatic experience, but Lawrence declined the offer. He hoped for a foreign mission.[19] Marcy then considered George Sumner, a brother of Charles Sumner, the outspoken abolitionist senator from Massachusetts. Interestingly enough, this idea came first from Jefferson Davis. Sumner was well qualified, but he, too, did not accept. His reason was different: Marcy had asked him for an assurance that he would not oppose the 1850 Compromise, and while this request was later waived, Sumner had still not accepted, believing that he would be out of place in the new administration. He did propose as a substitute for himself, however, and this was the individual who was finally selected, Ambrose Dudley Mann of Virginia.[20] Mann was a lawyer who had performed several diplomatic missions in Europe. Since his views were of the "Young America" stripe, however, it is rather surprising that Marcy offered him the position. But, after the two refusals, it was necessary to make a choice, and both Buchanan and Thomas Ritchie, the

[15] *Union* article of June 6, 1855.
[16] Buchanan's memorandum of June 25, cited above.
[17] Graham H. Stuart, *The Department of State*, 118-119.
[18] Nichols, 259.
[19] Lawrence to Marcy, Mar. 1, Appointments, D.S.; ditto, Mar. 13, M.P.; C. H. Hart, *A Discourse Commemorative of the Life and Services of the Late William Beach Lawrence*, 1-11; Lawrence to Cushing, Mar. 17, 1856, C.P.
[20] Geo. Sumner to Marcy, Mar. 19, 20, M.P.; Chas. Sumner to J. Bigelow, Mar. 26, Apr. 7, in Bigelow, *Retrospections of an Active Life*, I, 133, 134.

influential southern editor, endorsed him warmly.[21] The nomination
was announced on March 24. Mann was in Paris at the time and
did not arrive until May 2.

Besides choosing an experienced assistant, Marcy took another
step designed to make his way easier at the department. He voluntarily gave over to the office of the attorney general a number of
tasks formerly handled by the secretary of state. These included
advising the president as to the appointment of federal judges and
certain kindred officials, recommendations as to pardons, and the
conduct of such legal correspondence as the other department heads
wanted done for them.[22] Unhappily, these changes proved only a
minor mitigation of the work load, which was to be enormous.

For the first three months of the term the most pressing portion
of Marcy's work was not in foreign affairs but in the handling of
the general patronage of the government. This was a colossal task.
The paper work alone was bad enough. For one applicant from
New York, for example, there were petitions or letters from nearly
all of the top state officials, and from thirty of the presidential
electors, fourteen state senators and forty-four assemblymen, seven
judges of the state supreme court, the chairmen and clerks of two
county boards of supervisors, a sheriff, "other officials and numerous
distinguished democrats in both Counties," and so on, and so on.[23]
For one thing, there was much eyestrain involved with these documents, although Marcy used spectacles.[24] There were also the many
callers to interview. Marcy had the knack of saying "no," as everyone admitted, and normally said it early, but he was still swamped
with visitors. His room at Willard's Hotel, where he stayed for
many months, was simply beleaguered. Samuel Marcy, who twice
came up from Annapolis eager to tell about the arrival of the secretary's first grandson, was unable to get more than a few minutes
with him.[25] There was also the group discussion of the appointments by the cabinet as a whole, which met daily at ten for the

[21] Marcy to Buchanan, Sept. 2, 1855, B.P.
[22] Speech of Cushing at Newburyport, *Times*, Nov. 9, 1857.
[23] "William J. Hough for Solicitor of the Treasury," Mar. 12, 1853, M.P.
[24] Cf. the endorsement on the letter of Jas. A. Shields to Marcy, June 7, M.P., of
its having been "translated" for him; Newell to Marcy, Nov. 27, 1851, M.P.
[25] Samuel to Edmund, Mar. 31, M.P.

purpose. This was very time consuming. As for his own department, Marcy had little trouble. He simply told the clerks who were in office that none would be removed who did their duties properly and he held to this rule very well.[26]

For the appointments in New York state, however, the solution was more difficult. To put it in a nutshell, President Pierce insisted that here, as elsewhere, all of the elements in the party be treated equally, just as he had done in forming the cabinet. Softs, Barnburners, and Hards—all were to be on the same level. Marcy recognized that this would be an asinine policy, since it would displease everyone, but he found himself obliged to go along with it; as he wrote afterwards to Governor Seymour:[27]

I certainly did not approve the *Theory*, but when I found it *must be acted on*, I had much to do in carrying out the practical details and am satisfied with what I have done in that respect, so would you be if you could know how much worse things have been prevented.

Even so, the result was bad enough. The announcement of the New York City installment, March 29, had all the *éclat* of a bombshell. The biggest plum of all, the collectorship, had been marked for Daniel S. Dickinson himself, although very likely Marcy anticipated what proved to be true, that that worthy would decline it. Bracketed with Dickinson were Dix, to head the subtreasury, and Heman J. Redfield, Soft, as "naval officer" (a customs house post). Similarly, the six posts next in rank were also parceled out equally to the three factions. While Dickinson did decline and was replaced by Greene C. Bronson, and although Dix accepted only on a temporary basis, counting upon the Paris mission, the pattern had been set. Marcy's friends, to use George Newell's word for it, were quite "dumnfounded." Among those who were not in that class a rumor was started, in fact, that he would soon be out of the cabinet. For the time being, however, the administration's policy of neutrality seemed to gain a grudging acceptance.[28]

Marcy's personal friends fared much better. General John A. Thomas and his brother and also Colonel Berret, all of whom had

---

[26] *Journal*, Mar. 12; Stuart, *op. cit.*, 119.

[27] April 10, S.P.

[28] Nichols, *Pierce*, 254-255; Nichols, *Democratic Machine*, 192-193; Newell, Mar. 30, Geo. R. Davis, Mar. 30, John Knower, Apr. 11, all to Marcy, M.P.

actively worked for his nomination, received appointments. So, too, did Eames, while the secretary's son, William, became a purser in the navy and Abel French, Mrs. Marcy's sister's husband, was made a clerk in the state department.[29] If this was nepotism and favoritism, as it was, it was probably less extensive than was often true. What was more, Marcy was a shrewd judge of people and a stickler for good appointments.

The only pity, to tell the truth, was that Marcy was not given the chance to make every one of the new appointments throughout the foreign service or, as far as that went, to keep worthy men in office, as he did in the department. It is not anticipating too much what was to follow to say that the foreign missions would certainly have profited from the selection of more men of Eames' experience and cleverness and of more able and faithful workers such as General Thomas. (The former became *chargé d'affaires*—then the second rank in the United States foreign service—at Caracas, the latter the American advocate under the claims commission with Britain.) There was, of course, not only no career service, but the foreign posts were thought of as merely a part of the general patronage picture, the best of them being among the juiciest plums at the administration's command. The common rule was simple; each of the principal states which did not get a seat in the cabinet expected to have one of the main foreign missions.[30] And in following this pattern, the president deliberately sought to give the expansionists a healthy share, to compensate them for the fact that he had put a conservative like Marcy in as secretary. This might be good short-term politics, but it boded ill for United States diplomacy.

There is no point in going into too much detail as to the reasons for the particular selections which Pierce made, because previous accounts have done this[31] and Marcy had rather little influence in the matter anyhow. The choice of Senator Pierre Soulé as minister

---

[29] J. H. Thomas to Marcy, Mar. 11, M.P., telegram; George W. Cullum, *Biog. Register*, I, 430; *Union*, June 2 (*re* Berret); Charles Eames, *D.A.B.*; *Times*, Apr. 2, *re* Wm. Marcy; Marcy to Samuel, Apr. 10, M.P.

[30] Guthrie's letter, in Nichols, 252.

[31] H. B. Learned, "William Learned Marcy," in Bemis, VI, 174-182; Nichols, 255-257, 287-288.

to Spain to take up the ticklish Cuban problem, however, calls for a brief word. Marcy opposed the step as best he could. After all, Soulé's ardent and even irascible character, his status as a French republican refugee, which hardly qualified him to go to the capital of one of the most autocratic monarchies of Europe, and his frank talk of the need to get Cuba were all well known. Yet Pierce chose him, because he was the leader of one of the principal Louisiana factions and had campaigned busily for Pierce's election and because his chief rival, Slidell, had just declined a post which had been offered him![32] The choice of Solon Borland, a "fire-eating" expansionist of a rather ruffianly type,[33] for the new post of minister to Central America was hardly any better. Borland was a senator from Arkansas. As for James Gadsden, who was named the minister to Mexico because of his concern as a South Carolina railway man with the acquiring of lands from Mexico to round out a good south-westerly railroad route to the Pacific, his selection was more logical. At the same time, he was a southern nationalist, which did not augur well. The other two of the five most critical appointments were of an order less to be complained of. John Y. Mason, who was made minister to France, was a highly intelligent and agreeable man, if somewhat lacking in personal force. His choice was probably chiefly at Buchanan's instance, in view of his support of Buchanan for the presidency the year before.[34] As to the new minister to London, which was the most important assignment of all, Marcy was positively pleased at what was done. The nominee was none other than Buchanan himself,[35] who, besides having been secretary of state, had once been the minister to Russia. As such, he was the only one of the five who had had previous experience. He was also, it may be remarked, the only northerner. In view of his experience, his tact, and his considerable ability, the choice was a rather happy one. Very possibly, however, Marcy was also actively interested in having him out of the country, since he was a rival.

Buchanan proved to be in a very independent frame of mind,

[32] Ettinger, 133-138, 147-152; Nichols, 256.

[33] Cf. Gouverneur, *op. cit.*, 205.

[34] Maunsell B. Field, *op. cit.*, 62; Mason to Marcy, Apr. 22, 1852, M.P.

[35] Buchanan's account of his appointment, cited above; Buchanan to Marcy, July 27, never sent, B.P.

however. Long a major candidate for the presidency and possessed of an adequate personal fortune earned as a lawyer, he was disposed to be fussy. He was also angry because he feared that his Pennsylvania friends were not getting a large enough share of the spoils. But when he came to Washington, Pierce reassured him on this score. Pierce also told him, in his usual style of being willing to promise almost anything, that:

You know very well that we have several important questions to settle with England, and it is my intention that you shall settle them all at London.

When Buchanan naturally responded by asking "What will Governor Marcy say to your determination," the president replied hotly that he himself would make the decision. He also insisted that it was his impression that the cabinet favored such a policy. He said, however, that he would talk the matter over with Marcy. Marcy was later consulted as to this and apparently consented, for Pierce told Buchanan that Marcy was "entirely willing." The appointment was therefore made, being confirmed by the senate on April 11.[36] Apparently, it was all settled.

In regard to the other diplomatic appointments, much the same comment was in order as for the five chief ones. There were too many rabid expansionists. For one thing, the president had an obsessive concern for his beloved fellow officers of the late war, who were to compose a sort of "Mexico gang" in the administration. At least half a dozen such became heads of missions, namely Borland, Thomas H. Seymour (Russia), Seibels (Belgium), Jackson (Austria), Bissell (Argentina), and Trousdale (Brazil). In addition, Buchanan, while a civilian, had at one time favored the taking of all of Mexico. Marcy probably did not try to resist the "Mexico gang" as such, nor did he have any reason to. What he did try to do, however, was to keep out the extremists *per se*. As for Young America, as the *Times* said on March 16, "Gov. Marcy is rigidly conservative. His influence will be exerted directly against any recognition by this Government of the existence of tumult in Europe, except so far as may be necessary to preserve our own immediate material interests." As indicated with Soulé, he also op-

---

[36] Buchanan's account, cited above; his letters to Pierce, Apr. 2, 27, and to C. Johnson, draft, Apr. 27, B.P.

posed nominating the more wild-eyed expansionists. But he was largely unsuccessful. George N. Sanders of the *Democratic Review,* the very leader of Young America, was, for example, made consul at London. Similarly, Daniel E. Sickles, another hothead, was made secretary of legation there and August Belmont, the banker, who was supported by Sanders, was appointed *chargé* at the Hague. Marcy had resisted each one of these.[37] This is to say nothing of Edwin de Leon, who had even originated the name "Young America," and John L. O'Sullivan (the presumed author of the term "manifest destiny"), who had twice been indicted for breaking the neutrality laws. Each was given a position abroad! Taking the selections as a body, however, they were judged at the time to be at least no worse than under previous administrations. Such distinguished editors as Horace Greeley and William Cullen Bryant both testified to this.[38]

All the same, there were repeated rumors that Marcy would resign.[39] Nor was this to be wondered at. It was not only that so many of the extremists had been chosen. There was a personal factor involved. In an earlier day, the office of secretary of state had been the usual stepping stone to the White House. Marcy had been very conscious of this, from the time when Pierce had selected him, and his ambitions had been aroused. What was more, other people had sensed his desire. This was illustrated at a dinner which he attended at Brown's Hotel on May 21, given by Isaac Holmes. After the company had gotten into a high good humor, just how high we are not told, there was a good deal of jesting by Secretary Davis at Marcy and Buchanan, who also was there, on the subject of the presidency. Marcy "appeared to relish" this. After a time, Buchanan, who was mortally irritated at Marcy's rising prominence, remarked to the group and more particularly to Marcy that Marcy and he should consider themselves no longer candidates, as too old; this was especially true because Pierce, he added, was young and if successful might well seek another term. "The Governor [Marcy], to do him

[37] E. Everett to Col. Aspinwall, Aug. 8, Everett Letterbooks, M.H.S.; Field, *op. cit.,* 172; Belmont to Buchanan, Apr. 4, B.P.

[38] *Times,* May 25, June 14; *E. Post,* Apr. 18, May 25; *Tribune,* May 25.

[39] *Times,* May 30.

justice, appeared to take these remarks kindly and in good part, and said he was agreed." Buchanan was to find that Davis, Dobbin, and Cushing were all pleased at his advice, however, as was Pierce when he heard of it.[40] Indeed, there is not much doubt that the latter thought of Marcy as a rival and wished to keep him down. One of Pierce's close friends told a New York office hunter, for example, that Pierce would be very ready to gratify Governor Seymour's wishes in the patronage once Seymour had assured him that Marcy did not want to be nominated in 1856.[41] Likewise, Sidney Webster was quoted as saying that "we would now see whether Mr. Marcy is President or not."[42] Beyond these points, moreover, there was the plain fact that Pierce had thwarted Marcy on the New York patronage. There was also the fact that he gave more offices to Buchanan's friends than to Marcy's. Among the former were Belmont and Sickles—both, significantly, Hards—and also Sanders, to say nothing of John Y. Mason.[43]

In spite of all this and notwithstanding the competition of the several other chief candidates for the White House, Marcy was cheerful. On July 18, after the civil and diplomatic appointments had mostly been completed, he could still copy out of the book of *Ezekiel* the verses stating God's promise to prosper the mountains of Israel and make man and beast bear fruit.[44] He had high hopes for the administration and, through it, for himself.

---

[40] Buchanan's account of his appointment, cited above.
[41] L. B. Garvin to Seymour, Apr. 21, S.P.
[42] J. A. Thomas to Marcy, Nov. 24, M.P.
[43] Belmont letter, cited above; *Times*, Aug. 1 (*re* Sickles); Appointments file, D.S., on Sanders, contains letters from several of the Buchanan group.
[44] Date on *verso*, M.P.

XIX. THE DRESS CIRCULAR

"The American minister abroad should be an American;
he should look like an American, talk like an American, and
be an American example." (The New York *Evening Post*,
June 15, 1853)

IN THE first months of Marcy's term as secretary of state, as has
been said, he had little time for foreign affairs, for the patronage
problems were all-engrossing. In addition, as far as that went, both
he and the president were inexperienced in foreign affairs, while
Hunter was ill and Mann did not reach the capital until May 15.
By June, however, it was possible to get down to the foreign issues.
In fact, it was on June 1 that Marcy made his first splash in what
were to him the uncharted seas of foreign relations. This came with
the issuance of a notable set of instructions to the United States
diplomatic and consular agents, one of which dealt in part with
diplomatic costume.

A dozen years before, as a member of the Mexican claims commission, Marcy had been invited to President Tyler's dinner for the
diplomatic corps, an affair of much state. He had not been impressed. "The diplomats decked out in gewgaws made a truly
ridiculous appearance," he had written.[1] And yet, in that very year
the American minister—the minister of the world's leading republic—had worn at Queen Victoria's court a costume rich with
gold and embroidery and had ridden in a bright yellow coach with
liveried coachmen and outriders. This was hardly in keeping with
the aura of log-cabin and hard-cider simplicity which the Whigs
had affected in the campaign of the year before. Nor did the Democrats generally do much better,[2] despite their Jeffersonian tradition.
There had earlier been some efforts by the state department under
Democratic administrations to remedy the situation, but these had
been ineffective. Now, in the 1850's, the wearing of conventional

---

[1] To Wetmore, June 10, 1841, M.P.
[2] Weed, *op. cit.*, 512; R. B. Nye, *George Bancroft*, 162-163.

European court costume seemed positively indecent. Horace Greeley's paper, for example, called such garb "the baboon court dress,"[3] and Marcy's attitude was much the same.

The famous circular which Marcy issued on June 1 to the heads of missions directed each of them to conform in his dress to the customs of the country—in so far as was consistent with republican institutions.[4] It then went on to say:

but the department would encourage as far as practicable, without impairing his usefullness to his country, his appearance at court in the simple dress of an American citizen.

This every-day dress, although Marcy did not say so, was meant to be that worn daily by the middle classes throughout the western world at that time—silk hat and black coat and trousers—but which is now reserved for more ceremonial occasions. The circular added cautiously that should there be cases where this would be harmful to American interests, "the nearest approach" to that ideal was expected.

The simplicity of our usages and the tone of feeling among our people are much more in accordance with the example of our first and most distinguished representative [Benjamin Franklin] at a royal court than the practice which has since prevailed. It is to be regretted that there was ever any departure in this respect from the example of Dr. Franklin.

All previous instructions on dress were therefore withdrawn, leaving each diplomat to act "according to his own sense of propriety" but with a due regard for the wishes of his government.

Besides this circular to the heads of missions, there were also two others, to secretaries of legation and consular officers. Taken as a whole, these three documents laid down an important body of rules for the foreign service, touching upon a variety of matters. Even the hours of business were specified. Consular officials were told not to wear uniforms at all, and such foreign usages at the consulates as calling the consul's clerk "the chancellor" (or, worse, "le chancelier") were also banned. The most important feature apart from costume, however, was that all confidential work at the legations must be done by American citizens and that all consular

[3] *Tribune*, May 26, 1853.
[4] Texts of the three circulars appeared in the *Union*, June 14.

clerks and vice-consuls must be Americans. All in all, it was a sweeping move to make the service more efficient and also to Americanize it.[5] Later in the Pierce administration there would be other reform moves.

According to a statement by the Count de Sartiges, the French minister, the chief author of this program was Mann, the assistant secretary.[6] This is corroborated by other facts. Marcy had had no time to study the questions touched upon, by June 1, while Mann was an idealistic Young American who would relish such instructions. Beyond this, Mann had on February 7 urged in a private letter that American spokesmen wear plain black suits, had referred to Franklin as an exemplar of simple costume, and had proposed set hours for a legation's work.[7] This is really somewhat beside the point, however. For the fact was that Marcy made the circulars his own when he sent them out over his signature. Henceforth, the responsibility was his.

The reaction of the American people when the circulars were published two weeks after was one of immediate delight. John A. Dix, for example, regretted only that they had not gone so far as to require the ministers to live within their incomes. He cited the case of a minister to Russia who had left his estate in debt to the amount of $100,000 because of failing to do so; Dix argued that to follow such a pattern of expenditure was un-American.[8] Marcy, in fact, received favorable letters from all quarters and areas. As the *New York Herald,* which did not love him, had to concede: "all the country from Cape Cod to California, will cry amen." That paper went on to jibe, indeed, that the rule was just what was to be expected of a man who was never particular about his dress and didn't mind a patch on his breeches. Another newspaper remarked dryly that this was not the first time that Marcy had "made war upon feathers [an allusion to General Scott] and military trappings."

---

[5] The ban upon foreign clerks caused some difficulty, in view of shortages of Americans or their desire for high wages; cf. E. Everett to Marcy, July 15, 1853, and J. Y. Mason to Marcy, Mar. 15, 1854, M.P.

[6] Sartiges to Drouyn de Lhuys, Oct. 18, Corr. Pol. Etats-Unis, vol. 109, cited in Ettinger, 222.

[7] Mann's letter appeared in the *Herald,* Jan. 6, 1855. The addressee was not given.

[8] Dix to Marcy, June 13, M.P.

Even abroad, the abstract wisdom of the policy was granted by some. Thus, the London *Times*—"Jupiter" itself—admitted that it was no compliment to a civilized nation to have the envoy accredited to it dressed "as if he were intending to astonish Patagonians or Ashantees." But, the *Times* hastened to remark, "if custom is still for tinsel, it is hardly worth while to affect singularity in such a matter."[9]

During the autumn, as the first returns began to come in from the American spokesmen abroad, it none the less appeared that fancy dress was on the way out. The ministers at Berlin and Stockholm, it is true, had been told that only appearances in such costume would be suffered. Yes, and even the redoubtable Soulé, that "red-hot republican," had purchased modified court regalia—this, too, before leaving Paris! Yet Belmont and Seibels (at the Hague and Brussels) had worn plain clothes and Daniel (at Turin) had been told that he might. As a matter of fact, the *chargé d'affaires* at Paris, Henry S. Sanford, had also worn simple dress, despite public criticism of his course, and the timid Buchanan had done so at the lord mayor's dinner in London.

The real trials, however, came as the big royal receptions of the winter season approached. And the result proved to be far from satisfactory. For one thing, the new ministers had by this time learned that the costume which they were called upon to wear was identical with that of the servants at the royal palaces. More significantly, however, and this was in line with what the London *Times* had said, they did not want to start their tours of duty under a shadow of seeming disrespect for the crowned heads to whom they were accredited. After all, the instructions left the decision to them and the kings and foreign ministers soon found that out. Several of them accordingly decided, without much delay, to exercise the discretion given them and conform to local practice; what was more, the foreign offices or spokesmen at the palaces commonly requested—in a rather pointed manner—that they do so.

These circumstances proved to apply even in France, in spite of

---

[9] *Herald*, June 15; *Democratic Union*, in *The Daily Union* of July 8; cf. also *Daily Union* of June 23, *re* the general approval of the rule; *Times* (London), in *Union* of Aug. 23.

Sanford's course. When the cautious John Y. Mason reached there to take over, he found himself in a quandary. Sanford had been sarcastically dubbed the "Black Crow" because of his appearance in plain dress, while Soulé's conformity at Madrid to the previous custom was known—as was a more recent instance involving Seymour at St. Petersburg. Soon after Mason reached the French capital he accordingly took pains to consult the foreign minister, Drouyn de Lhuys. He stated that he meant to wear plain clothes when he presented his credentials to the emperor and asked if this would give offense. He was soon told that it would not, although a contrary course would have been preferred. He then discussed the whole matter with Robert McLane, who was on his way to China to be the American commissioner, and with General Thomas, who was also present. Both advised fancy garb for all social functions. Mason in consequence decided that this was the proper thing to do, while adhering to his plan of a simple costume for the proffering of his credentials. When he went to the Tuileries in February, 1854, for a social affair, he was clad in a blue coat with gold lace and in white cassimere breeches. Marcy was much annoyed. Although he did not quite reproach Mason, as such, for his act, he told him that Sanford's course "was so generally approved in this country as to amount to a public judgment in its favor" and that he had himself felt an "awkwardness" at Mason's reversal of the precedent which had been set.

The pattern of failure was not universal, on the other hand. Belmont continued to follow the circular, as did O'Sullivan at Lisbon. At Vienna, the *chargé,* Henry S. Jackson, did not, but he found a happy compromise. Recalling his one-time army service, he concluded to wear a military costume, which was common enough at full-dress affairs; he even decided to write to the governor of his state for a commission as a colonel of militia, in order to have a suitable rank. At London, by contrast, James Buchanan compromised as to the use of plain clothes themselves. His position, of course, was a highly amusing one, for he was exceedingly timorous and yet as ambitious as ever. He had not wanted the post there unless given a chance to score a major success that might bring him to the White House and he hence did not wish to imperil his mission by antagonizing the British ruling classes. At the same time, he had a deadly fear of being charged with "toadying" to British royalty! His solution was an original one. He wore a plain costume, but set it off with a sword and a three-cornered hat. Queen Victoria accepted this. If Marcy had mixed emotions upon hearing of this success by his rival, he did not show it. He wrote that he "heartily rejoice [d]." He added that "I know how little you regard popularity [and here, surely, Marcy smiled to himself!], but I hope you will not regard it impertinent in me to say that your course . . . has secured to you quite a large stock of this article."[10]

The circular, then, had had only a limited success. On the other hand, despite a "vast amount of small wit"[11] expended upon it by the Whig papers, the American people unquestionably approved of it. In an age when republics were on the defensive against monarchy, the people very naturally regarded the court dress as disgraceful in their spokesmen. This was true to a degree which a century later would be hard to understand. The only thing which was really lacking, in fact, was to make the new rule mandatory.

Under the circumstances, it was nothing to be surprised at that Marcy's precept soon became a fixed one, with no discretion allowed as to its observance. For some years, indeed, there was a good deal of variation in the practice on the subject, but in 1867 congress laid down a positive rule. Under the leadership of Senator Sumner, who had been a backer of the principle even before the circular came out, a joint resolution was passed which barred the wearing of "any uniform or official costume not previously authorized by Congress." Although this was not exactly law, the state department generally adhered to it and it helped to regularize the situation. The rule has since stood, for the most part. In the long run, then, and posthumously, Marcy won out.

*   *   *

[10] The sources for the above are *SED31*, 36th cong., 1st sess., 7-11, 23; Sanford to Marcy, Aug. 18, Des. Fr.; Buchanan, Nov. 11, Jackson, Jan. 30, Feb. 25, Daniel, Feb. 1, Dec. 25, Mason, Jan. 19, Mar. 15, all to Marcy, M.P.; Ettinger, 223; *Union* (*re* Sanford and Mason), Feb. 2, Mar. 10; Buchanan to Harriet Lane, Feb. 24, in Curtis, *op. cit.*, II, 114; Marcy to Mason, Feb. 21, priv., draft, Instr. Fr.; and copy of same, Feb. 20, M.P.; Marcy to Buchanan, Mar. 12, priv., M.P.
[11] Baltimore *Argus*, in *Union* of Mar. 4, 1854.

The dress rule produced some engaging anecdotes, by the way. One concerned Joseph H. Choate, a later ambassador to London who was celebrated for his wit. Choate's own opinion was that for one person to wear ordinary evening dress among dozens of persons in gilded costumes was "the most impertinent piece of swagger in the world," but he held to the rule.[12] On his leaving a certain function one evening, an English duke, a homely man, mistook him for a servant. "Call me a cab," cried the duke! "You're a cab," replied Choate quickly. "I wish I could call you a hansom cab."[13] The circular even produced its own folklore. By the following century, H. L. Mencken, in a famous book on American speech, could assert that Marcy had instructed American diplomats to use only "the American language" in addressing him.[14]

---

[12] Graham H. Stuart, *The Department of State*, 120, and his *American Diplomatic and Consular Practice*, 278-280.

[13] Cleveland Amory, "The Last Resorts," *Holiday*, August 1952, p. 75. Reprinted by special permission of *Holiday*, copyright August, 1952, by the Curtis Publishing Company.

[14] *The American Language*, 1936 ed., 79-80. In a letter to the writer on Sept. 21, 1955, Mr. Mencken stated via his secretary that he was unable to give the source for this assertion.

XX. SETTLING UPON A COURSE AS TO BRITAIN

"Recent developments have inspired the belief that the
fisheries, the reciprocity question, &c. will leave no ground
of concession which could be available in the settlement of
the questions in Central America." (Pierce to Buchanan,
June 26, 1853[1])

UNTIL late in May, as has been suggested, Marcy had little
time for diplomacy; indeed, he told Buchanan that he had
not had a single uninterrupted hour for such purposes. A few days
before he issued the dress circular, however, he began actively to
take up the complex affairs which were in dispute with Britain.[2] Of
all of these, the most immediately pressing item was as to the North
American fisheries, while the most involved and stubborn was the
Central American problem.

From the time of the first settlements, Americans had fished in
the coastal waters of what is now Canada. This privilege had been
maintained after independence. In a pact of 1818, it had been defined as unlimited on large parts of the coasts of Newfoundland
and Labrador, including the right to land and dry the fish so long
as the particular area remained unsettled; in return the United
States had given up its inshore rights elsewhere. For a long time
after 1818, however, American fishermen had been allowed a rather
liberal interpretation of the three-mile limit, commonly enjoying the
use of all bays more than six miles wide at the mouth.

Then, in the 1830's and after, there had been a rising resentment
over this in the provinces. Nova Scotia, in particular, had taken
the lead in restricting American access to those waters; she had even
ruled that the legal limit was to be a line drawn three miles offshore
from headland to headland, which meant a very drastic change. In
addition, Britain's abandonment of her mercantile system, which
had largely been affected in the 1840's, had deprived the colonials

---

[1] Curtis, op. cit., II, 86.
[2] Buchanan's account (June 25) of his appointment, ibid., II, 76-83; espec. p. 81.

of their preferred markets in the mother country. This had caused
a serious depression in the provinces. In turn, the depression had
led the provincials to talk of annexation to the United States. One
result of this was that imperial and provincial leaders had sought to
quiet such talk by securing a treaty for reciprocity in trade with the
United States. This had been declined. Indeed, the United States had
dealt rather coldly with the colonial commissioners who had come
to Washington.

The upshot had been that the colonial parliaments had insisted
generally upon an exclusion of American fishermen from their
coastal waters, partly with an eye to making the United States more
ready to negotiate. What made matters worse was that Secretary of
State Daniel Webster had conceded publicly that the headland-to-
headland rule was logical.[3] As far as trade went, the provinces
wanted a reciprocity in natural products, which they produced
abundantly, and not in manufactures, of which they produced but
little. On the other hand, the provincial duties on manufactures were
low, averaging 12%, and for all goods there was a world-wide
movement towards lower tariffs; the United States had taken part
in this last by the great tariff law of the Polk period. In any case,
there was much for it to gain by the right treaty.

While Edward Everett had been secretary of state, he had negotiated with John F. Crampton, the British minister, and the two
had drawn up a *projet* of a treaty.[4] It had not been finished, however. There were also certain complications. For one thing, the
provinces had no federal or "dominion" government as yet, so that
there were several parliaments whose desires must be satisfied. Beyond that, the southern states feared that reciprocity would lead to
annexation, which would wholly upset the sectional balance. But
the problem was an urgent one. American fishermen were in an

[3] J. M. Callahan, *American Foreign Policy in Canadian Relations*, 107, 241-249;
Hunter Miller, *op. cit.*, VI, 678-679; James Buchanan to Marcy, Apr. 14, 1854, I. D.
Andrews to Webster, July 9, 1851, and to Marcy, May 3, 1853, William R. Manning,
ed., *Diplomatic Correspondence of the United States, Canadian Relations, 1784-1860*,
vol. IV (hereafter referred to as *Can. Rels.*), 563-565, 433-436, 508; Marcy to
R. Rush, July 4, draft, 1853, M.P.; Report of the House Committee on Commerce, as
to reciprocity, *Union*, Feb. 18, 1853; H. L. Keenleyside, *Canada and the U.S.*, (1952
ed.), 221.
[4] Text in *Can. Rels.*, 57n.

angry mood and often carried arms, while both sides had stationed naval vessels in or near the disputed waters.[5] There was a real chance that war might result.

In Central America, there was a very real rivalry for control of the transit between the oceans. Since the American acquisition of California and Oregon, the gold rush, the British opening of the treaty ports in China, and other recent developments, this had become extraordinarily important to the United States and hardly less so to Great Britain, which power had a commerce even greater than the former's. The best prospects for a ship canal, if one was to be built, were at Panama or else up the San Juan River in Nicaragua and, after a passage of Lake Nicaragua, by a short cutting to the Pacific. The latter was considered the better route. In consequence, a charter for a canal there had been secured by an American company headed by Cornelius Vanderbilt.

Unfortunately, British influence lay in the path of such projects. Britain had footholds at a number of points on the eastern coast of Central America. In what is now British Honduras but which was then commonly called the Belize, she had undeniable rights to cut logs in a limited area and her subjects actually occupied a much larger region. There had also been a protectorate off and on over a motley tribe of Indians who lived around Bluefields on the shore of Nicaragua, some thirty miles north of the San Juan River. In the 1840's this had been revived and the British had declared that it ran as far as the south bank of that vital stream, which meant that potentially it would cut the canal route. They had forcibly expelled some Nicaraguan troops from the chief point in the area, the village of Greytown. This was on the northern bank of that river's principal channel. The British also claimed a paramount interest in the Bay Islands, a tiny but strategic archipelago off the shore of the republic of Honduras; a few Britishers had lived there at various times. None of the Central American states recognized any of these claims, nor did the United States except perhaps the quite restricted rights in the Belize.

After many moves and counter-moves by the United States and Britain in the region in the late 1840's, a stalemate had resulted. This had been perpetuated, if for the time being it seemed to have been

---

[5] Buchanan to Marcy, Apr. 14, 1854, *ibid.*, 563-565.

resolved, in the Clayton-Bulwer treaty of 1850, a pact which was one of the more masterly ambiguities of modern history. Each government had pledged never to obtain exclusive control over a ship-canal by the San Juan route. Of more interest to the United States, each had pledged never to

occupy, or fortify, or colonize, or assume or exercise any dominion over Nicaragua, Costa Rica, the Mosquito Coast, or any part of Central America. . . .

Nor (and here was the joker) was either to use any protection which it afforded to or any alliance which it had with any state or people to achieve any of the purposes prohibited above. The advantages of the canal, furthermore, were not to be obtained by one side and denied to the citizens of the other. Both also agreed to help in establishing free ports at each end. After the treaty was signed and before the exchange of ratifications, Bulwer, the British representative, had protested to Secretary Clayton at an alleged plot by some Americans to seize Ruatan, the largest of the Bay Islands. Clayton had replied that his government would not permit it, which remark might have been interpreted either as acknowledging the British claim or as merely barring American infiltration of the region. There had also been an exchange of notes confirming that the Belize and "the small islands in the neighborhood" were not covered by the pact. Which islands these were had not been stated. Aside from the question of the Bay Islands, which the British later insisted were the ones referred to, the United States believed that it had won a definite victory. The ambiguity as to protectorates was brushed aside and the seemingly unequivocal ban upon occupation or the exercise of dominion was viewed as having reduced the Mosquitian protectorate to a shadow or as having abolished it. The Belize was also regarded as likely to have a tenuous existence.

Regardless of what the Clayton treaty meant, the use of the isthmus was being started. A railroad had been begun across Panama; meanwhile, passengers could reach each of its shores by steamer and travel across by coach and by native canoe. In Nicaragua, it turned out that the idea of a canal was soon given up. But the Vanderbilt interests had put ocean steamers into operation and had set up a firm called the Accessory Transit Company. This enterprise operated river and lake steamers and stage coaches in the interior. Everything considered, the Vanderbilt route was both the shorter and the easier.

The importance of such routes had led to several attempts in Fillmore's period to come to a better understanding with Britain, but these had failed. In the course of that administration, though, the United States had consented to a temporary and *de facto* recognition of the municipal government at Greytown as independent and the British had removed their agent. On the other hand, the place had really continued under Britain's wing. The Accessory Transit Company had also recognized the township by securing a franchise from it to build a coaling depot across the river, at Punta Arenas on the southern bank. Later, in violation of the agreement, it had erected practically a town there. This had caused clashes between the two settlements. What was even more provocative to America than these last was that in March, 1852, the British had formally annexed the Bay Islands. One consequence was that both the Democrats, who had always criticized the Clayton agreement, and the Whigs, who had made it, had indulged in public tirades in congress against Great Britain. She had been accused of bad faith. The criticism of the Democrats in the recent campaign, which has been cited already, and since that time, had been especially virulent. To this the foreign office had replied through diplomatic channels that it favored the erection of both Greytown and Mosquitia as independent and separate states. Lord Clarendon, who in the spring of 1853 had become the foreign secretary, held to about the same line; in an instruction of May 27, however, he wrote that his government renounced neither the protectorate nor her own possessions in Central America, pending a settlement with the United States.[6]

In all of these relations with Britain, Marcy soon found that the one bright spot was Edward Everett's draft treaty. It was apparent that there was a considerable chance of having some such pact adopted. It

---

[6] The writer is much indebted to Mary W. Williams' work, *Anglo-American Isthmian Diplomacy*, on which the above paragraphs are largely based (see pp. 2-173, *passim*); for the location of the Mosquito Indians, see R. W. Van Alstyne, "British Diplomacy and the Clayton-Bulwer Treaty, 1850-1860," *Journal of Mod. Hist.*, XI, 149; for the text of the treaty of 1850, Hunter Miller, *op. cit.*, V, 671-675; for the senate debates in the special session of March, 1853, see *Union*, Mar. 17, 31, Apr. 6-9.

also seemed imperative to do so, if peace was to be preserved. The consequence was that when Buchanan came to town, late in May, Marcy showed him the draft and told him that he desired to handle this part of Anglo-American relations himself. Buchanan replied that the proposed concessions of duties on provincial products were "the great lever" by which Britain might be made to back down as to the isthmus. Marcy did not agree. He planned instead to use these trade concessions to exact the fullest privileges for his country in the fisheries and in the British North American waters generally, and saw quite correctly that there would be no bargaining power left over for the isthmus. When Buchanan went to see Pierce about it, furthermore, he found that the president was beginning to swing towards Marcy's view. The result was that Buchanan left Washington on May 31 without taking his commission.[7] Marcy did not worry, however. He was increasingly sure that Pierce would back him up and he knew that the Pennsylvanian could not very well decline the mission on the ground that all of the British affairs had not been entrusted to him alone.

On the other hand, as Marcy approached the isthmian part of the problem, he saw that it would take long and careful labor simply to draw up Buchanan's instructions. With respect to the Clayton treaty itself, he said that "The more it is studied, the more enigmatical it seems to be. It resembles more than anything of the kind I ever read a response of the Delphic oracle." He was accordingly very well content to have the negotiations on it taken from his shoulders. This was a very wise arrangement. In preparing the instructions, he none the less took pains to consult Buchanan and also Clayton himself as to their opinions.[8]

His first important instruction respecting the area, however, was to Joseph R. Ingersoll, the Whig incumbent at London. This was dated June 9. Under orders from the Fillmore administration, American marines had been landed at Punta Arenas to protect the property of the Accessory Transit Company. Lord Clarendon had protested at this and Marcy had replied by upholding the action, in reasoning which

---

[7] Buchanan's account of his appointment, cited above.

[8] To Buchanan, June 1, and to Clayton, June 1, M.P. Both men answered that Britain had not formally given up the protectorate but had essentially done so. June 4, 7, 11, July 1, M.P.

was decidedly American. He ruled that if Punta Arenas was in Nicaragua, the company's general charter protected it, while if it was in Costa Rica, as the latter insisted, then Greytown had no jurisdiction because that town had no pretense to a title from Costa Rica. As for the Mosquitos' claim to that part of the shore or to any part, he went on, the United States recognized that at best they could have only a "possessory right" to the land, as its owners but not its sovereigns. This was just as with Indians in the United States, he contended. Even if this was a mistake, he said, he did not believe that the title to Punta Arenas would be claimed seriously by Britain. To summarize, Marcy held firmly that only the Central American republics were entitled to sovereignty in the Mosquito area. His despatch was somewhat sharp in tone, partly because he wrote it without knowledge of the company's having secured from Greytown the franchise for the coaling depot.[9]

His next instruction, to Solon Borland, the new minister to Central America, had the same theme of resistance to British encroachments, but was also a useful indication of Marcy's conservatism as to the United States' own aims. This instruction was seemingly prepared in consultation with Borland himself. Marcy confessed that he was still not ready to give an official interpretation of the Clayton treaty. He stated, however, that he had been informed that Britain would be willing to give up the protectorate if Nicaragua could be induced to treat the Indians fairly and to compensate them for their rights as possessors. Nicaragua should be encouraged to buy them out, he said. After all, he went on, their "king" was "a mere effigy" and the protectorate simply a convenient political device. He also ordered the minister to try for a peaceable settlement of the Nicaraguan-Costa Rican boundary and for friendly cooperation between the several states, or even, if possible, for a reestablishment of the old Central American Confederation. The aim of all this was to make British interference more difficult. As an indication that he had already begun to appreciate Mr. Borland's shortcomings, the despatch several times cautioned him "carefully [to] avoid . . . the imputation of an

[9] William R. Manning, ed., *Diplomatic Correspondence of the United States; Inter-American Affairs, 1831-1860*, 11 volumes (hereafter cited by volume, as "Manning VII," etc.), VII, 80-82; Williams, 173.

improper interference in their internal affairs." And, it added: "This government has no object in seeking friendly relations with them inconsistent with their political rights and national prosperity."[10] Here spoke the true Marcy. As a veteran of the War of 1812 and the son of a revolutionary soldier, he had the nationalism and a mild version of the anti-British feeling of his generation. On the other hand, he sought no expansion unless it was accomplished honorably. He also was determined to act within international law.[11]

By the end of June, he was to write more specifically as to the isthmian tangle and had his instructions to the minister to London ready. These were debated by the cabinet at some length on July 1 and sent off on July 5.[12] They stated that the negotiations over reciprocity would definitely be carried on at Washington. As for Central America, they quoted the Monroe Doctrine and warned that the United States was resolved to sustain it. In the case of the Belize, Marcy conceded nothing more than Spain had granted, and denied that this allowed Britain any real colony there. As proof he cited the acts of parliament of 1817 and 1819 and the Anglo-Mexican treaty of 1826 which had renewed the Spanish grant. As for the Mosquito protectorate, he was just as positive. He called it "a most palpable infringement" of Britain's treaty of 1786 with Spain, citing as evidence the comments of Britain's responsible leaders in parliament in 1787. It was also, he said definitely, "contrary to the manifest spirit and intention" of Mr. Clayton's treaty. He insisted that the latter forbade all exercise of dominion by Britain in Central America, except her limited rights in the Belize. "The whole Central American question," he concluded, was "entirely confided" to Buchanan's management— "under such instructions as you may from time to time desire, or such as the President may consider himself called upon to furnish." This was fair enough, as Buchanan finally admitted.[13]

All the same, it was hard to persuade Buchanan to accept. Pierce wrote to him on July 2, urging that he do so. Then, when the instructions were sent to Wheatland, Marcy sent along a letter in which he

[10] Manning IV, 40-47; "Mr. Borelands [sic] mem. as to the matters to be embraced in his Instructions," 13 pp., M.P.

[11] Cf. his letter to L. B. Shepard, Apr. 15, 1855, M.P.

[12] *Times*, July 2; note of Buchanan on this, in Curtis, *op. cit.*, II, 89; text in M.P.

[13] Buchanan's notes, Curtis, *op. cit.*, II, 91-92.

said that he regretted that there was no time to talk the matter over with him personally before he sailed. This was because Buchanan had some time before set July 9 as his date for departing. Marcy was plainly hoping to avoid any arguments on the subject; in fact he was careful to say that Pierce had examined the instructions in detail and that they were such as he approved. A week later, when the acceptance still had not been received, he was none the less sure that it would come. He wrote to Everett jocularly that "The truth is old bachelors as well as young maidens do not alway [s] know their own minds. [But] If he ever meant to go he can assign no sufficient cause for changing his purpose." He was right. On the very next day, while passing through Philadelphia, Pierce obtained the needed consent, by this time at least thrice denied.[14]

During July, although busy with several other vital matters, Marcy began to take more time than previously for his negotiations with Crampton on the fisheries. To start with, there was the Everett-Crampton *projet*. This offered the United States the fullest use of the inshore fisheries of the provinces, plus the right to cure fish just about everywhere save on parts of Newfoundland. In return, provincial-caught fish could enter the United States free of duty and there would be free trade in a long list of other natural products. On the other hand, American shipowners were also to have the freedom of the St. Lawrence, except that Britain was tentatively given the right to set this aside, while British craft were to be allowed American registry if owned by Americans. Crampton, moreover, gave to Marcy a revised draft of the *projet*, sent from London in January.[15] This called for the use of American coastal waters by British fishermen and for an end of the bounty which the United States paid to its cod fishery; it also promised that if Britain closed the St. Lawrence the United States might cancel the free list.

As with the Central American issues, Marcy promptly began to seek out the best advice that was to be had; he consulted Everett himself and also Richard Rush, the now aged negotiator of the 1818 pact.[16]

---

[14] Pierce to Buchanan, July 2, Marcy to ditto, July 5, note of Buchanan, n.d., all *ibid.*, II, 89-93; Marcy to Everett, July 12, Everett Papers.

[15] Encl. in Russell to Crampton, Jan. 15, F.O. 115.

[16] Everett to Marcy, Aug. 15, Marcy to Rush, draft, July 4, M.P.

He also early called to Washington the United States consul at St. John, New Brunswick, one Israel D. Andrews, and kept him on hand for months. Andrews was an energetic man who had long been making exploratory moves in the matter himself.[17] By way of general policy, it may be noted, Marcy and Pierce early told Crampton that "It was the intention of the Administration to proceed, as long as they could gain the support of the Country, in the direction of Free Trade."[18]

At the end of July, Marcy invited Crampton to go off with him for a week of leisurely discussions at Berkeley Springs, in western Virginia, and Crampton accepted. The two men left for that place on July 29, each accompanied by a secretary.[19] It is too bad that no complete account of this interlude has survived, for it must have been one of the most agreeable during Marcy's tenure. We know that Marcy was increasingly finding Crampton a pleasant man to deal with.[20] During the daytime, there were the conferences in the special parlor which the hotel provided for the purpose, while every evening there was a round of whist. The latter left Marcy in a genial mood.[21]

Such details as we do have of the discussions, available from Marcy's diary of August 1-4,[22] reveal that they dealt largely with the free list. Nor were there many decisions reached on this score, even. Two of the very principal items suggested by the British for inclusion, metals and coal, were not cleared up. Marcy insisted upon barring metals; as to coal, he was privately undecided, observing that America's new gas industry wanted Nova Scotia's soft coal and that the Pennsylvania coal sent abroad was chiefly anthracite; he had some thought that American soft coal producers might be placated if the sales of their product to English shipping firms proved to be as large as he thought and if this fact was emphasized enough. Nor was there

---

[17] Andrews to Cushing, Apr. 8, 1854, C.P.; voucher for expenses, Sept. 30, 1854, Pierce Papers; Andrews to Marcy, May 3, 1853, *Can. Rels.,* 503-509.

[18] F.O. 5, Sept. 5, 1853.

[19] *Times,* Aug. 2; A. French to Philo White, July 30, M.P.

[20] Marcy to Crampton, priv., draft, Aug. 27, 1855, alludes to his friendly feeling for the envoy, M.P.

[21] As to the allegation of Henry Labouchere (Hesketh Pearson, *Labby,* 35) that Marcy was thereby made more ready to grant concessions, the story of the events refutes such an idea; Marcy was unyielding.

[22] Typed copy, J. B. Moore Papers, Library of Congress.

any exact decision as to the opening of the United States' seaboard to provincial fishermen. But the diary does tell us that Crampton disclosed that his country's *sine qua nons* were the placing of coal on the free list, the registry of provincial craft, and the end of the cod subsidy.

When Marcy went back to Washington on August 6 or 7 the task was not done and he was also far from rested up. This was unfortunate, because he secured no more vacation that summer. He wrote to General Wetmore disconsolately ten days after—in a very revealing letter:

> The weather has also had a more debilitating effect upon me than it ever had before. I have not been able to work—not even to write letters—after dinner. I have now more on my hands to do & which ought to be done within a brief period, than *ten able* men could do—and I hardly account myself one of that description. To tell you all—for this will be a letter of apologies—I had not given until recently much attention to our foreign relations and really was not qualified for the position assigned me. I have been obliged to make up this deficiency—with really no leisure to do it and without much assistance from any quarter. In looking back upon a public life unusually long—I find it has all been spent *in learning trades*, and I fear I have not acquired a high degree of skill in any of them —Tho not ambitious I naturally wish to appear to as good an advantage in the last—certainly the last—as in any of them.

It should be explained that he had not found Mann to be much of a help to him and that Mr. Hunter was still ill.[23]

Since Crampton lacked specific instructions as to the American coastal fisheries and felt obliged to insist upon the three *sine qua nons,* Marcy decided to prepare a full-blown *projet* for him to send on to London. By September 1, he had it ready. He had also drawn up a long explanatory memorandum which accompanied it. His *projet* began with the London proposals of January, but made vital changes. Taking it as settled that the inshore fisheries of both powers on the Atlantic would be available to each side, he threw in Newfoundland also. He further proposed, as he had at Berkeley Springs, that Florida be exempted, because the slaveholders would dislike having free negro fishermen come to their coasts from the Bahamas. He pointed out that Florida's vote in the senate might easily block the whole

---

[23] To Wetmore, Aug. 17, M.P.; Everett to Hunter (on Mann), May 26, Everett Letterbooks, M.H.S.

treaty. On the other hand, he suggested that all of the Pacific shores of both countries be included, reasoning to himself that the American people there would doubtless exceed the British.[24] He held that the cod bounty must be kept, since it had been started to countervail the United States tariff on salt and since the elimination of that duty was not feasible. As to registry and the opening of the coastal trade between America's Atlantic and Pacific seaboards, which Britain had also desired, he said that public opinion was not ready for the first and that only a constitutional amendment could open a part of the second without opening all of it, which was not expected or to be expected. And in regard to the free list, he said that he had granted all he could. If Britain was too insistent, he might want to strike out furs, he hinted, a step with which Canada would be displeased. He also demanded the use of the St. John River and the right to a duty-free passage of lumber *via* that stream.[25]

In short, Marcy had laid down a stiff program, not granting even one of Britain's three indispensable items.[26] As to his readiness to allow the provincials in American coastal waters, by the way, this was not a great concession, for shellfish were ruled out anyhow. Just as with the isthmian instructions, he played the game close to his chest, leaving himself room for bargaining later. He had incidentally reclaimed part of the ground which Secretary Everett had been on the verge of giving up.

At the same time, seeing that the desires of the British provinces were varied and conflicting, he and the president determined to send Israel Andrews to them as a special agent. Andrews was ordered to confer with their chief men, divulging Marcy's proposals when it was discreet to do so. This was all well and good, but there was also an objectionable part of the arrangements. Andrews was given funds to disburse for the shaping to opinion in the provinces and was told that vouchers would only be required "for such expenditures as [would] admit of them."[27] Marcy and more particularly the president had thus decided, cynically, to take advantage of human frailty in approaching

---

[24] Cf. Everett to Marcy, Aug. 15, cited above.
[25] Note to Crampton, Sept. 1, and *projet, Can. Rels.,* 71-80 and 71n.
[26] Everett's letter, Aug. 15, approved a concession on coal.
[27] Marcy to Andrews, Sept. 12, *Can. Rels.,* 81-83.

the provincial leaders.[28] It was a sorry decision. As evidence for the year 1854 will show, Marcy did not approve of this course and in all probability Andrews was the suggester of it. But Marcy did not prevent it.

It transpired that the draft treaty found a poor reception in London. Lord Clarendon told Buchanan that too much had been asked. Marcy waited patiently, supposing that the matter was being discussed with the provincials by the British colonial office. Also, however, if press statements were a proper sign, he began to dally with the idea of giving in on the subject of registry.[29] It must be added that Buchanan, for his part, was doing no better with the isthmus. Lord Clarendon made encouraging remarks on the subject and was always amiable in discussing it, but, as with the reciprocity items, he did not in the remainder of 1853 ever get around to study it out. Not a man of exceptional ability, he was already preoccupied with a rising threat of war between Britain and Russia over the Balkans and the Dardanelles.[30]

The failure for the time being to make any headway was certainly not Marcy's fault. He had stated the American position clearly and firmly and, with one exception, without rancor, on both the Central American and the North American problems. On each, also, he had put his country where it would be able to make some concessions without yielding the heart of the matter. If he had been slow to grasp all of the details of these difficult problems, as Buchanan charged,[31] he had come to master them completely before he was through. His exhausting labors over British affairs in the steaming summer of this year had therefore not been wasted.

---

[28] Andrews' reports of the disbursements were always kept in the Pierce Papers (*passim*, 1853-1854). Cf. also the document headed "Payments, out of the fund for Contingent Expenses of Foreign Inter-course, settled on the Certificate of the President," covering the years 1826-1852, which attests to Pierce's reflection upon the matter and his search for precedents, Pierce Papers, 1852 (n.d.).

[29] Buchanan to Marcy, Nov. 1, Marcy to Buchanan, Mar. 11, *Can. Rels.*, 532-533; 84-87; *Herald*, Nov. 29; *Times*, Nov. 30.

[30] Buchanan to Marcy, Sept. 22, Nov. 1, 12, Manning VII, 503-517; J. A. Thomas to Marcy, Oct. 21, M.P.

[31] Buchanan's memorandum on his appointment, cited above.

XXI. THOUGHTS OF EXPANSION

> "The Antilles flower—
>   The true *Key of the Gulf*
> Must be plucked from the crown
>   Of the Old Spanish Wolf"[1]

DURING July of the uncomfortable summer of 1853, although spending a good deal of time on the fisheries problem, Marcy also drafted the basic instructions for the American envoys to Mexico and Spain. These were difficult items to handle, because each of them involved a thought of territorial acquisition, a matter of much interest to the president. They were doubly difficult, however, because Marcy was surrounded by such unreliable counselors as Dudley Mann, whose head was buzzing with plans for Cuba,[2] and Caleb Cushing and the president himself. Marcy was alone during the period, incidentally, for his wife and Nelly had left for the north on June 30 and Edmund had gone on an ocean voyage. He played an occasional game of whist, but generally the heat simply forced him to devote his leisure time, if he can be said to have had any, to resting.[3]

Putting the topic of expansion aside for the present, one of the most difficult problems regarding Mexico was the transit route to the Pacific by way of the isthmus of Tehuántepec. The trouble was that concessions for the purpose, of a mutually exclusive character, were held by two rival groups of capitalists and both groups were American. The older one, the Garay grant, had been the subject of a convention which the state department had made with the Mexican foreign office, but the Mexican government had since repudiated it altogether, fearing that certain of its features would cause settlement there by Americans. The second grant, which did not have these clauses, had been made the month before Marcy came in. It was held by a man named Sloo. On March 21, moreover, the Whig minister of the United

---

[1] Transparency at the send-off to Pierre Soulé, *Tribune,* Aug. 6, in *Union,* Aug. 9.
[2] Mann to Marcy, Sept. 4, 1854, M.P.
[3] Marcy to Samuel, June 18, July 17; Samuel to Marcy, June 17; Marcy to Wetmore, Aug. 17, M.P.; Nichols, 285.

States, Mr. Conkling, had made a treaty by which his government and Mexico's were jointly to protect it. This had been done without authorization from Washington.

While the Garay and Sloo affairs were of interest chiefly to some busy lobbyists, the other Mexican difficulties were in several cases of much concern to Americans at large. These included a disagreement as to where the existing border should run and also—and related to that—a desire to locate the whole border farther south. The latter arose largely out of a wish to provide a good railway route to the Pacific. By the treaty of 1848, the boundary was said to lie along the southern limits of the Mexican state of New Mexico, then up its western margin to the first branch of the Gila River, and then down that stream to the Colorado, after which it went to the Pacific *via* the southern boundary of Upper California (the present state of California). The treaty stated that Disturnell's map of 1847 was the correct one for New Mexico's boundaries. But when the officials of the two countries met to examine the line they found that the map was incorrectly drawn and hence in conflict with certain other provisions of the treaty. The portion in dispute was a strip thirty miles wide in the Mesilla Valley. As it happened, this territory was regarded by many as containing the best route for the proposed railway. In consequence, there had been a deadlock, with the United States congress demanding the Mesilla but Mexico unwilling to yield it. There was also the further problem that this strip, if secured, would not quite do for the railroad but would in turn make it necessary to obtain a second piece. One other item remains to be told about. Under Article XI of the 1848 agreement, the United States was pledged to keep the Indians in the newly acquired lands from invading Mexico, or else to punish them and to obtain "satisfaction" from them. Mexico had, in fact, suffered severely from the inroads of these tribes. As a result, she had begun to make huge claims for damages. To this, the United States had answered that it had no financial responsibility in the matter, once it had done its best to keep order; but the government was quite ready to pay a large lump sum to get out of the article, lest such claims continue. The Mexican leaders knew this and were setting the price high. They were beginning to say that twelve or even twenty millions would be asked.

The immediate cause for haste, however, was the Mesilla dispute. The inhabitants of the area believed that they were now in the United States, but Mexican officials in Chihuahua had taken formal possession of it. This had caused William C. Lane, the governor of the territory of New Mexico, to announce that the region was under his jurisdiction. This had been on March 13. What was more, both he and Santa Anna (who had recently returned to the presidency of Mexico) had ordered in troops. Fortunately, neither order had been carried into effect, or there might have been war under way.[4]

Marcy's first step in the matter was to write to Conkling, on May 18, rebuking him for an official statement which he had made to the effect that Lane's course had been rash. Marcy held that Lane had been right in laying claim to the valley, although he admitted that to have taken physical possession would have been wrong.[5] The American object in avoiding an outright conflict there, of course, was to obviate getting Mexico's back up, since more land than that was wanted anyhow. The appointment of Gadsden, which was made at about the same time, evidenced this. For while Gadsden was appointed to secure a tract for a southern Pacific railroad, he also desired personally that a "natural" boundary be secured, such as at a mountain divide between two river basins.[6] This would mean much more than a mere adjustment of the boundary.

In the instructions to Gadsden, which were ready on July 15,[7] Marcy conceded that it might be no simple matter to get a proper pact with Mexico, because of the wounds which the recent war had inflicted upon her pride. He also thought it best to leave the Tehuántepec transit out entirely for the present, although he hinted that in the long run the United States might not uphold either of the claims anyway. As a matter of fact, he did not consider either of them very good.[8] As to the issue of a boundary, he was clearer. He not only upheld the Mesilla claim but pointed out that the 1848 treaty had authorized either country to build a railroad along the Gila River or as

---

[4] Hunter Miller, *op. cit.*, V, 213-216, 219-220, 419-420, VI, 307-309, 310-314; A. Conkling, Mar. 29, and A. B. Gray, Apr. 27, 1853, both to Marcy, M.P.; Paul N. Garber, *The Gadsden Treaty*, 16-17, 22, 70-73.

[5] Manning IX, 131-133.

[6] Garber, 81.

[7] Manning IX, 134-144.

[8] Cf. Crampton to Clarendon, Sept. 5, F.O. 5.

much as a league to the north or south of it; he argued that this last called for permitting some leeway in the matter anyhow. The land near the Gila had proved unsuitable, he said, so it would be necessary to go farther than a league south in any event. This problem of a railway line, it must be added, was a serious one to the administration, which had already come out in favor of federal support for a transcontinental railroad and had despatched army engineers to survey a number of suggested routes.

To come more to the point, Marcy held that the southern boundary of New Mexico should be run farther west than in the treaty and should then dip down to about the thirtieth parallel and proceed along such a line to the Gulf of California. Or, failing this, Gadsden should at least advance the frontier to the line of the San Pedro River and the Gila. The "sole object," said Marcy, was to win "an eligible route for a railroad." Finally, in the matter of the Indians, he cited the language of the treaty, that the United States must restrain them "in the same way, and with equal diligence and energy," as if they had tried to attack the American people, and said that that was all the United States was obligated to do. The government tried to do this, he went on, keeping large forces there while Mexico had left the frontier almost unwatched. All the same, it wanted to be released from Article XI. He consequently told Gadsden to offer a sizeable sum[9] for a settlement of all of the problems, including the minimum boundary. If, on the other hand, the larger area could be had, the amount would be increased. According to a newspaper account, by the way, Gadsden had tried to secure *carte blanche* powers to deal with Mexico, but Marcy had blocked this.[10]

A week later, Marcy had ready the first directive for Pierre Soulé, the new envoy to Madrid. This dealt chiefly with Cuba, the "pearl of the Antilles," and was therefore the first instruction relating to possible expansion into a wholly new area.

As has been said, that rather dusky and bloodshot "pearl" had figured importantly in the campaign of 1852. As far as that went, Presi-

---

[9] The amount has been disputed, because Marcy merely said he should offer for the whole what Letcher had been authorized to offer *re* Article XI and the latter sum had been left blank; as Hunter recalled, however, it was $3,000,000; Hunter Miller, *op. cit.*, VI, 309.

[10] *Times*, July 4.

dent Polk had offered $100,000,000 to Spain for it when Marcy had been in the cabinet in 1848. This had been refused. Then, during the Whig regimes which followed, there had been three successive efforts, one each year, by American filibusters who had planned invasions of the island in the hope of arousing the Cubans to revolt. The Whig presidents had endeavored to stop such moves, but when the participants or their accessories had been tried by American juries the latter had refused to convict them. Each attempt had failed, however. What had been accomplished was merely to arouse the Spanish people to a more stubborn determination not to give Cuba up. Beyond this, the governments of Britain and France had also been highly displeased. Both had sent naval vessels to Cuban waters to help intercept any further invasions. This had alarmed the Fillmore administration and caused it to tell the two powers that the United States would never consent to a transfer of the island to either of them; it had also led to a rejection of an Anglo-French proposal that the United States join with them in a declaration denying any wish to secure it. A statement that his government could not accept this plan had been made by Everett on December 1. He had remarked that the United States did not seek to secure the island, but would none the less look with disfavor upon any European power's doing so, for Cuba was "merely an American question." And, he added, his country would doubtless continue to expand. In turn, Lord John Russell, the British foreign secretary, had written a none too good-tempered reply. This in its train had touched off a series of heated responses in the senate, mainly by the Democrats. Lewis Cass had spoken in avowedly expansionist terms, for example, while Pierre Soulé had told the world at large that any thought of purchase was obsolete, which was true enough, and had hinted that outright seizure was the only course.[11]

Relations with Britain in the Cuban affair were made all the worse, moreover, by that country's continued efforts to end the slave trade upon the high seas. For one thing, she had secured a treaty from Spain allowing her to search Spanish vessels thought to be slavers. This had often led to the stopping of American ships by mistake, a notably sore point in the United States. Marcy had written a strong

[11] St. George L. Sioussat, "James Buchanan," M. W. Williams, "John Middleton Clayton," C. A. Duniway, "Daniel Webster," Foster Stearns, "Edward Everett," all in Bemis, V, 299-300, VI, 37-38, 104-107, 126-133; Ettinger, 87-100.

protest in one such affair as early as April 18.[12] There was also the fear that Britain might persuade Spain to free the slaves already in Cuba. This was a terrible bogey to the South, for it could produce the rise of a negro republic comparable to that in Haiti, which would offer a perilously contagious example to the slaves in the American cotton belt. Allied to this were the worries that further Cuban imports of negroes, of which there continued to be many under one subterfuge or another, or the possible arming of the blacks there in case of a war with the United States, might inadvertently bring the same result anyhow. Such anxiety over "Africanization" was no light matter to the "slavocracy."[13]

When the replies of France and England to Everett's answer on the tripartite guarantee of Cuba had been read to Marcy on April 16, he had received them in an attentive and conciliatory manner. He had declared that very likely no further correspondence would be needed, but had promised to study the matter.[14] Shortly after, he had in all confidence sent Everett a copy of Russell's note, "trusting that you will regard our personal relations such as to make it entirely proper. . . ." Everett had been pleased and had gone so far as to write a long draft reply, very strong in tone, for Marcy's use.[15] This Marcy concluded to set aside, but its contents had some faint reflection in a part of the aforementioned instructions to Buchanan of July 2.

In the latter, Marcy said of the Anglo-French replies that they included "a distinct intimation" that the two powers would resist a transfer of Cuba to the United States or else help Spain if there was "foreign" interference to aid a Cuban revolt. He added that their sending of warships to those waters had been "(to use the mildest expression,) not respectful to this Republic." Both countries, he added, had evinced a suspicion of an American design to "detach" (note that word) the island from its owner and appropriate it, without regard to Spain or to internationl law.

There is nothing in the history of our past course as a nation to justify such unworthy suspicions. It is true we have in the last half century greatly enlarged our territories; and so have Great Britain and France enlarged

---

[12] Marcy to Ingersoll, M.P.

[13] *Times*, in *Union* of June 3; *Union*, June 21; Ettinger, 21.

[14] F.O. 5, Apr. 18.

[15] Marcy to Everett, Apr. 19, and Everett's reply, addressed to Ingersoll, May, M.P.

theirs; but we have done it in a manner that may proudly challenge the most rigid scrutiny of mankind. In our territorial expansion international law has been observed; the rights of others rigorously respected; nothing in short has been done to justify the slightest suspicion of rapacity . . . every acquisition we have made has been obtained by an equivalent voluntarily accepted.

These sweeping statements had almost the tone of Everett's draft note. He went on to repeat the substance of the latter's no-transfer pronouncement of the year before and said further that the United States would regret to see outside aid given to Spain to preserve her rule. On the subject of "Africanization" of Cuba, he argued that if Britain was seeking the introduction of further negroes under the guise of "apprenticeship," she was pursuing a policy which would probably be little better than slavery and could be harmful to American interests. He therefore told Buchanan to try to discover her intentions. "If Cuba . . . enjoyed the political rights which have wisely been granted to Canada and other favored provinces," he added parenthetically, "if restrictions upon her foreign trade were relaxed our Government would be much less embarrassed in maintaining our neutral relations with Spain—and speculations upon the future destiny of Cuba" would cease to be a matter of much interest. He did point out, however, that the United States had early stopped all importations of slaves, but that while Cuba was under her present mistress the importations there would probably continue.[16]

Marcy's first step in instructing Soulé came on July 20, when he turned over to the new envoy Secretary Everett's plan of months earlier that a general commercial treaty be negotiated. This also looked to Spain's perhaps authorizing the American consul at Havana to "exercise some of the powers of a diplomatic agent" with the captain-general of Cuba. The idea therein was to facilitate the handling of local complaints (such as the stopping of American vessels) quickly and on the spot, obviating long and possibly angry exchanges with Madrid. As Everett had remarked, this would be quite in keeping with the almost vice-regal power which the captain-general already had.[17]

---

[16] Manning VII, 92-95.
[17] Everett to Calderon de la Barca, February 5, Manning XI, 150-152; Marcy to Soulé, July 20, Instru. Sp.

Marcy's own first directive to Soulé, who was in the capital and conferring with him,[18] came on July 20.[19] His instruction repeated much
of what he had said to Buchanan. He also reiterated in essence what
the Whigs had said, that for the big powers to help Spain as to Cuba
would be dangerously like their having a protectorate. "We have recently learned in the instance of Central America, what a protectorate
means, and to what uses it may be devoted," he said pointedly. As
for the United States, he promised, it would continue to be neutral so
long as Spain was in fact as well as in title the ruler of Cuba. Spain
should keep in mind, however, he told Soulé, that Americans tended
always to sympathize with those who rebelled against oppression and
that some enthusiastic spirits would always want to help them; besides
that, there were many natives of Cuba in the United States, many of
whom would have the same desire. Referring then to the suspicion
that the American people wanted to annex Cuba, he urged Soulé to do
what he could to allay such a feeling and to inspire confidence in "our
fair intentions." As to the previous effort to purchase the island, he
said that under certain conditions the government might be ready to,
"but it [was] scarcely to be expected" that Soulé would find Spain
prepared to sell, especially since she was thought to have promised
not to.

In the present aspect of the case the President does not deem it proper to
authorize you to make any proposition for the purchase of that island.
There is now no hope, as he believes, that such a proposition would be
favorably received, and the offer of it might, and probably would, be
attended with injurious effects.

Soulé was discreetly to explore, however, the relations of Spain with
the two big powers on the matter of Cuba and was told that future
American policy might be governed by his findings.

Marcy said further of Spain that "She cannot but see that at no
distant period Cuba will release itself, or be released from its present
colonial subjection." That being the case, Spain might as well be ready
to anticipate the inevitable.

If Cuba could be emancipated from a European domination, the United
States would probably be relieved from all the anxieties they now feel in

---

[18] *Times*, July 12.
[19] Instr. Sp.

regard to its future destiny. It would in that case fall necessarily into the American Continental system, and contribute to its stability, instead of exposing it to danger.

Soulé was to urge this step, if a suitable occasion offered. At the same time, he was to "take special care not to excite suspicions of sinister views on the part of this government nor to wound the sensibility of an ancient and proud nation." Under the right conditions, Marcy added, the United States would in fact be willing to contribute "something more substantial than [its] good will" towards so desirable an object. As with Gadsden, he hopefully cautioned Soulé to be discreet. Perhaps he also told him personally what he told John Y. Mason, who was to go to France, that his method should be to "pulse" the government to which he was accredited.[20]

All in all, Marcy had written the instruction in his own conservative style. This was a triumph for his policy. It is also very interesting, because there was planning secretly going on even at that very moment for a new filibustering effort. General John A. Quitman, who was to be its leader, was in Washington during the month and talked with Soulé, as apparently he also did with Attorney General Cushing, his cabinet friends. What is more, he is said to have received assurances from some administration leaders, and presumably this meant Cushing, that the federal government would not prevent the carrying out of the scheme. It is significant that his correspondence makes no mention of Marcy.[21] Obviously Marcy knew nothing of the plan, despite his talks with Soulé. The only reflection of the latter's influence in the instructions, indeed, was the statement in them that purchase was no longer feasible. In the light of the double game that Soulé was playing, it is amusing to consider how far his thinking and Marcy's diverged after that common point! While in Washington, Soulé also requested secret service funds for his mission, but was denied them.[22] This, likewise, was probably Marcy's doing.

As has been stated before, Marcy was not an expansionist as such. He was also not particularly eager for us to acquire Cuba,[23] even on the most honorable basis. Nor was he in favor of island acquisitions

[20] Mason to Buchanan, Mar. 5, 1854, B.P.
[21] Basil Rauch, *American Interest in Cuba: 1848-1855*, 266-273.
[22] Soulé to Marcy, Dec. 23, Manning XI, 733.
[23] Cf. A. H. Stephens to R. S. Burch, June 15, 1854, *Amer. Hist. Rev.*, VIII, 97.

in general. As he more than once told Crampton, he was against spending money for the large navy which their possession would require; he
believed that the cost of retaining them would be more than they were
worth.[24]

With the basic instructions completed, as most of them were by the
end of August, Marcy must have felt a deep satisfaction. Whereas he
had lost the first round in his battle for a wise handling of diplomatic
affairs, in the preference which Pierce had given to Young Americans
as diplomats, he had plainly won the second. Despite the gauntlet of
cabinet discussion which his leading state papers usually had to run,
he had managed to secure conservative directives. He had obtained the
adoption of a wait-and-see policy as to Cuba and one of only modest
territorial goals as to Mexico. Similarly, he had secured decisions as
to Great Britain which were marked by reason as much as by firmness.
As will be apparent with the Hawaiian Islands, which will be dealt
with in a separate chapter, and in general with the far-flung program
of fostering trade, which will also be taken up later, his moderate
attitude had been triumphant in those connections also. Thus far, he
had held Franklin Pierce rather firmly to the mark. To any contemporary who had access to the documents, it must have seemed clear
enough at the end of the summer of 1853, at least, that the con-
ductor of American foreign affairs would be William L. Marcy.

*   *   *

The most notable development as to Mexico and Cuba in the
remainder of 1853, it is true, did mark a divergence from this program. This was the sending on October 22 of new orders to Gadsden
at Mexico City. Inherently the product of Gadsden himself and of his
cabinet patron, Jefferson Davis,[25] they called for a "natural boundary"
in all earnest. The president was willing to pay up to $50,000,000 for a
huge new strip of land which would embrace roughly the southern half
of the Rio Grande Valley and a belt of about equal width from there to
the Gulf of California, plus all of Lower California. For this same
payment the United States would also expect to get out of Article XI

---

[24] F.O. 5, July 30, 1855 (citing earlier talks).

[25] Such is the logical conclusion, in the light of Marcy's favoring the treaty of
Guadalupe Hidalgo in 1848 rather than the acquisition of all of Mexico, the lack of
many documents on Mexico in his personal papers, and Gadsden's own interest in a
natural boundary (see above, and also his to Marcy, Sept. 5, Manning IX, 607-609).

of the 1848 treaty and the claims under it. There were also lesser lines proposed, such as the thirty-first parallel. The new orders, which were highly secret, were written after the receipt of Gadsden's news that Santa Anna was especially in need of funds. Before Gadsden received the orders, however, he was already pressing for approximately the watershed boundary just cited.[26] It seemed very likely, incidentally, that whatever negotiations there were would be made difficult by an incursion which one William Walker had started that autumn in Sonora and Lower California. Walker had with him a party of roughnecks from the gold fields and was out to conquer, or, as he blandly put it, to "liberate" that area.[27]

As to Cuba, the latter part of the year saw the issuance of a public reply by Everett to Lord John Russell, in place of the official one he had written for Marcy. Marcy dissociated himself from it, however, when talking with Crampton, "winking expressively, and laughing, very heartily." This was perhaps expedient, although rather surprising in view of his private letter of appreciation to the author.[28] On the subject of Africanization he was also cautious. He long disregarded the rumors of British action on that subject, as well as the inflammatory articles which the *Union* was printing.[29] Not until October 26 did he begin to question Clayton, the United States consul at Havana, as to the truth of the matter.[30] As for Soulé, his departure from New York was ominous, for it publicized the hopes of his friends for Cuban annexation.[31] Spain soon replied by appointing as her foreign minister a man versed in American ways, namely Calderon de la Barca, until then her minister to Washington. She was girding herself for a contest.[32] Soulé reached Madrid too late, however, for anything much to happen there before the year's end.

---

[26] Manning IX, 145-148, 600-601, 607-609, 617-619.
[27] Lawrence Greene, *The Filibuster*, 30-38.
[28] Everett to Marcy, Aug. 29, Sept. 26, Everett Letterbooks; F.O. 5, Oct. 3.
[29] Cf. *Union* of Aug. 20; *Times*, Oct. 15.
[30] Marcy to Clayton, Oct. 26, Manning XI, 166-167.
[31] *Union*, July 28; *Tribune*, Aug. 6, in *Union* of Aug. 9.
[32] Ettinger, 205.

XXII. THE KOSZTA NOTE

"His [Marcy's] State paper on the Koszta affair is one of the most profound arguments ever presented to the American people. It created a wonderful sensation in Europe, but no crowned head could find a man competent to reach his unanswerable logic." (George W. Bungay, 1854[1])

THE AUTUMN of 1853, as has been indicated, was largely a time of awaiting the next steps in the negotiations which had been begun. Since Marcy had put the Canadian reciprocity affair into shape and had secured instructions of the right sort for the chief ministers, it should have been a period of relative relaxation and even of happiness. But this was not to be the case. On August 21 there had come the news that his dear son Edmund had died. When Edmund had gone to sea, on the last day of June, it had been as a guest on the naval academy's practice ship *Preble,* of which Samuel was the sailing master. Far from proving beneficial to his health, however, the sea air had been harmful. He had died within five days. This was a cruel blow to his father, who doted upon him. Writing to Wetmore on August 27, Marcy explained that "Though I was hopeless as to his recovery, I did expect he would be longer spared to us." Even months after, he said sadly that "all things [were] passing away." Unfortunately, too, he was alone during these months, for Mrs. Marcy decided that she would stay in New York until their home was about ready.[2] This was to be in a house which Corcoran, the banker, had generously offered to build and rent to them. The site was on Vermont Avenue, a few blocks from the department.[3]

Under these bleak circumstances, it was well that there was maturing one of the occasions for pamphleteering which Marcy so much

---

[1] *Off-hand Takings, or Crayon Sketches of the Noticeable Men of Our Age,* 347.
[2] *Times,* Aug. 22; Marcy to Samuel, June 18, July 17, to Wetmore, Aug. 27, to J. Pierson, Nov. 24, M.P.; to Buchanan, Dec. 4, B.P.; Mann to G. T. Poussin, Aug. 23, Poussin Papers, L.C.
[3] Marcy to Samuel, July 17; insurance policy on the furniture, Feb. 14, 1854, filed under Feb. 14, 1855; both in M.P.

relished. The first facts in the case had been reported prior to his trip to Berkeley Springs. An Hungarian refugee, Martin Koszta, had come to the United States a few years earlier. Then, having gone to Turkey on private business, he had on June 21 been kidnapped at Smyrna by a band of ruffians hired by the Austrian representatives there and had been brutally beaten and tossed into the harbor, following which he had been put aboard an Austrian man-of-war to be returned to the jurisdiction from which he had once escaped. Early in August there had been additional reports. It transpired that the American consul at Constantinople and the acting American *chargé* had both protested in vain. The sequel to this was that the *chargé*, John P. Brown, had advised the captain of an American frigate which was present to interpose; that officer, Captain Ingraham, had placed his vessel (the *St. Louis*) between the Austrian warship and an Austrian packet on which it was intended to ship Koszta off, so that his transfer had been prevented. Ingraham had also given the Austrian commander three hours in which to release him. The Austrians had replied by yielding so far as to consent to Koszta's being placed in charge of the consul of France, pending an agreement between the home governments as to a final solution. Both upon his reaching Turkey, incidentally, and later, on the eve of his departure, he had applied to the American authorities for a *tezkereh* or recognition paper, which had been given to him.[4] Under Turkish practice, this supposedly accorded him United States protection.

On the morning after Marcy's return from Berkeley Springs and while he was having breakfast, the Russian minister had called to protest at the roles of the American agents in the affair. The minister had been deeply irked by an article which had just come out in the *Union* endorsing Commander Ingraham's conduct. Marcy had replied in his usual moderate tone, that, for himself, he approved of the piece; he might well have added that all of the American people would, if

[4] *Union*, Aug. 7; Mann to E. S. Offley, the U.S. consul at Smyrna, Aug. 6; Marcy to Offley, Aug. 13, *HED91*, 33rd cong., 1st sess., 78. For the official accounts, see John Griffith to John P. Brown, June 24; Brown to the Internuncio, June 27; D. Bruck, the Austrian minister, to Brown, June 27; Brown to Marcy, July 5; Brown to Ingraham, June 28; Offley to Brown, June 30, July 4; Ingraham to the captain of the Austrian warship *Huszar* (n.d.); and George P. Marsh, American minister, to Marcy, July 7, all in *SED40*, 33rd cong., 1st sess.

they read it.[5] As it happened, the formal protest from the Austrian *chargé* did not come until August 29, about a week after the news of Edmund's death.

This note, from the Chevalier Hülsemann, asserted that the capture of Koszta was warranted under the extraterritorial rights which Austria had by treaty over her subjects there. Hülsemann also held that since Koszta had merely declared his intention to become an American citizen, he was as yet still an Austrian subject. He further stated that the man, as one of the refugees who had for a time dwelt in Kutayeh, in the Ottoman empire, had pledged upon leaving Turkey never to return to that country; his release to the French consul, it was added, had been merely temporary, to avoid bloodshed. It was also argued that since he had left Austria without securing permission, he had left illegally. Ingraham's course, moreover, said Hülsemann, had been in violation of international law, as "a threat of an act of war" in neutral territory. The United States, in fine, was asked to call its agents severely to account for their conduct and give satisfaction for what had happened.[6] It may be noted, incidentally, that Prussia and Russia had also protested at what had taken place;[7] the three great eastern European despotisms stood shoulder to shoulder in the affair.

Marcy's reply to Hülsemann, officially dated September 26 but not published until the 30th,[8] was exceedingly long. It stated, to begin with, that the departure of Koszta and the other Kutayeh refugees from Turkey was by an arrangement in which Austria herself took part and that agents of hers had helped to oversee the removal. In short, Austria had accepted the fact of their leaving Turkey, essentially as in lieu of their extradition to her own territory. By this step, Marcy held, she had in reality renounced all claim to them.[9] Indeed, Marcy held that their abandonment of Austrian citizenship by their flight across the frontiers after the collapse of the Hungarian revolt was fully proper,

[5] *Times,* Aug. 9, Sept. 11.

[6] *Correspondence between the Secretary of State and the Chargé d'Affaires of Austria relative to the Case of Martin Koszta,* Washington, 1853, pamphlet.

[7] Nesselrode to Marcy, Aug. 10, in Notes from Rus.; Vroom to Marcy, Nov. 21, Des. Prus.

[8] Text in *Correspondence,* cited above; *Union,* Sept. 30.

[9] This, like a number of the other key points in the note, was derived from the forceful letter of George P. Marsh, the United States minister to Constantinople, to Marcy on July 7, cited above.

as with similar behavior by any political refugees. The soundest view regarding the alienability of citizenship in such cases, he said, was that:

When the sovereign power, wheresoever it may be placed, does not answer the ends for which it is bestowed, when it is not exerted for the general welfare of the people, or has become oppressive to individuals, this right to withdraw rests on as firm a basis, and is similar in principle to the right which legitimates resistance to tyranny.

In such an event, he said, continuing in this patriotically American vein, those who left their native lands might very properly indeed seek out the foreign country which offered them "the fairest prospect of happiness."

While Koszta's declaration of his intention to become an American citizen had not given him the full civil rights of an American, Marcy went on, he was in some sense "clothed with an American nationality." This was by virtue of domicil. As to the international law on the subject, he continued:

It gives the national character of the country not only to native-born and naturalized citizens, but to all residents in it who are there with, or even without, an intention to become citizens, provided they have a domicil therein . . . whenever they acquire a domicil, international law at once impresses upon them the national character of the country of that domicil. If a person goes from this country abroad, with the nationality of the United States, this law enjoins upon other nations to respect him, in regard to protection, as an American citizen.

While it might be feared that this doctrine was too broad, there were actually some restrictions to it, Marcy indicated. For one thing, he said specifically, if political agitators thought that they could come to the United States to get a cover of American protection and then return home "to carry on . . . their ulterior designs with greater security," they were quite wrong. Such action on their part would in itself divest them of their newly acquired nationality, he said. The chief point to notice in this application which Marcy made of the doctrine of domicil, however, was that he really used it in connection with the granting of the *tezkerehs*, which he discussed immediately after. He demonstrated that these papers given to Koszta were fully in accord with Turkish usage and had not led to a protest by Austria. They had, thus, confirmed his right to American protection. It was the two features

taken together, domicil *and* the *tezkerehs,* Marcy implied, which determined the case.

Marcy pointed out, further, that Austria had never charged that the
refugee's trip had had any political meaning.[10] As to the conduct of
the American agents, Marcy said that there had been no protest by
Turkey over their action at any time. By contrast, Turkey had indeed
complained at the course taken by the Austrians. As for Commander
Ingraham's threat of violence to the Austrian brig, he said:

The government of the United States exceedingly regrets that he was
reduced to this painful alternative; but it cannot find, after a full consideration of all the circumstances, any good reasons for disapproving the
course he pursued.

Under those circumstances, in fact, that course had been "right and
proper," and the same was true of the acts of the other United States
agents in the affair. On the contrary, Marcy voiced a confident expectation that after a full survey of the case the emperor of Austria would
agree to Koszta's liberation.

It was an exceedingly able note. As Marcy had said in it at the outset, moreover, he had endeavored to write it in "a friendly spirit,"
avoiding topics to which the Austrian government could take exception. Except for the remarks as to "sovereign power . . . not exerted
for the general welfare of the people," he had done this—within the
limits of the case. He had clung to the facts and to reason all the way
through, in decided contrast to Webster's insulting course in his
parallel reply to Hülsemann in 1852. It may be added that Marcy
while secretary of state did not ever engage in insults while dealing
with a foreign power. Not only was the note correct in its tone, however, it was also sound in its law. If it has been criticized at times as
too sweeping in its interpretation of domicil, this has been unjust, for,
as has been pointed out, Marcy did not intend his interpretation to be
too broad.[11] As a matter of fact, only two months after, in a second
case, he re-emphasized his narrow view of the matter. This involved

[10] Marcy was mistaken in this; she had eventually (July 29) made such a charge,
but the evidence of the truth of it was inadequate; Marsh to Marcy, Aug. 4,
SED40, cited above.

[11] Cf. the discussions of the point by John Bassett Moore, *A Digest of International
Law,* III, 811-842 (espec. 811-812, 817), and by Edwin M. Borchard, *The Diplomatic Protection of Citizens Abroad,* 491 and 491n, 558, 570-574.

a person with a status like Koszta's, who had been extradited to
Prussia by one of the lesser German states. Marcy held simply that in
view of the fact that his return to his native land had been by a lawful
process, there was no recourse.[12]

The American public naturally gave the Koszta note an instant and
happy approval. People were already jubilant to think, in fact, that the
Austrian agents had considered it necessary to hire over a dozen ruffians to seize him in the first place, since he was only a half-naturalized
American at that! Not long after Marcy left Washington for
Edmund's funeral at Albany, Assistant Secretary Mann wrote enthusi-
astically to him that "There is no other subject talked of. . . ." General Thomas, moreover, called the note the greatest paper since the
start of diplomacy, while Edward Everett, a cooler head, also praised
it fulsomely. Everett commented in a letter to Pierce that before he
had read it he had thought the subject one of difficulty and embarrassment. The press of all parties was similarly enthusiastic.[13] The note
was much praised in Europe, also. Kossuth naturally liked it thoroughly, but even Lord Palmerston, no admirer of Americans, said grudg-
ingly: "very clever paper, very clever paper."[14]

What was better was that the affair itself turned out well. On
October 3, when Marcy was still at Albany, he received an unexpected
visit from Hülsemann. The latter brought the news that his government had assented to the freeing of Koszta, on the condition that he
return directly to this country. Allegedly, his liberation came because
the Hungarian crown jewels, whose location he was supposed to know,
had been already found.[15] Since the tidings of his release, by a fortunate accident, came just three days after the publication of the note,
they appeared to many unthinking persons to have been caused by it.
Of such accidents is a reputation often made.

In the interim, the political world had on the contrary been assuming a sad countenance. The policy of Pierce as to appointments, of
course, had been murderous to Marcy's position in New York. Marcy's

---

[12] This was the case of Henry D'Oench, extradited to Prussia by the government
of Hamburg, in which state he was visiting. (Moore, *op. cit.*, III, 837-838).

[13] Mann to Marcy, Oct. 1; Thomas, ditto, Sept. 30, M.P.; Everett to Marcy, Oct.
1, 3, and to Pierce, Oct. 14, Everett Letterbooks; *E. Post*, Oct. 8.

[14] Buchanan to Marcy, Nov. 18; Thomas to Marcy, Nov. 29, M.P.

[15] *Union*, Oct. 5, Oct. 8 (from *Nat. Intel.*).

own friends had been hurt at the decisions to favor all factions equally, while the Barnburners had been furious over the rather shabby conduct towards John A. Dix, who after having been considered for the state department had been rejected, and who had been half promised the mission to France but had not yet received it.[16]

It was with the Hards, however, that the real trouble lay. Their fury at Marcy's elevation kept them at almost a white heat; they were particularly wrought up at the idea that he might be the next president.[17] Marcy, on his side, wanted to appease them, lest the Democracy of the state be cut entirely in two. His plan was therefore to get the Barnburners to toe the line on the sectional issues, so as to disarm their critics. If resolutions on these matters were brought up in the legislature by the Hards, he wrote to Seymour on May 27, the former free-soilers must not be "impracticable," but must if necessary even endorse the fugitive slave law by name.[18] These were sound tactics. They did not work out, however. Although there were resolutions passed by the lower house in July which were acceptable in themselves, a considerable number of the Barnburners abstained from voting.[19] In any case, the Hards were not even close to being mollified. By the start of the summer, in fact, these "Adamantines" or "Adders" (a poisonous species!) were already organizing on their own, determined to come out candidly against Pierce and especially determined to break Marcy down. One of their staunch allies was Collector Bronson, at New York, who helped them with his large patronage. In spite of all this, Marcy was unable to convince the president of their disloyalty. Bronson and his sort were not removed.[20]

At summer's end, as Marcy came to have an occasional hour free for politics and could see more readily what was going on, he was much concerned. He noted that "the disappointees," i.e. members of his coalition who had wanted offices and had not received them, showed a leaning towards joining the Hards. Both, he said, were tending in addition to collude with the Whigs. His main concern was to keep the

---

[16] Nichols, 228.
[17] J. A. Thomas to Marcy, May 17, M.P.; H. S. Brent to Cushing, June 7, C.P.
[18] S.P.
[19] Seymour to Marcy, July 9, unsigned, *ibid.*; *Union*, July 6.
[20] Marcy to Seymour, May 18, S.P.; John Van Buren, May 21, Tilden, June 21, I. Butts, June 25, F. Wood, July 1, all to Marcy, M.P.

record straight. As he urged his friends in a number of communications sent out by September 7, the state convention must be sure to adopt a platform acceptable to the Hards, thus giving them one last chance. Then, if they still decided to "bolt," it would be plain as to where the guilt was.[21] In brief, that was all that was accomplished. The Hards did secede, putting up a ticket of their own. Then, shortly after, the collector and another Hard incumbent, the federal district attorney at New York, proclaimed in public letters their support of the bolters. As Marcy said later, in reference to Bronson, the chief culprit, "I went zealously for his decapitation." But Pierce continued to temporize, weakly ordering the collector to divide the places fairly among all of the factions.

The result was that by the time of Marcy's visit to Albany his friends there were almost in a panic; many of them had been persuaded that the president preferred their enemies. Marcy soon wrote a firm letter to Washington asking that the two chief Hardshells be ousted at once. Significantly, however, he sent it to Cushing, not Pierce. When he returned to the capital, on October 7, he used all of his influence upon the president, mincing no words, but it was still in vain. Pierce did not give in until the second half of October, when John Van Buren threatened that if the president did not comply he would come out against him in a speaking tour which he was about to start. Then, and then only, was Bronson displaced and Heman J. Redfield, Marcy's own choice for the post, put in. At Albany, at about the same time, the state canal board also began to remove the Hards—a step which Marcy had likewise counselled.[22]

Such efforts were useless. So, too, was the widespread distribution of Marcy's Koszta note as a campaign document.[23] The Whigs swept the state. What was worse, the Hards actually drew as good a poll as the coalition Democrats.

This dismaying outcome was in part, unquestionably, on the order

---

[21] Draft of letter to Dean Richmond, Aug. 29, also "copy" of it sent to Richmond & "several persons" before the convention, M.P. Also his letter to Tilden, Sept. 7, Tilden Papers, N.Y.P.L.

[22] Thomas, Sept. 13, Seymour, Oct. 24, 1853, Redfield, Mar. 14, 1857, to Marcy, M.P.; *Times,* Sept. 19 (edit.) ; Bronson and O'Conor letters, *Union,* Sept. 27; *Union,* Oct. 23; Marcy to Seymour, Nov. 4, S.P.; to Cushing, Oct. 1, C.P., to Tilden, Oct. 8, 16, Tilden Papers; Nichols, 287-288.

[23] 10,000 copies were printed; Newell to "Dear Betty," Oct. 18, M.P.

of a vague protest against a variety of things, such as the canal issues and federal patronage. More especially, however, the rank and file of the Barnburner group were quite cool towards the federal administration. This was to some degree because of the final rejection of Dix in September for the Paris mission, after a rather humiliating demand for letters by him showing that he was not an abolitionist. After the results of the balloting were known, Marcy affected a certain degree of indifference. He wrote to his friend Redfield, on November 14:

That I have many enemies I know nor did I ever flatter myself that I had much popularity with the masses; but . . . I am quite sure I never deserved their enmity. . . .

　　With the consciousness that I have served the dem. party faithfully, I shall not allow myself to be much disturbed if I should be convinced that my services are not appreciated as I think that they ought to be.

He added that he felt that he could stand "a ruder shock" than this, in any case. He was less sanguine as to the New York Democracy, he wrote later; he doubted, in fact, if he would live long enough to see the party regain its ascendancy there.[24]

　　On the other hand, as the year 1853 drew to its close, matters generally looked quite promising. The success of Marcy's warfare upon knee breeches, to date, and, even more, his triumphant Koszta note, had put him upon the highest peak nationally that he had so far occupied. Although the Hard schism had been a grave matter, he was not entirely cast down by that. He had tried before the election to woo over to his side one of the leading New York City members of the Hard faction, the wealthy Francis B. Cutting, hoping thus to break up the clique in its principal stronghold. In talks with Cutting, he had indicated that the latter might well assume in the years ahead the same role as the symbol of party reunion that he had himself done in 1849. He had, in fact, taken him onto a mountain top, "intimating that he could easily take my place[,] which I in any event must leave to some one very soon." Although he had not succeeded at the time, a mutual friend was still working along that line.[25] In any case, there was a subject of rejoicing in the fact that the conservative element in the

---

[24] Nichols, 286-287, 292; J. G. Dickie to Marcy, Dec. 25, M.P.; F. P. Blair to Martin Van Buren, Nov. 27, V.B.P.; Marcy to Redfield, Nov. 14, to Chas. G. A. Nun, Jan. 24, M.P.

[25] Marcy to Wetmore, Nov. 4, Royal Phelps to Marcy, Nov. 28, *ibid.*

Democracy had won out everywhere in the North,[26] to say nothing of the fact that outside of New York state the party had been sweepingly successful.[27] In the foreign sphere, moreover, Marcy had managed to outmaneuver the *filibusteros*. He could thus be fairly confident of keeping the administration upon an even keel. All in all, he faced the opening of the regular session of congress with his usual equanimity, especially after the Democrats' first caucus, which was very successful. The new year promised well.[28]

* * *

Although Marcy did not attend the gathering of the party faithful at the Jackson Day dinner at Washington, January 9, he was not forgotten. The toast to his name was a humorous one, containing references both to his one-time feud with Scott and to the recent tussle with the Hards.[29]

The Secretary of State: The gratitude of a generous people for past services will ever protect his *rear*, and may the Lord have *Marcy* on an enemy who has the *hardihood* to assail him in front!

---

[26] Cf. the *Journal's* ironic query of Sept. 17: "Have we a Democratic Free Soiler among us?"; also *Union*, Jan. 5.

[27] Nichols, 291-292.

[28] Marcy to Buchanan, Dec. 4, B.P.

[29] *Union*, Jan. 12.

XXIII. PANDORA'S BOX

". . . this Pandora's box—the Nebraska question. . . ."
(Marcy to Horatio Seymour, February 11, 1854[1])

T HE COMPARATIVE calm which prevailed at the close of 1853
was very thoroughly disturbed in January of the new year. This
was done first, and only briefly, by the Hards, and then, lastingly, by
a mischievous plan put forward by Stephen A. Douglas, the energetic
little senator from Illinois. Before the uproar which ensued had died
down, it may be foretold, many of Marcy's dreams for the administration would have been shattered. And before the last echoes had quieted,
indeed, Marcy was to have been long in his grave and a civil war
would have been fought.

The Hards' move began on January 3, when Francis B. Cutting himself proposed in the house of representatives that a call be made upon
the secretary of the treasury for the letters which he and Collector
Bronson had written to each other.[2] It was plainly a step to open an
attack upon Marcy and the president. Just as plainly, it showed that
the wooing of Cutting had been a thorough and complete failure. As
that faction's organ, the *Albany Argus,* made clear ten days later, the
chief target was the secretary of state. The whole list of happenings of
the past fall, added the *Argus* unpleasantly, was on account of "*the
envious malice and unsated ambition of the ingrate who fills the highest seat among the councillors* [sic] *of the President.*"[3]

The main onslaught at Washington came just after the middle of
the month. At this time, Mike Walsh, another New York City congressman, led off with a violent attack in the house upon Marcy and
also upon Pierce. Cutting followed him. The main burden of their
argument was that the administration had the support of the ex-
freesoilers and allegedly had rewarded them handsomely with office.

---

[1] S.P.
[2] *Union,* Jan. 5, 1854.
[3] *Argus,* Jan. 13, in *Atlas* of Jan. 14.

As a matter of fact, this last was simply not true.[4] As for Marcy's friends, the Softs, they were indicted also; they were castigated for having, like their allies, supported him for a presidential nomination. It was really all akin to the type of attack made upon Marcy in the recent campaign, to the effect that he (as Dickinson had put it) was a "political mendicant . . . wanting principle, and wanting consequence . . . realizing . . . that . . . 'fogyism' could no longer count upon a monopoly of official honors and emoluments," who had hence sold his soul to the Van Burenites in order to regain office. The Softs replied by attacking the Hards for, among other things, having deserted the party in 1837 and 1838 (as some had done) and for thus producing a Whig victory. Since then, they said, the Hards had hoped that Marcy was "dead" and had considered it Pierce's greatest fault "that Marcy will not stay dead." The Softs also pointed out that Cutting had taken part in the 1849 reunion. The offensive of the Hards looked serious, especially when it was backed up by the general committee of the party at New York City. There was a danger that the Hards might, moreover, get southern friends to block the confirmation of Redfield as collector, thus disturbing the whole patronage pattern once more. Marcy was worried lest this take place.[5]

What occurred instead was that the issue was brushed aside by the plan of Douglas. This was in the form of a bill to open to slavery the huge territory of Nebraska, which lay wholly north of the Missouri Compromise line. Douglas's proposal was put forward under the guise of a mere extension of the alleged principle of the settlement of 1850, which, referring to a region south of the line, had at bottom left the issue of slavery to be decided by the first comers; he did not urge an outright repeal of the Missouri Compromise. His bill was brought in from his committee on territories on January 4.[6]

The motives of Douglas have often been argued about. An im-

[4] The *Union*, Nov. 10, 1853, said that of 41 principal postmasterships, the Barnburners had received ten; it cited a *Times* statement that of 35 treasury appointments in the state, that faction had had nine.

[5] *Times*, Jan. 18, 20; speeches of Perkins and Westbrook, *Atlas*, Feb. 14, 15; Marcy to Redfield, Dec. 13, M.P.

[6] It was a modified version of one first introduced by Dodge (P. O. Ray, *The Repeal of the Missouri Compromise*, 195, 205). In its original form, the bill did not refer to the alleged principles of 1850, but an accompanying report did. James Ford Rhodes, *History of the United States*, I, 425-428.

portant motive of his, certainly, was to get the Nebraska area open for settlement and thus for railroad building, partly with an eye to the profits which this would bring to his home city of Chicago, where he incidentally owned more than a little real estate. For one thing, his plan looked to the building of the much-talked-of Pacific railroad by a northern route. By contrast, as has been shown, the Pierce administration was seeking to obtain the Mesilla Valley and thus might be considered to be for a southern route. Since few men expected that more than one line would ever be put through, the decision as to where it would run was a critical matter. But Douglas's plan of applying "popular sovereignty" to Nebraska, thus giving slaveholders at least a chance there, was apparently meant to win the support of the South to his bill and away from the southern Pacific route.[7]

Many contemporaries, on the other hand, thought that his motive was different from that. As a presidential candidate in 1852, he had comparatively slight backing in the South and in the Northeast.[8] In the former section, the bill would win him friends. In the latter, it could overturn the regnant Pierce-Marcy-Cushing combination and bring his own adherents into a stronger position. These latter were chiefly Hards. As an alert politician who had been treated rather coldly by Pierce and company, he must have seen great advantages of this sort in the move. In particular, Marcy's coalition in New York might very easily be torn to shreds, for it was difficult to see how the Barnburners, those rebels of 1848, could swallow the pill. It was also difficult to see how President Pierce could oppose it, if the great leaders of the Northwest and of the South joined forces in its behalf. According to a *New York Daily Times* editorial of January 24:

> It is easy enough to detect the partisan purposes which lurk under this movement. Senator DOUGLAS is an aspirant for the Presidency. He is cunning, unscrupulous and desperate. He has brought forward this scheme, first, to strengthen himself with the pro-slavery interest in the Southern States; and second, to crowd Secretary MARCY, whose friends it is supposed will flinch from this test, out of his path for the nomination.

The Hards, added this paper, were doing their best to bring the trouble on. They hoped to expel the Softs from the government, or if

[7] Frank H. Hodder, "The Railroad Background of the Kansas-Nebraska Act," *Miss. Valley Hist. Rev.*, XII, 3-22.
[8] On the 33rd ballot, he had had 13 votes from the southern delegations, as against 20 from the northeast and 24 from the northwest, *Journal*, June 5, 1852.

that failed, to wreck the entire administration. Some of the old Barn-burners smelled the same rat. Judge Hammond concluded that the Hards, indeed, had been the real authors of the idea.[9] Prince John, in a letter to Marcy on February 12, was even more to the point:[10]

The Nebraska business was aimed mainly at you & incidentally at me. It is proper, therefore, that you should know my feelings, & views. While I was entirely opposed to your selection as a member of the Cabinet, I have uniformly said that you had dealt fairly & honorably by the radical Democracy, & had probably done them more service than Gen[l]. Dix could have done. . . . We shall oppose the Nebraska bill, & hope you will not urge our members to vote for it. But whatever you may do in this respect, so long as your conduct continues as fair towards us as it has been, we shall stand by you, & we want you to take any course on the Nebraska matter that you conscientiously can which will secure your remaining where you are.

Whatever Douglas's motives were, and undoubtedly his railroad plans were important among them, the going was not to be quite so easy as he may have expected. On January 16 Senator Dixon of Kentucky suggested an amendment explicitly repealing the Missouri Compromise ban; because of southern pressure, Douglas decided reluctantly to adopt this.[11] Meanwhile, in the administration, Marcy was urging the president to resist the bill. He was aided, moreover, by Senator Cass, who called upon Pierce for that purpose. As late as Friday, January 20, in fact, the *Union* was criticizing the Dixon plan. Then, on the Saturday, the cabinet came to a decision which was in essence a defeat for Marcy. It agreed to favor an alternative amendment, which said that the issue should be left to the supreme court to handle, subject to the provisions of the constitution and of "the acts giving governments," which obviously would include the Missouri Compromise itself. Thus the court would itself decide whether the latter was constitutional. On the other hand, the provision of the bill authorizing slavery in the area would be effective until such a decision was had. It is said that Pierce and Cushing were sure that the ruling would be unfavorable to the Missouri Compromise.[12] Perhaps Marcy hoped for just the opposite. Or perhaps he was merely fighting a delaying action. Judging that the administration would support some

---

[9] Hammond to Seward, Feb. 28, Seward Papers.
[10] M.P.
[11] Rhodes, *op. cit.*, I, 433-435.
[12] Nichols, 321-322.

version of the bill, however, he had already written to Newell to try to get the Albany *Atlas,* the Barnburner-Soft organ, to be noncommittal on it.[13]

Despite the strong current already in motion by that Saturday, the next day, Sunday, was a critical one in Marcy's career. He went off to take his dinner with a relative who lived in the city, unaware of the strength of the drive for the Dixon amendment by Douglas and the the southerners with whom Douglas was acting. That afternoon, Douglas and Secretary Davis went together to the White House to win Pierce over. They were accompanied by Senator Atchison of Missouri and by Hunter and James M. Mason, the two influential Virginia senators, plus two congressmen. Together, the group overpowered the president. The four senators were particularly irresistible, because (aside from Cass) they were the principal Democratic leaders in the upper house; as such, they could reject all appointments and also any of the treaties so much hoped for. Pierce resisted the less well, anyhow, because he considered that he had weakened his standing by proposing to appoint Dix and by actually appointing some other Barnburners. The recent attack by the Hards presumably also had some bearing upon his decision. Knowing Pierce's character, Douglas took the precaution of obtaining from him a commitment in writing on the main point involved. Its words, later copied in the amendment to the bill, stated that the Missouri restriction "is hereby declared inoperative and void." At the close of the conference, remembering well enough his secretary of state's views, Pierce asked his callers to visit Marcy and talk the matter over with him. This they tried to do, but he was absent. It was already too late, however.

As things worked out, Marcy did not hear of the amendment until the next day, at just about the hour at which Douglas introduced it in the senate in a substitute bill. The new measure, incidentally, called for dividing the area in question into two parts, Kansas and Nebraska. Marcy's friends in the house, the Softs, were at once alarmed. They held a conference to consider the problem, the upshot being a decision to question him and Pierce on it; for this purpose, Representative Reuben Fenton, of Chautauqua County, was selected. Fenton saw Pierce first and found him insistent that the bill be taken up; the

---

[13] Newell to Marcy, Jan. 23, M.P.

president argued excitedly that the Softs had been ready enough to receive their share of the patronage and must now in turn support this step. When Fenton saw Marcy, he stated how much he regretted that Marcy was for the bill, if he indeed was.

The Secretary seemed depressed, and remarked that if Mr. Fenton had made up his mind on the question it was idle for him to advise. He further stated that the proposition [popular sovereignty], as a fundamental principle, was Democratic, and that the only question was as to the application [of it] under the circumstances.

Marcy recounted how he had been absent when the delegation had called at his house the previous afternoon. He expressed his deep concern at the anger which the bill was sure to arouse and its likely consequences for the Democratic party. This undoubtedly was Marcy's true reaction: he probably could not take seriously the thought of slaves picking cotton on the plains of Kansas. He remarked only that "every person must judge of his duty for himself and walk in the light of his own convictions."

A few days later, still dubious and wanting some advice, he called in half a dozen of his personal friends in the delegation. He wanted to know, he said, if he should quit the cabinet. Most of those present replied that he should not. If he left, they reasoned, the Hards would come in, which it was held would be even more fatal to the Democratic party in the state and the union than the Hard secession had been. What they had in mind, naturally, was that the party split of 1848 would be renewed. Marcy accepted this advice, which was doubtless what he had wanted to hear.[14] As Ida Russell, house guest of the Marcys that spring, commented:[15]

He has so much trust in the New York managing policy & the idea that a great deal will come by getting up administration measures & then standing by them right or wrong. . . .

This was all too true. It should be recalled, however, that even John Van Buren, the Barnburner chief, advised him to stay.

None the less, Marcy did not press the Nebraska bill very strongly upon his friends or other associates. The most that he would say, often,

---

[14] Statement of Rep. Reuben Fenton, in Henry Wilson, *History of the Rise and Fall of the Slave Power*, II, 382-383; John Bigelow to F. P. Blair, n.d., Blair-Lee Papers, Princeton; Nichols, 322-323; Rhodes, *op. cit.*, I, 439.
[15] Ida Russell to Cushing, May 5, C.P.

when he did bring up the subject, was that *the president* expected them to sustain it. As a loyal friend of Pierce and a member of his cabinet, he felt that he could do no less; on the other hand, he at times simply avoided the subject.[16] In the ensuing battle for the control of public opinion, however, he did follow the administration line clearly in one respect. This was in regard to the newspapers. He wrote more than once to urge Newell and also Governor Seymour to try to keep the *Atlas* quiet upon the subject. Similarly, he was very cautious in performing his official duty to select papers to publish the laws in the various states. He wrote to Seymour that he supposed that he would have to follow the *"expedient"* rule in this and select ones which were not opposed to the Nebraska policy. "Can such be found which are not *hards*," he asked anxiously? In particular, as he told the governor in another letter at this time, he hardly dared to select the *Atlas*, although that sheet was his chief supporter among the papers of the state, because of its Barnburnerism in the past.[17]

My endorsement of it at this time will greatly impair the strength of my position here which it is important to the democrats of N.York should not be weakened. That act would receive a sinister interpretation in every quarter of the Union—I do not think I ought to select [the] Atlas. . . . To take two papers . . . or even one, distinctly opposed to that bill would in my judgment be unwise—On the other hand I am alike unwilling to do an act which will look like making the support of that bill a test of democracy. Though I go for it myself I would not withhold my confidence from those who honestly oppose it. I sincerely wish the measure had not been thrown upon us; but it has been and we must meet the exigencies as well as we can—

Meanwhile, feeling in New York was rising strongly against the program. The upstate—or Yankee—area, long one of the very centers of abolition, was soon aflame with indignation and by the latter part of February was busy with meetings of protest. As a loyal Democrat of Monticello, New York, wrote, the people there considered the Missouri Compromise "as sacred as the Ordinance of 1787." Marcy's old friend Samuel A. Shaw of the Cooperstown *Freeman's Journal* wrote in a like vein:

Governor, there is to my mind a moral principle at stake here, which I would adhere to, if it cost me every friend I have.

---

[16] Cf. *Times,* Feb. 21, and Fenton (*loc. cit.*).

[17] Newell to Marcy, Jan. 27, Mar. 26, M.P.; Marcy to Seymour, Feb. 11, 21, S.P.

It was only at the metropolis, where conservatism reigned and there were many ties with the South, that there was much support for the Douglas plan. At Tammany Hall, resolutions were adopted which were written by Marcy's friend Lorenzo B. Shepard. These contained an endorsement of the administration, which was voted unanimously, plus approval of the idea of popular sovereignty, which got two-to-one support. A resolution favored by John Van Buren, opposing the repeal of the Missouri Compromise, was voted down, also two to one. By March, however, opposition had risen so in the state that even the Albany *Atlas* was openly critical of the Nebraska program.[18]

At Washington, such rising hostility, which was general throughout the North, was seen with alarm. Marcy wrote to his son Samuel on February 11 that the party's ranks were likely to be thrown into confusion in all of the free states. He added gloomily: "but I hope it will not break them up." On the 20th, in a letter to John Y. Mason, he noted that passage of the Douglas bill in the lower house was problematical. "I fear the opposition to it is increasing and what worsens the case, is assuming a sectional form."[19] The senate passed the measure on March 4, however.

When, in the following week, most of the cabinet began to work busily to get it through the house, Marcy took no very active part.[20] One New York paper, whose language may be judged to have been more picturesque than accurate, said: "Marcy is sullen, sour, and swears out of both sides of his mouth."[21] But it presumably was not for nothing that he invited twenty of the New York state congressmen to the dinner parties which he gave that spring in his newly finished house. And when the final poll was taken, which was not until May 22, his namesake William Marcy Tweed was on the affirmative side, as he had urged, and eight of the others who had been his dinner guests also voted that way. A majority of the Democrats of the state, however, were in the negative.[22]

---

[18] *Atlas*, Feb. 23, Mar. 6; J. P. Jones, Feb. 7, S. M. Shaw, Feb. 14, L. B. Shepard, Jan. 18, Feb. 4, all to Marcy, M.P.

[19] M.P.

[20] *Atlas*, Mar. 11, citing the *Courier;* Allan Nevins, *Ordeal of the Union*, II, 154.

[21] *New York Morning Express*, Mar. 21, citing the [daily] *National Democrat.*

[22] Dinner memo. book, Moore Papers; *Union*, May 27; for Tweed, cf. Tweed to Marcy, Jan. 26, M.P. The parties in question were mostly those of April 12 and 27 and May 4.

And so Marcy had made his decision, perhaps the most important of his life and certainly the most unfortunate. Against his better judgment, he had stayed in the Pierce administration and had even used his influence, half-heartedly, in favor of the unwise policy. There was one real and valid argument, it is true, for his staying on. The Pierce administration would be less likely to make mistakes while he was in it and the filibustering element would be the better held in leash.

The regime had passed its principal crossroads, however. No more would it be able to count upon the support of most of the free states for its general program. And the United States had also passed the crossroads. While partisans like Seward were not too correct in saying that "slavery [was] wrapping us up in his black folds" and while demagogic figures like Garrison and Yancey were to have much to answer for at the bar of history, fierce and undying sectional hatreds had been stirred up. These were, furthermore, almost at once beyond the control of cooler heads like Marcy, to say nothing of the amiable but feckless Franklin Pierce. As for Marcy's coalition, it was weakened, but rather surprisingly was not destroyed. Most of its leaders remained loyal on most issues.

*   *   *

There survives a record of a bit of conversation between Secretary of State Marcy and a slave in nearby Maryland. Written down for the negro, in a letter which he had sent to George Newell,[23] it makes an interesting footnote to the general subject of this chapter.

The slave had become much attached to Newell, who was a very kind-hearted person. In the latter's absence, Marcy's friend James G. Berret hazarded that the man should get Newell to buy him. In the words of the slave, Samuel Chase, as given in the letter:

The man [i.e. Berret] with the gov. [Marcy] said that you & I were such great friends you ought to buy me—I said no indeed; I did not want any body to buy me. The Gov. [Marcy] asked why not, for, he said if Mr. Newl [sic] buys you he will take you to N York and then you will be free.—I told him I did not want that, for I had seen a good many niggers who had been made free—and I was better off than any of them.—They did not know how to take care of themselves and had no masters to do it for them & I had—

Of such complex strands is the cloth of history woven.

---

[23] Samuel Chase (the slave) to Newell, Oct. 13, 1856, *ibid.*

XXIV. MR. GADSDEN'S TREATY

"The Mexican Government needs money—Their necessities are great, and their pretensions very extravigant [sic]: The most serious difficulty in the way of extension of Territory will be: *The consideration* to be paid—" (James Gadsden to Marcy, October 3, 1853[1])

DURING the stormy months of the Nebraska debate, which were accompanied all too appropriately by very bleak weather out of doors, the Marcys as a family began to return to a rather more normal life. For one thing, as has been said, the new house on Vermont Avenue was finally ready. By January 25, Marcy was keeping bachelor quarters there and gave a dinner for John V. L. Pruyn, who was passing through; Secretary Guthrie and Postmaster General Campbell and a number of congressmen were also present, "in addition to the gentlemen of the family." With the subsequent arrival of Jane Knower, who helped to get the house more in order, and then of Mrs. Marcy and Nelly, the new *ménage* began to blossom to the full. By March, Marcy was beginning a whole round of stately dinners. It must have been a real comfort to him to have his family about him once again, especially in view of the loss of Edmund. If anything, by the way, he was to live on an even better scale when secretary of state than when secretary of war. His house, a three and one-half story brick affair, soon had furniture in it insured for $4,000. As for his carriage and horses, which had arrived during the fall, they made (in Abel French's words) "altogether the most imposing equipage in town."[2]

It was in diplomacy, however, that Marcy was to be mainly absorbed. For one thing, as early as January 4 or 5 it was rumored that Gadsden had been able to complete his pact at Mexico City. The tidings from there in December, it must be admitted, had not been cheer-

---

[1] Manning IX, 619-621.

[2] *Union*, Apr. 18 (weather); Pruyn's Journal, State Library; Marcy to Samuel, Feb. 11, Newell to Marcy, Feb. 15, insurance policy under date of Feb. 14, 1855, M.P.; dinner memo. book, Moore Papers; French to Newell, Dec. 6, 1853, N.P.

ful. Gadsden had written, alarmingly, that when C. L. Ward, who had borne the oral instructions as to the boundaries, had arrived in Mexico City, he had insisted that Pierce wished the Garay claim to be injected into the negotiations. He had even said that five million dollars would be required of Mexico for the purpose. Here, surely, was a pretty mischance, for Ward was the particular agent of the Garay interest! Yet Pierce had entrusted him with the oral directive to Gadsden—allegedly after having cautioned him to avoid the Garay affair entirely! After recovering from the shock of the news, Marcy had replied to Gadsden on December 22 to try to straighten him out, commenting that the Garay claim was to be omitted. Then, at the turn of the year, had come a despatch revealing that the Mexicans had raised their demands on the score of the Indian raids. Gadsden attributed this to Almonte, the Mexican minister at Washington; he held that the latter was probably being prodded by some of the persons speculating in such claims, who were worried at the American minister's tendency to drive a hard bargain. Marcy soon called Almonte in for an interview and laid down the law to him:

I expressed to him my regret that such erroneous statements should have reached Mexico in any way, and still greater should be my regret [he went on] if his government at all heeded them; for if it did, I was quite certain the attempt to settle the existing difficulties between the two countries would fail—I assured him, that, though it was desirable to get a feasible route for a Rail-Road in the vicinity of the Gila river, any idea that the United States would give an enormous sum for a tract of barren country in that region ought at once to be abandoned by his government, as also the idea that a cession of such a tract was not to be accompanied by an adjustment of claims for damages arising under the Treaty of Guadelupe Hidalgo. I also remarked to him that his government ought not to form any extravagant notions as to the amount of those claims. . . .

In the instruction which he sent to Mexico City on January 6, he expressed concern, however, at the roles of the two Tehuántepec groups; he knew that they were ready to set aside any scruple and that they had certain confidential connections in Mexico which would aid them.[3]

Although Marcy and Pierce at first denied that a treaty had been

---

[3] Gadsden to Marcy, Nov. 20, Marcy to Gadsden, Dec. 22, Jan. 6 (incl. account of the interview), Manning IX, 667-669, 150-152, 156-157; Garber, 90, 94-95.

made,[4] on Sunday, January 15, there was sure evidence that such was the case, for a telegram came from Gadsden to that effect. He was at New Orleans, on his way home. This was just a week before the fateful interview of the southern junta with Pierce over the Nebraska problem. "All issues with Mexico reconciled on conditions honorable and just to both countries. Particulars by mail," the message read.[5] Then, on the following Thursday, the scapegrace Ward arrived bearing the text of the treaty. Gadsden himself had stopped off at Charleston to see his family.[6]

The terms quickly showed why Ward had hurried on with them. They included a boundary close to the minimum demands, as some recent despatches had indeed warned would be likely. This left Lower California to Mexico, as likewise all the coastline of the Gulf of California; east of there, the boundary was between 31° and 32° north latitude. The United States was also released from Article XI of the 1848 pact and from any claims arising under it, i.e. for damages by Indians raiding into Mexico. For all of this the United States was to pay $15,000,000. But there was also a provision for American assumption of the claims against Mexico by American citizens. This was up to a limit of $5,000,000, "including the claim of the so called concession to Garay whose lawful existence Mexico does not recognize"![7] In short, Ward had been thoroughly successful. This was naturally a blow. Gadsden was later to write that but for his own efforts a $3,000,000 indemnity directly for the Garay group would have been included, for Santa Anna himself had been brought in as a potential sharer in the deal.[8] He also wrote that Santa Anna had first asked for $35,000,000 for Indian indemnities alone![9] On the other hand, Gadsden was reported in the Charleston *Daily Courier* to have said that the United States could have had Lower California if Mexico had not been so affronted by the Walker invasion of that area in the past year.[10] All in all, Gadsden declared, this was the only treaty for

---

[4] *Times,* Jan. 6, 9, 10.
[5] M.P.
[6] Gadsden to Marcy, Jan. 12, *ibid.;* Garber, 109.
[7] Text of treaty, Manning IX, 691n.
[8] Gadsden to Marcy, July 11, 1855, Des. Mex.
[9] Gadsden to Marcy, Jan. 17, M.P.
[10] Jan. 21, cited in Garber, 98.

years "without 'Brokerage' [,] a Mexican signification, where the Broker greezes [sic] the officials: & retains all the tallow. . . ."[11]

Looking at the pact as a whole, Marcy decided without much hesitation that it ought to be approved. After all, it gave the land needed for the railroad, which, as his talk with Almonte shows us, was his chief interest. This would also, incidentally, take care of the Mesilla dispute. In addition, the Indian claims had been cleared up. While he opposed the Garay grant, he no doubt argued that the treaty would leave the disposition of that problem entirely to the United States government anyhow. In the cabinet's long series of debates on the treaty, which began on the very day it arrived, he therefore urged its acceptance. With him were the pro-southern members. President Pierce, on the other hand, was at first in the opposition, largely because of the Garay claim; Pierce was upheld, moreover, by McClelland and Campbell. While the cabinet's secret debates went on, however, public opinion began to mobilize on Marcy's side. Not only was the South mostly pleased—although not enthusiastic—but many northerners were, too, including such influential editors as Henry J. Raymond of the *Times*. Such northern leaders could point out, rightly enough, that the territory did not promise to be of much value to the cotton kingdom, while the ending of all the existent disputes would be worth much to both sections. Aided by such public comments, Marcy and his allies were able to save the pact from oblivion.[12]

By the last day of January, Marcy had begun a series of consultations with Señor Almonte and with General Gadsden, who was now on hand, in a move to amend the document so as to make it more fully satisfactory. Several changes were made. These included dropping any reference to the Garay rights. More interestingly, a pledge to use the navy to overtake and arrest filibusters who had left American shores for Mexico was also left out; Marcy perhaps consoled himself on this score with the thought that there was still included a general promise to suppress filibustering and that at bottom the matter would rest upon the good faith of his government anyway. The pact was sent to the senate on February 10.

Of the disillusioning story of the action of that body, the less said

---

[11] Gadsden to Marcy, Jan. 2, M.P.
[12] Garber, 109-119.

the better. And, in any case, Marcy had little to do with what happened. In brief, the Nebraska issue made the North hostile towards the territorial gains involved; and the role of Ward in the affair, which soon became public, together with shameless lobbying on the part of both of the Tehuántepec interests, was also hurtful. One result was that the senate put the Garay item back in, which enraged the Sloo people. The latter then checked the passage of the agreement as a whole. By April 6, the *Times* concluded that it was "essentially used up," i.e., had failed.

Then, surprisingly, under the leadership of Senator Rusk of Texas, it was altered drastically, among other things being made less obnoxious to the North by means of a reduction in the area to be acquired. Then, finally, the Sloo interest, which had won over a small coterie of senators, had the rival claim knocked out, had its own put in, and even secured a guarantee of an American right to intervene in Mexico to protect it, if need be! The price to be paid, by the way, was cut to $10,000,000.

Once again, the secretary decided to swallow the pill. He found Pierce very hesitant to do so, however, from a feeling that his administration had been badly treated and because of his hostility to the Sloo amendment. According to Garber, the historian of the pact, it was not Marcy but Rusk and its other southern adherents who won the president over.

In any event, by May 6 Marcy was able to write to our *chargé* at Mexico City telling him to get Santa Anna's government to ratify the altered version.

The only question which that Government has to pass on is the acceptance or rejection of the Treaty in its present form [he explained]; for any attempt to change it will, as I am persuaded, involve its defeat.

He warned that speed would be necessary, because those who had lobbied against the present terms—i.e. the Garay group—would probably try to prevent Santa Anna from approving them. As it turned out, the Mexican dictator was too desperately in need of money to decline. His ratification arrived on June 20. Despite some opposition by the house of representatives to voting the necessary appropriation, Marcy was therefore able to complete the administration's first important treaty. He exchanged ratifications with Señor Almonte at noon on June 30, six months to a day after the signing of the original text.[13]

Thus ended the significant period in United States relations with Mexico during Marcy's term. In the remaining three years, it may be added, nothing more was achieved. The United States secured no settlement of the claims, won no commercial treaty, and, on its own part, failed to check some further filibustering moves.[14] It was really an era of worsening relations. As for his choleric and increasingly meddlesome envoy, Marcy had little to do with him; following some insulting communications from that quarter in the spring of 1855, indeed, he sent no further instructions of importance to Gadsden for nearly a year[15] and probably sought to have the man removed, as, very certainly, did Mexico.[16] When a recall was finally decided upon, in June of 1856, John Forsyth of Mobile was given the mission, and Marcy and Pierce began to be more interested in Mexico again.[17] But nothing was accomplished. All in all, the Mexican chapter had been one of only limited success.

----

[13] Marcy to Almonte, Jan. 31 (copy), Feb. 4, M.P.; Marcy to John S. Cripps, May 6, and Almonte, June 29, Manning IX, 160-161, 166; *Union,* July 2; Garber, 116-145.

[14] Garber, 158, 174, 147, 163.

[15] Marcy to Gadsden, Mar. 14, 1855, Feb. 4, 1856, Gadsden to Marcy, Apr. 17, 1855, Manning IX, 179-181, 201-202, 754-763; Marcy to Gadsden, priv., May 7, 1855, M.P.

[16] Cf. Garber, 150-152.

[17] Marcy to Gadsden, June 30, 1856, Manning IX, 205; to Forsyth, August 16, M.P.; Garber, 178-179.

XXV. WAR IN THE CRIMEA

"1st. That free ships make free goods. . . . (Marcy's convention with Baron de Stoeckl, July 22, 1854)

IN THE underlying causes of the great war which had for a year been threatening in eastern Europe, Marcy really took but little interest. Count de Bodisco, the Russian minister and a man whom he liked very much,[1] had kept him informed of the repeated efforts to escape hostilities through negotiation. But, like other Americans, Marcy felt no great concern. He considered the rivalry of Russia on the one hand and of Turkey, Britain, and France on the other for the control of the Balkans and of the Bosphorus to be of no especial import to the United States. If war should come, he did tell Mr. Crampton, the United States would be neutral.[2]

When the war did materialize, moreover, first between Turkey and Russia in 1853 and then, in the spring of 1854, with an Anglo-French declaration of hostilities against Russia,[3] the fact of it seemed if anything likely to be beneficial to the United States. It could hardly be very damaging to the United States to have Britain and France, its two chief potential antagonists, tied up in "the East," even at the price of some dislocation of trade. And Marcy, like his countrymen, wanted Russia to win. For, strange as it would seem a century later, Russia, ruled by the worst despot in Europe, Czar Nicholas I, and the United States, the "model republic," were traditional friends. Yet there was a factual basis for this. Russia was simply too remote from the United States to present serious difficulties, while the United States and she were almost always in opposition to England.[4] As Marcy himself put it:[5]

---

[1] Cf. Marcy to C. Catacazy, Feb. 3, 1854, Notes to Rus.

[2] F.O. 5, Oct. 3, 1853, priv.

[3] Sir Spencer Walpole, "Great Britain and the Crimean War," *Cam. Mod. Hist.,* XI, 311-317.

[4] F. A. Golder, "Russo-American Relations during the Crimean War," *Amer. Hist. Rev.,* XXXI (hereafter referred to as "Golder"), 462.

[5] Draft, priv., to Carroll Spence, minister resident in Turkey, Mar. 27, 1854, M.P.

In relation to the political organization of her government [,] the people of the U. States never can have any sympathy with Russia & will always regret to see her political system extended; but in regard to our international relations no nation on the face of the earth has used us more fairly. . . .

His cordiality towards Russia, however, was of a very mild sort. Even during the coming war, it was hardly observable; the correspondent of the *New York Daily Times,* for example, while considering Pierce and most of the cabinet pro-Russian, held Marcy to be entirely neutral.[6] In view of Marcy's equable mind and conservative temperament, of course, this was not surprising. In addition, he could see plainly enough the potential perils which Anglo-French naval power held.

Even before the news of the Anglo-French declaration of war upon Russia, which came out in the *Union* of April 15, this danger had become troublesomely obvious. In a speech to the house of lords on January 31, Lord Clarendon had stated that:[7]

The happy accord and good understanding between France and England [which were moving towards a formal alliance] have been extended beyond Eastern policy to the policy affecting all parts of the world, and . . . there is no portion of the two hemispheres with regard to which the policy of the two countries, however heretofore antagonistic, is not now in entire harmony.

This was a very different kettle of fish from a mere war in the Black Sea! Marcy acted at once. He called Crampton and Sartiges in to see him, to explain what was meant, but found that neither was able to give an authoritative answer. Then, on March 11, he wrote to Buchanan to look into the matter, with especial emphasis as to Cuba and Hawaii. By this date, in fact, the thought of cooperation by the Allies (i.e. Britain and France) in western hemisphere affairs seemed particularly ominous, for news had come of the arbitrary seizure of an American steamer, the *Black Warrior,* at Havana, and it was possible that Anglo-French interference was the cause of it. In the instructions to Buchanan, the angriest of his career, Marcy warned that: "This assumed guardianship by these nations over the political affairs of this part of the world will not be acquiesced in by the United States."

---

[6] *Times,* July 26, 1855.
[7] Hansard, *Parl. Debates,* 3rd ser., CXXX, 43, Jan. 31, in Golder, 464n.

Next day, Sunday, he found time to prepare a private letter, also, to Buchanan, commenting gloomily that if Russia lost the war such meddling could be even more serious. "This view of the subject is Russianizing some of our people," he added. By April 1, it is true, word came that Lord Clarendon insisted that he had meant to allude only to certain Anglo-French cooperation in the Plata area, to which the United States had no objection.[8] But this was too clearly a lame answer to be very reassuring.

Meanwhile, some Americans had been talking freely and happily of going out to raid Allied shipping upon the high seas, under cover of privateering commissions from the czar.[9] This was naturally an intriguing thought—as, in fact, it was to the Russian government. The latter had already asked its representatives at Washington if the United States would allow this, presumably hoping that the latter's ports might be open for the sale of prizes.[10] This last was a key point, for it was to be expected that Russia's own harbors would be blockaded. As the Anglo-French declaration of war began to loom up, moreover, and in the absence of any statement to the contrary by the United States, rumors began to fly about of actual plans by its shipmasters. One Captain McKay, for instance, the brother of the famous clipper-ship builder, was thinking of using a clipper to capture a British mail steamer when it left Vera Cruz with the customary consignment of silver.[11]

When Marcy was first questioned on the subject of privateering, by Catacazy, the Russian *chargé* (Bodisco having died), he had not taken time to think out a clear answer.[12] Shortly afterwards, however, when Crampton and Sartiges saw him (i.e. about February 26) he spoke directly to the point. He stated flatly that in so far as he was concerned there would be a full and complete neutrality. He was then asked if his country would be willing to sign a treaty banning privateering by its men while it was at peace. To this he answered that the American

---

[8] Marcy to Buchanan, Mar. 11, Buchanan to Marcy, Mar. 17, Manning VII, 102-105, 533-535; Marcy to Buchanan, copy, Mar. 12, M.P.

[9] *Times,* Feb. 27, March 4.

[10] Russian Foreign Office to Bodisco, Nov. 28/Dec. 10, 1853, cited in Golder, 462 and n.

[11] F.O. 5, Mar. 6.

[12] Catacazy's of Feb. 14/26, in Golder, 462 and n.

neutrality laws were quite explicit enough to dispose of the matter.[13] Such was to be the department's policy throughout the war. It was also upheld honorably.[14]

A few weeks later, indeed, Marcy did cause a flurry of excitement at the Russian legation. Chatting casually at home one evening, he told Baron Edouard de Stoeckl, who had been given a temporary assignment as Bodisco's successor, that he did not care what American ship captains did, provided that it was done after they left American ports. This unguarded comment caused Stoeckl to begin conversations with some American shipmasters, with an eye to their going to Alaska or Siberia and taking out Russian citizenship. As it turned out, however, the Russian home government overruled the idea,[15] and Marcy himself would doubtless have opposed such a practice had it really developed. In the broader picture, however, as he pointed out, there was little danger of privateering, because there was little profit to be made;[16] presumably he referred to the fact that the Allied blockade of Russia had indeed left no ports available to which prizes could be taken for sale. The event proved him to be right.

Much more serious, to Marcy, was the problem of upholding his country's rights as a neutral. As early as December, 1853, when discussing a certain treaty with Sartiges, he had proposed that there be included in it a statement of the rule for which the United States had long contended, that free ships make free goods.[17] This meant that enemy goods, except contraband, could not be seized when on neutral carriers. Nothing had come of the suggestion, however. Similarly, in the opening months of 1854, he had written to Buchanan to ask for a statement of what Britain's policy on neutral shipping would be. He had added that the United States would not submit to the rules Britain had employed in earlier wars and considered that it was time to secure a general change of international law on the subject.[18]

---

[13] F.O. 5, Feb. 27; *Times,* Feb. 27.

[14] One alleged instance of laxity on his part in enforcing the neutrality laws came in the case of the steamer *America,* which was built in this country, and, according to Golder (*loc. cit.,* 474) was destined for Russia.

[15] Stoeckl to Nesselrode, Mar. 17/29; Nesselrode to Stoeckl, Apr. 10/22, Golder, 466-468 and notes.

[16] Draft, to Buchanan, April 10, M.P.

[17] Marcy to J. Y. Mason, April 17, *ibid.*

[18] Statement of Stoeckl, in despatch to Nesselrode, date not given, quoted in Hunter Miller, *op. cit.,* VI, 800.

Time was to show that the Allies were ready to take such suggestions in all seriousness, for the very reason that if the American government and people became openly hostile to them, because of harsh treatment of their shipping, the bogey of American privateers might become a reality and the long sea lanes to the East, among others, might be harassed. There was a further point, moreover, in that France herself had always held about the same views on maritime law as the United States had, so that the Allies did not see really eye to eye anyhow. This proved to be the immediately deciding factor, although the combined pressure of Buchanan at Whitehall and of John Y. Mason at the Quai d'Orsay—to say nothing of that by the lesser European states—was also helpful. On March 30, an Allied agreement originating with Drouyn de Lhuys, the strong-headed French foreign minister, was issued. Although for the duration of the war only, this proved rather acceptable to the United States, because it asserted what Marcy had mainly in mind, the historic American contention that free ships made free goods. In addition, however, the Allies declared that neutral goods would not be subject to capture if on enemy vessels. The latter point was the less contested one. (In each case, contraband of war was excepted.) [19] As Buchanan explained, in reference to Britain's role in this decision, she *"earnestly desire* [d] *to be on good terms with the United States."* [20]

Although the decision was satisfactory for the moment, as Marcy soon wrote to Buchanan, it was also unsatisfactory. The latter was because it publicly made a virtue out of necessity and also because, as Marcy told Stoeckl, it was "not responsive to our idea" of a lasting change in the rules. [21] Writing to Buchanan officially on April 13, Marcy also said that Britain would be wise to be very cautious about the right of search of American merchant ships. [22] At this time, he had heard only of the British part in the decision, and only informally at that, but he assumed that France would take the same

---

[19] Buchanan to Marcy, Feb. 24, Mar. 17, B.P.; Mason to Marcy, Mar. 22, *HED 103*, 33rd cong., 1st sess., 14-15; Mason to Marcy, June 11, M.P. For Drouyn de Lhuys' role see Warren F. Spencer, "Drouyn de Lhuys and the Foreign Policy of the Second Empire," unpublished doctoral diss., U. of Penna., 1955, p. 59, which cites Drouyn de Lhuys' own *Les Neutres pendant la Guerre d'Orient*, 30-32.

[20] Buchanan to Marcy, March 31, priv., M.P.

[21] Statements of Stoeckl, in Hunter Miller, *op. cit.*, VI, 800-801.

[22] Copy, M.P.

course and that it was safe to proceed upon that assumption. Next day, accordingly, in a note to Stoeckl, he announced that the United States looked to Russia for a role parallel to that of the Allies. He remarked that Russia had always been Europe's chief upholder of neutral rights. Explaining in a firm tone the American tenets on the two main points of free ships making free goods and neutral goods going free on enemy ships, he proposed that the United States and Russia sign a convention including these points, as a first step towards a permanent change in the law of nations. At the time that he presented this note to Stoeckl, he added in conversation that for tactical reasons he would leave out all the other traditional American doctrines on the subject. He went on to say that:[23]

> We are going again to ask France and England to sign this convention; if they refuse, as I have every reason to think [they will], we will conclude it with you alone in the first instance. We will then put forward the same proposals to the maritime powers of the second rank. Having less means of defending their rights, they are, because of that very fact, interested in seeing them determined by rules in a definitive manner; and we have no doubt that they will give their consent to them, provided that they succeed in escaping English influence.

In instructions to Seymour, his envoy at St. Petersburg, later, he noted also that if the United States, Russia, and the Allies should all cooperate to this end, the other nations might be expected to follow suit; he expressed some optimism as to the outcome.[24] When the Allied declaration was officially handed to him, he accordingly replied to Crampton and Sartiges with a statement of his desire to see the twin rules made law.[25]

Before answers on this came from the three chief belligerent capitals, however, there arose a project of American mediation to end the war itself. Earlier, in the preceding autumn, any mention of the idea had been largely gossip.[26] Similarly, although Marcy spoke of the subject at his diplomatic dinner on April 21, the day of the presentation to him of the Allied policy on neutral shipping,

---

[23] Notes and conversation, both in Hunter Miller VI, 798-801.
[24] May 9, M.P.
[25] To Crampton, April 28, incl. memo. that similar one went to Sartiges, Notes to Brit.
[26] F.O. 5, Oct. 3, 1853.

he did so in a largely humorous style.[27] It appears to have been only after the arrival of a private letter from Seymour, written on May 26 and stating that Russia would probably accept such a plan,[28] that the administration took it up.

Marcy broached the mediation scheme to Stoeckl in the first half of July. He commented that in view of Russia's offer of mediation in the war of 1812, it would be only right for the United States to reciprocate. He explained that the cabinet had approved in principle and that he was working out the details; he expected to be ready to make a proposition to the belligerents in about ten days or two weeks. He did disclose, however, that it would essentially be one of simply lending the United States' good offices, with no implication of an intent to coerce. The Russian *chargé,* whose reports are the chief source for this bit of history, then asked what likelihood there was that Britain would refuse. "Let her do so," he quotes Marcy as having replied. "It will be one more count against her in our eyes. You surely can not object to that." From this remark and because of the unresolved Cuban crisis, it was supposed at the Russian legation that the plan was essentially political in character, designed to embarrass the Allies in case they later thought of mediation in the American dispute with Spain; it was also suspected that Cushing was its prime mover. In spite of all this, they urged their government to accept.[29]

The first reply from St. Petersburg, however, was on the subject of the neutral rights convention. The news was good. Stoeckl had been given full authority to negotiate a pact of the type Marcy wanted;[30] this was all the more cheering because of reports that the British government felt that it had already yielded too much on that score.[31]

The news found Marcy laboring through one of the worst heat waves in Washington history, worse than that which had so bothered him in the preceding summer. He wrote to John Y. Mason that:[32]

---

[27] *Times,* Dec. 30; dinner memo. book, Moore Papers.
[28] M.P.
[29] Stoeckl to Nesselrode, July 2/14, July 29/Aug. 10, Golder, 471-472, 472n.
[30] Hunter Miller, *op. cit.,* VI, 803-805.
[31] Mason to Marcy, May 11, M.P.
[32] *Union,* July 21; Marcy to Mason, July 22, M.P.

The Thermometer is at 99°—the nights afford no relief—This State of the Weather produces a lassitude which incapacitates for mental labor, and the pressure of incidental business attending the close of the session of Congress was never in my experience so great. . . .

He none the less was happy to hasten the matter along. After taking time only for consulting the foreign relations committee, as was his wont, on Saturday, July 22, he signed a convention with Stoeckl. The pact covered his twin rules—always excepting contraband and lawful blockade—and also had a provision that any country which later formally declared its adherence to the agreement would automatically enjoy its rights to the full. As David Hunter Miller's analysis has shown, the initiative had been Marcy's throughout, as were the terms in detail. The czar and the Russian foreign minister, Nesselrode, delighted at the prospect, had been only too glad to leave everything to him. As for the multilateralization feature, Marcy told Stoeckl candidly that it was meant to "give to our convention more importance" as well as to speed the proposed change in international law.[33]

The treaty was highly popular in the country. It was approved by the senate on July 25, the day it was first read, and by a unanimous vote.[34] On July 31 and in the first week of August, Marcy submitted identical *projets* to the envoys of the Netherlands, Prussia, Britain, and France.

If the incentive for the mediation proposal had come from Cushing, as Stoeckl thought, it may well have been Marcy who now obtained an abandonment of it. For the Allies, who had learned of it as early as the end of June, had been very bitter over it—the private French remarks being singularly acid.[35] Yet it was these very powers which held the key to the proposed revamping of international law. While other problems, such as Cuba and the port of San Juan (of which more later), may well have entered into the thing, the administration at any rate suddenly dropped it. On the very day after Marcy presented the *projet* of the neutral rights treaty

[33] Stoeckl to Nesselrode, July 11/23, 14/26; text of agreement; and Hunter Miller's statements; all in Hunter Miller, VI, 791-794, 801-809.
[34] *Union*, July 27; *Times*, July 24, 26.
[35] Sartiges to Drouyn de Lhuys, June 26, Cor. Politique, Etats-Unis, vol. 111, French foreign ministry; Drouyn de Lhuys to Sartiges, July 20, *ibid*.

to the Allied representatives, in fact, Stoeckl wrote home that Marcy had said that the president had reconsidered the mediation plan and decided to give it up. Marcy added frankly enough that the administration had important negotiations pending with the Allies, which might otherwise be jeopardized.[36] Nor was it ever brought up again.

Later in August, following the termination of the session on the seventh and the writing of some important instructions to his European ministers, Marcy took a fortnight's holiday. As in the year before, this was at Berkeley Springs, but this time it was largely for relaxation. His going there was probably partly to be able to spend some time with Senator James M. Mason, the chairman of the foreign relations committee, with whom he was developing a cordial friendship.[37] He was absent from August 21 to September 4.

The reason that the mediation proposal was not revived later was probably simply that the neutral rights convention was making but little headway. Great Britain was not at all ready to give in on the latter, while France, somewhat surprisingly, followed her lead. As for the European neutrals, they were told the Allies' views plainly enough and by the end of the year only the Kingdom of the Two Sicilies had dared to flout them. The reply of the Netherlands, received on September 22, also showed the Allied influence very clearly. As for Prussia, it declared as a result of British coaching that it was ready to sign the convention, but only if privateering as a means of war were ended for good. This was obviously meant as a jab at the United States. When Marcy learned of it, he said sourly that "The English found the use of privateers excellent until they discovered that there is another nation which can derive greater advantage therefrom."[38]

The privateering issue was a serious one, for privateering had enabled Americans to capture hundreds of British vessels in both the revolutionary war and the war of 1812; in short, it was one of the country's major tools. Fortunately, a way out had been suggested by Buchanan months before. In a despatch in which he had

---

[36] Stoeckl to Nesselrode, July 29/Aug. 10, cited in Golder, 472.

[37] Cf. Marcy to Berret, Aug. 26, 1855; also Mason to Marcy, Aug. 13, 1854, M.P.

[38] Mason to Marcy, Sept. 3, 1854, M.P.; ditto, Feb. 28, 1855, Des. Fr.; *Mess. & Pap.*, 276; Hunter Miller, VI, 812; Stoeckl to Nesselrode, Nov. 6, *ibid.*, 812-813; Notes from Prus., Nov. 22.

written of his talk with Clarendon on the subject, the American minister had told of stating to the foreign secretary that the United States would be willing to give up the practice permanently, if it was agreed that henceforth all private property at sea was to be wholly exempt from capture.[39] Marcy soon took up this bold idea and made it his own. In the foreign affairs portion of the annual message of December 4, he laid the proposal officially before the world.[40] He pointed out that the United States merchant marine nearly equalled that of "the first maritime power," but that the United States navy was only a tenth of hers, if that large. Such being the case, privateering was a necessary part of American national policy, he said, and to give it up would be like renouncing the use of volunteers on land. The way out was a noble one:

The proposal to surrender the right to employ privateers is professedly founded upon the principle that private property of unoffending non-combatants, though enemies, should be exempt from the ravages of war; but the proposed surrender goes but little way in carrying out that principle, which equally requires that such private property should not be seized or molested by national ships of war. Should the leading powers of Europe concur in proposing as a rule of international law to exempt private property upon the ocean from seizure by public armed cruisers as well as by privateers, the United States will readily meet them upon that broad ground.

We are to hear more of this scheme in the year 1856.

With the close of the year 1854, the principal problems of neutrality had been dealt with. On the matter of privateering, Marcy might, indeed, have done better, in that he could perhaps have used the bogey of American privateering under the Russian flag to extort concessions from the Allies. Although he had not done so, Buchanan and Mason had, however, found it a convenient lever themselves. At the same time, in avoiding allowing such activity he had escaped a precedent that could have been very dangerous to the United States itself in a comparable situation. He had very probably been responsible, also, for the decision to abandon the mediation idea, which would surely have been fruitless. This latter decision was

---

[39] Buchanan to Marcy, Mar. 24, B.P.

[40] That he wrote this portion is the natural conclusion, in view of the draft passages in his papers; cf. also letters to Buchanan, [Dec.] 3, 1854, and J. A. Thomas, of about the same date but filed under Mar. 14, 1855, M.P.

adhered to, despite much interest in the idea in congress in December. Indeed, he advised house leaders that it would be "inexpedient" to revert to it.[41] He had also made a useful beginning on the subject of a neutral rights pact, whatever the final answer might prove to be. All in all, moreover, the United States had maintained a very proper neutrality.

On the other hand, despite the continuing strength of the "happy accord" between the Allies and American concern lest those powers should in case of victory be even more meddlesome, their busy state left the United States comparatively free for great enterprises, if it should care to embark upon them.

---

[41] *Times,* Dec. 29; speech of Rep. Clingman, Jan. 6, 1855, in *Union* of Jan. 7.

XXVI. NEGOTIATING WITH LORD ELGIN

"No one was prepared to learn that so momentous a matter
as the fisheries should have been brought to so speedy and
favorable a termination." (*The Daily Union*, July 12, 1854)

IN THE latter part of the spring, while the ratification of the
revised Gadsden treaty was being sought in Mexico and the
projet of a neutral rights convention awaited a reply from St. Petersburg, Marcy's plan for a pact on the fisheries came to its culmina-
tion.

Early in 1854, the outlook for such a treaty had not been bright.
The draft which Marcy had given to Crampton to be sent to London
had, as will be recalled, been considered too demanding. It was
known that Lord Elgin, the governor-general of Canada, was in
London, but Buchanan reported that a talk with him had given
but little reason for optimism.[1] When Andrews came back from the
Maritimes, moreover, he brought word that prospects there were
equally bad, because the colonies were prosperous and increasingly
contented. He explained also that they had received no word from
Britain as to the draft treaty, so that it was not officially before
them. This shortcoming was gotten around, indeed, by Andrews'
persuading Crampton to put it before them himself. This move was
helpful. What was more, Mr. Francis Hincks, the prime minister of
Canada, the province most interested in the plans, decided to go
to London to push them. And, finally, Andrews made arrangements for a convention of provincial spokesmen to discuss the whole
business. This would very possibly be at New York, where Marcy
would be able to meet with them himself.[2]

Early in March, however, Crampton read to Marcy a despatch
from Lord Clarendon in which the latter cited his many objections
to Marcy's *projet* and stated a wish to suspend the discussions "for

---

[1] Buchanan to Marcy, Nov. 1, Dec. 22, Jan. 10, *Can. Rels.*, 532-537.
[2] Andrews to Marcy, Mar. 31, April 3, 1854, *ibid.*, 544-556.

a while." Marcy was naturally depressed. Six months had already gone by since the *projet* had been taken across the Atlantic. Writing to Buchanan on March 11, he said that the news was quite alarming, for the United States would continue to insist upon the older interpretation of the 1818 treaty "at any hazard," and it had been only with difficulty that American fishermen had been held in check in the past two seasons. The department might accept a temporary arrangement, he went on, such as Buchanan's proposal of a certain amount of free trade in return for full freedom in the fisheries, but, as he added in a private letter of the next day:

The fishery negotiation looks dubious. If the negotiation falls through and England insists on excluding us from the open Bays, there will be trouble.

He hoped, however, that Elgin's presence in London and the trip of Hincks would prove useful.[3]

As it turned out, affairs did go better, in all truth. Andrews wrote that his plans for a convention and the movement of opinion were both proceeding well. The only hitch was in his demand for more "sinews of war," to the tune of $8,000 or $10,000! Marcy was not pleased. He wrote in reply, on April 10, that:

I am not hopeful of improving it [the prospect] in the way you propose. I have always been distrustful of attempts to change the public opinion of any community by such means as you refer to.

He promised, none the less, to refer the request to Pierce. The president proved to have fewer qualms. Andrews was promised $5,000. In a letter notifying him of this, incidentally, Marcy spoke of important news which he had, the most cheering thus far. Crampton, he said, had apparently been told to yield just about any point which the provincials seemed ready to concede themselves. This was a prophetic intimation. Marcy ended by urging Andrews to press on speedily with his work, before the fishing season began.[4]

The solution was to come, however, not by way of a convention of delegates, nor yet through Mr. Crampton. The convention was to be postponed and then, as it happened, given up, while Crampton

---

[3] To Buchanan, Mar. 11, 12, *ibid.*, 84-87.

[4] Andrews to Marcy, April 3, cited above; Marcy to Andrews, April 10, 15, *ibid.*, 88-90. For some of Andrews' actual disbursements, see C. C. Tansill, *The Canadian Reciprocity Treaty of 1854 (J.H.U. Studies)*, 69-73.

was to be set aside in favor of a special plenipotentiary. This last was to be Lord Elgin himself. Lord Clarendon had instructed Elgin to include a stop at Washington on his way back to Canada, to try in person to see how the situation lay. While he was authorized to negotiate, the shortness of time before the opening of the provincial parliament would call for his presence made a full settlement unlikely until later.[5]

The traditional account of what followed has been based upon the sprightly but extremely questionable version left by Laurence Oliphant, Elgin's secretary. It runs somewhat as follows. The British negotiators spent the first ten days of their visit in social activities designed to conciliate the southern Democrats who controlled the senate, quieting their fears of an annexation of Canada; wine and conversation were both so abundant as to bring a charge later that the treaty was "floated through on champagne"; in the negotiations, Marcy was helpless because he had been "completely taken by surprise"—in short, it was Elgin who "achieved this remarkable diplomatic triumph." The above quotations are of Oliphant's own words. The facts, however, were otherwise. For, despite the specious authenticity of his narrative, which was in part, he alleged, based upon a diary, it is grossly inaccurate. Indeed, much of it was obviously based upon his recollections as written down thirty-two years after. Among the less important instances of his unreliability may be mentioned his repeated references to the British minister as "Sir Philip Crampton" and his statement that he met Lincoln in Crampton's house at this time, plus his references to Marcy as a reputed duellist and a man who had started life as a cabinet maker and had been the minister to Mexico.[6] The main fault of the account, however, that it denies Marcy the credit for being the real maker of the treaty, will be proved below.

Marcy may well have had a week of warning of Elgin's coming,[7] but that fact can have made little difference. He was too loaded down with work to do much preparing. As he was to write to

[5] On the convention, see Elgin to Clarendon, Aug. 25, 1855, in J. L. Morison, *The Eighth Earl of Elgin,* 183. Clarendon's instructions to Crampton and Elgin, both of May 4, are in F.O. 115.

[6] Laurence Oliphant, *Episodes in a Life of Adventure,* 44-59.

[7] Andrews to Marcy, May 4, private (no date of receipt), warning that Elgin might come, M.P.

John Y. Mason on May 25, his post called for enough work *not* connected with foreign affairs to take up his whole day, he would have needed all of his time simply to peruse the documents received at the department, had he been able to—and nearly all needed answers—and he had about twenty unfinished treaties on hand.[8] In addition, the Kansas legislation was coming to a climax; it was finally adopted by the house, to the salute of one hundred guns, a few hours after Lord Elgin's arrival, which was on May 22.[9]

Despite this, Marcy welcomed his visitor and the latter's suite, which included Mr. Hincks, very warmly—as Clarendon was to say, "in a spirit of the most friendly candor."[10] Although Marcy may never have known it entirely, Elgin bore instructions like those which Marcy guessed that Crampton had received, namely to try to get any terms which the United States and the provinces could agree upon. This was a reflection, of course, of Britain's desire to placate the United States, since the coming of the Crimean War; her recent statement on neutral shipping had been a comparable step. More interestingly, Clarendon showed that he was afraid of Marcy as a bargainer. He desired that the real purpose of the mission be concealed to the last, so that Marcy should not be encouraged to increase his demands; Elgin was to pose as coming for an exploratory visit only. He also warned him explicitly to avoid giving in on *anything* unless in return for a *quid pro quo* and said that at all costs he should not talk in a "yielding tone." As Clarendon wrote to Crampton, Marcy's own "unyielding spirit" made this necessary. Obviously, Marcy had already inspired Clarendon with a healthy respect![11]

The first days after Elgin's arrival do seem to have been spent largely as Oliphant says, namely in social functions. Although the pact that was finally concluded was perhaps not "floated through on champagne" or even written "amid the soft footfalls of fairy feet . . . [and] the graceful sweep of $500 dresses," there were many entertainments, including a big dinner which Marcy gave to the visitors and to several members of the diplomatic corps. Such affairs

[8] Letter to Mason, May 25, *ibid.*
[9] Oliphant, *op. cit.,* 45; *Herald,* May 23.
[10] Clarendon's statement in the house of lords, *Union,* July 18.
[11] The two instructions of May 4, cited above.

were doubtless very agreeable, for the social season was at its height
and it was a relief to everyone at the capital, no doubt, to turn away
from the Nebraska problem. In addition, Lord Elgin was a man of
notable wit and charm,[12] while Marcy's dry humor and cynical yet
playful wit were present as usual. We may conclude, however, that
these two negotiators did more than dissolve by social means the
tensions of that angry springtime. The very presence of Elgin, as
the governor-general of Canada and at the same time so obviously
a top-grade British spokesman, was in itself a denial that Britain
had any thought of facilitating the annexation of her majesty's provinces to the United States. Presumably Marcy discreetly indicated
this salient fact to those who would be interested in it.

Despite Oliphant's statement regarding ten days of amenities and
three of negotiations, the serious discussions appear to have begun
on May 28.[13] On the matter most vital to the United States, the
fisheries, the two men in general agreed that the United States
should have a wide use of the coastal waters; the only trouble was
to say where these left off and the rivers began. To the provincials,
the latter were their own special preserve. On the other hand, Marcy
was determined to uphold the American right to the use of the
bays, as has been said. For the moment, no decision was reached.
By contrast, it was early decided that Americans should be allowed
to land to dry their nets and cure their fish on all the coasts of the
colonies, but they were not to touch the shell fish; Marcy's draft
had included these points. He and Elgin seem to have agreed fairly
soon, moreover, as to what broader regions should be open to both
countries for fishing. Because of Britain's objections to American
use of her waters on the Pacific, on account of the charter rights of
the Hudson's Bay Company, that region and the whole American
west coast were alike left out. Similarly, the reservations as to
Florida led to limiting provincial fishing on the American east coast
to the area north of the thirty-sixth parallel, i.e. starting at Albemarle
Sound, North Carolina. Each side was to use the other's fisheries on
the same terms. As to the much debated cod bounty, Marcy stood
firm on keeping it.

[12] Oliphant, *op. cit.*, 45-59; Marcy's dinner memo. book, Moore Papers.
[13] Marcy to Buchanan, June 5, stating that he had been with Elgin constantly
for the last ten days, M.P.

In the discussion of the reciprocal trade provision, however, Marcy made the concession which he had long debated, that coal be added to the free list. This was partly offset, though, by the inclusion of "unmanufactured tobacco." The old request, that colonial craft be allowed in the United States coastal trade, does not seem to have been much discussed. Elgin did press hard for the registry of colonial built vessels, but Marcy would not give in. He offered as a partial compensation to recede from the demand for a free navigation of the St. John River. Elgin judged from this that the passage of lumber down that stream without payment of duty would also be abandoned. Marcy replied to this, in a written note of Sunday, June 4, that Elgin was mistaken. He enclosed a draft paragraph, possibly the one that was finally used, reserving the right to a free movement of the timber, explaining that: "Such a clause seems to me to be just and right. It is due to the lumber interest and will break or weaken the force of opposition to the Treaty from that quarter." He had his way. Besides the point regarding the St. John, he also made some other minor concessions as to navigation. While the United States obtained the use of the St. Lawrence and of the canals linking the Great Lakes to it, if Britain later chose to stop this, the United States was no longer authorized to suspend the free list entirely. Instead, the latter would be denied only to the province of Canada. This was, however, precisely the area which most wanted it. The federal government also granted the use of Lake Michigan, so long as the St. Lawrence was open to Americans, and pledged to recommend to the states that British subjects never be treated differently from Americans in traversing the state canals.

The last points of difference were not settled until the morning of Monday, June 5, the very day the treaty was signed. These included the treatment of estuaries and a decision as to Newfoundland. On the latter, indeed, special instructions had arrived from Lord Clarendon just a day or two before. His lordship had urged caution as to that island and perhaps deferment of any solution, pointing out the sensitive matter of French fishing rights there and the excessive dependence of the population upon fishing. Elgin therefore suggested that the treaty simply contain a promise by both parties to make a separate agreement as to Newfoundland later. But *"Mr. Marcy, who I am bound to say evinced in all his communications with me great candour and firmness,"* was extremely unwilling to accept this, Elgin found; Marcy was sure that the senate would disapprove. He was even surer that a plan to reserve to France the privileges given her by Britain would be held unsatisfactory. The result was a special article stating that the provisions of the treaty would extend to the island—"so far as they are applicable to that Colony"—only if approved by its parliament. If the latter rejected the plan, this was in any case not to block the rest of the treaty. Incidentally, from a note which Andrews, who was in the city aiding Marcy, wrote to Cushing (seemingly on June 5), it may be supposed that Marcy and he expected to be able to get a separate pact with Newfoundland later, if need be. As to the estuaries, a compromise wording was found. There was also a provision for a board of arbitrators to handle most points in that connection. In closing, it is to be noted that the treaty specified that its terms, except for Newfoundland, were to go into force only after being approved by the British parliament, the legislatures of Canada, Nova Scotia, New Brunswick, and Prince Edward's Island, and the United States congress. Once so sanctioned, they would remain in operation for ten years; thereafter, either side could bring them to an end after one year's notice.[14]

In a letter written on this last day, to Buchanan, Marcy had said modestly of his treaty that "I believe it is in a shape to be acceptable to this country," but it was better than that.[15] In reality, he considered it "very satisfactory"—according to the *New York Daily Times* correspondent.[16] And he was right. As he sat, blinking with sleepiness, late that night, while Elgin read the text aloud for final corrections, he can only have felt greatly pleased.[17] Essentially, it was he who had made the treaty, and he had done it largely upon his own terms.

---

[14] The account of the negotiations is based upon Elgin's report to Clarendon from Quebec, June 12, F.O. 115, including the quotation beginning "Mr. Marcy . . . ," to which italics have been added; Clarendon's instructions of May 19 *re* Newfoundland, F.O. 115, and ditto, F.O. 5; Marcy to Buchanan, June 5, already cited; Andrews' voucher for expenses, Sept. 30, Pierce Papers; Marcy's note to Elgin, June 4, Notes to the Brit. Leg.; Andrews to Cushing, n.d., C.P.; several bits of drafts, in D.S. "Reciprocity Negotiations, 1848-1854"; and the final text, Hunter Miller VI, 667-672.

[15] To Buchanan, June 5, cited above.

[16] *Times,* June 8.

[17] For Marcy's sleepiness, I have taken Oliphant's word; *op. cit.,* 55.

He had, indeed, shown consummate skill all the way through the twelve months of discussion. At the outset, for instance, he had established an extremely strong bargaining position, as Clarendon's instructions to Elgin show us so well. Since the arrival of the British party, moreover, he had made fewer concessions than Elgin had. Thus, of the three British *sine qua nons* of the year before, coal, cod bounty, and registry, he had yielded only on the first. As to other points, he had receded from his *projet* only on the score of the west coast and, perhaps, Newfoundland—which afterwards did, in fact, accede to the treaty—together with the navigation of the St. John and of Lake Michigan. By contrast, the coasts of the United States had in general been omitted, the cod bounty was kept, the United States secured the duty-free passage of its timber *via* the St. John and the inclusion of raw tobacco on the free list, and it conceded nothing as to registry and the coastal trade.

The main features of the treaty, of course, were that the United States received the fullest use of the historic fisheries, the finest in North America, and agreed in return to a free commerce in most of the natural products of the two countries. If this latter be objected to, as chiefly helpful to the British colonies, as of course it was, it should be kept in mind that the duties which the provinces imposed upon American manufactures were low, as has been commented, and were likely to fall.[18] It was to be expected, furthermore, that the colonials would more readily buy American goods once they had the dollars which their natural products would now earn. In sum, Marcy had proved himself a shrewd bargainer, a fact which, as has been noted, was fully acknowledged by Clarendon and Elgin. Taking a broader view, the pact was also commendable in being reciprocally beneficial and tending to link the two areas together in an economic sense. This was all Marcy had sought and he had done it in a noble style. In addition, he had ended a growing crisis in United States relations with Britain.

Space forbids a discussion of Marcy's private letters to win support for the treaty.[19] Its hearty approval in the American press, how-

---

[18] They averaged about 12% and those on British goods were the same; *Union*, Sept. 13, 1854, edit.

[19] Cf. June 9-11, M.P.

ever, was a great adjunct. As the *Times'* correspondent put it, it was a treaty valuable to both sides and the congress ought to hasten it through while Britain was in a good humor. Or, in the words of the *Boston Post,* it "create[d] a thousand new ties of peace between two great countries." Or, to quote the *Palladium,* published at Oswego, where the interest in it was more immediate:[20]

It is a measure of more direct and practical importance and benefit to the people than all the abstract questions of mere agitation for the past twenty years.

Under these circumstances, it proved possible to get the treaty through the senate fairly easily. It was not so in the house, however. Whether the services of Israel Andrews were so crucial in the passage of it there, as that worthy later claimed, cannot be said exactly, but the vote was a close one.[21]

In due time, the various British parliaments concerned would likewise give their approval. Before that time, however, the making of this great treaty, following upon the Koszta note, the completion of the Gadsden pact, and the expectation, so soon to be borne out, of a neutral rights convention with Russia, saw Marcy's achievements at their very apex.

---

[20] For the press comments, see *Times* correspondent, in issue of July 14; *Sun* correspondent, in issue of July 18; *E. Post* edit., July 14; *Journal of Commerce,* in *Union* of July 23; *Boston Post, ibid.,* July 20, Oswego *Palladium, ibid.,* Aug. 13; *Courier & Enquirer, ibid.,* Sept. 17; *Detroit Free Press,* March 27, 1855. Hostile comments: *Herald* correspondent, in issue of June 14; *Tribune* edit., July 18. Cf. also Abbot Lawrence's very favorable comment, letter to Marcy, June 17, private, "Recip. Negots." volume, D.S.

[21] Andrews spent a good deal of money with the members, as he did afterwards with leaders in the provinces. (Hunter Miller, *op. cit.,* VI, 733-738; Morison, *op. cit.,* 177-186; the latter includes some moneys advanced by the Canadian provincial government). As before, however, Marcy did not encourage this, as the pencilled note to him by Andrews on July 15 (M.P.) shows. This indicates that on the night of the signing of the pact Andrews had suggested "external measures" and Marcy had not gone along with him. Yet Andrews' expenditures for the treaty as a whole, from first to last, were very extensive, perhaps as high as $200,000. (Thomas H. Le Duc suggested the latter figure in his article on Andrews in the *D.A.B.; D.* C. Masters, *The Reciprocity Treaty of 1854,* was cited by Le Duc, but contains $118,000 as its highest figure—p. 84, note 1.) He received funds not only from the United States and provincial governments but also from private individuals. In the following year, in fact, a committee of the Boston Board of Trade launched a rather public drive to raise some $53,000 allegedly still needed to settle his accounts. Its printed letter (June 23, 1855, C.P.) stated that "several times that amount" had been used to effect the Webster-Ashburton treaty, which it termed far less valuable.

XXVII. GREYTOWN

"O Pierce! O Marcy! were you not content
To let your axe speak for you? Is your bent
For fame so strong that Greytown must be made
A smouldering pile ere Bronson's ghost be laid?"[1]

WITHIN four days after Marcy signed the epochal treaty with Lord Elgin, he issued instructions which had a share in bringing on the bombardment of San Juan de Nicaragua (or "Greytown"). The reasons for this act were quite involved, like everything else connected with that so strategically situated and yet so miserable place.

Although Great Britain was ready to placate the United States regarding the fisheries and neutrality, she seemed unwilling to yield anything at all as to Central America. Doubtless her reasons were varied. They would include Whig fumbling, Democratic bluster in the senate and in the *Union*, the failure of Vanderbilt to construct a canal, ministerial instability, and, as has been noted, Lord Clarendon's being so busy with eastern matters as to fail to learn the real nature of the problems involved.[2] This was all the more unfortunate, however, for London had the best of reasons for wanting to build good relations with the United States. On the American side, also, there was a comparative absence of provocative incidents. Yet the ministry took a more uncompromising attitude than ever before. As a despatch of Buchanan's which arrived on January 30, 1854, revealed, Clarendon and his associates stated that they held the Clayton treaty to have been "entirely prospective in its operation." Buchanan did write that there was some disposition to take up the idea of handling the Mosquito Indians as mere proprietors of certain lands and he did predict that Britain would finally and "after a struggle" get out of the Bay Islands, but Marcy was increasingly convinced that all this would take a long time. The British appeared much too stubborn, much too ill-informed as to the merits of the American

---

[1] Contributed to *E. Post,* Aug. 3, 1854.
[2] Cf. Williams, 157-158.

case, to make a settlement likely soon. Such a remark as Lord Clarendon's recent one, moreover, as reported by Buchanan, that the present Mosquito "king" was not a worthless drunkard but "a decent and well behaved youth of between 22 and 23 *who resided in Mr. Green's family*"[3] (Mr. Green being the British consul), was simply infuriating.

Although Buchanan had asked for detailed instructions as to the size of the territory of the Mosquitos, Marcy did not, therefore, send a reply. He had enough other concerns. At the same time, he hoped that his envoy's able statement of the American position, in a note to Lord Clarendon, a copy of which reached Washington on or before February 7, would lead to favorable results.[3a] One step only did he take, in the interval. He rejected flatly, in a note of February 21, a *projet* which Marcoleta, the Nicaraguan representative, had drawn up. This was an outwardly workmanlike effort at a general settlement with Britain and had tentative British approval. But, as Marcy said, the United States simply denied that that power had any rights in the area to give away.

Although angry and frustrated, Marcy long held unreservedly to a peaceable course. When he was questioned by Crampton about the Central American Land and Mining Company, an American organization which had a dubious patent to most of the region claimed by the Mosquitos and which was suspected of a filibustering design, he said he would oppose the project if it became clear that it was of that variety. He would be against any filibuster at all, he added, commenting candidly that such a move would embarrass relations with England. This was early in March. Likewise, he avoided any steps towards a one-sided abrogation of the Clayton treaty. His attitude was wholly unsatisfactory to Solon Borland, who had more than once complained of it. When that hot-blooded Arkansan received Marcy's mild rebuke of late 1853 on the score of a suggested abrogation, indeed, he decided to resign, as the department learned on April 20.[4]

---

[3] Italics added.

[3a] Buchanan to Marcy, Jan. 10, 20; Buchanan's note of Jan. 6 to Clarendon, Manning VII, 518-533.

[4] Marcoleta's note to Marcy, Jan. 24, and Marcy's reply, Feb. 21; Marcoleta to Marcy, May 4; Borland to Marcy, Feb. 22 (encl. letter to Pierce), Manning IV, 381-383, 381n, 55-56, 404-409, 387 and 387n.; F.O. 5., Mar. 6.

When Borland arrived back in Washington at the end of May,[5] i.e. during the Elgin discussions, he brought a story of events which to him were highly annoying and which were to produce the crisis over Greytown. For one thing, there had been a new friction between the inhabitants of that place and the Transit employees at Punta Arenas. This had involved some destruction of property. Then, when Borland was on his way home, he had interceded in behalf of an American captain who had quite without warrant shot a negro boatman. He and the captain had been mobbed. Later, Borland had had his face cut by a broken bottle which had been flung at him. When a party from an American steamship had at one point tried to rescue him, it had been driven off by firing. Before leaving the area, Borland had arranged for a guard of fifty men to protect American nationals and property there. Meantime, the entire municipal government of San Juan had quit and none had taken its place. Besides Borland, one J. L. White, the aggressive general agent of the Transit Company, was soon at the capital. He demanded stern measures.

What appears now to have happened is that White and men of his ilk persuaded Marcy and Pierce, and more likely chiefly Pierce, that a threat of armed action would be enough to make the inhabitants of San Juan stop all interference with the company. A similar threat had, by the way, been used successfully by the French against the city of Cartagena, Colombia, two months earlier.[6] If such a result could be had in this case, Marcy may well have reasoned, there would be the added gain of lessening British prestige.

To a later reader, the instructions which Marcy wrote anent Greytown on June 9 were certainly ominous.[7] These were to Fabens, the commercial agent at that point. They told him that Commander Hollins and the U.S.S. *Cyane* were to proceed thither at once and demand redress for the damages at Punta Arenas. Since the government had collapsed, Marcy said, Fabens must take the matter up with the leading residents. It was to be hoped that the townsmen would have adjusted the matter before Hollins' arrival,

---

[5] *Union*, May 30.

[6] W. O. Scroggs, *Filibusters and Financiers*, 75-76; Williams, 175; Marcoleta to Marcy, "Rec'd June 6th," M.P.; *Union*, Apr. 25.

[7] *HED126*, 33rd cong., 1st sess., 19-20.

and in that way Commander Hollins will be relieved of the disagreeable necessity of taking any action in regard to that subject. . . .

Alluding then to the treatment of Borland, Marcy said that it was an "indignity offered to the nation as well as to him. . . ."

Nothing short of an apology for the outrage will save the place from the infliction that such an act justly merits.

As stated above, this was just four days after the conclusion of the Elgin treaty. The instructions of Secretary of the Navy Dobbin to Hollins, of which Marcy presumably was aware, were even more forthright.[8] If a letter[9] which the newspapers afterwards printed, allegedly written by White to Fabens on June 16, was authentic, White himself had aims which went beyond a threat of force and a peaceable settlement and he counted upon Hollins to fulfill those aims. White stated that he hoped that no mercy would be shown to the town; he also spoke of hopes that "we can . . . put in our own officers, transfer the jurisdiction, and you know the rest. . . ."

Needless to say, Marcy was not ready to tolerate a filibuster now, either. It is difficult to believe, moreover, that he accepted the idea that Hollins might really take drastic action. This would have been too inconsistent with the plans which he was making for continuing the peaceable negotiations with Britain. As his previously cited letter of June 5 to Buchanan and instructions which he sent to him on June 12 make clear, such negotiations were still his intent. He was as before ready to concede little beyond possessory rights in the Belize and he rather agreed with Buchanan that the chances for a success of the negotiation were small. And yet he said—and here was the key—that the United States must keep on trying for such a settlement.[10] On the other hand, it must be said that for him to be willing to take the risk that there *might* be violence employed at Greytown, especially on the very morrow of his friendly negotiations with Lord Elgin, was one more sign that he was not as sensitive to moral issues as he once had been.

In the following six weeks Marcy was working quietly to win approval for his reciprocity treaty, seemingly unworried as to Hollins'

[8] These were dated June 10, *ibid.*, 2.
[9] Williams, 177-178.
[10] Manning, VII, 105-107.

mission. Then the news came, like a bombshell. The *Union* had it on July 26. Captain Hollins had told the inhabitants of Greytown to pay a total of $24,000 in damages and make apologies—or suffer the consequences. No amends had been forthcoming. Then, after giving public warning and sending a steamer to take away any persons who cared to leave, he had bombarded the town. Afterwards, a landing party had set fire to its remains. There had been no bloodshed.[11]

Writing to Buchanan on July 28, Marcy insisted that "it was not anticipated that circumstances would require a resort to violence." Soon after, he told Crampton that he had been sorry to learn that such measures had been used. He added that he would refrain from commenting on how far Hollins was justified in them until the cabinet had finished debating the matter. It is significant that, after reading the instructions in the case, Crampton reported to London that he was ready to believe that a resort to violence had *not* been expected. The American people, however, were not so understanding. Instead, they were furious. The administration therefore decided to play for time. Although the instructions were released to the press, no public statement was given as to whether Hollins would be rebuked. As a means of delaying, moreover, it was decided to send agents to appraise the damages which had been done and incidentally to look for evidence of any other person's being to blame! Nor was there any desire to hurry their departure. But it was also ruled, secretly, that Hollins would be sustained in full; this was largely because he had, of course, acted within the scope of his orders. Marcy expressed this attitude in a letter to John Y. Mason some weeks after, adding that if it became his duty to comment upon Hollins' course he would "endeavor to make out a good case." The decision to stand by the man was also, no doubt, taken because to back down might put the United States at a disadvantage psychologically in dealing with Britain. And, wrote Marcy to Buchanan, serious embroilment over it was unlikely.[12] He swallowed his pride, therefore, and went ahead.

---

[11] Scroggs, *op. cit.,* 77-78.
[12] To Buchanan, July 28, B.P.; F.O. 5, July 31, Aug. 7; to Fabens, Sept. 20, draft; to Mason, Aug. 30, draft, M.P.; to Buchanan, Aug. 8, Manning VII, 108-109.

The reaction across the water, as he expected, was not a warlike one, but it was bad enough. Indeed, even before the news of the affair, there had privately been a low enough opinion in Britain of the United States' conduct. As an American had put it after a recent visit:

> . . . on arrival [in England] I found the public mind to my surprise fully *convinced* that we were all in a *bad way* in U.S.—that we had a Govt. at Washington administered by a sad set of worthless persons, who were encouraging all sorts of violations of Law—pushing on the Filibusters—and determined to *Steal Cuba.* . . .

Now, there was condemnation in all circles. Lord Clarendon remarked acidly that the news was not conducive to a happy settlement. He directed Crampton to demand compensation for any losses by Britishers; more seriously, he quietly put aside a memorandum he had lately prepared which went a considerable way towards meeting the United States' demands.[13]

When Crampton read to Marcy the instructions concerning reparations, Marcy listened very attentively and replied that Pierce had not yet fully made up his mind on the point. He hinted, however, that Hollins would be upheld. He said also that he believed that Lieutenant Jolly, the captain of H. M. Schooner *Bermuda,* which had been present in the harbor, was really largely to blame. Jolly was reported to have urged the citizenry not to comply, Marcy said. But let Crampton's report tell the story:

> ". . . Now," said Mr. Marcy, "what took place in the present instance? The people of Grey Town not only refused satisfaction, but they did worse: they refused even to discuss the question of whether any satisfaction was due. It was well known that all the Members of the Municipality, and all the leading Merchants were at Grey Town, and yet not one of them came forward. . . . I will not pretend to determine whether the indemnification demanded was too great or too little; or whether the charges made were strictly true or not. These were points which Captain Hollins would have been ready to discuss with any body from or belonging to the Place, and he certainly would not have proceeded to the extremities he did, had even a single individual interested come forward: but nobody came, and

---

[13] Davis to Marcy, July 10, M.P.; Buchanan to Marcy, Aug. 18, Manning VII, 579-579; F.O. 115, Aug. 31; undated memo. in Clarendon Papers, printed in *Amer. Hist. Rev.,* vol. 42, 496-497, in R. W. Van Alstyne's documents on "Anglo-American Relations, 1853-1857."

Captain Hollins was left the choice either of weighing his anchor and going away, quietly, after having made an empty threat, or else of resorting to force, the necessity of which nobody can regret more than I do."

It was here that Mr. Marcy animadverted upon the supposed conduct of Lieutenant Jolly: "it was by his advice and encouragement," said Mr. Marcy, "as it has been stated to me, that the Authorities and People of Grey Town were persuaded to adopt the extraordinary and useless course they have pursued, and which alone has led to the catastrophe we will have so much reason to regret. It was on board Lieutenant Jolly's vessel that the principal ringleaders (as Mr. Marcy termed them) had been received, and it was by his influence, contrary to the solicitations of Captain Hollins to Lieutenant Jolly, to exert it upon them to adopt a more conciliatory line of conduct [,] that they persisted in an obstinate refusal to pay any attention whatever to the representations of the government of the United States."

Marcy ended by stating his deep regret at the whole affair, particularly that it should give rise to such discussions just when the happy result of other dealings promised so well for relations with Britain.[14]

A few days later, he wrote to Fabens, who was in the United States, asking him to come to the city to discuss Jolly's role in the incident. He also wrote to White that Jolly was said to have charged that Hollins "dared not" carry out his threat of bombardment.[15] This hope of shifting the burden to the British themselves, however, was not borne out by events. No direct proofs of interference by Jolly were found; in fact, his own and the British consul's reports, both written at the time, tended to show that there had been none. Copies of these papers were soon sent to Washington for Marcy to see.[16]

There were also a number of other causes of friction. Sanders, whose nomination had been rejected by the senate, had stayed on in London and was causing trouble, as likewise was Daniel Sickles.[17] American vessels, furthermore, had begun to take guano from Avis Island, a point which Britain claimed, near St. Croix.[18] But the

---

[14] F.O. 5, Sept. 18.

[15] Marcy to Fabens, cited above; Marcy to White, Sept. 20, draft, M.P.

[16] Jolly to Commo. Henderson, July 14, in Clarendon's of 6 Oct., and J. Geddes' letter of July 20, in Clarendon's of Sept. 21, F.O. 115.

[17] Letter of Sanders "To the President of the Swiss Federal Council," Aug. 16, printed, M.P.

[18] Crampton's note, Nov. 2, Notes from Br., and Marcy's reply, Nov. 18, Notes to Br.

Falkland Islands troubles were the worst of all. This archipelago was a sore point anyway, because the British had seized it long after Mr. Monroe's enunciation of his "doctrine." Yet American seamen had been harshly punished for taking wild pigs there, two whaling vessels had been detained long enough to lose their season, and an American captain had been given a lengthy jail sentence for a seemingly minor offense. On the other hand, when Commander W. L. Lynch of the U.S.S. *Germantown* had heard of the imprisonment of the shipmaster, he had threatened to destroy the battery at Port Stanley, the island capital, unless the man was let go. The threat had fortunately not been fulfilled, because it was learned that the captain had been released, but its utterance had caused rancor.[19] As a British official said, Hollins had tried to outdo Captain Ingraham's conduct in the Koszta case, and now Lynch had sought to surpass Hollins![20]

The investigators of the Greytown affair did not reach the latter place until December 20. They found the village "slowly rising from its ashes," with the Mosquito flag flying over its thatched huts and three British warships protecting it. Well before this, however, Marcy had taken up the subject in a long passage for the annual message of December 4. This was a full-blown defense of the whole operation. Although Buchanan had written some weeks earlier that "No person doubts that you can make a strong argument upon any subject," the passage was not one of the secretary's happier statements. It was more plausible than sound. Terming the Greytowners "marauders," as he had weeks before in a letter to Buchanan, he alleged that their claim to jurisdiction over Punta Arenas was unfounded and that the Transit Company held the place "under a title wholly independent of them." Lacking the proof that he had hoped for that Jolly had definitely obstructed the meeting of Hollins' demands, he turned around and criticized the former for not urging the inhabitants to comply with them. He also hinted that foreign powers which had complained at what had transpired should be careful, lest worse misconduct by themselves should be cited in

---

[19] Marcy's notes *re* Falkland Is., July 1, Oct. 7, 16, *ibid.*, and Crampton's notes *re* same, Sept. 12, 21, Oct. 20, and enclosures with these, Notes from Br.

[20] Philip Griffiths, priv., to Clarendon, Aug. 21, F.O. 5.

rebuttal. This last was "a cut direct at Lord Clarendon," in return for Clarendon's remarks upon the affair, as Marcy admitted privately. He hardly mentioned the stalemate in Buchanan's negotiations.[21]

Although the message contained some skillful flights of rhetoric, it was a pity that they could not have been devoted to a better cause. For relations with Britain had come to an *impasse*. Not only had the United States resolved to yield nothing as to Greytown and Central America at large. The British, for themselves, had given the whole matter up as a bad job, determined to leave the United States severely alone. They had become convinced that its government was being lax deliberately in regard to filibustering and other forcible measures, as part of a deep-laid design of expansion. Accordingly, they refrained from protest, so that the United States would not be encouraged to be even more aggressive.[22] As Aberdeen wrote to Clarendon on November 5, Britain's best course was a waiting game, "by means of civil negotiations for some indefinite period."[23] In short, there would probably be no solution for some time to come. Marcy recognized this, as is revealed by the circumstance that after the receipt of the news of Greytown he wrote no despatches on the Central American issues in general during the remainder of the year. At the same time, the events which had occurred were to be laid in part at his own door. He had acquiesced in the mission of Hollins.

---

[21] John H. Wheeler to Marcy, Dec. 22, Manning IV, 432-433; Buchanan to Marcy, Oct. 25, M.P.; *Mess. & Pap.,* 280-284; Marcy to J. A. Thomas, copy, M.P., filed at end of March, 1854.

[22] Williams, 194-195.

[23] Aberdeen to Clarendon, Nov. 5, *Amer. Hist. Rev.,* vol. 42, p. 498, as cited above.

XXVIII. THE *BLACK WARRIOR,* OSTEND, —AND DISILLUSIONMENT

"Alas! that in her men abroad
Our land is so ill-starred,
That foreign influence should make
Our softs so very hard."[1]

MEANWHILE, there had been continual excitement over Cuba. Threats of a filibuster and of revolt in the island, two revolutions in Spain, the flagrant misconduct of the United States envoy, Mr. Soulé, and a vainglorious despatch from the chief American ministers in Europe had kept the Cuban pot boiling in grand fashion. And meantime, too, the mid-term elections had been held.

In the very first week in January, tidings had come that Soulé had fought a duel with the Marquis de Turgot, the dean of the Madrid diplomatic corps, who, as France's ambassador, was also its most influential member. While some of Soulé's hot-headed friends at home had had only raucous laughter at the idea of his hitting his adversary, since he was a wretched shot and Turgot was said to have unusually thin legs,[2] Soulé had managed to wound the other man just above the knee, laming him for life. Ostensibly, the dispute arose because of an alleged insult to Madame Soulé, who had worn a very *décolleté* dress to a ball. Soulé, however, declared that Turgot had been trying indirectly to force him out of his post in Spain. Marcy's response to the news was a cold one, for Soulé had plainly much impaired his usefulness at that court. By February 6, however, the president had decided not to remove him. According to the president's private secretary, Sidney Webster, this was from a fear that such a step would have led the southern extremists to bring up the whole Cuban business in the senate. This, in turn, would have endangered the Nebraska bill. The best that Marcy could do, therefore, was to tell Sartiges that the administration "re-

---

[1] Contributed to *E. Post,* Aug. 3, 1854.
[2] Edwin De Leon, *Thirty Years of My Life on Three Continents,* I, 84.

gret [ted] sincerely that it [had] happened." He did so with obvious embarrassment. According to Sartiges, he and others of the cabinet hoped, however, that Soulé would resign.[3]

As for Cuba itself, Soulé's despatches told of a hostile reception for all of Marcy's plans. He was trying none the less, he said, to win the support of the dowager queen, Christina, who had huge interests in Cuba and was very mercenary. On the other hand, he warned that the new captain general of the island, Pezuela, was opposed to slavery and that it was likely that large classes of slaves would be freed. This would be done in order to render the property owners uneasy and hence more dependent upon Spain. Meantime, word had been coming to Washington from Havana of decrees such as Soulé predicted. This was very alarming to the South. There were also widespread reports that the Anglo-French alliance was backing the new program.[4]

Then on March 9, came the exasperating news that the crack American steamer *Black Warrior* had been seized at Havana while on her usual run from Mobile to New York. Since she was not allowed to land cargo there, she had as was customary been cleared in advance as "in ballast." This was a routine long sanctioned by the local authorities, although technically illegal. Her cargo of cotton had also been confiscated and a heavy fine had been imposed which her captain had refused to pay.

There was great excitement at Washington. Marcy, for one, was very angry. He told Sartiges that he was sure that Spain had done the thing deliberately, to provoke the United States, and he said to the Russian *chargé* that "if he had had the available vessels he would have sent them to Havana." A more feasible step, advocated by leaders from both sections, was to suspend the neutrality laws, as a warning to Spain that if she did not make amends, and quickly, the government would unleash the filibusters. On March 11, he wrote in very strong terms to Soulé regarding the affair. On the same day, he penned his wrathful query to Buchanan about the

---

[3] Soulé to Marcy, Dec. 23, Manning XI, 729-734; Sidney Webster, "Mr. Marcy, the Cuban Question and the Ostend Manifesto," *Pol. Sci. Quarterly,* VIII, 20; Sartiges to Drouyn de Lhuys, Jan. 8, Feb. 6, Cor. Pol., cited in Ettinger, 233-234.

[4] Soulé to Marcy, Dec. 23, Jan. 20, Manning XI, 729-736; Nevins, *Ordeal,* II, 348.

extent to which the "happy accord" of Britain and France would go. As it turned out, the belligerent attitude of Marcy and most of the rest of the cabinet alarmed the anti-Nebraska men, who raised a violent outcry that the administration was seeking to use the episode as a way out of its sectional troubles. As a result, Pierce decided upon a discreet course. This was by March 15. By that time, also, Marcy's usual common sense had doubtless reasserted itself.[5]

The upshot was that on that day, March 15, Marcy sent instructions to Soulé simply to seek an indemnity of $300,000 and the disavowal of the officers involved. The outrage was so grave, he said, that the United States would have been justified in taking it up at Havana itself and, he implied, at the cannon's mouth. But the president, "anxious to preserve peaceful relations," had decided against this. Soulé was, however, to obtain as early a reply as possible; the messenger who took this despatch to him would wait for the answer. On this day, also, a special agent was sent to Cuba in the most secret manner to find out the truth as to "Africanization." Lastly, in a public message, congress was told of the diplomatic representations being made to Spain and was promised that if they failed the president would "use the authority and means which Congress [might] grant" to him to uphold the country's honor. It was hinted that a big appropriation ought to be made, for use in case an emergency should arise. In short, the document talked in large terms, but with intentional vagueness. Sidney Webster relates that the purpose was to keep the South in line, while pressing for a peaceable decision.[6]

The evasive quality of this message made it in the long run unsatisfactory in all quarters.[7] By early next month, however, the administration was ready for a new departure. The fact was that the policy of Pezuela had given pause to those in the cabinet who sympathized with the actual filibustering element, since the negroes

[5] W. H. Robertson to Marcy, Mar. 1, Marcy to Soulé, Mar. 11, Manning XI, 740-742, 168-170; *Atlas,* Mar. 11; F.O. 5, Mar. 12; *Times,* Mar. 11-16; H. L. Janes, "The Black Warrior Affair," *Amer. Hist. Rev.*, XII, 280-298, incl. docs.
[6] Marcy to Soulé, Mar. 15, Manning XI, 174-175; Marcy to C. W. Davis, Special Missions, D. S., Mar. 15; *Mess. & Pap.,* 234-235; Webster, *loc. cit.,* 13.
[7] Cf. Nevins, *Ordeal,* 349, and *Times,* Mar. 16, 17.

who were being freed would doubtless fight if a filibustering invasion occurred. In consequence, there was a shift to a policy of purchase. To Marcy, who wanted the acquisition of the island only if by peaceful means and showed no great enthusiasm even for that, the step can have caused no great concern. Its chance of success was too slight. The gullible Pierce, on the other hand, must have found very tempting the reports which came from Soulé on March 30 and Buchanan on March 31, that Spain was so weak financially as to be just about helpless and that the Allies had no thought of joint action as to Cuba.[8]

The resultant of these factors was the fateful instruction which Marcy had ready on April 3. Should circumstances allow it, he wrote, Soulé was to renew the effort to buy Cuba, for as much as $130,000,000. ". . . this will be a delicate and difficult negotiation, and the manner of conducting it is left wholly to your discretion." Should this not prove feasible, however,

you will then direct your efforts to the next most desirable object, which is to detach that Island from the Spanish dominion and from all dependence on any European power.

Though Spain's pride might revolt at the thought of a sale, he went on, it had been suggested that she might be induced to agree to its independence. For its part, the United States would be ready to assist the inhabitants in such a move. He did not specify how. As a first step, Soulé might press Spain to relax somewhat the arbitrary character of her rule, so that native leaders could organize. In such an event, the United States would be ready to assist these leaders to work for independence. Was this a covert way of saying that it would help foment revolution, once Spain had made it practicable? Probably not. If that had been the idea, it would surely have been conveyed more privately. It should be noticed also, in regard to the part about the delicacy of the negotiation for purchase, that there has never been evidence of provision at any time of federal secret service funds to Soulé, in striking contrast to the case of Israel Andrews. Although seemingly ambiguous, the instruction probably meant what it ap-

---

[8] Rauch, *op. cit.,* 281; Soulé to Marcy, Feb. 23, Manning XI, 737-739. Buchanan to Marcy, Mar. 17, Manning VII, 534.

peared to. As it said, a sovereign Cuba (if not black) would offer the United States little anxiety.[9]

To the more radical southerners, however, this was by no means enough. They wanted a conquest of the island right away, either by filibuster or by American national forces. It was known in diplomatic circles, indeed, that the would-be filibusters at New Orleans had raised upwards of $500,000[10] and acquired thousands of stands of arms, while the newspapers kept telling of the presence in the Gulf of the bark *Grapeshot*, which was laden with army-surplus muskets. In the senate, moreover, Slidell was calling for a suspension of the neutrality laws. Beyond that, there were reports from Cuba that negro regiments were being formed, while native white leaders were threatening that if there was no American invasion by the end of May they would themselves revolt. Then, also during May, there came the report of the secret agent sent to Cuba. He said that Africanization was indeed to be expected.[11] While Marcy questioned this conclusion, more excitable persons thought differently.

Under these circumstances it was well that Spain had recently returned the *Black Warrior* to its owners, complete with cargo. This was offset, however, by the arrival of news from Madrid that Soulé had presented the indemnity demand in a thoroughly high-handed style. He had turned it over as an ultimatum, allowing forty-eight hours for a reply, and had made insulting remarks in his notes to the foreign minister.[12] Marcy was furious. He told Sartiges that Soulé had gone beyond his instructions; what was more, he allowed Sartiges to send a record of his remarks to Paris and even certified them as correct.[13] This proved to be merely his own reaction, regrettably. Pierce declined to remove Soulé and even made some further concessions to the radicals.

Within five days, indeed, there was a secret crisis. James M. Mason, Douglas, and Slidell himself—in short, the Democratic majority of the foreign relations committee—told Pierce that they wished to approve of Slidell's motion. The outcome was a conference at the White

---

[9] Marcy to Soulé, Apr. 3, Manning XI, 175-178.

[10] F. O. 5, Nov. 13, 1854.

[11] Robertson to Marcy, Apr. 26, May 11; report of C. W. Davis, May 22, Manning XI, 768-795, *passim.*

[12] *Union,* Mar. 28; Soulé to Marcy, Apr. 13, and encl., Manning VI, 751-759.

[13] Sartiges to Drouyn de Lhuys, May 7, Cor. Pol., cited in Ettinger, 268.

House. Marcy was not present; at the same time, he apparently approved of what was done. This was that Pierce proposed to his callers the creation of a three-man commission to go to Madrid to present to that government in all seriousness the desire for Cuba and to warn that probably only a cession would stop the filibusters. The three visitors accepted this plan, although far from eagerly. As a part of the arrangement, Marcy was called upon to telegraph to the district attorney at New Orleans that decisive measures were on the way. This was to help him hold the filibusters in line. Pierce also promised that before the session ended he would explicitly ask for a big appropriation, big enough for war purposes, in case the commission was unsuccessful. On May 31, i.e. the next day, Pierce issued a proclamation calling for an observance of the neutrality laws.[14]

The aftermath of this series of decisions was, for one thing, a killing off of the filibuster movement. Quitman and its other top men were even obliged to give bond for their good conduct. Another result was a more open policy of conciliation as to the *Black Warrior*. First, Marcy notified Cueto indirectly of the new attitude.[15] Then, in an able and important instruction of June 22, he reviewed the whole case. The government was pleased to know that the vessel had been let go, he said, and also to learn, as it had done more recently, that the fine had been remitted. None the less, it wanted satisfaction for the insult involved. He pointed out the repeated prior use of the procedure employed in this instance for the declaration of cargo and said that the statutory twelve-hour period of grace for altering the declaration had been denied. All the same, he said, it was desired that "extreme measures" be avoided. Because of this, the president had "determined to make a solemn, and he hope [s] an effectual, appeal to Spain," to adjust this case and similar extant disputes and also to lay a sounder basis for future comity. Soulé was therefore told to make no further moves in the matter, although he was "at liberty" to read this note to Calderon. It was a "masterly reply," as the head of the department's diplomatic bureau told a correspondent. Two days later, in a more confidential instruction, Marcy directed Soulé more explicitly as to how it was to be used. He was to tell the foreign minister of its nature and was authorized to present a copy of it. Marcy now

[14] Nichols, 342-343.
[15] Cueto to Calderon, June 7, July 4, both in Janes, *loc. cit.,* 296-298.

also told Soulé of the plan for the commission.[16] Copies of the two instructions were sent, moreover, to Buchanan and Mason.

By midsummer, as things turned out, Pierce had not dared to send congress the proposal for the commission, although that body was still in session. Marcy wrote to Mason that[17]

To tell you an unwelcome truth, the Nebraska question has sadly shattered our party in all the free states and deprived it of that strength which was needed & could have been much more profitably used for the acquisition of Cuba—

While Marcy and the president had had hopes that the sectional feeling in the North would blow over, that had not transpired. As the end of the session came on, it was arranged that a call should be made by the senate to ask if the emergency appropriation was still needed; Pierce replied that that was the case. But the senate foreign relations committee decided that discretion was the better part of valor, and buried the idea.[18]

There had been a revolution in Spain in July, however, and even Marcy, for all his conservatism, had a faint hope that it might prove helpful. Now, on August 8 or a week after the ill-fated message as to emergency funds, there returned from Europe the ebullient Daniel Sickles, with a head full of plans and a case full of despatches. He was soon the president's guest. He bore the news that Orense, the chief of the Spanish republicans, a minor faction, was ready to give Cuba its freedom if he gained power.[19] Soulé was writing also that Cuba would be sold at a fair price if the United States would put up $300,000 to help this faction gain office. On the day before Sickles' arrival, moreover, a despatch from Mason had come, denying that there was any chance that Spain would be given military aid by the Allies. Soulé had written on July 23, it may be added, that he considered the moment a favorable one for sending a commission.[20]

The discussions that followed Sickles' arrival produced a pair of

[16] Marcy to Soulé, June 22, 24, Manning XI, 179-190; Dallas to F. Markoe, July 10, Markoe Papers, L.C.
[17] To Mason, July 23, draft, M.P.
[18] Nichols, 353-354.
[19] *Union*, July 29, Aug. 2, 10; Nichols, 358-359; Ettinger, 326 (as to Sickles' message).
[20] Soulé to Marcy, July 15, Manning XI, 798-799; Mason to Marcy, July 20, Manning VI, 652-658; Soulé to Marcy, July 23, priv., M.P.

instructions to Soulé which Marcy had ready on August 16. The first of these merely said that there was no change in policy, i.e. that purchase was still the objective, but that the current revolution would perhaps in time produce beneficial results. The second was the important one. Essentially it meant something like the old commission idea. Alluding to the importance of the Allies in Spanish and Cuban affairs and to the need for harmonious action by the ministers at all three capitals, Marcy said that it seemed desirable for Buchanan, Mason, and Soulé to meet "as early as may be at some convenient central point, (say Paris,) to consult together . . . and to adopt measures for perfect concert of action in aid of your negotiations at Madrid." Soulé was therefore, if he assented, to make the necessary arrangements. If the meeting was held, the government was to be advised at once through a special agent. As the simultaneous despatch to Mason said: "This whole subject in its widest range is opened to your joint consideration."[21]

The reasoning behind this move was to be found in a plan which August Belmont had proposed in 1852 and which Buchanan had since taken up. The European holders of Spanish bonds, which were very depreciated, were to unite in a sort of international conspiracy to compel Spain to sell Cuba in order to pay her debts. Since the bondholders included men of vast wealth and influence, there was some prospect of success. In addition, by the way, a portion of the proceeds of the sale would be used to build Spain a network of railroads, which she lacked; it was argued that the economic benefits from this would far outweigh the loss of Cuba. As Marcy explained:[22]

Mr. Buchanan having suggested as I understand in a private letter to the President that it was probable that an influence might be brought to bear on Spain in regard to the sale of the Island of Cuba by the Spanish Creditors & bondholders in London & Paris the President was induced to believe that a conference of Mr. B. & Mr. Mason with Mr. Soulé might possibly result in some thing favorable to our negotiation with Spain. Mr. S. was therefore authorize [d] to have a meeting with those two gentlemen at some convenient place to be designated by him. . . . I was not myself very hopeful of any very useful result from such a conference but did not think, it would in any event be harmful. . . .

[21] Marcy to Soulé, Aug. 16, Manning XI, 190-193, 193-194; Marcy to Mason, Aug. 16, Manning VI, 482.

[22] W. J. Staples to Marcy, Nov. 26, 1852, M.P.; Rauch, *op. cit.,* 259; Marcy to P. D. Vroom, Nov. 4, M.P.

Marcy's scepticism was well justified. Even on the 14th, the *Union's* New York correspondent was writing that the new Spanish ministry was just as monarchist, i.e. conservative, as its predecessor. According to a statement made by Buchanan in 1856, however, it was Marcy himself who urged the idea of a three-man move, as such, his purpose being to have the other two act as checkreins on Soulé. Sidney Webster agrees that this was the purpose involved. But what Marcy did not know was that Pierce secretly told Sickles, verbally, that he would be on the watch for any revolt in Cuba, ready to exploit it to the best advantage. In his vague style he also gave Sickles to understand that he was ready for a drastic policy in general. As Buchanan said in 1856, Pierce thus destroyed the chance of keeping Soulé in line.[23] But Marcy did not know that he had been betrayed.

Despite his ignorance of this, Marcy was not very optimistic, as has been said, as to the outcome. But the driblets of news which came from Europe in the next two months were positively alarming. For one thing, there were reports that Soulé had been active in promoting a second uprising, this one by his cherished republicans. Then, after its failure, and it fortunately had been bloodless, he had departed in a blare of publicity for French territory just across the border, where he consorted with a number of French and Spanish republican refugees who frequented that area. All of this was well known to the governments of the two countries and to the press. Marcy himself learned many of the facts, however, from a series of confidential letters which Perry, Soulé's secretary of legation, began to write to him after his superior had left. Perry said also that Soulé had deliberately tried to foment trouble and for this purpose had withheld the June 22 note on the *Black Warrior*. Once again, Marcy was outraged; he told Sartiges that he was ready to abandon Soulé. At the same time, he was as impotent as before. What was equally bad was the revelation by O'Sullivan from Lisbon, that a certain "V. Frondé," an agent of the continental republican committee at London, had been given a passport there as bearer of American despatches to Portugal and Spain and had used the privilege to carry messages to would-be revolution-

---

[23] *Union,* Aug. 20; despatch from Lancaster, Nov. 15, 1856, obviously based on a statement by Buchanan, by the Philadelphia correspondent of the *Times,* in issue of Nov. 17; Webster, *loc. cit.,* 20; Nichols, 359 (what Pierce told Sickles).

aries in those countries. Frondé was also said to be planning to go on to France to arrange a revolt and the assassination of Napoleon III by an "infernal machine." Marcy at once wrote to Mason to give warning to the emperor and wrote to Buchanan to enquire as to this misuse of American passports.[24]

These difficulties with France were especially embarrassing, for the United States already was having problems with that power. In the previous spring, the French consul at San Francisco, Patrice Dillon, had assisted in recruiting men under the banner of Count Raousset de Boulbon, a filibuster who had made an incursion into Sonora in 1852. Even more prominent in the affair, it is true, had been the Mexican consul, one Del Valle, although he was perhaps at first only a dupe. When Del Valle had been prosecuted for a violation of the neutrality laws, in April, however, he had called for the services of Dillon as a witness in his defense. Dillon had been made to attend the court, in violation of a recent treaty with France which gave consuls certain immunities. Although the judge had later released him, after learning of the treaty, Dillon had arrogantly struck his consular flag, demanding atonement. The matter had since involved Marcy in a number of warm conversations with Sartiges and, since Mason had requested him to handle it personally, in a great deal of writing of notes to Drouyn de Lhuys. Marcy was disposed to be conciliatory, but the emperor's government had been very demanding and no settlement had been secured. The case was complicated by Dillon's own involvement in the recruiting. He had himself been tried, later, for violating the neutrality laws, but the jury had disagreed. Perhaps unfortunately for the American position in the case, the prosecutor had then dismissed the charges. Meantime, by the way, the *Union* had on October 1 reported the end of Raousset de Boulbon's dream. That brave but foolish man, who earlier had been defeated in battle, had been shot by a Mexican firing squad.[25] As it happened, the Dillon affair was not to be cleared up until the following year.[26]

---

[24] Ettinger, 303-327, 377; Nevins, *op. cit.,* II, 358-359; Perry to Marcy, Sept. 6, priv.; Marcy to Mason, Sept. 29, draft, and to Buchanan, Oct. 8, copy, M.P.

[25] "Raousset de Boulbon," *Biographie Universelle; Rufus K. Wyllys, The French in Sonora,* 178-180; as to the correspondence, which is voluminous, a convenient brief reference is Hunter Miller VII, 162-205; as to the "spats" with Sartiges, Marcy to Buchanan, priv., Nov. 3, B.P.

[26] It was finally arranged that when a French warship appeared in the harbor

To return to the Cuban matter, by September the plans for the three-man conference had begun to leak out into the press of Europe and America. The accounts given were far from accurate, but there were all sorts of rumors of impending American action. Besides this, a regular host of United States diplomats had begun to congregate at Paris, whether for private reasons or out of a desire to be "in" on the great event. Not only did Sickles return there, after going to the Pyrenees to see Soulé, but Lewis Cass, Jr., had come up from Rome, as had Daniel from Turin; O'Sullivan was present while passing through; and Belmont had been summoned by Sickles as a potential advisor.[27] Worst of all, A. Dudley Mann, who had been given leave by Marcy to visit Europe but had been told strictly to refrain from talking about public affairs, was there working openly for Cuba and making the maximum use of his title of assistant secretary of state. The newspapers of the continent, mostly hostile to the United States anyhow, were having a heyday over it all. In disgust, Marcy wrote to recall Mann. He commented to Mason that[28]

In my own judgement the chances of a good result are much diminished by the unfortunate notoriety which has been given to the movement.

* * *

In the interim, the mid-term elections were shaping up. In the months following the signing of the Kansas-Nebraska act, as has been hinted, there were wholesale desertions from the Democratic party everywhere. In many states, the Republican party had been formed, out of mergers of all of the anti-Nebraska elements. This was not so in New York, but Marcy did not hope for too much there, notwithstanding that. He used what influence he could to persuade Governor Seymour to run again, commenting that he hoped Seymour would be the governor for at least two and one half years longer. He found his own influence rather weak, as before, however, because Pierce did not back him up. Thus, when a new federal attorney was to be chosen for the southern district, Marcy made a most stubborn effort to have L. B.

Dillon's flag would be hoisted, the United States' forces there would salute it, and the French vessel would return the salute. Mason to Marcy, Des. Fr., Sept. 7, 1855.
   [27] Ettinger, 348-349, 354; Buchanan to Marcy, Oct. 3, M.P.
   [28] Marcy to Mason, Sept. 20, priv., copy, Marcy to Mann, Oct. 18, priv., and Mason, Oct. 19, ditto, M.P.

Shepard, a personal adherent, named. But Pierce overruled him, selecting a Hard. As Marcy explained to another applicant at about this time:

I am so situated that I cannot do . . . as much as you may expect. There are men here willing to strike at me indirectly—they would gladly wound me through the sides of my friends.

Marcy commented of Pierce that "In other respects he has treated me with great personal kindness," but the president's political non-support was a serious matter.[29]

As the state conventions approached, Marcy sought to get his coalition group, which still had much strength left, to straddle the slavery issue. This was the best that could be counted upon, under the circumstances. He suggested that the Softs approve of the idea of federal non-intervention in the territories and that they assert that neither the Nebraska act nor hostility to it was a party test. This was approximately what their convention did. One result, however, was that a number of additional freesoilers deserted. While the convention was sitting, Marcy also wired to Seymour, who was still reluctant to be renominated, urging him to consent. The latter finally agreed, but said honestly that if he won he knew that "the jealousy of your colleagues will be aroused" and if he lost they would censure him and call his defeat a sign of weakness on Marcy's part! He was promised administration support, however. Marcy was eventually able to send a messenger to Albany with a letter to this effect.[30]

Despite Seymour's hesitation, he made a good race and nearly won the plurality which would have given him the election. The circumstances were that the Hards had a candidate of their own, but drew a small poll; that the Whigs had the support of abolitionist and free-soil groups; but that there were also the Know-Nothings or nativists in the field; the latter had considerable power, because they avoided the slavery issue and because there was rising enmity for the immigrants who were now flooding in. The man who defeated Seymour was Clark, the Whig nominee. In all of the other northern states except two, by the way, the Pierce Democrats did equally badly. Nor

---

[29] Marcy to Seymour, May 3, 28, July 12, S.P.; to Guthrie, July 7, and Dickie, July 1, M.P.; *Union,* July 11, *Times,* July 12.

[30] John Bigelow to F. P. Blair, Aug. 30, Blair-Lee Papers, Princeton; *Union,* Sept. 7-9, 19; Seymour to Marcy, Sept. 9, M.P.; Nichols, 363-364.

were such gains as were made in the South much compensation. The ineluctable fact was that in the test to which "popular sovereignty" was being put, under the new law, the North was resolutely determined that both Nebraska and Kansas should be free states. "Emigrant aid societies" were springing up everywhere to see to it. Nor could the exploit of Commander Hollins or the meddling and bumptiousness of the spokesmen abroad have helped very greatly. As for Marcy, he received much abuse during the campaign, not only from the Hards, as when James E. Cooley described him as one of the "unkennelled pack of political vermin" which made up the Pierce administration. What was worse was the attitude towards him of the growing legion of anti-Nebraska voters of all stripes. "They fear," wrote Newell unhappily on October 28, that "you are too much mixed up with things."

*   *   *

It was on the very day of the election that there came the expected despatch from the three conferees in Europe. This proved to be as crushing a blow, almost, as the balloting. It recommended an immediate effort to buy Cuba, by a proposal "through the necessary diplomatic forms to the Supreme Constituent Cortes about to assemble," and in an "open, frank, and public" manner. The money would be offered for debt payment and railroad building, as has been outlined. More seriously, the despatch went on to allude to the danger of Africanization. This was discussed in a most flamboyant style and with a startling conclusion:

> After we shall have offered Spain a price for Cuba, far beyond its present value, and this shall have been refused, it will then be time to consider the question, does Cuba in the possession of Spain seriously endanger our internal peace and the existence of our cherished Union?
> Should this question be answered in the affirmative, then, by every law, human and Divine, we shall be justified in wresting it from Spain, if we possess the power; and this, upon the very same principle that would justify an individual in tearing down the burning house of his neighbor, if there were no other means of preventing the flames from destroying his own house.

Accompanying it, there came a letter from Soulé telling Marcy that the three ministers had met first at Ostend and then at Aix-la-Chapelle and that Soulé himself had written the essence of the joint despatch, aided in part by his colleagues. In a second missive, of October 20, moreover, he wrote that he regretted that the product had not been even more outspoken, for the time to act was now.[31] What had happened was that Soulé's zeal and charm, aided by the president's messages *via* Sickles, had won out to a greater degree than Marcy had expected, in other words that Buchanan and Mason had not been successful in holding him in check. There were two conditions, it is true, which lay in front of the policy of "wresting" Cuba from Spain, first a rejection of the offer to the *cortes* and second that there should arise a real danger of Africanization of the island. Even so, the passages which have been quoted above were highly inflammatory and were certain to attract more attention than the conditions cited. As for Buchanan, Marcy's old rival, it seems rather apparent, in fact, that he had now consciously cast his lot in with the extremists. According to the *Herald*, his aim had been to hoist Marcy out of his path to the presidency; similarly, Marcy was told privately that Sanders and Sickles were now working in the Pennsylvanian's interest. There is also the evidence of the alignment of these men and the other expansionists on his side in 1856.[32]

Marcy was deeply perturbed. While there was no thought of accepting the advice of this "manifesto," its terms were soon known in substance to the press, bringing the administration in the public eye to the lowest point of its term. The *Herald* said, for example, that the conferees had stated "that our safety demanded and our interests required [that] we purchase or take Cuba at once."[33]

It was something of a relief, five days later, to learn that the French government had barred the passage of Soulé across its territory on his way back to Spain, for this gave the cabinet a chance to appear in a more righteous garb. Marcy was even moved to write an article for the *Union,* perhaps his only one of the Pierce era, in support of Mason's stern query to France as to the meaning of the affront. At other times he sought escape from his disappointment by reading the new volume of George Bancroft's history of the United States.[34]

When the cabinet debated the recommendations from Ostend, how-

---

[31] Manning VII, 579-585; Manning XI, 824-826.
[32] *Herald,* Dec. 29; Newell's letter of Oct. 28, M.P.
[33] Nichols, 368.
[34] *Times,* Nov. 10; Marcy to O'Sullivan, Nov. 12, copy, M.P.; Marcy to Mason, Nov. 14, Instr. Fr.; pencil draft, at end of 1854, of article for *Union,* M.P.; Marcy to Bancroft, Nov. 5, Mass. Hist. Soc.

ever, Marcy was able to win a complete victory. The fact was that the *filibusteros* had now so far overreached themselves, even leaving out of the reckoning what the elections had shown about northern opinion, that they had ruined themselves completely. Marcy was accordingly able to reply to Soulé in a very cold style. This was on November 13.

Marcy told Soulé that for the present he must propose purchase only very diffidently, and not at all if he found that individual members of the *cortes* were hostile. He then referred to the ambiguity in the despatch as to *"wresting"* Cuba from its owner and said that he concluded that a recommendation of wresting was not really intended. "The President concurs in this view of the subject." In any case, Marcy said, extreme measures were to be avoided, desirable as was the acquisition of the island in principle. As for a threat to American security *via* Africanization, he went on, there was no such danger at present. On the other hand, he stated that the plan which the Spanish foreign minister had recently voiced to Mr. Perry for a mutual commission to settle all oustanding disputes would not do, because some of the problems affected the United States' national honor. Soulé was told, however, to present the *Black Warrior* note without further delay. In effect, then, Marcy replied not only to the Ostend paper but also to Soulé's despatch of the 20th, and denied about every argument in each. Copies of his instruction were sent also to Buchanan and Mason. Not long after, significantly, Sartiges wrote home that Marcy showed a marked "tranquillity of spirit and a confidence in himself which indicate that he is today master of the situation as he never had been in the past." What had happened was that he had defeated Cushing for good, barring one or two later exceptions. As to the Ostend despatch, the administration suppressed it and managed to prevent for a time a call by the house for the documents in the case.[35]

In the annual message, Marcy did not even mention the Ostend business. In alluding in general to possibilities of expansion, however, he took a swipe at what he termed the "jealous distrust" shown the United States on that score by the European countries. This distrust

---

[35] Marcy to Soulé, Nov. 13, Manning XI, 196-201; Sartiges to Drouyn de Lhuys, Nov. 26, Cor. Pol., in Ettinger, 380; *Times,* Dec. 9.

was surprising, he said, in states which had recently "absorbed ancient kingdoms, planted their standards on every continent, and now
possess [ed] or claim [ed] the control of the islands of every ocean."
As to Spain, he remarked merely that its recent revolution would perhaps in the long run permit the establishment of better relations. On
the Dillon case, he wrote that "There being nothing in the transaction
which could imply any disrespect to France or its consul, such explanation has been made as, I hope, will be satisfactory." He deliberately linked with this a reference to the fact that France had let Soulé
cross her territory, as she had finally done, and mentioned in an amicable tone France's denial that the barring of him had been intentional.
As he explained in a letter to Mason, he hoped that this would induce
that country to accept his statements on the Dillon episode.[36] Despite
the message's full-blown defense of Hollins, which has already been
summarized, it was in general highly peaceable in tone. Accordingly,
it was much praised in commercial circles. It was also strongly commended in Europe.[37]

As that *annus mirabilis,* 1854, closed, however, Marcy enjoyed a
far less favorable position than he had at the beginning of the summer. Back then, with the wisely modest terms of the Gadsden pact
ratified, the statesmanlike treaty with Elgin finished, and the far-
sighted policy as to neutral rights well in train, his status had been
very high. Even since then, an admirer might present him with "a
plain, substantial, unadorned hickory cane, corresponding in these
respects with his character," or the *Union* might speak properly
enough of his "days and nights of toil" in advancing American interests in every quarter of the globe.[38] Yet the good had in the second
half of the year been overlaid with much that was less creditable and
for which Marcy as the secretary of state had to bear a part of the blame.
For one thing, there was the rascally behavior of the representatives
abroad, of which there had been many unfortunate instances besides
those mentioned here. As Marcy wrote to General Thomas, with an
eye especially to Sickles and Sanders and the case of "V. Frondé:"

---

[36] *Mess. & Pap.,* 274-284; to Mason, Dec. 13, copy, M.P.
[37] *Nat. Intel.,* quoted in *Union,* Dec. 6; N. Niles to Marcy, Dec. 6, M.P.; Vroom
to Marcy, Jan. 2, 1855, Des. Prus.
[38] J. G. Davis to Marcy, July, 1854, M.P.; *Union,* Dec. 6.

Our diplomatic character in Europe, which I acknowledge with shame, is now miserably low, has been damaged by the Legation at London more perhaps than by any other, though Soulé has inflicted deep wounds on it. The disrepute of this thing falls with the greatest weight upon my department and it is the result of the conduct of men who are my enemies and against whose appointment I made a strenuous opposition—

For this, indeed, the president was more largely responsible. Then there had been the Greytown and Ostend affairs. The Central American and Cuban problems seemed, in fact, as far from settlement as ever. And, finally, the North had repudiated the administration in the recent election.

In writing to George Bancroft, a few days after the receipt of the Ostend despatch and of the election news, Marcy commented that such an historical work as the latter's must bring its author a more "enduring" fame than anyone could hope to acquire in public office.[39] On the other hand, he still kept his aplomb. When the *Herald* predicted that he would quit the department and take the mission to London, i.e. exchange places with Buchanan, and when Buchanan had the effrontery to suggest that this would be a good arrangement, Marcy could write to Buchanan in his old, teasing style, pulling the Pennsylvanian's leg. As a letter to Mason tells us, however, he had not the slightest intention of taking the London post.[40] Old fighter that he was, he was still ready to go a few more rounds.

---

[39] To J. A. Thomas, copy, M.P., filed at end of March, 1854; to Bancroft, cited above.

[40] Buchanan to Marcy, Nov. 10, and Marcy to Mason, Dec. 31, M.P.; Marcy to Buchanan, "November 3," B.P.

XXIX. THE LAST OF PIERRE SOULÉ

"I like all who with a *sound good Conservative* spirit are engaged in administering [the government's] laws and duties—and . . . I feel that we are in good hands now." (C. A. Davis to Marcy, March 7, 1855[1])

THE FIRST two months of 1855 were relatively quiet ones. There was a lull in British affairs and also, for the moment, in Cuban matters. Indeed, after the fiascoes of the Ostend despatch and of Soulé's fishing in the troubled waters of the Spanish revolutions, Marcy and even Pierce had quite given up any thoughts of securing that "pearl" of the Antilles and Cushing and the others who favored a violent policy had been defeated. The result was that Marcy had at least a trifle more leisure for social activities.

The social season of 1855 was a short one, confined to the weeks between New Year's and the adjournment of congress early in March. All the same, it was busy. Marcy himself gave a formal dinner at least once a week. Besides this, there were Mrs. Marcy's various morning and evening receptions, the fashionable wedding of Marian Campbell to go to (she was a former New Yorker), and divers calls by diplomats, fellow cabinet members, and others, sometimes at the tea hour and sometimes in the evening. Mary Olcott, the daughter of the Albany banker, was the Marcys' guest during about half of this period and recorded many of the goings-on in a diary. The household included only one child, Nelly, but Samuel was on call at Annapolis, where he was teaching and rather lazily writing a textbook; in addition, there were Mrs. Marcy's sisters Jane and Beppy, the latter an invalid, her brother John, and George Newell, while Sarah and Abel French seem to have been living elsewhere in the city. When the servants were taken into account, it made one of those large households so typical of the Victorian era. This was all very much to Marcy's taste, although he had none too much time for family and other pri-

---

[1] M.P.

vate affairs, the business of the department being always in arrears. For one thing, he seldom went to church now.[2]

From March until the middle of the year, however, to say nothing of other problems, Marcy was busy winding up various details of the sorry Cuban affair. These involved two points, essentially; first, keeping an eye upon his own reputation in connection with past episodes in the matter, and secondly, a new and final outburst of trouble as to that island.

When the irascible Soulé had read Marcy's reply to the Ostend memorandum and to his own letter about it, he had resigned at once. He had felt that the administration had betrayed him, and was quick to attribute the result to Marcy. His picturesquely phrased letter of resignation arrived on January 13.[3] In view of all that occurred, Marcy and his associates in the cabinet did not need to be offered the resignation a second time. Within two days, there was sent to the senate the appointment in his place of John C. Breckinridge, an able young state-rights congressman from Kentucky. And, when the latter shrewdly declined the doubtful honor, Pierce—for it must have been his doing—hit upon Augustus C. Dodge. Dodge had been a senator from Iowa, but had been remanded to private life because of his support of the Nebraska act. He had few qualifications for the office.[4] But, as the Philadelphia *Public Ledger* remarked:

With the return to the conservative policy of Mr. MARCY, the duties of our Minister to Spain will be light.

Marcy's own comment was fully as pointed: "He will follow instructions [,] at all events"![5] It was possible to adopt such an attitude, of course, because by this time even the South, in general, had ceased to expect much as to Cuba. The filibusters, it is true, were still hopeful, and Mann, the assistant secretary of state, offered his resignation, disgusted at the turn of events, but that was about all. Even the latest

---

[2] Dinner memo. book, Moore Papers; Miss Olcott's diary, in possession of Douglas W. Olcott, Rensselaer, N.Y.; Gouverneur, *As I Remember*, 265-266; Samuel Marcy to Marcy, June 1, M.P.; Marcy to Buchanan, Feb. 6, B.P.

[3] Soulé to Marcy, Dec. 17, Manning XI, 831; Field, *op. cit.*, 75-76.

[4] *Union*, Jan. 15; L. C. Pelzer, *Augustus Caesar Dodge*, 196-198.

[5] Philadelphia *Public Ledger's* correspondent, Feb. 10, in *Times* of Feb. 13; same paper, Mar. 10, cited in Ettinger, 467.

crop of rumors by Buchanan's friends, that Marcy was about to leave the department, was soon repudiated.[6]

The administration went ahead placidly. Late in January it had a steamer which was loaded with muskets seized. Then, when news came, next month, of an abortive Cuban revolt, which the captain-general had caught just in time, Marcy and Pierce told Cueto that they were confident they could prevent any parallel move from the United States, although they doubted that one would arise. Interestingly enough, moreover, Marcy made no protest at the reports that British and French warships had helped move troops to danger spots along the island's coasts. Times had changed.[7]

Although administration leaders in congress had held off any call in December for the papers relating to the Ostend despatch, as has been remarked, it was not possible to do this forever. The best that could be done was to delay until the very end of the session, so that debate would be impossible. Aside from the pressure in that body, however, there was a direct demand for the documents from Soulé himself, who was now in the city. He was breathing fire, especially against Marcy, and there was even a report that it was to be Marcy's turn to be "called out" for a duel. Marcy said nothing to this. When Soulé threatened to denounce the government if his case was not sufficiently explained to the public, on the other hand, there was quite a problem. Should Marcy's purchase or "detach" order of April 3, which had been so misinterpreted, be included? If so, should not Pierce's oral instruction *via* Sickles also be sent in? This last, no doubt, was not feasible. The answer, which was of course a cabinet decision, was to suppress the "detach" paragraph, together with portions of one or two other documents. Marcy afterwards wrote to Mason that he had doubts as to the desirability of sending in much of the correspondence, and that, because of Soulé's insistence, more was sent in than otherwise would have been.

Of course, to omit anything at all, was unfair to the conferees. On the other hand, to have sent in the "detach" item would have been un-

---

[6] C. G. Baylor to Marcy, Jan. 17, M.P.; Mann to G. T. Poussin, May 28, 1855, Poussin Papers; *Times,* Jan. 19-25.

[7] *Nat. Intel.,* Jan. 27; F.O. 5, Feb. 18; Robertson to Marcy, Feb. 14, Manning XI, 838-840.

fair to Marcy, under the circumstances. It was a bad business, either way, and the expedient path was chosen. According to the *Herald*, the papers were withdrawn from the public printer on March 5 for several hours for a last-minute cabinet discussion. Their publication in the press began the next day. The *Black Warrior* documents, incidentally, were included.[8]

The reaction of the public, which did not know of the ambiguous "detach" item, was mostly favorable to Marcy; the "three wise men of Ostend," as the *Post* dubbed them, were lashed unmercifully for their part. Among those who praised Marcy was Lewis Cass. Marcy replied on April 2 that:

Situated as I was the conduct of our Spanish affairs was attended by many difficulties, and I sincerely rejoice that the results have your approbation. [He went on to say that] Mr. Soulé has thus far been quiet, but he will not keep so long. He will soon break ground, and gradually work into opposition to the administration, or at least to me.

As this letter indicates, Marcy accepted the situation with few qualms. Indeed, he mailed out copies of the correspondence to a good many persons to show them how well he was doing. And when the news came, on March 19, that Perry, as the *chargé* at Madrid, had been able to settle the *Black Warrior* incident—and on the basis of Marcy's June 22 instructions—he was quite pleased. He even took time for a letter to Prosper Wetmore, to point out that "The Sp. Govt. have subscribed to all its positions." His attitude plainly was that if the conferees had been so stupid as to write a stump speech into their despatch, and one which was unwarranted by their regular instructions, it was up to them and not to him to take the consequences.[9]

Meantime, there had been a repetition of Spanish provocation in Cuba and its coastal waters. This arose out of the state of siege which had been proclaimed at the time the would-be revolt had been detected. On March 14, the steamer *Crescent City*, itself once the focus of an unpleasant happening in that quarter, had brought tidings that another steamer, the *El Dorado,* had while outside of Cuban territorial

[8] *Union*, Mar. 6, 7; *Herald*, Mar. 6, 9; *Times*, Mar. 6; Marcy to Mason, Mar. 19, draft, M.P.; Slidell to Buchanan (on the threat of a duel), June 17, Sears, *loc. cit.*, 722; Marcy to John Van Buren, Mar. 25, M.P.; texts in *HED93*, 33rd cong., 2nd sess.

[9] *E. Post*, Mar. 6; Cass to Marcy, Mar. 24; Marcy to Cass, Apr. 2; draft to Mason, Mar. 19; letter to Wetmore, Mar. 20, M.P.

waters been fired upon in a dangerous manner by a Spanish gunboat and briefly stopped. In a first note on the subject, on March 28, Marcy had demanded prompt redress. Then came the news that the United States consul at Sagua la Grande, Cuba, had been arrested for allegedly conspiring with the rebels. As earlier in such cases, Marcy reacted angrily.

In instructions to Horatio Perry on April 9, the first and only ones he sent to that man, Marcy wrote that "Spain must be given distinctly to understand that her pretensions to visit and search our vessels upon the open sea in the vicinity of her West India possessions, will not be acquiesced in."[10] Next day, furthermore, he agreed with a cabinet decision to send Commodore McCauley and the home squadron to the neighborhood of the island to prevent any such infractions of American rights. McCauley was specifically told, however, that if American vessels were molested when inside the three-mile limit, such cases were merely to be reported to Washington. There was some element of risk in this, but in principle it was right and Marcy felt justified; he did take pains, however, to explain to Cueto the exact character of the orders which had been issued. Beyond this, he was not ready to go. He wrote to Shepard, the Tammany leader, on April 15:

> I am entirely opposed to getting up a war for the purpose of Seizing Cuba; but if the Conduct of Spain should be such as to justify a war, I should not hesitate to meet that State of things. . . .
> The robber doctrine I abhor, if carried out it would degrade us in our own estimation and disgrace us in the eyes of the civilized world. Should the administration commit the fatal fault of acting upon it, it could not hope to be sustained by the country, and would leave a tarnished name to all future times. Cuba would be a very desirable possession if it came to us in the right way, but we can not afford to get it by robbery or theft.

He added that the opinions of the *Union*, which was behaving in an especially inflammatory manner at this time, were far from his. Instead, he cited as sound the statements of the Charleston *Mercury* in 1852, which the *Intelligencer* had just reprinted. These included the remarks that Cuba could be gotten only by war, that if such a war occurred it would be an unjustified one, and that the chief European powers would take part in it.

The sending of the squadron aroused a good deal of criticism. This

---

[10] Nichols, 394; *Nat. Intel.,* May 24; Marcy to Cueto, Mar. 28; to Perry, Apr. 9, Manning XI, 201-205.

was largely because the exact nature of the orders was a secret and it was thought that the aim was to provoke war, which made the commercial cities and the anti-Nebraska elements notably hostile. Marcy resented this criticism especially because he was simultaneously under attack from the extremists, as usual; when an acquaintance wrote to ask "what the Devil is in the wind" and to inquire if Marcy's "big anchor" had "fouled its cable," Marcy, meeting him on the street soon after, said that he had better write for the newspapers than to him. At the same time, his very presence in the cabinet was a source of reassurance to conservatives. Lewis Cass, for one, said "I trust you will stay where you are, and do as you have done."[11]

The uproar gradually subsided. While it lasted, however, a final blow was given to the filibustering junta. General Quitman was called to Washington, where Marcy and Pierce had Cueto explain to him in their presence how strongly defended Cuba was and, presumably, voiced again their complete unreadiness to support an invasion of it. The result was that by April 30 the filibuster leader resigned from the movement.

As a last sop to Quitman's adherents, however, some instructions which Marcy had been preparing for Dodge were altered to suit the pro-Cuba group. Marcy had said that "it is not presumed that you will be able to do anything to cause her [Spain] to change her present purpose" as to Cuba. In place of this, a bombastic draft by Cushing was employed which resurrected the idea of purchase. This was only a sham, of course. What were more realistic were the proposals, taken from Marcy's draft, of the old plans for direct communication by the United States consul with the captain-general and for a thorough commercial treaty. This despatch was dated May 1. On May 10, incidentally, Marcy directed Dodge to accept a smaller figure than had been planned for in the *Black Warrior* case. We wanted to avoid asking for "remote consequential damages," he explained. In a private letter to Dodge, moreover, he suggested that the Spanish government discreetly be asked to end the state of siege in Cuba and the stringent instructions to its naval commanders there, if it could see its way to

---

[11] F.O. 5, Apr. 9, 17, June 12; to Shepard, Apr. 15, Albert Smith to Marcy, Apr. 11, 13, M.P.; *Nat. Intel.*, Apr. 14, incl. press comment of the day; Cass to Marcy, Apr. 9, M.P.

that. "I have hopes that by pressing this view of the subject upon the Govt. of Spain it will see the wisdom of a course which will go far to allay irritation here and in Cuba." He also said he hoped that self-government would now be permitted. Here spoke the real Marcy.

By May 28, the Cuban crisis had so far passed and the volume of business at the department had so much diminished that Mann's resignation was accepted. A replacement had not been chosen, however.[12]

In the interim, a chain of unpleasant repercussions had begun to emerge from the repudiation of the Ostend policy. The first of these had been the fact that back in March, at the time that the correspondence had been printed, someone in the department had told a *Times* reporter of the existence of the bad-tempered letters which had passed between Soulé and Horatio Perry and also of the secret letters Perry had sent to Marcy describing Soulé's conduct. It has been suggested that the divulger of this confidential information was Marcy himself. In this case, the motive must have been the natural one of whittling Soulé down to size in the face of an expected attack from him. This may well have been so. If it was, it was not in itself a grievous fault, in the light of the conduct of that "envoy extraordinary." On the other hand, we have Marcy's subsequent statement to Perry, on June 4, that he had told only Pierce even of the very existence of these letters; furthermore, Perry himself was convinced, by August 21, that Mann had been the one to reveal the story. In that case, naturally, Mann's motive would have been to defend Soulé, by showing that Soulé had had to cope with a disloyal secretary of legation. Whatever the explanation of the disclosure was, Soulé had replied by sending a letter to the *Intelligencer* calling Perry "a spy and a traitor." Also, some one had written a letter to the *Herald* to say that Perry had been two-faced.

As a result of this last, Perry wrote a long and bitter screed to the *Intelligencer*, indicting his former superior and sparing not one detail of his record. In substance, he said what he had written confidentially to Marcy. This was published on May 22. In form a letter

[12] Marcy to Vroom, May 14, M.P.; Rauch, *op. cit.,* 300; drafts of instructions of May 1, some filed at end of April; Marcy to Dodge, #7, May 10, and priv., May 12, M.P.; Mann to Poussin, cited above.

to the president, his missive called upon Pierce and the American people to have done with the radicals for good. It also asked Pierce to publish every line which Perry had written to Marcy, whether in official despatches or otherwise.

To Marcy, the letter was personally very welcome. He wrote to Dodge that it was generally rather well received and he even called it "discreet." As might have been predicted, however, the president insisted upon Perry's removal. When this was done, it was Marcy's unpleasant duty to write the despatch, on May 26, notifying Perry of the decision; and in doing so, Marcy included some words of criticism of the writing of such a public letter. This was unfortunate, for in the past year he had quietly permitted the man to keep on sending his indictments of Soulé and had told the president of them. In addition, he had refrained from even acknowledging their receipt, let alone thanking Perry.

It was not until a week after Marcy sent this letter of removal that he wrote Perry a sympathetic private letter, explaining the president's action. From its tone, the preparation of it had been a painful matter. Apparently sent on June 4, it explained that Perry's correspondence with Soulé was on file in the department but that the private letters to himself had been shown to no one and that only Pierce had learned of their contents. He refused to publish them, but told Perry to do so if he wished.

It was on the next day, as it happened, that the response of Soulé to Perry's blast appeared. This was only a brief statement. It contained the threat, however, that the public would soon be given a full history of Soulé's mission, including appropriate comments upon Marcy's role in it. While there were some who, like Senator Slidell, Soulé's mortal enemy, hoped that this would in turn cause Marcy to pen a devastating, and in fact an "à la Scott," reply, Marcy kept quietly at his work. He wrote to Dodge that he awaited the onslaught "with unconcern." This was probably true. As he had told August Belmont the year before when Belmont was under fire from Captain Gibson: "I am so hardened to Newspaper attacks that I may err by disregarding them too much." It was a sound attitude, to be sure. At the same time, he had in the process become callous to a good many considerations. His treatment of Perry tells us this.

While the attack from Soulé, which was expected to be *via* a book, did not ever materialize, Marcy was instead confronted with one from Perry. This appeared on September 18 and, like the other missives, in the *Intelligencer,* it was insulting in tone but at least had the virtue of being brief, the latter probably because the writer had little to go on. Its main point was that Marcy had never communicated with him, either privately or through despatches, except at the time of the *El Dorado* case, as has already been cited. Perry's complaint was not surprising. It should be added that later, when he had received Marcy's June 4 letter, he wrote to thank him for treating the correspondence confidentially. It was at this time that he blamed the March revelations upon Mann.[13]

Nor was anything accomplished later in Spanish affairs. Marcy did write to Dodge, on July 7, to propose officially the making of a sweeping commercial treaty. In fact, since Dodge was not very competent in such matters and because Dodge asked him to, he drafted a suitable *projet* for him. Then, on July 16, in a private letter, he alluded once more to the independence of Cuba. "This is a primary object with this govt.," he added. With neither of these approaches, however, could anything be accomplished, in 1855 or afterwards. Although Dodge proved an acceptable envoy and was favored with an expression now and then of good will or even more than that from the foreign ministry, Spain was rife with suspicion of the United States and would make no agreements with it, even if beneficial to herself. Nor was it possible to get satisfaction for the *El Dorado* case or for any of the older items.[14] So ended the Spanish chapter. It was a futile one, and very discreditable to the United States. Although it was in the main not of Marcy's doing, Marcy could not be separated from it entirely. On the other hand, if he had been more successful in keeping his country's Spanish relations under his own control, he would have derived more in the way of reputation from them.

---

[13] Soulé letters in *Nat. Intel.,* Mar. 24, June 5; Perry letters, *ibid.,* May 22, Sept. 18; Perry to Marcy, Apr. 10, 28, Aug. 21, M.P., and Apr. 28, Moore Papers; Marcy to Perry, official, May 26; priv. draft, [June 4], M.P.; Slidell to Buchanan, June 17, cited above; Marcy to Dodge, May 12, July 16, to Belmont, Nov. 5, 1854, M.P.

[14] To Dodge, July 7, 16, draft, C. A. Davis to Marcy, Dec. 8, 1856, M.P.; Dodge to Marcy, Aug. 26, 1855, with encl., Jan. 13, with encl., Apr. 10, Dec. 5, 1856, Dodge to Pidal, Nov. 24, 1856, Manning XI, 886-913.

XXX. MR. CRAMPTON GOES RECRUITING

"The information in his [the President's] possession does not allow him to doubt that yourself, as well as the Lieutenant Governor of Nova Scotia, and several civil and military officers of the British Government, of rank in the Provinces, were instrumental in setting on foot this scheme of enlistment; have offered inducements to agents to embark in it, & approved of the arrangements for carrying it out. . . ." (Marcy to Crampton, September 5, 1855[1])

WITH the passing of interest in Mexican affairs after the middle of 1854 and in Spanish relations after the middle of 1855, British problems became more than ever Marcy's chief concern. This remained true to the end. The one notable exception was the great filibuster of Walker in Nicaragua, but even this was as a matter of fact closely entwined with British relations. The two will be discussed together. The end of the Cuban dream, it may be added, meant a considerable slackening of the pressure upon the state department.

As it happened, relations with Britain were the subject of rising tensions until the middle of 1856. Although the joint claims commission completed its work at London to the full satisfaction of the United States[2] and although the irritating and mischievous Sickles was replaced by a mild-mannered man,[3] affairs simply did not go well. Richard W. Van Alstyne, writing largely from British sources, has concluded that the Pierce administration deliberately sought to take an unconciliatory attitude in order to regain some political backing.[4] There is some truth to this charge. It was also true that the Greytown affair had rather rightly angered the British government. On the other hand, the enlistment trouble, which is to be the theme of the present chapter, was only one instance of provocative action or at least of provocative statements on that government's part. On February 2, 1855, for example, Marcy heard from Buchanan that there was no

---

[1] Notes to Br.
[2] Buchanan to Marcy, Jan. 26, 1855, Des. Br.
[3] This was John Appleton; *Union*, Feb. 23.
[4] As cited already (*Journal of Mod. Hist.*, XI, 172).

chance at all for the neutral rights convention and none for a consular treaty; he was also told that Lord Clarendon seemed very little inclined to make concessions as to the isthmus. When the news came over the telegraph on February 21 that the generally conciliatory Lord Aberdeen had been replaced by the aggressive Palmerston, moreover, the prospects of adjustment seemed nil. Then, on March 14, came the unkindest cut of all. Lord Elgin, who had finished his Canadian assignment, had remarked at a public dinner in Great Britain that there never had been an administration so discredited as Pierce's. Coming from him, this was hard, even if true. As a result, Marcy and his associates were in no very affectionate mood towards the former "mother country."

At the start of January in this year 1855, there had been reports of a bill in parliament authorizing the recruiting of foreigners for the British regiments. The fact was that the British army, weak in logistics and poorly led, had done badly in the Crimea. The Light Brigade had charged bravely enough to make history, but the casualties and deaths through disease for the army as a whole had been tremendous. Nor had Tennyson's comment that "some one had blundered" helped matters very much. The British, who were relying upon volunteering, found it a difficult means of raising men. The first reaction of Marcy upon the subject of recruiting outside of the British Isles, in any case, was one of scepticism that the United States would be resorted to. Not only was there the stringent American neutrality law, but there had been the long train of British protests at the alleged laxity in enforcing it against the filibusters, so that it was hardly to be expected that Britain would now turn about and violate that law herself. In addition, assurances had been given in parliament that no efforts would be made abroad until the governments in question had been approached. American sympathies, as has been said, were on Russia's side, not Britain's; some American doctors, for example, had enlisted in the Russian cause.[5]

It was wholly a shock, therefore, for Marcy to learn on March 22

---

[5] Buchanan to Marcy, Jan. 19, Manning VII, 598-599; *Union*, Jan. 2, 5, Feb. 22, Mar. 14; Stoeckl to Nesselrode, Dec. 28/Jan. 9, cited in Golder, 469-470; statement of Newcastle, in Marcy to Buchanan, Dec. 28, 1855, Instr. Br.; Vroom to Marcy, Aug. 7, Des. Prus.

that handbills were being circulated in New York which quoted British bounties for enlistment and invited natives of the British Isles and Germany to go to a "passage office" on Pearl Street as a means of getting to Halifax to sign up. When the district attorney sent Marcy a copy of such a handbill, he at once turned it over to Cushing for action. The latter, next day, ordered the practice stopped.[6] Meantime, Crampton had come to the department and shown Marcy a copy of a letter which he had just sent to the British consul at New York. This told the consul that his acts were disapproved. Marcy was also deliberately given the impression that Crampton would not tolerate recruitment in any form. During the interview, Marcy took pains at least twice to say that it was his firm intention to enforce the neutrality law, although he did concede that there was nothing wrong in a person's going to one of the provinces to enroll.[7]

Actually, recruiting was thereafter merely carried on more secretly. Early in May, Crampton himself took hold of it, as Marcy later learned. He set off to Quebec and Halifax to make the necessary arrangements.[8] His attitude was that it would be improper to enlist anyone in the states or to "hire or retain" any person to do so when in Canada, but that anything else was all right. He hired agents to seek out prospects, set up depots in the provinces to receive them, arranged free passage by water to Halifax, and spent liberally from his legation's secret service funds for these purposes. Although he was later to deny that this had actually been "recruiting," he called it exactly that in his private letters to Lord Clarendon. This was all done without telling Marcy, although he had been ordered by Clarendon to "have no concealment" from the latter.[9]

---

[6] Letters of McKeon and Cushing, *SED35,* 34th cong., 1st sess., 80-81.

[7] Marcy to Buchanan, June 9, conf., B.P., and Dec. 28, Instr. Br.; Crampton to Clarendon, Mar. 3, 1856, F.O.5. This document gives Crampton's defense of his course. For a good analysis of the whole story, see Learned, *op. cit.,* 237-262.

[8] J. B. Brebner, "Joseph Howe and the Crimean War Enlistment Controversy between Great Britain and the United States," *Canad. Hist. Rev.,* XI, 324.

[9] He was also naive enough to think that the agents he selected, men of no very good character, would adhere to his detailed instructions not to violate whatever he conceded to be the letter of the law. He misled Clarendon by writing, April 9, that "I am upon a perfectly good understanding with Mr. Marcy on this subject," when really he had never told Marcy of what he was doing; indeed, his March 12 letter reveals that he had thought it wiser not to! (R. W. Van Alstyne, "John F. Crampton, Conspirator or Dupe?," *Amer. Hist. Rev.,* vol. 41, 492-502. Many quotations are given from his letters.)

After Crampton had left for the north, Mr. Lumley, who acted as *chargé d'affaires* for him, called at Marcy's house and asserted that the trip was intended for the prevention of any violations of the neutrality law. Mr. Lumley also read to Marcy Lord Clarendon's recent instructions on the subject, by way of substantiating what he said, and also an earlier instruction, dated April 12, which stated that the minister's procedure in the affair was approved. This last, as read by Lumley, went on to say that

the law of the United States with respect to enlistment, however conducted, is not only very just but very stringent, according to the report which is enclosed in your despatch, and her Majesty's government would *on no account* run any risk of infringing this law. . . .

What he did not tell Marcy was that the part underlined above had in the original copy read *"at once relinquish rather than"*—and Lumley had altered these words to conceal the fact that recruiting had been started and had been ordered stopped. As Lumley's despatch to Clarendon of May 7 records, Crampton himself had suggested the change before leaving. Lumley further tells us that Marcy was much pleased with the interview and asked for a copy of the instruction to show to the cabinet. He was given one, but Lumley shrewdly stipulated that it was a private communication. Marcy thus supposed that there was no official sanction for such recruiting as was from time to time reported. Later, however, as he read the instruction over at leisure, a phrase in it startled him. For there was a distinct hint in it that the British ministry had authorized recruitment and had given Crampton a role to play therein.[10]

As it transpired, the British agents received encouragement in their work from no less a person than Judge Kane of the United States federal court at Philadelphia. On May 22, in hearings as to certain recruiting suspects who might be held over for trial, Kane ruled that the making of enlistment contracts in the United States violated American law. On the other hand, he said that conversations to promote enlistment, or even the paying of a person's way to Halifax, did not. Although these statements did not constitute law, they were taken as such by the British. Soon after, moreover, a notice published by the lieutenant governor of Nova Scotia was learned of in the

[10] F.O. 5; to Buchanan, June 9, cited above.

United States. This made it plain that even real commitments to enlist might not be avoided.

The upshot was that Marcy swung into action. Late in May he wrote privately to Buchanan to look into the proceedings and to express his antagonism to them. Then, on June 9, he sent his first regular instruction. Enclosing a copy of the Nova Scotia notice, he directed the envoy to call Britain's attention to it. He pointed out that the recruiting was more than a violation of the act of 1818. It showed a lack of "respect for our obligations of neutrality" and went against "the comity due to us as a friendly power." In view of Britain's concern that the United States had been lax as to the filibusters, he hinted, this came with bad grace.

The President will be much pleased to learn that her Majesty's government has not authorized the proceedings herein complained of; and has condemned the conduct of her officials engaged therein, called them to account, and taken most decisive measures to put a stop to the illegal and disrespectful proceedure.

A month later he had his answer. Lord Clarendon had referred to the April 12 despatch and had said that a fortnight previously, i.e. about the middle of June, instructions had been sent to Halifax which would have effectively ended the program. To this, Marcy answered on July 15 in a note to be presented to Clarendon that the work was going on more vigorously than ever. He added that the administration would now want Britain to do not only what had been asked earlier but also to dismiss such men as had been recruited.[11]

A week later, Marcy left for a brief vacation at Old Point Comfort, rather expecting the president to join him there soon after; most of the diplomatic corps were already away from the capital. Mrs. Marcy had wanted him to meet her in New York state, where most of the rest of the family were. By this time, however, he was becoming confirmed in his preference for the Virginia resorts. They were nearer and enjoyed a more friendly political climate. He left Washington on July 21 and soon wrote, punningly, from Old Point that he was "comfortably" situated there.

As it turned out, however, his stay at Old Point was eventually

---

[11] Clarendon to Buchanan, July 16, Marcy to Buchanan, June 9, July 15, *SED35;* Learned, *op. cit.,* 243; Buchanan to Marcy, June 29, Des. Br.

cut short by a presidential summons to return to the capital.[12] On August 4 there had come to the department Lord Clarendon's note of July 16 on recruitment. This may well have been sent on to Marcy and read by him before he left Old Point. Clarendon flatly denied that there had been any violation of United States laws by British officials, claiming that what had happened was merely that "many persons in various quarters [had] give[n] themselves out as agents employed by the British government," in the hope of earning rewards,

but such persons had no authority whatever for their proceedings from any British agents, by all of whom they were promptly and unequivocally disavowed.

He cited Judge Kane's opinion to prove that nothing that had been done had been illegal. He also held that Crampton had been directed to have no concealment from the administration. He even quoted the April 12 instructions, *in their altered state,* as witness to his government's good intentions! In short, his note was disingenuous, as Marcy could tell even then, ignorant as he was about the falsification of the earlier despatch. By a coincidence, it was just after this new despatch came to Washington that the American legal officers uncovered explicit evidence that Crampton himself was personally involved. It was the knowledge of this which caused President Pierce to write to Marcy, August 7, to come quickly back to the capital.[13]

Upon his return, on August 9, Marcy seemingly found the evidence against Crampton sufficiently incriminating. Accordingly, he disregarded the minister's calm suggestion, in a note of the day before, that since the authorities in the provinces had been told to accept no more recruits from the United States, the United States should drop any pending prosecutions. Marcy also found that there was ready or nearly ready an opinion by Attorney General Cushing on the whole matter. Cushing declared that the government would be entitled, if it chose, to dismiss Crampton and to withdraw the *exequaturs* of certain consuls who were implicated; in short, he agreed with Marcy that Britain must be held solemnly to account. It was a policy in which

[12] Diary, July 21-Aug. 5, and letters, M.P.

[13] Des. Br., July 20; Pierce to Marcy, Aug. 7, Diary, Apr. 18, 1857, M.P.; Nichols, 420.

the American people heartily concurred. As it happened, however, no action was taken for the time being, because the president soon went off for a vacation at White Sulphur Springs. Indeed, this led Marcy to take a further respite himself. He went now to Berkeley Springs. It was not until early in September that the administration was functioning fully again, the first cabinet meeting being on September 3.[14]

In the light of what followed, some authors have concluded that Marcy disliked Crampton. This was not so. He stated on September 2 to Buchanan that:

I confess that I regret to be obliged to strike a blow at Crampton for our personal relations have been pleasant. Though a full-blooded John Bull he is probably as acceptable as any other of the race which we should be likely to have among us.

In a private letter to Crampton, on September 5, Marcy likewise voiced his regret. He also said, though, that "Our national sensibility has been wounded and is somewhat tender in consequence of the unscrupulous charges against our good faith in regard to the maintenance of our neutral relations." This was the crux of the matter. In his formal note, on the same day, he dealt chiefly with the affront to American sovereignty in the fact that the British agents, such as Crampton, had deliberately violated the spirit of the laws, even if instructed to obey the letter of them. Their conduct, he said, had been "disrespectful to the United States and incompatible with the friendly relations between the two countries." Crampton replied that he was sending the matter on to London. This led Marcy to despatch to Buchanan copies of the correspondence and part of the evidence which had been secured. The latter probably was largely that given by Max F. O. Strobel in the trial of Henry Hertz and his accomplice Perkins, near the end of the month, which showed that the minister had discussed recruiting with Strobel as early as January and that in February he had told him that he had received letters from home and was able to go ahead.[15] When the trial of the two men took place, on September 21 and after, there were some added proofs and Hertz, by the way, was convicted.

---

[14] Notes from Br., Aug. 8; *Opinion of the Attorney General . . .*, Wash., 1856; *Times,* Sept. 4.

[15] Buchanan, B.P., and Crampton, M.P.; to Crampton, Sept. 5, Crampton to Marcy, Sept. 7, Marcy to Buchanan, Sept. 8, and encl. *SED35,* pp. 18-22, 112-143.

In the meantime, Crampton was raising every issue he could as a distraction. On October 11, he presented the case of a bark, the *Maury,* which was fitting out at New York, alleging that it was to be a Russian privateer. Marcy replied almost at once that the matter was being investigated and was soon able to turn over Cushing's report that the vessel was destined for the China trade and mounted merely a few cannon for dealing with pirate junks. Before this was over, the minister presented with apparent seriousness the case of the Irish clubs in several cities, which talked of liberating Ireland from British rule.[16] Marcy did not bother to reply.

The answer of Clarendon, which came in a note of September 27, was not what was wanted. He said that he had hoped that his statements of July 18 would have been deemed acceptable. As to giving any affront to United States sovereignty, he doubted that British agents could have done such a thing. He then referred disparagingly to methods allegedly used to obtain the evidence which had been sent to him, saying that they might be "sometimes resorted to under despotic institutions, but . . . are disdained by all free and enlightened governments." He also complained of the American sales of munitions to Russia as unneutral. "This is a very laconic, but certainly a very unsatisfactory answer," said Marcy. It was also one easy to counter. In instructions to Buchanan, on October 13, he denied that his government had used means, to get evidence, which Britain would not have employed. No protest had been raised against the evidence at the trials by the British officials present, he argued; actually, he was at fault here, for the latter had not been allowed to participate. He pointed out slyly, however, that it should be proof enough of the reputable character of the witnesses, that the British had used them as their own agents. As to the munitions for Russia, he cited the fact that immeasurably more aid had been given to the Allies and that in each case it was fully proper under international law. In sum, the assurances of Lord Clarendon as to the work of the agents could not be accepted. On the contrary, the administration awaited the amends which it had demanded.[17]

---

[16] *Ibid.,* 26-27, 90; Fuess, *op. cit.,* II, 169-173; Notes to Br., Oct. 12, 20, 25; Notes from Br., Oct. 13.

[17] *SED35,* 23-25, 29-33.

In October, 1855, then, as, for a variety of reasons, a crisis approached in Anglo-American relations, no satisfaction had been obtained in the enlistment controversy. The practice itself had been stopped, and on October 20 the attorney general had ordered further trials of offenders given up, also.[18] At the same time, Marcy and his fellow cabinet officers had no intention of letting the British ministry or its chief agents off scot free. Not only did they wish to take advantage of the opportunity to hit Lord Palmerston and his foreign secretary hard, between the wind and the water, perhaps gaining something on the Central American issue in the process. They also were naturally angry at the persistent deception which had been used against them.

---

[18] Cushing to McKeon, Oct. 20, in *Opinion,* cited above.

XXXI. THE GREAT NICARAGUAN FILIBUSTER

"It appears that a band of foreign adventurers has invaded
that unhappy country, which, after gaining recruits from
among the residents, has by violence overturned the previously existing government, and now pretends to be in
possession of sovereign authority." (Marcy to John H.
Wheeler, November 8, 1855[1])

THROUGHOUT the whole of the year 1855, while the storm
over recruitment was blowing up, there were also the old questions as to Central America. In addition, the long period of private
talk about a filibuster in that area was replaced by positive action.

As before, Central America was pitifully weak. On the other hand,
the filibustering movement was at its apex. Manifest destiny and the
easy triumphs of the Mexican War, the old frontier tradition of using
force, the sympathy of some members of the administration and of
the *Union* with filibustering, and a desire to keep Britain out of Latin
America all contributed to this. Besides the efforts of Walker and
Raousset de Boulbon in Sonora, both of whom had gone unpunished
so far as the United States was concerned, there were the tentative
plans of Gibson in Sumatra and the private wishes of General
Cazneau in Santo Domingo, flurries anent an invasion of Hawaii—
all three of which topics will be discussed later[2]—talk of taking the
Falklands or even Australia, and a similar interest in the properties
owned by the Hudson's Bay Company in the United States' northwest.
Nor is this the full list. It was a lurid age.

In the first half of 1855 the project receiving the most regard was
that of the Central American Land and Mining Company, now
headed by Colonel Henry L. Kinney. According to the *Boston Post,*
this firm's aims were merely to *start* in Mosquitia; it would soon turn
to overrunning the transit route and would then gobble up everything
from Panama to the Rio Grande, preparatory to annexation of the

---

[1] M.P.
[2] For Hawaii, see chapter 34, below. For Gibson and Cazneau, see chapter 35.

whole area to the United States.[3] And if some Americans feared taking lands there, lest slavery be strengthened, there were many in both
North and South who had not the slightest interest in slavery as a
moral issue or who were not much concerned over it on any other
score.

Against such a background, so violent if also so colorful, Marcy
played his usual role as the representative of a more conservative,
more law-abiding America. Seated in his big arm-chair in the state
department, he was as watchful and shrewd as ever, if more tired.[4]
While Sidney Webster, the president's private secretary, was, by the
spring of 1855 at least, directly involved in the Kinney project and
got Pierce to make some helpful gestures,[5] and while Cushing sometimes seemed friendly to it, Marcy held firm. He also had two great
advantages. The American people as a whole were not inclined to
put up with such adventures. Moreover, if the government wished
any reputation abroad, it must not stand for them.

As has been stated, Marcy had held in 1854 that there was no clear
proof of illegality on the part of the Kinney project and that the
United States could not check peaceful migration. He was not alone
in this. The *Times* said, for instance, that there was no adequate evidence against the company. But when a note by Marcy which conceded
these things was published in the *Union* on January 9, the Kinney
men became bolder. It was soon given out that there were sixty recruits ready in the capital alone and at least 700 more in the country
at large, and that the first vessel would leave from Baltimore on the
25th, while two more would depart from Gulf ports later. Towards
the end of the month, Colonel Kinney's headquarters, now at the
National Hotel in Washington, were literally buzzing with his aides
and subalterns and samples of weapons were being examined openly.
After seemingly hoping that the enterprise would fail from its very
improbability, Marcy now hesitated no more. He was also able to
carry Pierce with him. As a start, he called Kinney in to see him, but
he found him evasive. He would not tell where the land grants lay,

---

[3] Quoted in *Union*, Dec. 19, 1854.
[4] Cf. Henry Wikoff's description of an interview, *op. cit.*, 290-297.
[5] *Journal*, Mar. 2, 1857; *Day Book*, Mar. 3, 1857; Fabens to Kinney, July 3,
1855; Nichols, 398.

lest it be pointed out how shadowy they were. As a result, Marcy demanded a letter from him, giving his purposes. This was on January 27. Kinney complied next day. He still would not say where he was going, but did remark that it would be his purpose "to establish municipal regulations for the immediate government of the colonists," so as to be able to enforce order from the beginning.

This gave Marcy his opening. In a public reply, dated February 4, he said that the term "municipal regulations" suggested that the party would go out as a hostile expedition. In such case, "the procedure will be in contravention of our neutrality laws, and all those engaged in it will subject themselves to severe penalties." More to the point, he gave warning that if they got into trouble with the Mosquito Indians or with the British, the United States government would not help them. This was printed in the *Union* on February 7 and at once dealt the project a serious blow. When, in March, moreover, there was evidence that the filibusters were determined to proceed anyhow, although now quite furtively, Marcy had no trouble in obtaining preventive action: Kinney was prosecuted in the courts, as was Fabens, who was conspiring with him, and Marcy removed Fabens from his post; also, the steamer which the group had chartered was detained. The outcome was that by May 31 all thought of a large-scale expedition had been given up. While Kinney and a few adherents did later slip away secretly to Greytown, they accomplished nothing.[6]

In the interim, the isthmian discussions had not prospered. When Aberdeen was still the prime minister, the British had proposed that the negotiations be taken up directly by Marcy himself. They had not cared for the odor of Ostend which hung about Buchanan, and after the Elgin pact they had come to recognize that Marcy was a reasonable man if a hard bargainer. Crampton had suggested the plan to Marcy in January; he had divulged that the idea was to proceed eventually by arbitration. Marcy had rejected it, however, stating that "delicacy about Buchanan" was the obstacle. Presumably the delicacy was felt mainly by the president, who either did not want to antagonize the Pennsylvanian's many friends or wanted to continue to

---

[6] *Times,* Jan. 4, 29, 30, Feb. 1, June 1; *Union,* Jan. 11; *E. Star,* Oct. 18; Kenney & Marcy letters, in *Union,* Feb. 7; Marcoleta to Marcy, Mar. 14, 18, and encl., Manning IV, 446-451; Nichols, 399; Fabens to Marcy, Sept. 6, M.P.

play him and Marcy off against each other.[7] On his own side, Marcy took no initiative in the matter, apparently convinced that with Palmerston premier nothing at all could be accomplished.

Nor was Marcy receptive to a new British departure in April. This involved a suggestion from Crampton that San Juan be made a free port and be independent politically, subject to a quitrent to Mosquitia to aid in extinguishing the Indian title as a whole. Before Marcy could reply, he heard from Buchanan that Clarendon had repeated his old stand, that the Clayton pact was merely prospective. When Marcy did answer the proposal, on May 9, therefore, it was in no favorable vein. He pointed out curtly that Greytown was not and had never been a part of the Mosquito domain, that its residents were simply not of the calibre needed for "a wholesome political community," and finally and most importantly that the United States viewed the place as a part of Nicaragua and therefore could not approve of such a solution. The proper answer was to put the town under Nicaragua, he said, and to compensate Costa Rica by giving it commercial privileges there.[8]

Later that month, however, Marcy became positively angry with the British government. This was in the first place because of Clarendon's hot-tempered criticism of the annual message for its upholding of Hollins, and then because of a rather naive article in the London *Times,* which claimed not to know why the American people did not sympathize with Britain in the war. This was too much, Marcy felt. Britain and France, he wrote to Buchanan, had tried "to obstruct us in whatever direction we [had] attempted to move [sic]." British lack of good faith as to the 1850 treaty, the offensive articles in her press, Clarendon's "happy accord" speech and a subsequent one on the same order by Napoleon, and the violations of American laws by British agents were all reasons for hostility, he declared. So also were Britain's acts of interference in American negotiations

---

[7] Crampton to Clarendon, priv., Jan. 15, 28, *Journal of Mod. Hist.,* XI, 176-177. Before the discussion had been concluded, Crampton had decided that there was a certain amount of ill will between Marcy and Buchanan; this was probably jealousy.

[8] Crampton to Marcy, Apr. 25, Buchanan to Marcy, Apr. 7, Marcy to Crampton, May 9, all in Manning VII, 601-605, 112-114.

with other powers, he said, although he did not bother to list them.[9] Had he done so he would doubtless have included American relations with Hawaii and Santo Domingo and the tolls upon the Sound.

By the time Marcy went to Old Point Comfort in July, he and Pierce were in a mood to make a strong demand upon Palmerston for a solution of the Central American issues and had in fact quite resolved to do so. Their motives were a compound of annoyance at the long delays which had been encountered and a desire to take advantage of the recruitment affair. In addition, there was a rising conviction on President Pierce's part that he should seek reelection in the coming year, or at least have a large role in the national nominating convention. Marcy was ready enough for a strong stand. After arriving at Old Point he prepared a new set of instructions which he sent to Washington; these were highly satisfactory to the president and were soon transmitted to Buchanan by Mr. Hunter, the acting secretary. In the first place, they asked Buchanan, who desired to return home, to stay long enough to obtain a settlement, or at least to get the issues clarified. The president had been willing to wait for a time, Marcy commented, because Britain was engrossed in the war, but now he wanted answers. For one thing, Buchanan was to tell Britain that the United States held her to be "solemnly bound" by the Clayton treaty to evacuate the Bay Islands. As for the Mosquito protectorate, it was a "mere fiction" and the administration expected her to give it up; and as to the Belize colony the United States "had a right to insist, and [did] insist," that it should be limited to its earlier extent. In short, the despatch was almost an ultimatum.[10] Taken together with the thoroughly unsatisfactory note from Clarendon on enlistment, which came to the department on the same day that this arrived there from Old Point, plus the discovery immediately afterwards of the evidence against Crampton, it laid the foundations for a crisis.

The foreign office took no heed, however; in a formal reply, Clarendon held to his earlier position. Marcy soon wrote to Buchanan

---

[9] Buchanan to Marcy, Apr. 6, *ibid.,* 599-600; Marcy to Buchanan, May 28, priv., B.P.

[10] Pierce to Marcy, Aug. 4, 6, M.P.; Marcy to Buchanan, Aug. 6, B.P.

with some heat that this would not do. Commenting in particular upon the "wholly prospective" idea, he said that:

> . . . Her position in that respect raises a very serious question. The U.S. will never acquiesce in that interpretation of the convention, and Great Britain cannot, it seems to me, believe that this Government will do so. That she is wrong, no reasonable, calm-judging man can doubt; and the judgment of this country and, I should think the reflecting portion of the English people, will look upon it as something more and worse than an error.
>
> . . . From the course of the British Government on the Central American controversy and the recruiting scheme, I am inclined to conclude that it cares very little about maintaining cordial relations with the U.S. I can discover nothing in the present condition of Great Britain or her future prospects to justify her in holding her head so high. . . . With her, as with all others, this country desires to maintain the relations of friendship; but from her and them it claims a respect for our sovereign rights, and good faith in international compacts,—and neither will be sacrificed for the sake of peace.

His view was typical of those held by most of the cabinet and by the American people.[11] Meantime, however, a further irritant to Anglo-American relations was developing, in the great Walker filibuster in Nicaragua.

After a California jury had acquitted Walker in 1854 of the charge of violating the neutrality laws by his invasion of Mexico, he had turned to greener pastures. He had seen the enormous value of the transit route in Nicaragua and the great usefulness of the connecting steamers on either side for bringing recruits, who might indeed be had from the miners constantly passing through. In addition, a civil war was going on in that country. What Walker had proceeded to do had been to obtain a contract with one of the warring parties, the Liberals, to bring in Americans as immigrants; once naturalized, they would fight on the Liberal side—for the moment, at least! In May of 1855, accordingly, Walker and fifty-seven other heavily armed men had sailed from San Francisco in an old brig, after outwitting the efforts of United States officials to stop them. For the next few months, as it happened, they gave Washington little concern. When Marcy first took note of their departure, in June, it was to make light of it.[12]

---

[11] Clarendon to Crampton, Sept. 28, Manning VII, 615-617; Marcy to Buchanan, Oct. 22, B.P.; Williams, 199, 203.

It was not until October that the reports were serious. On the 15th, the department read that Walker's men, who were now far more numerous, had taken the lead in a great defeat which the Liberals had inflicted on the Legitimists at Virgin Bay, at the western end of Lake Nicaragua. The minister, Mr. Wheeler, moreover, wrote so cheerfully of Walker's hopes for more recruits from the steamers which were expected that it was obvious that he was himself a Walker adherent. Then, in the first week of November, there came Wheeler's despatches of October 14 and 23, telling of the taking of Granada, the Legitimist capital, and of the securing of a peace in which Walker would be the dominant figure. What had transpired had been that a coalition government had been set up, representing both parties, with one Señor Rivas the president but with Walker as the commander-in-chief of the army. Letters accompanying the October 23 despatch, moreover, showed that Wheeler had himself early gone to the captured city, perhaps with the victorious army, to help arrange this peace.

Marcy's response was what was to be counted upon. On November 8 he penned an instruction in which he did not hesitate to call the filibusters "a band of foreign adventurers" and indicate that his sympathies were wholly with the native people. He said that there was no proof that the inhabitants acquiesced in the new regime. If they should do so later, he added, recognition of it as a *de facto* government would perhaps follow, but Wheeler was carefully to avoid dealings with it until given orders to that effect.[13] Here, then, was a correct attitude. As to choking off the source of Walker's power, however, by stopping the flow of recruits, Marcy was unable to do anything very much. As he said in a note to one of the Central American envoys on December 6, probably most of the men travelling on the Transit steamers were miners. It was hard to tell if they were or were not, he added, for some of them only decided to enlist in Walker's army after they began their journey. The administration did make some efforts, however. At about the close of the

[12] *Union*, Nov. 15; Greene, *op. cit.*, 58-59; Scroggs, *op. cit.*, 92; note to Marcoleta, June 5, Manning IV, 69-70.
[13] Wheeler to Marcy, Sept. 21, Oct. 14, 23, *ibid.*, 478, 481-483 and notes; Greene, *ob. cit.*, 123-24; Marcy to Wheeler, Nov. 8, M.P.

year, a number of alleged recruits who were to sail on one steamer were arrested and another steamer was held back entirely, but such attempts hardly cut the flow of enlistment at all. When they were made, moreover, it was to the jeers of the bystanders, which indicated what juries would do if any of the supposed recruits were brought to trial.[14]

In spite of this, Marcy held determinedly to his policy of non-recognition. When he learned that Wheeler had made a formal call upon President Rivas, for example, he wrote: "You will . . . at once cease to have any communication with the present assumed rulers. . . ." Three days later, in a note to Molina, the Costa Rican *chargé,* he said sympathetically that he was "aware that the independence of States which may be comparatively weak in physical power is as dear to them as that of the strongest." When a request came from Rivas' secretary of state for the dismissal of Marcoleta, moreover, Marcy postponed any action by ruling that since that incumbent was recognized at Washington on the basis of a letter by the president of Nicaragua himself, a similar document would be needed to supplant him. But when a new envoy did soon after arrive who, as it happened, met this criterion, he was rejected also. This was Parker H. French, a former member of the California legislature. The *Times* reporter predicted on December 18 that should French go to see Marcy he would meet with a cold reception, for "I know of no man who possesses greater facility than the Secretary of State of turning an unwelcome visitor into an icicle." As it turned out, Marcy had no need to summon this talent of his into play, for the man did not call in person. Marcy wrote a note to him on December 21 saying that he could not be received, because the Nicaraguan people had not really given their sanction to the government he represented.[15]

In the light of all of these developments, in Nicaragua, in the old isthmian tangle, and in recruiting, it is not surprising that a crisis did truly come. What happened was that news arrived on November 6 that the pugnacious Palmerston was despatching a large and ex-

[14] Marcy to Irisarri, Dec. 6, Manning IV, 76-77; *Times,* Dec. 25, 26, Jan. 10; Scroggs, *op. cit.,* 145.
[15] Manning IV, 77-80; *Times,* Dec. 21, 24.

tremely powerful squadron of war steamers to American waters. No official explanation was offered, but the British newspapers which bore the tidings showed well enough the tenor of ministerial thought. The London *Times,* for example, said that Britain's aim was to impose a strong wall between herself and North America and that while this would, as the editor commented sarcastically, doubtless call for "mild and temperate comment" from the American press and give American leaders political capital, the squadron might later even be enlarged. The *Morning Post,* Palmerston's usual organ, went so far as to say, boastfully, that the step would cool the arrogance of the Pierce administration.

Marcy was furious. He wrote to Cushing, for once in agreement with that gentleman, terming the *Morning Post's* article even "more mean & outrageous" than the *Times'* squib. In instructions to Buchanan on November 12, he said that these statements left little room to doubt that they were issued by command. As to the repetition by the British press of Crampton's charges that an invasion of Ireland was threatened and that Americans were fitting out vessels to be used as privateers under the Russian flag, he termed such statements utter nonsense. No sane man would believe such an "idle fear" as the former, he said, while as to privateers there had thus far been not one case in the entire war. In the matter of an alleged filibuster upon Cuba, of which the British papers also spoke, he remarked simply that not for many years had there been less likelihood of it. If, on the other hand, it was the ministry's intention to influence the United States actions as to the probable dismissal of her officers, Marcy added, "they have yet something to learn in regard to the character of the American people." He naturally heartily approved of a request which Buchanan made for an explanation. Finally, he called upon the latter to seek a speedy reply on the enlistment problem, so that "final measures" could be determined upon before congress met. His stern position was in accord with the sentiment of the American public. There was open talk in the papers of the possibility of war, but little support for backing down.[16]

---

[16] *Times,* (N.Y.), Nov. 7; London *Times, Chronicle,* and *Morning Post,* all in *Union* of Nov. 14; to Cushing, Nov. 10, C.P.; to Buchanan, Nov. 12, Manning **VII.** 123-124; letters to Marcy, Nov. 15-22, M.P.

Marcy's uncompromising spirit was also seen during these weeks in the first drafts of items for the annual message. One paragraph reads as follows:

I therefore recommend that congress should give authority to the executive to notify the Br. Govt. that in consequence of the practical abrogation of an important part of the Convention [of 1850] so far as it affects G.B. —by an erroneous construction [—] the U.S. are absolved from the obligations of that compact.

As to enlistment, moreover, he specifically mentioned the administration's demand for the release of those men who had already been recruited. According to the newspapers, Marcy believed that Britain perhaps meant to interpose in Nicaragua, to check Walker; it was also said that the president had remarked that if this were the case there might be serious trouble. At about this time, also, the navy department began to get the vessels of the home squadron ready to sail.

Within a few days, however, the administration quite reversed itself. By November 16, judging from a *New York Daily Times* article, word had come from Buchanan that Lord Clarendon had condemned the London *Times'* statement and had asserted that the squadron being sent was aimed solely at dealing with supposed privateers. More significantly, a slightly later despatch and a private letter from Buchanan revealed that the British business community was being aroused and would not long stand for Palmerston's "reckless act." These advices led Marcy and Pierce to adopt a conciliatory course. They wished, certainly, to avoid hostilities, and they also reasoned that if they themselves adopted a moderate line, Palmerston would appear at a disadvantage in Britain. Thus, although the cabinet decided that it would still send a naval force to San Juan to show the American flag, only one vessel was to be so employed. More importantly, it was settled that the annual message should be toned down and that action on the enlistment problem should be cautious.[17]

The quality of the message, as finally written, was firm but reasonable. The Central American issue was reviewed fully, in order to bring it before the British public. It was remarked that to consider

---

[17] Drafts of message, *ibid.*; *Times*, Nov. 13, 15, 19-21; Buchanan to Marcy, Oct. 30, and Nov. 1-2, B.P.; ditto, priv., Nov. 2, M.P.

an amicable solution "hopeless" would be improper, but the ministry was none the less warned that:

There is . . . reason to apprehend that with Great Britain in the actual occupation of the disputed territories, and the treaty therefore practically null so far as regards our rights, this international difficulty can not long remain undetermined without involving in serious danger the friendly relations which now exist.

As to recruiting, there was now no mention of a return of the men already signed up. Such a transition to a peaceable line was made the easier by receipt of Clarendon's admission that the advice as to privateers had been incorrect and his promise that the squadron, which would not come near the United States coasts anyhow, would be withdrawn as soon as possible.[18] This is not to say, however, that Marcy and his associates did not gravely resent Palmerston's bullying act. Quite to the contrary. Nor did they relish backing down from their Central American ultimatum.

On the matter of recruiting, however, they likewise leaned over backwards. For Lord Clarendon's reply on this, in a note of November 16, was not nearly acceptable. He asserted that no specific charges against the officers had yet been made, which was a curious comment, and asked to be supplied with such. He also claimed that the trials held had been concerned chiefly with inflaming opinion against his country.[19] As Marcy sat down to write his rejoinder, however, he said that "I am determined that in manner it shall be unassailable." His reply was dated December 28. Declaring that he desired to avoid any inflammatory features of the issue, he did indeed take a reasonable attitude. He quoted several authorities to prove that it was not justifiable to enlist men in neutral countries and pointed out that the administration had already shown well enough the guilt of the agents involved, but he went on all the same to give the evidence. On the other hand, he closed by asking the recall of Crampton and of the consuls at Cincinnati, Philadelphia, and New York. This note, as it happened, went out on the same steamer which bore the annual message. The latter had been delayed because the new house of representatives, in which no party had a majority, had

[18] *Mess. & Pap.,* 328-333; Buchanan to Marcy, Nov. 16, B.P.
[19] Clarendon to Crampton, Nov. 16, *SED35,* cited above, 38-43.

been unable to organize; on December 31, however, Pierce had sent the message in none the less, the purpose being to put the case before the British parliament prior to its opening. This, in turn, was meant to put pressure upon the ministry to come to terms.[20] The enlistment correspondence, however, was not published. At year's end, therefore, despite the adoption of a course of placating the foe, there was still a crisis.

It had been a trying autumn. Marcy had had the aid since November 1, it is true, of a new assistant secretary, his loyal friend General Thomas, an able man who in his conservatism was an agreeable contrast with his predecessor. For a long time, also, he had been receiving the help of George Newell, who handled some of his private correspondence and served as an analyst of the European press; Newell, who was growing wealthy from private investments, worked without pay. Notwithstanding all this, Marcy was increasingly feeling the burden of his duties. "No one but a person who is with him at his house, as I have been [wrote George Newell] can know what an ever pressing burden is upon him, and how difficult it is to get his mind away from the engrossing official matters which constantly weigh upon him & from which there can be no escape." He was also becoming slightly bent with age.[21] Unpleasant as his tasks often were, however, he was none the less resolved to finish the course.

---

[20] To Buchanan, Dec. 9, B.P.; Instrns. Br., Dec. 28; Nichols, 436-437.

[21] Cullum, *op. cit.,* I, 430; *E. Post,* Jan. 23, 1862; inventory of estate, in hands of Harry C. Newell, Southbridge; Newell to Seymour, Dec. 22, Seymour Papers, State Library; *Charleston Standard,* Oct. 26, 1855.

XXXII. THE SHADOW OF THE
DEMOCRATIC CONVENTION

"The attention of officials & unofficials here is much engrossed with what is to be done in the first week of June at
Cincinnati." (Marcy to G. M. Dallas, April 29, 1856[1])

FROM January, 1856, until the first week in June of that year,
the old issues of British recruiting and of Central America continued to be featured. There was also, however, a new and overriding
factor, the approach of the national Democratic convention at Cincinnati. Although Marcy was not directly preoccupied with this, he
could not wholly forget it, because President Pierce wanted a renomination. This, in turn, had a considerable bearing upon American
foreign relations.

The controlling element in the picture was Kansas. As has been
said, the North had from the beginning organized emigrant aid
companies to help settlers to go there. Since that time, moreover, the
South had responded with a weapon of its own. In March of 1855,
when a territorial legislature was to be chosen, thousands of Missourians had gone across the line for the occasion, flooding the ballot
boxes, with the result that a proslavery legislature had been elected.
When the federal governor, Andrew Reeder, had criticized the steps
which had produced this result, the South had demanded his removal and Pierce had acquiesced. As it happened, the removal was
well justified on the basis of some improper real estate speculations
which he had made,[2] but this was essentially beside the point. The
North was wholly outraged. What followed was that the freestaters
in the territory decided to boycott the legislature; in October, 1855,
they held a constitutional convention, and soon after sought admission for Kansas to the union, as a free state, hoping thus to by-pass
the proslavery government which was in power. With such a division
of power, friction was of course inevitable. As winter came on, there

---

[1] M.P.
[2] Nichols, 407-417.

were scattered outbreaks of violence in the territory, including a number of killings, which were magnified by eastern newspapers as constituting virtually civil war. One thing, at least, was certain: in most people's eyes popular sovereignty had proved a disastrous failure—and the Pierce administration was held to be to blame.

Although Marcy had disapproved of the ousting of Governor Reeder and had criticized the role of the Missourians,[3] he was of course tarred with the same brush as Pierce by the very fact that he was a member of the administration. In the autumn elections of 1855, he and the other Softs, as supporters of Pierce, were naturally unpopular, and their faction suffered grievously at the polls. Although he was able to secure federal patronage for his group, this was no longer of much avail. The Softs were attacked on the left by the Republicans and other freesoil elements and on the right by the Hards and the Washington *Union*. In fact, when the ballots were counted, Marcy learned that the Softs had drawn less than a fourth of the total cast, having been beaten by both the Nativists and the Republicans. This was a new low. The Pierce administration had generally done better elsewhere, it is true, having recaptured several northern states and carried most of the South.[4]

It was some time during the summer of this year that President Pierce had made his decision to try for reelection. He had presented his desire to the cabinet about November 1, i.e. just before the balloting, and had asked if the members had approved.[5] The answer had been what he sought, although few of the members could have believed that he would make a strong candidate. From this time on, Marcy's official position was one of supporting his superior and he held honorably to that determination. While he may have toyed idly with the thought that friends of the administration might want him as their candidate if Pierce could not be carried, he certainly did not take the matter very seriously. As it turned out, however, Pierce had little backing outside of the federal officeholders of the nation and none too uniform a backing among them, even. What happened in-

[3] Marcy to Vroom, May 14, M.P.
[4] *Times*, Aug. 28; as to the *Union*, see issue of Oct. 26 censuring John Van Buren; *ibid.*, Nov. 10; Nichols, 426.
[5] *Ibid.*, 425-427.

stead was that the leaders in the party swung to the only prominent Democrat who had been quite apart from the searing domestic problems of the past two years, in other words to James Buchanan. It even proved that "Old Buck's" share in the Ostend business was used but little against him; what was more, he had the great advantage that his state, Pennsylvania, had gone for the party as usual in 1855. It is agreeable to notice, incidentally, that Marcy displayed no resentment towards him. On December 23, 1855, for example, in alluding to Buchanan's repeated denial of wanting to run, he wrote to him good-humoredly that:

This is a strange world in which we live. Every body here takes Genl. Cass' declaration that he is unwilling to have his name used as a Presidential candidate for all he means by it—but nobody seems to heed your wishes upon that subject. I see I am getting into deep water [he added, however] & will therefore turn back to the shore.

He often found it convenient to use such a half serious, half joshing style, for he had found Buchanan difficult to address in private letters. Buchanan was "sometimes all easiness and confidence and friendliness, and then again all of a sudden . . . as captious and jealous as can be," he had once told Crampton.[6]

Within a fortnight after this letter to Buchanan, Marcy had quite decided that he would not seek or accept a nomination himself under any condition. More than ever before, he was conscious of his advancing age. He was also shrewd enough to see that even if the president's candidacy went awry, his own chances would be extremely small; the defection of New York state, for one thing, had been quite sufficient to ruin them.

It was true, of course, that Marcy had made some compensatory gains in the opinion of the country as a whole. The publication of the *Black Warrior* and Ostend documents had made it thoroughly plain to the reading public that he was the bulwark of caution and of honorable methods in the administration's handling of foreign affairs. Such a reputation had won him a host of admirers, especially among the businessmen in the larger cities, as well as among conservatives generally; this was notably true with both the Democrats

---

[6] To Buchanan, Dec. 23, B.P.; Crampton to Clarendon, Nov. 18, priv., 1854, Clarendon Papers, *Journal of Mod. Hist.*, XI, 176.

and the cotton Whigs. "Had not your balance wheel kept the administration machinery steady," wrote Justice Robert H. Morris of the New York state supreme court after the Ostend papers appeared, "we should ere this [have] been nationally compromised." After the annual message of December 31, 1855, came out, there were more comments of the same type. At the New Year's gatherings at the capital, the very next day, likewise, his treatment of the British problems was approved by all as both strong and discreet. Similarly, after weeks of worry at the thought of war, the businessmen at New York City were delighted. As one of their more illiterate members put it:

> . . . I go from my house in Bond St. to Wall, every day *Sunday excepted,* & without any distinction of party, *Whig Soft hard Repub[lican] Nigger Greeley.* I will say take any *faction* & *colour,* their [sic] is but one Opinion which I will give, *and its true,* I [k]now nearly every *Merchant, Commercial man, Mechanic & retired man from business* & every man of any standing talks in this way: Well I should feel some what alarmed if Marcy was not in the Cabinet, another says there will not be war for Marcy is so conservative that he will not plunge the Country into difficulty another says Marcy will carry us safe except he is out voted in Cabinet Council, another says it's a *damned* lucky thing that Marcy is in the Cabinet. . . .

Then, when the enlistment correspondence was given out, on February 27, the comments were almost as favorable. Royal Phelps, another New York merchant, declared that all parties agreed that his letters had been the best which had ever left the department. There were even those who called Marcy "beyond question the ablest statesman of the age."[7]

This was all very gratifying, and Marcy took a good deal of pleasure on each occasion in mailing out sets of the correspondence to his admirers and friends. He was none the less not interested in a nomination. This is seen, for example, in his continued failure to visit his own state. There was also his persistent effort, in January of 1856, to get Pierce to appoint Seymour, his most important backer, to the vacancy arising at London out of Buchanan's wish to

---

[7] Morris to Marcy, Apr. 14, 1855, M.P.; *Journal of Commerce,* Jan. 3, 1856; G. Davis to Marcy, Jan. 19; Phelps to Marcy, Mar. 1, 1856; C. Jones to Marcy, March, 1856, M.P.

come home. As far as that goes, he was in February trying to get Seymour to take a special assignment of importance in Kansas. In either case, Seymour would be of little help politically, so far away. But, most of all, there is the conversation which he had at the turn of the year with L. B. Garvin, an intimate of Seymour. He spoke unequivocally:

The Govr [wrote Garvin] Says he is not a candidate for any position whatever & intends to retire to private life at the close of the present Administration—He talks [added Garvin] fully & freely & without reserve on all political questions. . . .

Or, as Marcy said some months later regarding the presidency, "When that topic is introduced, I say & say truly that 'I am in favor of the present administration.' "[8] There was always the possibility, of course, that his political friends might try to draft him. Not only was he their patron, but they knew of his willingness to accept office on previous occasions. This was rendered somewhat the more likely when the Softs, in their state convention in January to choose delegates to the national convention, adopted the unit rule and passed resolutions highly acceptable to the South. At the same time, it was recognized that the Hards would also be sending a delegation.

But to return to foreign affairs. For several months, Marcy patiently awaited the replies of Great Britain on the two big questions. When he discovered that Lord Clarendon, for instance, had sent Crampton a copy of the note on enlistment, so that Crampton might prepare an answer, he announced that the administration would wait for it. By April 28, however, when there was still no result, he wrote to George M. Dallas, who had been selected instead of Seymour as the replacement for Buchanan, that he must ask the British explicitly what their intentions were.[9]

As to Central America, there had by this time come a proposal for arbitration. Such a resort had been mentioned in some of Buchanan's despatches in the past year, as well as in Crampton's pro-

---

[8] L. B. Garvin to Seymour, Jan. 3, Marcy to Seymour, Jan. 18, 25, Feb. 10, S.P.; to J. Y. Mason, Apr. 20, copy, M.P. His sending out of 2,000 copies of the enlistment note, in March, was presumably to aid Pierce, for it was a cabinet project; Davis, Dobbin, and Guthrie helped furnish names. (Checklist of states, in Newell's hand, March, *ibid.*)

[9] To Dallas, Mar. 14, Apr. 28, Instr. Br.

posal of direct negotiations at Washington, but Marcy had never
considered such matters very seriously. But now, when on February
26 came news of a speech by Clarendon in the house of lords urging
such a procedure, Marcy recognized the move as a major one. He
was inclined to believe that it represented another step to delay a
solution, but he also knew that the American people and congress
were much interested in the preservation of peace and that therefore
the proposal must be shown attention. Even so, his response was a
cautious one. He wrote to Dallas on February 29 that he thought
that Pierce would decline to accept it; then, two weeks after, he
hinted that it was still being discussed, and rather more favorably,
but added that "Indeed it is no very plain matter to settle upon the
course proper to be pursued."[10] The trouble was that the arbitration
idea had two jokers in it. One was that crowned heads, which were
customarily anti-American, had usually been the arbiters in the
past; the other was that the interpretation of the Clayton treaty was
a matter of principle, which the United States did not want compromised.

As to the great Nicaraguan filibuster, Marcy kept watching it
anxiously. As before, he was unable to stop the flow of recruits
thither, but as spring came on a very real obstacle to Walker did
arise. By a stroke of great folly, Walker had invalidated the charter
of the Accessory Transit Company, a step which was justifiable
enough in view of the firm's failure to observe its contract but which
alienated the tremendously powerful Commodore Vanderbilt. That
he then gave the franchise to Vanderbilt's rivals, Morgan and Garrison, was doubly infuriating to Vanderbilt. When news of the
change reached Washington, the doughty commodore and J. L.
White, his henchman, soon came to see Marcy to ask for assistance.
This was rather amusing, because these men had clearly been aiding
Walker previously by giving free passage to his recruits; according
to the *Times*, Marcy "peremptorily refused to do anything." In conversation with Crampton, who at the end of March came in for one
of his rare interviews of this period, Marcy did, however, voice

---

[10] Dallas to Marcy, Feb. 29, priv. M.P.; Buchanan to Marcy, Feb. 8, draft, B.P.;
Marcy to Dallas, Feb. 29, M.P., and Mar. 14, Manning VII, 126-127.

more concern. He termed Walker "a pirate and an assassin" and declared that the United States government would be as glad as Britain's to see him "rooted up." He then went on to allude to a plan, probably of his own devising, for blockading both sides of the isthmus in order to accomplish this; the cabinet had discussed the idea, but had not given its approval. As Marcy explained with regret, "a blockade is an act of War and would be illegal without a declaration of war with the advice and consent of Congress. . . ."[11] Here, no doubt, was the voice of the timid Pierce.

Not only would Pierce not take such a step as this, however, but he was also beginning to veer in the direction of actually favoring Walker. In his quest for a renomination, the president knew that his chief reliance must be upon the South, and many of that section's leaders were demanding a recognition of the Rivas-Walker regime by the government. In particular, the friends of that regime feared that without such official sponsorship by the United States the filibuster would be crushed. It had already been attacked by an army from the neighboring state of Costa Rica and there was a likelihood that the other little Central American states might do the same thing. It was also known that Great Britain had offered to sell Costa Rica a large parcel of muskets. In view of the great resources of Commodore Vanderbilt, moreover, such developments might be increasingly common. By the end of April, furthermore, there was news of a major defeat of Walker at the city of Rivas.

Meantime, James Buchanan had returned to the United States and was enjoying a triumphal reception. Before he reached Washington, on May 14, his journey had come to resemble a royal progress and it was clear that the president's popular support was fading rapidly. Pierce and Marcy both wined and dined Buchanan.[12] But on the very day of his coming, significantly, the president yielded to the demands of the extremists and recognized the filibustering government. This was a step likely to be popular in other quarters besides filibustering ones, because it represented a defiance of Lord Palmerston, who was reported to have ordered 20,000 troops to Canada and who had in-

---

[11] *Times*, Mar. 24, Apr. 4; F.O. 5, Mar. 31.
[12] *Times*, Apr. 24, 25; Marcy to Dallas, priv., draft, May 12, M.P.; *Herald*, May 15, 16.

vited Mr. Dallas in a rather pointed manner to attend a vast naval review.[13]

For himself, Marcy had held out against recognition to the end; as the *Times* had editorialized on May 5, the country had "reposed upon [his] conservative influence and . . . prudent counsels. . . ." He simply did not have enough influence to check the move, unfortunately. But it was a proof of his firmness that the president felt obliged himself to write the message to congress which would announce the step; as he wrote to Marcy on the evening of May 12, after completing this task, he regretted that he could "not have what would have afforded [him] great relief, the approbation of your judgment. . . ." "I can never fail to appreciate a friendship so generous and true, as that which has been exemplified by you in all our intercourse," he added. Two days later, when Padre Vijil, who had replaced French as the filibusters' representative, called at the department, Marcy none the less had the unpleasant duty of escorting him to the White House.[14]

The other decision which Pierce came to in his electioneering drive was by contrast thoroughly in accord with Marcy's own views. This was to expel Crampton and the three consuls. When Lord Clarendon's reply at long last came, on May 17, it was found as had been expected that his lordship had not recalled them. His note was very conciliatory in manner, and contained a sort of apology, but it denied that his government had had any intention of breaking the American laws. It also took Crampton's explanation at its face value, namely his allegation that he had sought to inform people as to the advantages of enlisting but had not engaged in what he had considered recruiting. The note was accompanied, morever, by a mass of affidavits collected by Crampton and his subordinates, designed to impeach the reputation of the federal district attorneys and of their chief witnesses in the trials of 1855. In spite of this, when Marcy read it he was at first embarrassed. On the one hand, the recruiting business had given the United States government the best weapon in years to use against the British government and he did not want to relinquish it. In addition, the many deceptions practised by Crampton and his subordinates barred an abandonment of the affair. On the other hand, as Marcy

---

[13] R. B. Campbell to Marcy, Apr. 18, J. Y. Mason to Marcy, Apr. 17, M.P.

[14] Pierce to Marcy, May 12, M.P.; *Herald,* May 15.

wrote to Dallas on May 19, "After what it has now said, to hold the British govt. *particeps criminis* might be regarded as severe & unwise." He had none the less found a solution, he added: "A door, it seems to me, is pretty fairly opened for an allowable separation of the govt. from the implicated officials."[15] And this was the line which he followed.

In his reply, dated May 27, Marcy declared that the assurances that the British government had not wished to set aside the laws were satisfactory, but as for Crampton and the consuls, he went on, the weight of evidence was too convincing. He was aided in writing his reply, by the official British correspondence in the case, recently published at London. As he pointed out, this showed that the recruiting had not been stopped until Crampton had given the word, namely on August 5; it indicated, furthermore, that the envoy had used such hostile language in referring to the United States and its government that the retention of him in his post would have been quite unsuitable anyhow. Marcy explained that Crampton had therefore been given his passports and the three consuls their *exequaturs*.[16] It was a very good note, for it satisfied the demands of American self respect and at the same time turned an amicable face towards the British ministry. As for putting the blame upon Crampton, that was proper enough, for it was quite clear that he had disobeyed his instructions, both as to having no concealment from the state department and as to running no risk of violating American laws.

Marcy's note was pretty generally lauded by the newspapers. The stock market was also gratified; whereas stocks had fallen when news came of Crampton's expulsion and conservative papers like the *Times* had been writing editorials "Counting the Cost of War," on the publication of the text stocks rose sharply.[17]

Three days before, the long-preparing instructions on Central America had also been finished. These contemplated a settlement by direct negotiation, if possible; Dallas was told, however, that if this was not feasible, arbitration might be used for some of the points in-

---

[15] *Times*, May 19; Notes from Br., dated Apr. 30; Marcy to Dallas, May 19, priv., Huntington Library.

[16] Instr. Br.

[17] *Times*, May 21; *Post*, May 30; correspondent of Natchez *Free Trader*, clipping, M.P.; C. P. Clinch to Marcy, June 5, *ibid*.

volved. In general, Marcy said that Britain was entitled to nothing
beyond the Belize, and that only as granted under her treaties with
Spain. There were many points, he went on, which the administration
could not allow to go before arbitrators; on the other hand, he was not
prepared to say that some of the questions of fact should not—such
as what were the proper limits of the Belize and to what lands the
Mosquitians had possessory rights; he pointed out, furthermore, that
if arbiters were used, the United States would prefer "eminent men of
science" rather than heads of state.[18] It was a firm instruction. At the
same time, it showed a readiness to take a fresh look at the problems
involved.

*　　*　　*

Meantime, on the afternoon of May 27, Senator Mason had wired
the news of the dismissal of Crampton to Cincinnati to give a fillip
to the Pierce movement. Marcy was not optimistic as to Pierce's
chances, however.[19] He saw well enough, by about this time or shortly
after, that the Buchanan forces should be able to check a renomination
for Pierce, even though the Douglas backers had been combined with
the Pierce men. On the other hand, he did not think that the "Buchaneers" were powerful enough for a clearcut victory; he thus had
some fear of a stalemate. If anything, however, his chief worry as to
politics was over the obvious danger to the Union itself in the rising
sectionalism. And yet even this left him less alarmed than it would
have done a few years before; he confessed privately that he was
simply too tired and worn to take a keen interest in the matter:[20]

> . . . I look on the coming storm with more calmness than is befitting a
> Patriot—for I am satisfied that it is quite time for me to retire from the
> turmoils of active life—Those who have a right still longer to occupy the
> stage, naturally take more interest in the play whether it is likely to be a
> tragedy or a comedy—I long for retirement & it rejoices me that it will
> come in the fleeting space of nine months.

Marcy's forebodings as to Pierce's chances were to be justified. For
one thing, the Soft delegation, which planned to be for the president

---

[18] To Dallas, Manning VII, 128-138.

[19] Marcy's friends still had some hopes of drafting him. John Stryker plainly
did, while Seymour, Pruyn, Shepard, and Richmond, who were also at the convention, doubtless agreed. Their talking point, of course, was Marcy's conservatism.
(Stryker to Marcy, May 9, 27, M.P.; *Atlas & Argus,* May 27, *Herald,* May 29.)

[20] To J. Y. Mason, June 2, M.P.

at the outset at least, was admitted to the proceedings with no greater voice than the Hards were; this was a decision of the mounting Buchanan element in the convention. It was a ruling harmful to the president, of course, but also quite fatal to any plan to draft Marcy, and Marcy's name was not even put up. When the actual balloting began, moreover, the Pierce cause itself bogged down, and by the second day of voting the "Buchaneers" had swept all before them. As to the platform, a move was made by William B. Lawrence, who was a member of the Rhode Island delegation, to praise Marcy's principal achievements item by item, but this was voted down. The fact was that the Buchaneers wanted to disown all connection with the unpopular Pierce regime. What they did instead was to call for promoting the freedom of the seas and worldwide trade and to uphold the Monroe Doctrine (all of which had been important in Marcy's program) but in language such as to suggest that these were new schemes. What was more, the platform urged direct American control over the isthmus and approved the efforts to "regenerate" that area, i.e. to filibusterize it. The Nebraska act was also explicitly endorsed.[21]

Marcy took these results without complaint. On the day of Buchanan's nomination he wrote to Dallas signifying his acceptance of it and commenting briefly that "The next step is to elect him." Four days after, in a communication to the chairman of the coming ratification meeting at New York City, he expressed publicly his approval of the choice; he declared that the selection of Buchanan would unite the Softs and the Hards and that he would himself use his best efforts to aid in winning the victory.[22] He did not comment upon the platform. In brief, he assumed his usual position. His loyalty to his party, together with an honest enmity for the Republican Party, that new form of Whiggery, and a fear that the open sectionalism of the Republicans would endanger the union, forbade him to do otherwise.

---

[21] J. V. L. Pruyn Journal, June 2-6, State Library; Lawrence to Marcy, June 11, encl. copy of his resolutions, M.P.; *Official Proceedings of the National Democratic Convention held in . . . 1856, passim.*

[22] To Dallas, June 6, priv.; to Horace F. Clark, etc., June 10, M.P.

XXXIII. BRITAIN AT LAST CHANGES HER TUNE

"It would be wise if Britain would at last recognize that the
United States, like all the great countries of Europe, have a
policy, and that they have a right to have a policy." (Speech
of Disraeli, June 16, 1856)

IN ADOPTING a firm stand on the enlistment affair, Marcy had
done so only with some misgivings. Similarly, he had been somewhat hesitant to write his note on Central America and to put up with
the recognition of Walker. He had half anticipated that a rupture of
relations with Britain would come and had even told Dallas what to
do if he was given his walking papers. At the same time, he had hoped
that these steps would contribute to the ousting of Lord Palmerston
from office. He knew well enough that there was a latent respect for
the United States in Britain and also that the ministry's conduct on
both recruiting and the isthmus had been criticized increasingly. Beyond this, however, the Crimean War had at last come to an end, and
upon terms none too popular with the British people. There was a
fair prospect, consequently, that the prime minister might be over-
thrown when the peace terms came up for debate. This was a very
gratifying thought: "I shall not mourn his fall—indeed on phil-
anthropic principles I wish it," conceded Marcy. He was to be disappointed, however. On the very day after that comment, Dallas was
to write from London that Palmerston had gotten the treaty through
parliament and had even done so by large majorities![1]

Notwithstanding this first setback, the result of the stern attitude
was in some ways to be successful beyond Marcy's wildest dreams.
Although the British press was critical of Pierce's recognition of
Walker, as Washington learned by mid-June, it was not nearly so
much so as it might have been. When the crucial instructions on
Crampton and Middle America reached London, moreover, they too
were received in passably good style. In an interview on June 11,

---

[1] *Cam. Hist. of Brit. For. Pol.*, II, 276-277; Marcy to Dallas, May 12, 27, Dallas
to Marcy, Apr. 7, May 13, M.P.; Buchanan to Marcy, Feb. 1, B.P.

Dallas read the isthmian despatch aloud to Clarendon. "When I had finished [Dallas wrote] . . . he was obviously much gratified by its tone and import; and he remarked with some warmth, that it would be disreputable to both Governments, if, upon a platform written with so much clearness, and in a spirit so candid and conciliatory, they failed to reach an adjustment of the whole difficulty." Dallas wrote further that there was now a genuine disposition to wind up the whole affair in a process of give and take. As to Crampton, Dallas said little, but there was no hint of anything alarming.

The real answer as to Crampton came in Palmerston's comments in the house of lords on June 16. These, fortunately, had been preceded by an outburst of attacks in London upon the British government's role in the matter; there had also been demand after demand for publication of the pertinent papers. In the house of commons, moreover, there had been an historic speech by Benjamin Disraeli, the rising Tory leader, who had laid down what he termed the proper attitude for the government to take towards the United States in general. His most telling comment, that it was high time that Britain recognized that the United States had a policy of its own and was entitled to, has been quoted already, at the start of this chapter; it probably reflected the thinking of the better informed statesmen of Great Britain. It was in reply to this and to other attacks that Palmerston announced on the same day that no action would be taken to remove Mr. Dallas and that there would be no interruption of friendly relations. When Parliament debated the dismissals problem, on July 1 and 2, the ministry was not turned out. At the same time, it was amply warned that it must stop swaggering and get down to business.

In commenting upon the helpful turn foreshadowed by Disraeli's speech, which after a century would still be viewed as one of the more important in the history of Anglo-American relations, Dallas predicted that even more favorable developments were on the way.[2] As soon as "a somewhat natural sense of wounded self esteem" had been overcome by reflection, he said, the ministry would very likely be entirely ready to seek closer and even cordial relations. He added, significantly, that:

---

[2] Williams, 215; Dallas to Marcy, June 13, 20, Manning VII, 654-658; *Cam. Hist. of Brit. For. Pol.,* II, 276-278; Dallas to Marcy, June 10, July 3, M.P.

It is due to the President and yourself to say that so auspicious an aspect in our public relations is exclusively, and by almost unanimous opinion, ascribed to the equally able, firm, and conciliatory despatches last sent to be laid before Lord Clarendon.

It might have been well if he had also said that the filibustering and the bombardment of Greytown had doubtless served a purpose, too, in forcing Britain's attention to western hemisphere problems. It was against that background that Marcy's statesmanship had been put into play. It was also true, of course, that Great Britain was much impressed with the enormous material progress of the United States in the boom of recent years[3] and simply had to recognize that she was dealing with a major power.

In the matter of Central America, affairs went decidedly well. By July 18, for example, Marcy was reading that his envoy had begun his talks on isthmian affairs and that the approach on both sides had been one of finding agreement rather than conflicts. When, on July 26, Marcy sent Dallas further instructions, his tone was suited to the new spirit. He suggested that the powers try to persuade Nicaragua to set out a reservation for the Mosquitos, with a proper indemnity and with guarantees of the tribe's security. In the case of San Juan, he held that it should be separate and also a free port. The Bay Islands, he argued, must certainly go back to Honduras; if, however, the British thought that there must be safeguards for the residents there, the United States would be willing to discuss the matter; its one qualification would be that British sovereignty must be wholly ended. This was a concession. There was also a readiness to yield on another point, in connection with British Honduras. Marcy said that the administration might consent "in the last resort" to allow a larger territory to that colony than the old Spanish treaties had.

By August 29, after some further instructions from Marcy, Dallas was sending a full-blown *projet* for the solution of all of the troubles; its main text dealt chiefly with Nicaragua. There was to be an Indian reservation, with safeguards, and there was provision for the treatment of past land grants. Greytown, furthermore, was to be a free port, with self-government under Nicaraguan sovereignty, but Costa Rica was to have certain trade rights; boundary disputes in the area,

---

[3] Dallas to Marcy, Dec. 26, 1856, priv., M.P.

moreover, were to be arbitrated by the United States and Britain. Beyond all this, however, there was an important separate article dealing with the Bay Islands. It stated that since a convention had just been made between Honduras and Britain, by which these islands were to be "a free territory" under Honduras, the two big powers recognized that territory's "independence and rights." In return for this, the United States agreed that the Belize (right down to the Sarstoon River) was exempted from the provisions of the Clayton Treaty. As to the Honduran pact referred to, it provided quite specifically that all control by Britain was to end in the islands; in a manner comparable to the Greytown arrangement, these would have free-port status and also self-government.

Marcy now showed himself to be the hard bargainer that Lord Elgin had found him to be. In a despatch on September 26, he demanded that the area specified for the Mosquitos be cut down, that the lands given to San Juan as such be the subject of Anglo-American arbitration, that some changes be made in the rules as to previous Mosquitian land grants, and that free trade *via* the isthmus be safeguarded. In a confidential despatch sent as a supplement, he explained that the first two of these were the more important and that the second, as to the size of San Juan, was a *sine qua non*. Dallas was appalled and told Marcy so quite plainly. He found, however, that he was able to get every one of the alterations accepted; he also acknowledged very generously that Marcy's instructions had given him an effective weapon.[4] Even aside from these alterations, however, the finished convention was a triumph for Marcy's diplomacy.

On November 7, having received the revised treaty, Marcy wrote that it would be submitted to the senate. Even this early, however, he was doubtful if it would be approved. He had learned that Senator Mason himself, that mainstay of the administration in foreign affairs, was inclined to make war upon the pact, to say nothing of men like Cass, Douglas, and Slidell; in fact, there was a genuine uneasiness over it in the upper house. Many senators reasoned that if the Bay Islands were to enjoy self-government they would do so only if they

---

[4] Dallas to Marcy, July 1, Aug. 29, Marcy to Dallas, July 26, Sept. 26, Manning VII, 141-159, 663-687; text of Honduran treaty, *Times,* Sept. 16; Dallas to Marcy, Oct. 10, 14, 17, priv., Marcy to Dallas, draft, July 13, M.P.

leaned upon Britain for protection from Honduras. In short, an informal link with Britain might thus survive. To those unaware of the change in British thinking, such a fear was not unnatural, for the Clayton treaty had taught the United States quite a lesson. There was also a further objection, it may be added, this one brought up solely by southerners. The latter's criticism was that the British pact with Honduras barred slavery in the Bay Islands and they were worried lest the Dallas agreement gave countenance to this ban. In short, the prospects were not very good; Marcy wrote to Dallas on January 4 in a private letter that "The whole filibustering interest" was in opposition. "That faction now looms up larger than heretofore because they believe that the incoming administration will favor all their designs." As the weeks wore on, moreover, the opposition grew. During February, when the subject was in a critical stage, Marcy gave it continual attention, writing to Dallas repeatedly; he noted that minor alterations would satisfy Mason, but not the other senators; he was also dismayed to find that Buchanan, who was now the president-elect, was not urging his followers to endorse it. By February 23 he had concluded that it would not be passed—"unless it is made an unilateral instrument, loosing the U.S. and binding G. Britain."[5]

As it turned out, the answer did not come until after Marcy's term had ended. At that time, in March, the senate adopted a lavish series of amendments to the pact, some fifteen in all. These were mostly concerned with protecting the rights of Nicaragua, or with making a show of doing so, some of them being very petty. There was one considerable change, however; this was the removal of the paragraph on the Bay Islands and the substitution for it of a flat recognition of those islets "as under the sovereignty and as part of the said Republic of Honduras." Thus altered, the treaty was approved, March 12. President Buchanan accordingly had it sent to Britain; as was to be expected, however, the British government turned it down.

Although the Dallas-Clarendon convention failed and although Crampton was knighted by the queen[6] and no new British minister

[5] Marcy to Dallas, Nov. 7, Jan. 4, Feb. 6, 9, 16, 23, M.P.; Slidell to Buchanan, Dec. 27, Sears, *loc. cit.,* 727; *Times* edit., Feb. 18.
[6] Text of ratification by Buchanan, Mar. 19, Manning VII, 629n.; Dallas to Marcy, Dec. 12, priv., M.P.

was sent, the last seven months of Marcy's term were the most friendly ones which he experienced in Anglo-American relations. There was a real wish for conciliation, by both sides. For one thing, the American stand on the Walker filibuster was reversed. What transpired on this subject was that by the time Mr. Wheeler, on instructions from Marcy, resumed dealings with the filibuster regime, a break had come between it and most of its native supporters. To Marcy's great concern, this meant that the United States had recognized a government which now could hardly pretend to have any local backing at all and which from the outset was at war with a local rival and with the latter's allies among the neighboring states! The result was that in September Marcy obtained Wheeler's recall altogether from Central America. The administration also had nothing to do with Walker's new envoy. As for the filibuster itself, it was on the decline; it had been cut off from major reinforcements and the end seemed not far away. It is quite possible, incidentally, as the press warned, that the refusal of Marcy and his associates to continue their recognition of Walker was a reason why Douglas and Cass and many of their ilk declined to approve of Mr. Dallas' convention.[7]

To contemporaries, however, the most spectacular development of the era was Marcy's letter on privateering. It will be recalled that Britain and France had at the outset of the Crimean War proclaimed that for its duration they would observe the twin rules that free ships make free goods and that neutral property on enemy ships should be allowed to pass freely, except contraband of war in both cases. As has also been discussed, Marcy had since that time worked steadily to have these rules made permanent parts of international law. He had found, however, that Britain and France had blocked him and that Russia had been the only major power to sign a convention of the sort he wanted. What was more, he had learned that Prussia—and subsequently France (in 1855)[8]—had held that they could accede to this only if the United States would agree to a permanent ban upon privateering. He had responded in the passages which he wrote for the annual message of 1854 by proposing American abandonment of the use of private

---

[7] Manning IV, 539n, 543-544, 86-88; correspondent of *Times,* issue of Nov. 29.

[8] For France, see Walewski's note to Mason, Dec. 18, 1855, cited in Leland, *op. cit.,* 674.

armed vessels, *if* the other powers would agree that all seizure of private property on the high seas in wartime should be given up. His bold idea had not been accepted, however.

At the peace conference at Paris in the spring of 1856, on the other hand, a move had been made by the Allies which had brought the subject up again. Count Walewski, who had replaced Drouyn de Lhuys as France's foreign minister, had proposed four basic principles for incorporation into international law; he had done so with Clarendon's advance approval. These included the ban upon privateering and Marcy's two rules as to free goods. A fourth item, that blockades must be effective if they were to be regarded as binding, was merely a statement of the traditional doctrine on that score and hence added little, as such. Essentially, then, France, as another traditional "little navy" power,[9] had succeeded in getting the twin rules adopted where the United States had failed. She had been able to do so because of British friendship and also, of course, because of the inclusion of the privateering item. Upon his return to London, by the way, Clarendon had gone so far as to tell a critically-minded parliament that the United States would surely accept this last. This, of course, was very doubtful, as Clarendon should have known from the 1854 message. Indeed, in view of Britain's failure even to present the declaration to the United States government during Marcy's term, Clarendon may well have been deliberately disingenuous. As far as that went, the whole "Declaration of Paris," as the agreement was called, was received in the United States as a direct and intentional blow. Not only had the country not been consulted in regard to the "free goods" rules, in which it had shown such a great interest. It had also been affronted by a step which would, if effectuated, deprive it of what had been its greatest offensive weapon in case of war at sea. The one consoling feature was that Russia, which had signed the declaration, had indicated that she had no intention of applying its terms to any power not a signatory of it.[10]

When Marcy was formally presented a copy of the declaration by

---

[9] Despite her huge naval armament of the moment.

[10] *Cam. Hist. of Brit. For. Pol.*, II, 279-280; Marcy to Dallas, Aug. 4, priv., draft, M.P.; Gortchakoff to Stoeckl, May 1, in Notes from Rus.

France, he commented simply that it did not go far enough.[11] His first instructions to American spokesmen abroad, sent to Seibels in Belgium and a number of others on July 14 and just after, was to voice his "sincere regret" at the move and to ask that those governments be persuaded, if possible, not to adhere.[12]

His noteworthy reply to Count de Sartiges came two weeks later, on July 28.[13] Throughout it, he held closely to the position of the 1854 message. The Paris proceedings, he said, would of course defeat the efforts which the administration had been making *via* negotiation; the second and third points of the declaration, he added, were those which his country had sought to have adopted, but the first, as to privateering, set far too high a price for these other changes. "The right to resort to privateers," he asserted, "is as clear as the right to use public armed ships, and as incontestable as any other right appertaining to belligerents . . . and most nations have not hesitated to avail themselves of it. . ." Only two treaties had called for its abandonment, he said. These were the one between Sweden and the Netherlands in 1675, soon after violated by both, and the United States' own agreement with Prussia in 1785, whose privateering ban had ended in 1799.

Turning then to his main point, Marcy said that:

The prevalence of Christianity and the progress of civilization have greatly mitigated the severity of the ancient mode of prosecuting hostilities. War is now an affair of governments. . . . It is a generally received rule of modern warfare, so far at least as operations upon land are concerned, that the persons and effects of non-combatants are to be respected. The wanton pillage or uncompensated appropriation of individual property by an army, even . . . in possession of an enemy's country, is against the usage of modern times. . . .

It was fair to presume, he went on, that the Congress of Paris had had such considerations in mind, in reference to the sea, in adopting the privateering rule. The United States, moreover, he added "yield [ed] a most ready and willing assent" to this—*provided that national ships were no longer to be allowed to seize private craft.* After all, he argued, if it be objected that the distribution of prize money to a priva-

---

[11] Sartiges to Walewski, June 30, cited in Leland, *op. cit.,* 676.

[12] To Seibels, July 14, and note at end of same, *HED1,* 34th cong., 3rd sess., 33-34.

[13] *Ibid.,* 35-43.

teering crew excited its greed, then what of the prize money given to naval men? Beyond that, he said that it would be difficult to draw the line between privateers and naval vessels because the former might well continue to operate by assuming the guise of the latter.

The United States consider powerful navies and large standing armies, [he said further], as permanent establishments, to be detrimental to national prosperity and dangerous to civil liberty. The expense of keeping them up is burdensome to the people; they are, in the opinion of this government, in some degree, a menace to peace among nations. A large force, ever ready to be devoted to the purposes of war, is a temptation to rush into it. The policy of the United States has ever been, and never more than now, adverse to such establishments; and they can never be brought to acquiesce in any change in international law which may render it necessary for them to maintain a powerful navy or large regular army in time of peace. If forced to vindicate their rights by arms, they are content in the present aspect of international relations, to rely, in military operations on land, mainly upon volunteer troops, and for the protection of their commerce in no inconsiderable degree upon their mercantile marine. If this country were deprived of these resources, it would be obliged to change its policy and assume a military attitude.

He therefore proposed that to the first proposition of the Declaration of Paris there be added: "And that the private property of the subjects or citizens of a belligerent on the high seas shall be exempted from seizure by public armed vessels of the other belligerent, except it be contraband." Thus amended, the United States could accept the declaration, although it was willing to agree to points two, three, and four without the first. Should the proposal be taken up, "some modification, if not an abandonment" would be necessary in *re* the doctrine of contraband, he added. A few days after the completion of this remarkable state paper, Marcy sent a copy of it to Dallas, in case Lord Clarendon should bring up the matter.

The letter was universally commended in the United States, although many observers had some doubts as to its acceptance. Elihu Burritt, for example, the leader of the American peace movement, praised it loudly, but said that thousands of people on both sides of the Atlantic would wait, trembling, for the result.[14] But, as the European editorials on the subject began to arrive at Washington, it was

[14] Letters of Lieber, Aug. 11, Burritt, Sept. 5, Thomas, Sept. 8, Wikoff, Sept. 19, Bancroft, Sept. 24, M.P. Also *Times,* Aug. 12, *Nat. Intel.,* Sept. 16, *Journal of Commerce,* Aug. 12.

found that they were overwhelmingly favorable, except for those of the controlled press of France. Even the *Times* of London spoke favorably; the *Telegraph*, also of London, called Marcy's letter unanswerable. Among the diplomats accredited to the Vatican, it was said to be unanimously approved. The attitude of the British commercial cities was so favorable, that when Palmerston spoke at Liverpool during the autumn even that staunch nationalist found it discreet to declare that "in the course of time" such an amendment to the law of nations might well be made.[15] By early October, there was more substantial ground for optimism. Russia, for one, had agreed to the plan, subject to its general approval by the powers, and for a time, moreover, France appeared to be on the verge of acceding. Marcy actually heard from Mason on November 24 that Count Walewski had said that she would; privately, Mason was also writing, to Buchanan, that all of Continental Europe except Austria was favorable. Prussia, in fact, later presented a conditional approval.[16]

In spite of these indications, the project collapsed. When Russia approached the Allies on the subject, she received a refusal from France and an evasive answer from Britain. This letter had been foreshadowed by the comment of the *Morning Post*, Palmerston's organ, at the outset. The *Post* had dryly pointed out that Marcy's note had essentially refused to give privateering up, under the cover of an outwardly humane but essentially impractical suggestion. When Marcy went out of office, he had himself received no reply from France. Early in the Buchanan administration, in consequence, the United States quietly dropped the whole matter.[17]

Meantime, in any case, a considerable sector of American opinion had turned against the amendment. It was pointed out that privateering would soon be obsolete, since only large and fast steamers, i.e. ones too costly to gamble with, could be expected to engage in it with success. Such vessels, furthermore, might well be taken over by the

---

[15] Voluminous clippings and copied-out excerpts (by Newell), Moore Papers, incl. London *Times,* Aug. 21, 28, *Telegraph,* Aug. 21.; L. Cass, Jr., to Marcy, Sept. 25; Dallas to Marcy, Nov. 21, and attached clipping, M.P.

[16] Marcy to Dallas, Oct. 4, Nov. 24, *ibid.;* Mason to Buchanan, Nov. 26, B.P.; Notes from Prus., Mar. 7.

[17] T. H. Seymour to Marcy, 16/28 Nov., Des. Rus.; *Journal of Commerce,* July 31, 1857.

country's navy anyhow, as the ocean mail-steamer contracts already had begun to provide. The main argument, however, was that there was a serious flaw in the proposal that private property be exempt from capture on the high seas. This was that item four of the Declaration of Paris specified a continuance of blockades. As the *Journal of Commerce,* which had at first lauded Marcy's letter, began to point out, if American ports were all blockaded, the amendment would be but cold comfort.[18] On the other hand, of course, Marcy might have altered his proposal somewhat, if it had come nearer to adoption. Viewed merely as a cover for an American refusal to go along with the Declaration of Paris, however, it was most excellent, for it left the former Allies, rather than the United States, in the unhappy position of opposing a seemingly liberal and humanitarian step.

*   *   *

During these last months in office, Marcy had felt older and more tired than ever before. In keeping with this, and because of the incessant load of work which he bore, he had in the warm months of 1856 given up any thought of travelling off on a regular vacation. Instead, he had leased a comfortable estate, "Grassland," outside of the city, three miles beyond Georgetown. Here he could do his work in a more relaxed atmosphere and with fewer interruptions.

It seems, however, that after he knew fairly definitely that his tenure of office would not be renewed, that is, after Buchanan won the election, he had a considerable feeling of let-down. When Washington Hunt wrote late in June anent the need for making some changes in their joint investment in the water rights at Lockport, Marcy replied at once that he was ready to, but said further that "my affairs must be put in such a condition that they can be shortly closed. I can now number my political days and am conscious that my natural days cannot be greatly extended." As one sign of his increasing age, he experienced a swelling in the feet and ankles, which he assumed was gout. It was

---

[18] R. W. Russell, *The New Maritime Law,* pamphlet, N.Y., 1856; Phila. *American and Gazette,* Dec. 27, clipping, Moore Papers; W. B. Lawrence, "Laws of War and Privateering," in *Nat. Intel.,* Feb. 11, 1857 (a favorable article); W. M. Addison, *Ought Private Vessels to be Exempt from Capture in Time of War? The Negative Maintained,* pamphlet, Balto., Mar. 11, 1857, Moore Papers; W. C. Jones, "Letter to the Secretary of State," Apr. 28, 1857, in *Nat. Intel.,* May 1; *Journal of Commerce,* Sept. 29, 1856.

really something more serious than that.[19] He watched the election that autumn as closely as usual and was extremely relieved when the Democratic party won; he thought Buchanan immeasurably better qualified than John C. Fremont, the Republican candidate, and he could take pleasure, of course, in the fact that the Democrats had recaptured congress. At the same time, he looked forward with satisfaction to his retirement.

To a large number of thoughtful Americans, on the contrary, the prospect of Marcy's stepping down was most unwelcome. As the *Times* said, in urging that he be kept on, it would be hard to find anyone else so suitable. This thought was general throughout the North, especially in the larger cities. A friend at New York City, for instance, wrote humorously if none too tactfully that people hoped that Marcy would stay on as secretary until there was nothing left of him but his eyebrows and his snuff box! In the South, too, notably in the border states and on the eastern seaboard, this was generally the case. The only groups actively against him were the filibusters and the original Buchanan men. Early in February, however, when a petition in his behalf was being arranged among the New York business men, Marcy quickly discouraged it.[20]

There had long been rumors that Lewis Cass was to be Marcy's successor, although there were some predictions that Buchanan would end by asking Marcy to continue in office. When, in the middle of February, Senator Cass's daughter visited the Marcys' house to pay a call upon Nelly, Marcy accordingly decided to find out the truth. He slyly told Miss Cass that he was very glad to be about to retire from the worries of the state department. His answer came out at once. "And we shall be so glad to come in," said Miss Cass![21] It was obvious that Buchanan meant to be his own foreign minister, as his experience had qualified him to be, for Lewis Cass was not the man he had been.

---

[19] "Agreement for rent of country house," May 28, 1856; Hunt to Marcy, June 23, and Marcy to Hunt, June 29; Dr. G. Tyler to Newell, Aug. 3, 1857, M.P.

[20] To Samuel Marcy, Aug. 30, M.P.; *Times,* Nov. 14, Dec. 5, Feb. 17; Louisville *Courier,* cited in Rochester *Daily Union* of Nov. 22; C. A. Davis to Marcy, Dec. 4; misc. clippings; T. N. Carr to Marcy, Dec. 16; R. Withers, Feb. 4, R. Phelps, Feb. 5, to Marcy, and Marcy to each, Feb. 6, all in M.P.

[21] Henry Hervey to Clarendon, Feb. 23, F.O. 5.

XXXIV. SOME HAWAIIAN MISADVENTURES

"It seems to be inevitable that they [the Hawaiian Islands] must come under the control of this Government. . . ." (Marcy to John Y. Mason, December 16, 1853[1])

ENTANGLED with the whole skein of problems with which Marcy had to deal, and particularly with the British and French threads, there was that of the Sandwich Islands, also known as the Kingdom of Hawaii. When Marcy wrote the angrily questioning despatch anent the "happy accord" of Britain and France, at the time of the *Black Warrior* crisis in 1854, for example, he had much to say about Allied interference with United States interests in the Hawaiian archipelago, and very properly. Yet it is convenient to take up this subject by itself. In brief, the Hawaiian story came in two parts, a project of annexation, in 1854, and a program of reciprocity, in 1855.

By the early 1850's the Hawaiian Islands (for we may as well use the present-day name for them) had for three generations been ruled by a single family of native kings, of which the present representative was Kamehameha III. Given to drunken bouts which sometimes lasted for weeks,[2] this man was no paragon of royal virtue; at the same time, like his predecessors, he had much common sense and a good understanding of his people's problems. In addition, his domain had been considerably westernized. Thanks to American missionaries, a large proportion of the people could read and even write their native language, Christianity had been adopted, and there was even a rather western-style government, with a council of ministers who were largely American and English and an elective representative body. American influence was also much felt economically. Sugar plantations had been begun, there was much foreign trade—chiefly by American vessels—and the large American North Pacific whaling fleet used the islands as a base. As for Honolulu, with its white frame houses,

---

[1] M.P.
[2] David L. Gregg to Marcy, Mar. 4, 1854, Des. Haw.

warehouses, and steepled churches, it looked like what it in a sense was, the westernmost extension of the American frontier.[3]

Anxious lest their independence be lost, the rulers of the islands had in 1842 been able to win a partial recognition of their sovereignty from the Tyler administration; it had been accompanied, however, by a statement that the United States had a special interest there. Soon after, the native regime had secured British and French recognition of its sovereignty. Although the United States had declined to join in an Anglo-French proposal not to seek hegemony there for itself, it had behaved very correctly. When the French had acted aggressively, in 1851, and the native king had asked the United States to declare a protectorate, Secretary Webster had replied that his government simply favored Hawaiian independence. In a confidential letter to Luther Severance, his commissioner, he had in fact added that if that self-reliance was endangered, no American agent was authorized to threaten the use of the navy to protect it. The power to declare war, he explained, lay exclusively with congress. Nor were Americans to be led to expect annexation.[4]

Early in Marcy's term as secretary, there were further reports of French aggression. Accordingly, he tried to get the new American commissioner, David L. Gregg, over there quickly to look out for things. He instructed Gregg to continue the policy of sustaining the independence of the islands and to seek to preserve relations of the "kindest" sort; indeed, he was to hold to Webster's instructions to Severance. On the other hand, Marcy told him in private conversation that should any legitimate offer of annexation be made by the island government, it would be accepted. Here, then, as with Cuba and part of Mexico, there would be no "timid forebodings of evil from expansion." As a matter of fact, Marcy had as early as June sounded out Sartiges as to France's attitude towards the United States' setting up a coaling station there.[5]

---

[3] R. S. Kuykendall, *The Hawaiian Kingdom, 1778-1854, passim;* H. W. Bradley, "The American Frontier in Hawaii," Pacific Coast Branch of the Amer. Hist. Ass'n., *Proceedings,* 1930, 150.

[4] Kuykendall, *op. cit.,* 194-203, 400-402; Webster to Severance, July 14, 1851, *SED77,* 52nd cong., 2nd sess., 95-97; also conf. to Severance, July 14, Instrns. Haw.

[5] *Union,* May 6, 20; Marcy to Gregg, July 8, 30, Sept. 22, 1853, Instr. Haw.; Gregg to Marcy, Apr. 5, 1854, Des. Haw.; Sartiges to Drouyn de Lhuys, June 7, Corr. Politique Etats-Unis, vol. 109, French foreign ministry.

In the very next month, as it happened, there were reports which suggested that annexation itself might be possible. News in the capital on October 11 and after was to the effect that Elisha Allen, a former American consul, had become Kamehameha's chief minister and that the regime at Honolulu was on the verge of transferring its power to the United States. This prospect arose in part out of discontent in the islands in the wake of the gold rush boom in California and also of a recent and disastrous epidemic of smallpox. As despatches from Gregg in the following months were to tell, however, the prospect arose also because of fears by the native leaders of an uprising by Americans or other foreigners there, or of a filibuster from California, or both, which would overthrow the monarchy. There were Americans in the islands, however, who were openly urging the king to permit annexation. On November 20 or earlier, Crampton protested in Britain's behalf at the reports of such a possibility. Marcy's answer was that:

We have certainly no desire to precipitate such an event, and, above all, we would discountenance and do all we could to defeat any attempt to bring it about by force; but, if it must come; if the present Government of the Sandwich Islands must fall, and their admission to this Union be desired, I will not conceal from you that it is highly probable that the Government as well as the Congress and People of the United States would be disposed to receive them.

Over the next few weeks, Marcy had a number of conferences with the Britisher, as also with Sartiges. He found them both strongly against American acquisition of the islands. They even implied that war would ensue if this were accomplished. With his usual common sense, the secretary doubted this. He believed that the most that England and France would do would be to take steps short of war. All the same, he wrote to Buchanan and Mason on December 16 to try to find out discreetly what the actual response of the two might be. The reply from Buchanan was gloomy, while Drouyn de Lhuys' comments on the subject to Sartiges were highly hostile. It is only fair to add, by the way, that the machinations of French and British agents in the islands were themselves among the causes of the king's alleged interest in annexation. In any case, for the moment nothing happened.[6]

---

[6] *Union,* Oct. 11, Nov. 8; Severance to Marcy, Sept. 5, Gregg to Marcy, Feb. 11,

By March 11, 1854, however, when Marcy wrote to Buchanan to ask about the meaning of the "happy accord," he had received advices that the rulers there were about to tender their sovereignty to the United States. He notified his envoy that this was "probable" and if so would be done with "the very general acquiescence of the people." If that were so, it would be his country's duty to accept. He also hinted to Buchanan that the French acquisition of New Caledonia, not long before, in a part of the Pacific where Britain had important interests, might be used to raise doubts in British minds about the value of the "accord." Then, less than three weeks after, there was official news from Gregg of a heart-warming variety. King Kamehameha, with the approval of Prince Alexander Liholiho, the heir apparent, and of the cabinet, had truly decided to open negotiations for a cession. So Gregg's despatch of February 7 ran. As it happened, a despatch of two days after, which was sent by a separate vessel, was delayed because that craft foundered; this and other important papers were saved and taken back to the islands, but did not reach Washington until June 10. The February 9 missive, if it had been at hand, would have explained the vital fact that the royal order on the subject stated the purpose as one of "being fully prepared to meet any sudden danger." A further royal order, dated February 21, likewise called for annexation "in case of necessity." In short, as a secret article to the subsequent draft treaty was to make plain, the intention of the native leaders was to have "annexation" only as a weapon to fall back upon in case of armed attack by any American private group. An American protectorate would at once be proclaimed, to ward off such a move, but after the crisis had passed the government would still be able to reclaim its full powers by simply failing to ratify the treaty. As D. A. Ogden, the American consul at Honolulu, was to write to Marcy in May of 1855, concerning annexation: "I do not believe there ever was an intention on the part of the Govt. here to consumate it [sic]."[7]

Uninformed of these schemes on the part of the king and his

Mar. 4, Des. Haw.; Kuykendall, *op. cit.,* 412-422; F.O. 5, Nov. 20; to Mason, Dec. 16, Instr. Fr.; to Buchanan, Dec. 16, B.P.; Buchanan to Marcy, Jan. 28, 1854, M.P.; Drouyn de Lhuys to Sartiges, Nov. 3, cited in Leland's *Guide,* 670; S. K. Stevens, *American Expansion in ' awaii,* 42, 61.

[7] Gregg to Marcy, Feb. 7, 9, 11, Mar. 4, Apr. 5, Des. Haw.; Kuykendall, *op. cit.,* 423; Ogden to Marcy, May 25, M.P.

ministers, who included Robert C. Wyllie, the Britisher who was foreign secretary, Marcy went ahead to order an acceptance of the supposed proposition and to specify the terms upon which it should be
accepted. The United States did not desire a protectorate, he averred.
As to a transfer of sovereignty, the federal administration would take
it for granted that the existing island government would be super-
seded or at the least made subject to the American government. The
latter would be ready to compensate the king and the chiefs with annuities, he went on, to the amount of $100,000 per year. As for in-
dividual property rights, they would be guaranteed to the islanders in
the fullest way, he declared. He urged that the government at Honolulu ratify the pact in advance, if possible, and also be persuaded to
send an agent or agents to Washington with power to agree to any
last minute alterations which the United States might want to propose.
"I have good reason to believe that some of the leading powers of
Europe would be very unwilling to see the Sandwich Islands become
a part of the United States; and, if an opportunity occurred, would
endeavour to defeat any negotiation for that purpose." For this reason
and others, he urged haste. He added that the treaty should be in
Washington before the senate ended its session. These instructions
were dated April 4.[8]

Busy as he was in the following months with the Elgin negotiations, the neutral rights convention, Greytown, and the Ostend Conferences, Marcy can hardly have been too impatient at the delay which
ensued. Even so, it was a long one. Word did come, alarmingly, in
June, that Prince Liholiho was now leading a party of native opponents of annexation. In July, moreover, it was learned that $300,000
would be the amount asked in annuities. By September, however,
when there were rumors that a pact had been made, Marcy showed
that his basic optimism on the subject had not been overcome. He told
Crampton in carefully chosen words that the administration would
accept, if a satisfactory offer came, and he seems not to have been
bothered by that minister's comment that the news would have an unfavorable effect in Britain. On October 28, however, there was bad
news. A despatch from Gregg revealed that the authorities had in-

---

[8] Kuykendall, *op. cit.*, 248, 416; to Gregg, Apr. 4, Des. Haw.

sisted upon immediate statehood for the archipelago and that the American commissioner had reluctantly agreed to have such a provision included in the treaty which was being prepared. This was a serious point. It was very clear that the 70,000 natives of the islands were not ready for self-government of a sort suitable for equal partnership in the American union, and, similarly, that the 1500 permanent white residents would not be able or allowed to run things, if statehood were granted. In all probability the provision had been inserted as a means of defeating annexation, perhaps by Liholiho or through the agency of Mr. Wyllie, who was in contact from time to time with the British and French representatives there. The latter were both actively opposing the step. When the text of the draft treaty came, on November 11, it was on the basis of which Gregg had warned, namely immediate statehood plus $300,000 annually. It also had the revealing secret article as to immediate proclamation of annexation, if the king desired it, subject to final ratification of the treaty on each side.[9]

Marcy did not reply at once, being busy with the annual message and other matters and perhaps uncertain as to whether some device could be employed to get around the difficulty. In the end he found the president, at least, positive that no such expedient could be used. As he wrote to Gregg on the last day of January, 1855: "There are in his [the president's] mind strong objections to the immediate incorporation of the Islands in their present condition into the Union as an independent State." Pierce perhaps was alarmed at the thought of what Ogden had recently written, that there might be two "colored" spokesmen in the senate and one in the house. "How would the South like [this]," Ogden had asked? Marcy told Gregg, however, that probably no treaty which differed much from the terms laid down by the United States in April could be accepted. He was to pass this on to the native government. The policy as to the islands would be as it had been before the annexation proposition had been made, said Marcy further. This was about the end of the matter, on the part of

---

[9] *Union,* June 28, from correspondent of Boston *Post;* Gregg to Marcy, May 12, Aug. 7, Sept. 15, Des. Haw.; Crampton to Clarendon, Sept. 11, cited by R. W. Van Alstyne, *Pac. Hist. Rev.,* IV, 21; F.O. 5, Sept. 11; Ogden to Marcy, Nov. 7, priv., M.P.; Van Alstyne, *loc. cit.,* 20-21; Kuykendall, *op. cit.,* 423-425.

the United States. As for the negotiations in the Sandwich Islands, they had already come to a standstill. Then, abruptly, they were ended by the death of King Kamehameha; Marcy learned of the king's passing on February 9. Liholiho, who succeeded him, was the known enemy of annexation.[10]

The second part of the story deals with the making—and failure— of a treaty for commercial reciprocity. This was the result of a proposal by the native leaders, as was annexation. There were, in fact, two new suggestions which were closely linked: one for commercial reciprocity, to obtain duty-free entry for their sugar, so as to stifle the desire of the Anglo-Saxon planters for American annexation, and the second for a joint guarantee of the islands' independence by the United States, Britain, and France. To accomplish these things, that government sent over Judge William L. Lee, the Hawaiian chief justice.[11]

Lee arrived in San Francisco in April, 1855. He talked freely of the reciprocity plan there and soon had Senator Gwin on his side; Gwin wrote to Marcy that such a pact would be very useful to the west coast people economically. What was more, said that ardent expansionist, such freedom of trade would "produce an identity of feeling & interest" and thus smooth the way for an eventual annexation.

Lee arrived in the capital on July 10 and at once got in touch with Marcy, who was entirely disposed to go ahead with the reciprocity plan; the two began their negotiations on July 12. On the first day thereof, Marcy raised the key objection, namely that the United States had several commercial treaties with other countries giving them most-favored-nation status, and that, if Hawaiian products such as sugar should be free of duty, the Louisiana sugar producers might suffer in turn from rival cane growers in the Atlantic area. An examination of existing United States treaties proved this to be unlikely, however; indeed, when the items to be included were discussed, Marcy suggested that there be instead a reciprocity on all articles. He found that Lee could not accept this, because the island government depended upon tariff receipts for much of its income. But the two

---

[10] Instrns. Haw., Jan. 31, 1855; Ogden letter, cited above; Kuykendall, *op. cit.*, 425-426; Gregg to Marcy, Dec. 19, Des. Haw.

[11] Kuykendall, *The Hawaiian Kingdom, 1854-1874*, 38-40.

negotiated in an amicable style and finally assented to a suitable list of articles. The cabinet gave its approval and the pact was signed on July 20.

Despite the friendly style of the negotiations, Lee was secretly consulting with Crampton and the French *chargé d'affaires,* Boilleau, on the other point, namely a territorial guarantee. A few days after his arrival, he had done so but had at once been told, by Crampton at least, that the United States would quickly reject it and would blame Britain and France for its having been brought up. This was a natural reply, for Marcy had had such a plan suggested to him by the Allied ministers in March and had turned it down. In spite of this, the friendly attitude and the good faith which Marcy had shown led the special envoy to bring the matter up. This was on July 18. What followed was described by Lee in a letter to Hawaii later that day:

Mr. Marcy said he could not entertain any proposition for a tripartite treaty with France & England, for he could not recede from the ground taken in the case of Cuba. I then urged him to enter into a stipulation on the part of the United States, to guarantee our independence from all external and internal pressure. After much conversation, in which Mr. Marcy manifested the warmest friendship for the King & people of the Hawaiian Islands, he promised to receive any proposition I had to make, and to submit it to the Cabinet.

After further discussions with Crampton and Boilleau and after some weeks' absence from the capital, Lee on September 13 brought up the subject again. This was *via* a note to Marcy calling attention officially to the danger of unlawful incursions into the islands and voicing a hope that the United States would direct its naval vessels in the Pacific to turn back any such invasion, whether by Americans or by foreigners, if assembled in American territory. The note also asked that the government have one such warship cruise regularly in the region of the islands, as France and Britain were about to do.

The upshot was that Marcy proposed such a declaration to the cabinet. Although he found that it met with considerable opposition from some of the members, he succeeded in getting it adopted. He replied officially to Lee on September 21 that:

. . . the United States would not regard with unconcern any attempt on the part of any foreign power, and especially, of any European maritime power, to disturb the repose or interfere with the security of the Hawaiian Government.

This Government will exert on all occasions the power it possesses to prevent the organization or fitting out of any unlawful expedition within the United States against the Hawaiian Islands and to defeat any unlawful attacks which any such expedition may meditate upon the same.

It is the intention of the United States to station some portion of their naval force, at or in the vicinity of the Sandwich Islands, instructed to watch over and protect the interests of American citizens in that quarter.

According to Boilleau, the French *chargé*, Marcy had had great difficulty in getting this official statement. In particular, there had been "objections of the most lively sort" from Jefferson Davis, who was not in agreement with the seeming pledge to pursue and combat any filibusters which had succeeded in getting away from American shores. Indeed, the United States had been quite generous.

The reciprocity pact did not go well with the senate, however. Although it was sent to that body early in the following session, the efforts of Senator Slidell in behalf of the Louisiana sugar producers kept it bottled up in the foreign relations committee. American wool raising interests also opposed it. At the next session it was again obstructed. Marcy worked hard to get it through, arguing that the United States had no treaty of a most-favored nation sort with any sugar producing country. He was aided, moreover, by Elisha Allen, the Hawaiian, who was in the United States on private business and also as a special envoy to work for the treaty's passage. The pact came up for consideration at long last in the executive session of February, 1857, but it did not reach a vote. In a special session called by President Buchanan later, moreover, it was filibustered to death by the Louisiana senators.[12]

In short, Marcy had no success with Hawaii. The annexation proposal had not been a genuine one, while weakness of the administration in congress had made even the reciprocity pact impossible. On the other hand, he deserved praise for the thorough reasonableness of his policies all the way through. He had not let the official protests of

---

[12] Gwin to Marcy, Apr. 20, M.P.; Lee's despatches of July 14-20, Sept. 18, to Wyllie, in Kuykendall, *op. cit.*, 40-43 and notes; the account of the negotiations in the text, 45-46; both of the above are cited by permission of the University of Hawaii Press; Sartiges to Drouyn de Lhuys, Mar. 17, cited in Leland, *Guide*, 673; F.O. 5, July 30; Lee to Marcy, Sept. 13, Notes from Haw.; Marcy to Lee, Sept. 21, Notes to Haw.; Boilleau to Walewski, Sept. 24, Corr. Pol. Etats-Unis, vol. 113, foreign ministry; Marcy to Sen. J. M. Mason, Aug. 15, 1856, N.Y.H.S.; Marcy to Allen, Aug. 30, Notes to Haw.; Allen's notes to Marcy, Notes from Haw.

Lord Clarendon—as for example in a note of October 6, 1854—[13] and the advices of Sartiges deter him. And he had kept the record of the United States clean and honorable. For example, on the major point of the potentially violent stirrings of Americans in the islands in the year 1854, his instructions to Gregg had been identical with those of Webster earlier: that Americans must not be led to expect annexation. In his instructions of January 31, 1855, moreover, in which he turned down the draft treaty of annexation, he had reiterated such orders. The United States policy, he had said, was "not to accelerate or urge on any important change in the government of that country . . ." His conduct, in short, was beyond reproach.

[13] Notes from Brit.

XXXV. THE TOLLS UPON THE DANISH SOUND

". . . it is a paramount object of this government, as it is its
imperative duty, to remove every obstruction to free commerce by vessels sailing under our flag." (Marcy to Henry
Bedinger, July 18, 1853[1])

THERE remain to be taken up the varied avenues by which Marcy
sought to open the trade of the world to American producers and
shipmasters. Taken together, these constituted a bold and sweeping
program, of which the most celebrated feature, the removal of the
tolls upon the Danish Sound, was merely the most important.

To begin with, it should be noted that just about every treaty which
Marcy suggested with the countries already discussed had called for at
least some measure to advance American commerce. With the countries around the United States borders, including Hawaii, Marcy came
to advocate in each case a general policy of reciprocity.[2] With the
more remote ones, he commonly tried for a commercial treaty as such,
but for something less than full reciprocity. With the most distant
ones of all, such as those of the Far East, South America, and the
Baltic, his policy more often meant not a mutual tariff reduction particularly, so much as obtaining the free right of entry or passage for
American vessels, by removing obstacles which had restricted or even
wholly barred them from certain harbors, rivers, or seas.

In China and Latin America, Marcy had no successes. In China,
this was largely because the Tai-Ping Rebellion left conditions too uncertain, too unripe at the moment for useful results,[3] while in the
Plata basin the interference of Brazil in Uruguay and the monopolistic
measures of Lopez, the dictator of Paraguay, were very serious obstacles.[4] In both China and the Plata, Marcy showed himself ready to
cooperate with the other chief maritime powers, i.e. with Britain and
France. In these remote areas, the "happy accord" of the two latter

---

[1] Hunter Miller, *Treaties . . .*, VII, 534.
[2] For Mexico, see Marcy to Forsythe, Aug. 16, 1856, Manning IX, 209-210.
[3] Cf. Marcy to Marshall, June 7, 1853, Instrns. China; to Peter Parker, Sept. 27,
1855, M.P.
[4] Cf. Manning I, 540-556, 569-571, 613-614, X, 104-114, 140, 148-149.

powers commonly included the United States and Marcy was willing to have it so. As for the effort to open the Amazon, Marcy made this more or less unilaterally; his approach was hampered, however, by a certain lack of realism and also by increasing South American fears of filibusters.[5]

With the movement of Commodore Perry and his squadron to open up Japan, Marcy had no contact; it had been begun by the Fillmore administration in 1852 and was in any case under the navy department. After Perry's treaty reached the United States, as it did in the summer of 1854, and after congress had belatedly authorized the appointment of a consul general, by an act of March 3, 1855, Marcy did become directly involved. What Perry had obtained, in his tactful negotiations, was chiefly the opening of two minor ports, Shimoda and Hakodate, as places for provisioning American vessels and for a limited trade. It would be up to the consul authorized by the pact to seek a general commercial treaty. Marcy now quickly offered the new post to John Romeyn Brodhead, the New York historian, who had had considerable diplomatic experience. Brodhead would probably have made a good choice, but he declined.[6] It was then that Marcy turned to another New Yorker, Townshend Harris, who was an acquaintance of his from a time long before;[7] even more to the point, Harris was a bosom friend of Wetmore's. At the time, he was in the Far East on a trading trip. As a matter of fact, Marcy had himself offered him the consulate at Ningpo, one of the lesser Chinese treaty ports, the year before, but Harris had declined it.

In the history of the making of this famous appointment, the great trouble in Marcy's mind was a doubt as to the man's sobriety: "Was he not when he left the U.S. a little inclined to intemperance?" he asked Wetmore in a letter of March 20. Wetmore replied on the 24th reassuringly. He also said:

I have never known a man so well qualified by a general knowledge of business, domestic & foreign, as Harris, to manage such a mission as you suggest. [He has] . . . an enlarged and enlightened knowledge of commercial relations between nations. . . . He is a great reader, a fluent speaker, a ready writer, and has his intellectual resources always at com-

[5] *Times,* Aug. 5, 1853; Manning II, 20-22, 28-30, 170-172, 454, 470-473, X, 683-685.
[6] Brodhead to Marcy, Mar. 15, 1855, M.P.
[7] Cf. Harris to Marcy, Aug. 8, 1855, *ibid.*

mand. . . . He is a good linguist—Speaking & writing French, Spanish & Italian. . . . In one of the letters he informed me that he was engaged on a history of the Island of Formosa.

Upon Wetmore's repeated affirmations in later letters on the subject of temperance and his statements that Harris was on his way home and yet would be willing to leave again for the Orient without much delay, Marcy managed to hold the post for him. This went on until late in July, when Harris suddenly appeared at Old Point Comfort, where Marcy was vacationing. Marcy was at once taken with him, seeing no signs at all of dissipation and being vastly pleased with his broad attainments. He wrote to Pierce, urging the appointment. His expectations of a good result were to be borne out, for few American envoys to the Far East have ever been more praised. At the same time, the first leg of Harris's trip to Japan was far from auspicious. When journeying to Europe, on the liner *Pacific*, he seems to have tippled heavily and was the focus of an angry dispute involving the ship's officers and a great number of the passengers. Marcy was overwhelmed with an "avalanche" of complaints about him and debated his recall, but luckily decided against that.[8] It was not until 1857 and after, too late for Marcy ever to hear of it, that the patient and resourceful diplomacy of Harris produced the rich fruit for which Marcy had hoped.

With Santo Domingo, the administration's desire was for a coaling station. William L. Cazneau, who went there as the American agent, was directed to seek such facilities at Samaná Bay, if that was the best place, and was told that a square mile of land would do. In return, the United States was ready to give recognition to the Dominican government by means of a general commercial treaty. Even this modest purpose was thwarted, however. For one thing, Cazneau was himself a notorious annexationist, who later offered to raise a thousand "colonists" for Walker, while his wife had been the editor of a publication put out at New York in the interest of the Cuban junta. In addition, the two Cazneaus talked freely of "regenerating" the republic—presumably in a Walkerian manner—by an infusion of American immigrants. Even more seriously, however, there was the opposition of

---

[8] To Wetmore, Aug. 5, 1854, Mar. 20, Apr. 20, May 14, Aug. 4, 1855, Jan. 24, 26, 1856; Wetmore to Marcy, Mar. 24, 31, Apr. 17, July 17, 26, 1855; Pierce to Marcy, Aug. 2; Harris to Marcy, Aug. 8; Marcy to J. Y. Mason, Jan. 25, to Harris, Jan. 27, 1856, all in M.P.

the partners in the "happy accord." Britain and France sent a number of war vessels to the Dominican capital and forced President Santana to alter the treaty in such a way as to make it unacceptable to the southern senators.[9] As a matter of fact, American prestige quickly fell to a new low there, from the very fact that the United States failed to meet such threats with counterthreats.[10]

By contrast with these varied efforts, Marcy's handling of relations with the Dutch East Indies produced a triumph. The circumstance was that, like other powers, the United States had been allowed only commercial agents to represent it there. Yet it wanted to have consuls admitted, partly because they might have influence enough to protect American mariners who got into difficulty.

Marcy's instructions on this topic went out to Belmont on the same day as the ones to Trousdale in Brazil. He cited the case of Walter M. Gibson, an American shipmaster who was in jail at Batavia on a charge of encouraging the native chiefs of Sumatra to throw off Dutch allegiance; this was merely an instance, Marcy said, of the sort of thing Americans had to face at present. He therefore told Belmont that if it was necessary in order to win the entry of American consuls, the administration would denounce the existing commercial treaty with the Netherlands, which indirectly gave that country large consular privileges in the numerous and busy ports of the United States. As it happened, Captain Gibson arrived back in the United States on August 9, the very next day after Marcy sent this instruction, having escaped from his prison. He was soon in Washington, demanding $100,000 in damages for his imprisonment and the confiscation of his schooner, the *Flirt*. His story was that he had stopped while quite innocently in East Indian waters, and had been arrested because his mate had set off in a native boat to take a message to the sultan of Jambee. He claimed that a letter which the Dutch allegedly had found upon the mate was a forgery. Finding Gibson a plausible and impressive figure, but having only his statement to go on, Marcy wrote to Belmont on September 6 to look into the matter.[11]

---

[9] Scroggs, *op. cit.*, 236; Crampton to Clarendon, Oct. 9, 1854, F.O. 5; Manning VI, 16-19, 127-150; Mrs. Cazneau to Marcy, Dec. 11, 1855, M.P.
[10] Despatches of Elliott and Pereira, Manning VI, 166-184.
[11] To Belmont, Aug. 8, Sept. 6, 1853, Instrn. Neth.; *Times,* Aug. 10, 31; Belmont to Marcy, Oct. 8, Des. Neth.; Walter M. Gibson, *The Prison of Weltevreden . . .,* New York, 1855; *Union,* June 4, 1854.

Investigations of this case and discussion of a consular convention
now went on simultaneously and for many months. The outcome,
however, was that the Dutch ministry was convinced that Gibson was
guilty and produced damaging evidence against him. What was more,
Gibson appeared in person at the Hague in the affair, which affronted
the ministry and also led to embarrassing criticism of it in the chamber as allegedly weak in its dealings with him; this in turn made difficult any concessions by that government on the consular problem. For
a time, there was a crisis. Belmont closed the Gibson case in a note in
which he told the Dutch that "it now only remains for my Government to take such measures for the enforcement of Mr. Gibson's
claim, as it may deem fit and proper in the premises." Fortunately,
however, both Marcy and Belmont soon became convinced that Gibson
was a liar and that the Netherlands was right. Marcy told the man to
his face what he thought of him.[12]

Then, on December 7, 1854, Marcy penned to the Netherlands a
note of a stiff-sounding variety, but one which in effect adroitly
shrugged off any claim in Gibson's behalf. The Dutch quickly understood. Early in the following year, as a result, they signed the consular
agreement, which had already been discussed in detail. Both the East
and West Netherlands Indies were opened very freely to American consuls. Since the Dutch felt obliged to make the same concessions to the
other maritime powers (fear of British encroachment having been a
factor which had delayed their yielding to the United States), Marcy
had won a victory for the world at large. The congratulations which
the other diplomats at the Hague at once showered upon Belmont
proved this. As for Gibson, he went on to new fields of adventure,
for a time was a Mormon leader, and ended his career as prime minister of Hawaii![13]

The removal of the tolls upon the Danish Sound was an even
greater victory. These levies, which were imposed by Denmark upon
all vessels and cargoes going into and out of the Baltic Sea, were in
principle no better than the former exactions of the Barbary states

---

[12] Belmont to Marcy, Mar. 5 (and encl.), Sept. 9 (and encl.), 1854, Des. Neth.;
Tribune, Oct. 28, 1854; Marcy to D. Piatt, Jan. 15, 1854 (1855?), Belmont to
Marcy, Sept. 15, Nov. 14, M.P.

[13] To Belmont, Dec. 7, 1854, Belmont to Marcy, Jan. 23, 1855, M.P.; Kuykendall,
Hawaiian Kingdom, 1854-1874, 102-104; convention is in Hunter Miller, *op. cit.,*
VII, 3-13.

upon commerce in the Mediterranean; they were also burdensome not merely in terms of the fees paid but because of the hours or days lost while stopping for examination; on the other hand, time had hallowed them. While the American share in the Baltic trade was not large, the Washington government objected to the duties and had never given them a direct assent. In 1826, it is true, a commercial treaty with Denmark had provided for most-favored nation treatment, and in 1842 Webster, after getting the levies cut, had expressed his satisfaction at the outcome. Under President Polk, on the other hand, the Democrats had suggested the payment of a lump sum as a means of escaping the duties permanently. But the Whigs who had succeeded him in office had finally dropped the matter.[14]

Marcy's instructions to Henry Bedinger, the new *chargé* to Denmark, were very pointed. Dated July 18, they directed him to leave upon his mission without unnecessary delay, because the president desired the matter to be taken up at an early date. It was to be presented to the Danish government "in emphatic, but respectful terms" and United States policy would be to "press . . . [it] to a conclusion."

It is clear that no defence can be made in behalf of a "principle" so flagrantly at variance with the established right of each of the nations of the earth to the *liberum mare* [free sea].

Like Buchanan in Polk's day, Marcy brushed aside any thought that the United States had acquiesced in the principle, while admitting that "we have offered no positive resistance." He pointed out that the American merchant marine now was of not less than four and one half million tons size and that American trade was burgeoning. He also showed that the levies were especially obnoxious to the United States. Raw cotton, the country's chief export, he said, bore a levy of three percent *ad valorem*, while cotton twist, which Britain manufactured in huge amounts from cotton raised in the United States, paid only one percent. In conclusion, the instructions to Bedinger demanded the ending of the duties as a right. His further directive of November 8 denied that any compensation was intended.

The response of the Danish foreign minister, Bluhme, in an interview of December 1, was that the practice had gone on since time immemorial. He added that while the total levy upon American craft was small, to exempt them meant an obligation to exempt all powers'

[14] Hunter Miller, *op. cit.,* VII, 524-534; Instrns. Den., 1849-1853, *passim.*

ships. After some further correspondence in the matter, Marcy read on April 21, 1854, that Denmark had asked the United States not to press it any further until European affairs should be "more tranquil." Bluhme had added that as soon as possible Denmark would be willing to enter into arrangements with the nations of the world to give up the duties, upon receiving *"a certain compensation,* which he did not distinctly explain—in lieu thereof." Perhaps partly because Britain also urged delay, Marcy quietly let the matter rest for several months. Then, in the annual message of December 4, 1854, it was brought up. That document urged that the year of notice provided in the 1826 pact for setting that agreement aside should be given.[15] This the senate authorized, on March 3, 1855.

In informing Bedinger of the senate's vote, Marcy expressed the administration's regret at having to perform this duty and referred to its previous hope that an appeal to Denmark's sense of justice would be enough. A further such appeal might be tried, he went on, if Bedinger thought that there was any point to it, but if that failed the notice must be presented. As it turned out, Von Scheele, the new Danish minister, replied flatly that the levies would not be given up without an equivalent; he went on to say that Britain, Prussia, Sweden, and some other countries were ready to talk of compensation. On April 14, therefore, the word was given.[16] This meant that the great test would come just a year afterwards; should some American vessel try to pass through the straits without stopping to pay, it might be fired upon and a war could ensue.

While Marcy was fairly confident of success without such a trial of arms, the indications were that he was ready to face that alternative, if necessary, despite reports[17] that Denmark was arming. Thus, in September, 1855, when there were signs that Prussia would follow the United States' lead, he asked the American envoy at Berlin if that was truly the case, since events "might lead to collision"; would Prussia be ready to take "efficient measures," he asked? He had some fear that Britain, France, and Russia would support Denmark. There was some criticism in the United States of the administration's bold

---

[15] To Bedinger, July 18, 1853, Inst. Den.; Bedinger to Marcy, Dec. 3, 1853, April 1, 1854, Des. Den.; F.O. 5, Apr. 23, 1854; *Mess. & Pap.,* 279.

[16] To Bedinger, Mar. 12, Instr. Den.; Bedinger to Marcy, Apr. 20, 1855, Des. Den.

[17] Tal P. Shaffner to Marcy, Jan. 25, M.P.; *Union,* Feb. 16, 1855.

stand, but it was not always very serious. The *Times'* correspondent suggested jokingly, for instance, that the solution would be to send Captain Hollins and the *Cyane* to Copenhagen. By the end of October, however, Marcy must have had Buchanan's private letter of the 12th. This stated that the Danish envoy to London had declared that his government's purpose was to settle the question before the deadline and that the three powers especially friendly to Denmark had all agreed to a conference to discuss how to end the tolls.[18]

By October 29, in fact, Marcy had learned directly from Bedinger of Denmark's call for such a conference, which was to be held at Copenhagen in November. It had been summoned, said Von Scheele, because of the desire of Britain and Prussia for it. When Bedinger had protested that there would not be time for the United States to get delegates there, even if it chose to, Von Scheele had replied that the meetings would doubtless go on for months. According to Bedinger,

many of the powers . . . are becoming, every day, more restiff [sic] under those burthens, and while hesitating themselves to take the first step in the matter, they do not object to see the U.S. disposed to lead the way. . . .

This was very true.

After consulting with Pierce, Marcy replied (November 3) that the United States would take no part in the gathering. The trouble was, he said, that it would assume as the basis for its assembling that Denmark did have a right to collect the duties, which the administration so strenuously denied; also that it would pass upon a lump sum to be paid by the world at large as compensation and the proportions each country should bear, which it had no authority to do. He also objected to the terms of the summons, which stated that the tolls should be considered as a part of the general European settlement then about to be made. Paraphrasing Canning's celebrated comment, he declared that "The Government of the United States will never consent to the pretension that the *new* world is to be appropriated to adjust the political balance of the *old*." The country was unwilling, he said, to be drawn into the "vortex" of that balance of power. Having gotten all this off his chest, presumably with an eye to helping Pierce in

---

[18] To Vroom, Sept. 20, 1855, Inst. Prus.; *Times,* Sept. 4, Oct. 3; *J. of Commerce,* in *Nat. Intel.* of Oct. 2; Buchanan to Marcy, Oct. 12, B.P.

1856, he then came to the chief business of the despatch. While the administration was not ready "to purchase a right which [it] consider[ed] indubitable," it would be ready to make a liberal compensation for the expenses Denmark had incurred in providing navigational aids such as lighthouses and buoys in the waters in question. Here was the milk in the coconut! He also told Bedinger to invite Denmark to submit a proposition to this effect. In a confidential despatch of two days after, he asked Bedinger to read it to Von Scheele at once and also to make every effort to learn the views of Denmark and of the other states at the conference. He also sent copies of the main despatch to the American ministers at the chief European courts.[19] This was well received, incidentally, by the diplomats of the other powers; they praised it for its dignified but moderate tone.[20]

As a letter to John Y. Mason of November 5 shows, Marcy was already thinking tentatively that the United States might simply pay its full proportion of whatever capitalization was agreed upon.[21] This was a dark secret, however. When Torben Billé, Denmark's *chargé*, in pursuance of instructions from home, sought to sound him out, he virtually refused to answer and at the most would only say, as to the course after the treaty came to an end, that "of *that* I cannot inform you."[22]

On hearing from Bedinger on February 5 that the conference had opened and that Denmark showed a conciliatory disposition but asked for delay, Marcy none the less consented. He wrote on the 19th that the president had agreed that sixty days should be added to the waiting period, running it to June 14; meantime, the United States would take no step which would embarrass Denmark in its relations with the other powers. No added extension should be expected, however, he said, "except upon the express condition of a discontinuance to collect [sic] tolls on American vessels and their cargoes." Subsequently, after learning that Denmark had cut her figure for the total capitalization nearly in half and that Von Scheele had promised to be ready to negotiate with the United States as soon as he was "half

---

[19] Bedinger to Marcy, Oct. 7, 1855, Des. Den.; Marcy to Bedinger, Nov. 3, Inst. Den.

[20] Mason to Marcy, Dec. 3, Des. Fr.; Vroom to Marcy, Dec. 4, Des. Prus.

[21] M.P.

[22] Crampton to Clarendon, Nov. 13, F.O. 5.

through" with the other powers, the administration granted a further respite. "Upon the express condition" that Denmark agree that all sums paid by Americans as duties should be considered as paid under protest and subject to claim, Marcy and the president on May 30 extended the period to a full additional year of grace. The new date, then, would be June 14, 1857.[23]

This left matters on such a basis that there might be no solution before Marcy left office. And so it proved to be, although Marcy did what he could to prod the Danes into action. Mr. Billé did present him with a draft of a convention on the subject, which after some minor changes he considered satisfactory. He said in a note to Billé on January 27 that he had left the amount of payment blank, but added significantly:

I suppose your government will require the United States to pay a sum proportionate to that to be paid by other powers.—We claim to be placed in this respect on the most favored terms, and if so, shall not refuse to enter into the arrangement by any disagreement as to the amount to be paid.

The sum finally set was $393,011, which was the United States' share of the amount finally agreed upon at the conference. What held up the completion of the agreement was the failure of Billé to receive his full powers. When Lewis Cass completed the pact, however, on April 11, 1857, everyone knew whose the accomplishment was. Meanwhile, on March 14, at Copenhagen, all of the European powers most concerned and nearly all of the lesser ones had signed a general treaty for the abolition of the dues.[24] Marcy had thus won one of his greatest victories and done all the world a service. He had achieved what Frederick the Great, Sir Robert Peel, and all of the American secretaries of state beginning with Webster in 1841 had failed to do.[25]

---

[23] Bedinger to Marcy, Jan. 9, Feb. 7, Mar. 12, 1856, Des. Den.; Marcy to Bedinger, Feb. 19, May 30, Inst. Den.

[24] Notes to Den., Nov. 18, Jan. 27; to Bedinger, Dec. 8, Inst. Den.; Notes from Den., Feb. 19, Mar. 14; Bedinger to Marcy, Mar. 15, Des. Den.

[25] *Journal of Commerce,* in *Union* of Oct. 26, 1854.

XXXVI. L'ENVOI

"But keep in mind, that you yourself have gained distinction enough to have your own account to settle with posterity." (George Bancroft to Marcy, December 20, 1856[1])

INAUGURATION day came, none too soon, on March 4. It was marked by "a pleasant atmosphere of revelry, but no disorder," as "Buchaneers" swarmed into town; the president-elect, dignified as always, took the oath of office, the ceremonies passing off brilliantly amidst great crowds of people. The Pierces had moved out of the White House and, for the time being, in with the Marcys. Later, the new cabinet was announced. And on the seventh, Marcy, his hair still black and his eyes still bright—hardly looking his seventy years—turned over the seals of the department to Mr. Cass.[2]

On April 30, the Marcys left Washington for the north. They stopped for a few weeks at New York, enjoying the applause which their old friends had to give Marcy; there were a great many invitations to dinner and many sittings for painters and photographers. It was very pleasant, but rather tiring. Late in May, Marcy was glad to go on to Albany and Lockport, at which latter place he talked over his investments with Hunt. In general, they were in good shape, totalling in all about $100,000 and at last giving him the financial independence which he had craved. Later, he went on to Rochester and Niagara and then back to Albany. By this time, a plan which he and his family had been discussing for months had crystallized; they were going to visit Europe, and the date of departure was to be August 1. In preparation for this, the family scattered about to say farewells and Marcy went with an Albany friend to Ballston Spa for an interlude of rest. They stayed at the famous old Sans Souci Hotel.[3]

---

[1] M.P.

[2] Elizabeth L. Lomax, *Leaves from an Old Washington Diary,* 67; *Atlas & Argus,* Mar. 10; Pierce to Marcy, Apr. 5, 1857, M.P.; *Journal of Commerce,* Mar. 2; to Wetmore, Mar. 8, M.P.

[3] *Evening Star,* May 1; Marcy to Berret, May 3—June 14; diary, May 14ff., all in M.P.; *Atlas & Argus,* May 26, July 6; Marcy to Hunt, Jan. 22, M.P., copy; list of assets [1857?], copied by J. B. Moore, Moore Papers; *E. Post,* July 10.

Throughout these last weeks, Marcy had shown an unusual pallor, but had otherwise seemed quite well. As he confided to his wife, however, he was beginning to have serious palpitations of the heart. He tried to avoid over-eating and the use of coffee, but he recognized that his health was precarious. While posing for Brady, the photographer, at New York, for example, his heart had bothered him so that he had been unable to stand still for the picture and had instead sat. According to the conclusion of his doctor afterwards, the trouble was *angina pectoris*. After his western trip, he had a long talk with Seymour, his old follower, at Albany, about the latter's career. "Governor Marcy said [recorded Seymour] that the trouble with him was to know how to die; how after so long an active career to sit down quietly to meet the coming future." Unquestionably he was learning, though. He wrote his will. He also showed to the world an exceptional "buoyancy of health and . . . exhiliration [sic] of spirits," as on a visit to Albany and Troy from Ballston on July 2 and 3. In talking with Mary Pattison at Troy, on his way back, moreover, in a conversation in which he was led to give his opinion of a number of the other political leaders of the day, he did it discriminatingly but with a charity in his judgments which that discerning friend had not always found before. When at Ballston, he would take his chair out under the elms by the hotel and have long chats with the proprietor and other friends, entertaining them with stories and anecdotes and with the old twinkle in his eye. At other times, he would read his chosen classical authors.[4]

On the morning of July 4, fatigued after his trip and a restless night, he had pains which he thought to be rheumatic. Finally, at about 11:30, he walked over to see the local doctor, a quarter of a mile off, but failed to find him and walked back. In his room, he put on his dressing gown and slippers and lay down, his snuff box at his side. He picked up his favorite little red-bound edition of Bacon's *Essays* to read. Then, in a few minutes and very quietly, he died, his features perfectly composed.

---

[4] Diary, June 5-27; Marcy to Mrs. Marcy, ca. June 24, M.P.; *Atlas & Argus,* July 9; Mary Pattison to Newell, Oct. 5, 1859, M.P.; Dr. Grafton Tyler to Newell, July 23, 1857, *ibid.;* statement of Seymour to Pruyn, Dec. 6, 1859, in *Knickerbocker Press,* Mar. 9, 1913 (from Pruyn's journal); *Atlas & Argus* of July 6, in *Journal* of same day; *E. Post,* in *Journal* of July 10.

His friends and admirers were much grieved at his abrupt death. As a New Yorker wrote to Weed:

And [so] our old Friend Govr Marcy has passed through "the valley of the shadow of Death." He was full of years & full of honors yet would we that his green old age might have been with us to cheer & charm us a few years more & that he rather might have glided to the Tomb than thus to have been precipitated into the vast invisible ocean of Eternity.

I know how sadly you have felt & will feel at this removal. The event must carry you back many years & tracing down the times how many scenes of varied interest—of political excitement—combinations, struggles, reverses, defeats, triumphs mix in with social gatherings, pleasant evenings enlivened by his quiet humor & made interesting by the warmth & attention he gave, relaxed from great labors, to the game [whist] of which he was so fond! Peace to his spirit! We could better have spared a better Man, if such there be.

His old associates and his neighbors honored him very fulsomely, however. While his body lay in state in the assembly chamber at Albany, 10,000 people filed past it. Two ex-presidents and the governor and four ex-governors were present at the rites which followed, scores of militia and fire companies marched in the procession, and fifty thousand spectators looked on.[5]

To revert to the date, exactly four months before his death, when Marcy had quit the state department, he had left United States foreign affairs in better order than they had seen in a long time. As the *Intelligencer* had commented on December 3, after citing some minor exceptions, "there is no cloud on the foreign horizon." For example, isthmian affairs were in general nearly adjusted. Walker was on his last legs and would surrender on May 1. Better than that, the turn of British opinion which has already been noted, towards a friendly attitude *vis-a-vis* the United States, was not to be reversed. Lord Napier, who arrived in the United States as the new British minister in March, was decidedly well disposed, to give but one illustration. It would not be long before he would make his generous remark that "peaceful and legitimate expansion of [the] U.S. is a cause of satisfaction and pride for every thinking Englishman." While this must have made Palmerston squirm, it stood. Beyond this, the old "happy accord" had pretty well vanished.[6] While the shift in British policy

[5] *Journal*, July 6-10; *Atlas & Argus*, July 9; John E. Develin to Weed, July 10, Weed Papers, U. of Rochester; Newell to Tyler, cited above.

[6] Quotation from Napier and comment of Sartiges on it, Sartiges to Walewski, Apr. 26, in Leland, *Guide*, 677.

was of course in great degree out of recognition of America's rising material power, it was only fair to give Marcy some of the credit. And this he was undoubtedly given, even in London. As Robert B. Campbell, an American there, reported, the foreign office considered him "very superior in intellect to the Ministers of any foreign Court in Europe," and regarded his despatches as "unrivaled," to say nothing of his being "the very Devil in controversy."[7] Unquestionably his firm if tactful diplomacy had done much to produce the changed British view. Under these circumstances, the Buchanan administration should have found it comparatively easy to bring the isthmian troubles to a conclusion. Indeed, although Buchanan revived much of the old disputation and indirectly aided Walker in a further attempt, a general solution was finally had.

Except for the modest Mexican purchase, it is true, all of the efforts at expansion had come to nothing. But Marcy had never made such efforts aggressively. As for the bad conduct of men like Soulé, that was not his fault but Pierce's. If Manifest Destiny, incidentally, had been a casualty, so, too, had Young America; the effort to Americanize the foreign service, for instance, had been only partly successful. Marcy was to be seen at his best, however, apart from the coming solution of the isthmian troubles, in other ways. These included his statesmanlike attempts to reform international law, his preservation of American neutrality from infringement, whether by American privateers or by British agents, his splendid treaty in *re* the British North American provinces, and, almost as well, the removal of the tolls upon the Sound. Even more, the true Marcy was felt in his continual effort to restrain the filibustering interest, whether from private conflict or from pushing the government into a war of conquest. This was very well understood by his contemporaries. It was the basic cause for comments more than once made by the *Times* (which had become the country's leading paper) that "his steady and shrewd conservatism" had kept the Pierce administration from really serious mischief abroad.[8] Or, as the *Evening Post* put it, on the day Pierce and Marcy went out:

The affairs of the State Department have been, in the main, well managed under Mr. Marcy—with great ability and great discretion. If we must

---

[7] Campbell to Marcy, Apr. 15, 1856, M.P.
[8] *Times,* Mar. 7, July 6, 1857.

make any exceptions to this commendation, we suspect it will be found that they were owing to the folly of Mr. Pierce.

Under this second sentence, of course, would have to be included such items as the appointments, Pierce's private communications through Sickles which had brought on the "manifesto" character of the Ostend meeting, and the recognition of Walker. If it be argued that on some other points the roles of the two men are less easy to disentangle, this is of course true. But the difference in their characters was all too clear, as was their divergence on filibusterism and Manifest Destiny.

It should be added that one topic of importance in American foreign relations in the era, which has not yet been taken up, was not identified with either the president or his secretary. This was the reform of the diplomatic service under the important and lasting laws of 1855 and 1856. Marcy did help somewhat in the revision of that program, however.[9] He also made a real effort to have its most forward-looking feature become a reality, namely the plan for consular pupils, on a career basis.[10]

In short, Marcy had on the whole been a very able secretary of state. In this writer's opinion, he deserves to be numbered among the dozen best ones the United States has had. As a recent student of his career has said, he was sometimes pushed and he yielded and sometimes he was pushed and he pushed back; but on the whole he usually got his way, often by sitting quietly until time had proven him to be correct.[11] Considering his lack of experience in diplomacy, his was no slight achievement. His state papers, in particular, had been exceptional. If he be compared with the other leading secretaries of the mid-century era—Webster, Seward, and Hamilton Fish—his stature is not lessened. He was their equal. This is particularly clear if the fact is kept in mind that these other men served under presidents and beside congresses inherently conservative in their foreign outlook and little inclined to meddle in external affairs.[12]

---

[9] Speech of Rep. Perkins, Jan. 11, 1855, in *Union* of Jan. 14; acts of Mar. 2, 1855, Aug. 18, 1856; Marcy to Charles Eames, June 20, 1855, M.P.; Perkins to F. Markoe, July 17, 1855, Markoe Papers, L. C.; J. A. Thomas to Vroom, Sept. 8, 1856, Vroom Papers, Low Library, Columbia Univ.

[10] Henry Brooks Adams, "Civil Service Reform," *North American Review*, CIX, 461-463.

[11] Robert L. Scribner, "The Diplomacy of William L. Marcy," unpublished doctoral dissertation, Univ. of Virginia, 1949.

[12] Marcy's stature as secretary was attested to by John M. Clayton, who said he

It may be observed in passing that Marcy had mellowed a good deal by the 1850's. He was less gruff and more kind. His humor was also more apparent. Mostly, it was of a bantering type, as in his explanation to Mrs. Clement C. Clay of Alabama anent the reason for his "unusual poise and uniform complacency" (to use her words). He told her that he had his secretary daily clip out the news items of a flattering sort and put them prominently on his desk, while throwing those of a different order into the waste-basket. He was also affable with reporters—while not going out of his way to win their approval; he liked to tease them. Once, incidentally, at a party at Seward's he entertained the company with a mock paragraph in the style of these men, purporting to describe the speculations which could arise out of the fact of his being there. He was also a loyal member of the administration. He kept its secrets, even in his own household. He also kept on at least passably good terms with each of its other leading members, while with most of them he worked on a very amicable basis indeed. To the staffs of the foreign legations he was also a friend; his redoubtable foe on many issues, Sartiges, finally said that Marcy's home had been "throughout [his] four years the home of the diplomatic corps."[13] But above all, Marcy was industrious: in spite of his advancing age, he worked incessantly; he cannot have fallen much short of Clarendon's figure—fourteen hours a day.

There remains the task of appraising Marcy's career as a whole. To begin with, it had been a long one. From those early days as a law student, militia ensign, and assessor of the federal direct tax, down

---

had done better than any secretary for forty years previously (Geo. Chipman to Marcy, Nov. 3, 1856, M.P.); Martin Van Buren had a very kind feeling towards him, at the end (Pierce to Marcy, Apr. 5, 1857, *ibid.*); and Edward Everett was his cordial and approving collaborator, until the Nebraska measure. Similarly, Señor Marcoleta said he was ready to take his seat beside Marcy in the next world, and was confident that it would not be in one of the hotter areas (Marcoleta to Marcy, Feb. 16, 1857, in French, *ibid.*). Long after, John Bassett Moore would term him "a great secretary of state." ("A Great Secretary of State," *Pol. Sci. Quarterly,* XXX, 377-396); cf. also Graham H. Stuart, *The Department of State,* 122, who praises him, but in a more qualified way.

[13] Cf. letter of the dept. clerks to Marcy, Mar. 3, 1857, M.P., headed by Hunter's name; Virginia Clay-Clopton, *op. cit.,* 62; B. P. Poore, *Reminiscences,* I, 479; Ida Russell to C. Cushing, May 5, 1854, C.P.; Sidney Webster, *Franklin Pierce and his Administration,* p. 52 (a portion reprinted from *New York World* of Jan. 31, 1892); Sartiges to de Vertigny, May 13, 1857, M.P.

through his work as recorder, master in chancery, adjutant general, comptroller, justice, and United States senator, his three terms as governor, and his roles as the receiver of the City Bank of Buffalo, Mexican claims commissioner, and secretary of war and secretary of state, his had been an unusually full career. From 1816 on he had held high office almost uninterruptedly—except for the interval when he helped reunite the New York Democracy and became its presidential favorite. In almost every one of these positions, moreover, his services were given at a critical time.

Marcy was an admirable administrator, a discreet and tactful party organizer, and a talented writer. He also had great common sense. Had he been nominated by his party in 1852, as he nearly was, he would almost certainly have been elected and as president he might well have prevented the Civil War from developing; this is to say that as president he would have been better able to resist the Nebraska bill. He was the ablest of the men considered for the nomination at that time, of larger caliber, for example, than Pierce and Buchanan. At the close of his career in the state department there continued to be many, as four years earlier, who thought that he had no peer alive.[14]

His great shortcoming was the one which these men also had, although he had it in a lesser degree. At least by mid-career, and probably far earlier, he had become much too willing to let other men do the determining of policy. Left to himself, he had decided shrewdly and well, and New York state or the United States had been the gainer. But too often, despite his commanding figure and his distinguished, craggy face, he had as a cabinet officer accepted the decisions of his superior even when this meant going against his own better judgment. This was pointed out very strikingly in an editorial in the *Evening Post* on May 7, 1857. That "conscience" of the New York press praised him for his sagacity and moderation; yet it went on as follows:

Without questioning his [Marcy's] general fidelity to democratic principles, we do him no injustice in saying that long service as a disciplinarian has made him overestimate the importance of mere party ascendancy. The success of democratic principles if possible, but the success of the democratic party at all hazards, has been his watchword. Hence, unquestionably,

---

[14] Cf. Dobbin to Marcy, Apr. 8, M.P., and *Atlas & Argus*, July 8.

his acquiescence, as Secretary of State, in the blundering appointments of the late administration, in the Greytown bombardment . . . and in the crowning folly of the Nebraska-Kansas bill.

No doubt, added the *Post,* he had resisted these moves strenuously, but he had stayed in the cabinet all the same. The paper was right, of course.

And he also had a second fault, eagerness for office. He had seldom sought office in any overt way and indeed had clung fully to the proprieties in such matters. Yet he had early admitted to himself the overpowering pull which public life had for him and how corrupting this influence could be. For if "power corrupts," the desire to retain it does also. It had been this which in 1846 had made him acquiesce in the first decision for war against Mexico, prior to the news of conflict in the disputed area north of the Rio Grande. And it had been this which had made him accept many things in the Pierce administration, including those which the *Post* cited. Had he left that regime when the Nebraska bill was brought out, in particular, and put himself at the head of the forces which were combining against it, his position in history would today be a greater one. Regrettably, the "spoils of victory," to use his own term, had held too much of an attraction for him. And in seeking them, he had been compelled to forego a part of the victory itself.

On the other hand, it would be very wrong to close without recognizing that in other respects he had served his country well. Judged by the canons of his own conservatism, which always meant loyalty to the Union and to the great party which had done so much to build the Union up, he had worked usefully. In the period of Jacksonian Democracy, for instance, he had labored to keep his party from extreme measures in regard to banking. He had also tried to curb the speculative business tendencies of the day. Then, under the expansionist regimes of Polk and Pierce, he had stood for a moderate course in foreign relations, whether in regard to compromising the Oregon issue, opposing the seizure of all of Mexico, or escaping an aggressive war for Cuba. His largest contributions, of course, were in the state department, in which connection he had shown signal ability. All in all, he has deserved far better treatment at the bar of history than he has customarily received.

NOTES ON THE ABBREVIATIONS AND SHORT TITLES USED IN THE FOOTNOTES

Argus   *The Daily Albany Argus*

Atlas   *Albany Evening Atlas*

B.P.   James Buchanan Papers, Historical Society of Pennsylvania

Bemis   S. F. Bemis, ed., *The American Secretaries of State*

Budget   *The Northern Budget*, Troy

B.U.A.   Brown University Archives

C & E   *Morning Courier & the New York Enquirer*

C.P.   Caleb Cushing Papers, Library of Congress

Can. Rels.   Vol. IV of Wm. R. Manning, ed., *Diplomatic Correspondence of the United States, Canadian Relations, 1784-1860*

D.S.   Department of State records, National Archives

D.A.B.   *The Dictionary of American Biography*

Des. Br. (or Fr., etc.)   Despatches from the United States minister to Britain (or France, etc.), National Archives

Ettinger   Amos A. Ettinger, *The Mission to Spain of Pierre Soulé*

E.Post   The New York *Evening Post*

F.O. 5 and F.O. 115   Photostats, Library of Congress, of British Foreign Office records, the first the despatches of Mr. Crampton, the British minister, the second the instructions of Lord Clarendon, and the correspondents these two men—*except as noted.*

F.P.   Azariah C. Flagg Papers, New York Public Library

Garber   Paul N. Garber, *The Gadsden Treaty*

Golder   F. A. Golder, "Russo-American Relations during the Crimean War," *American Historical Review*, XXXI, 462-476.

H.S.P.A.   Historical Society of Pennsylvania

Hammond   Jabez D. Hammond, *The History of Political Parties in the State of New York*

HED   *House Executive Document*

HED60   *House Executive Document No. 60,* 30th cong., 1st sess.

Herald   *The New York Herald*

Instr. Rus. (or Neth., etc.)   Instructions from the State Department to the United States minister to Russia (or the Netherlands, etc.), National Archives

Journal   *Albany Evening Journal*

L.C.   Library of Congress

McCormac   Eugene I. McCormac, *James K. Polk*

M.H.S.   Massachusetts Historical Society

Manning I   Vol. I (or as given) of Wm. R. Manning, ed., *Diplomatic Correspondence of the United States; inter-American Affairs, 1831-1860*

M.P.   Marcy Papers, Library of Congress

Messages   Charles Z. Lincoln, ed., *State of New York. Messages from the Governors,* vol. III

Mess. and Pap.   James D. Richardson, *A Compilation of the Messages and Papers of the Presidents*

N.P.   George W. Newell Papers, New York State Library, Albany

Nichols   Roy F. Nichols, *Franklin Pierce*

N.Y.H.S.   New York Historical Society

N.Y.P.L.   New York Public Library

P.D.   James K. Polk, *The Diary of,* M.M. Quaife, ed.

P.P.   James K. Polk Papers, 1st or 2nd series, Library of Congress

SED   Senate Executive Document

S.P.   Horatio Seymour Papers, typescript, New York Historical Society

Smith   Justin H. Smith, *The War with Mexico*

State Library   New York State Library, Albany

Times   *The New York Daily Times*

Union   *The Daily Union* (Washington)

V.B.P.   Martin Van Buren Papers, Library of Congress

Williams   Mary W. Williams, *Anglo-American Isthmian Diplomacy*

BIBLIOGRAPHICAL NOTE

ALTHOUGH the bibliographical references in the footnotes have been kept to a minimum, especially since the cutting of the length of the text, they will give some idea of the rather wide scope of the research done for this book. A further statement seems called for, however, regarding the principal sources used.

Among the personal papers consulted, the William L. Marcy Papers in the Library of Congress have been by far the most important. They consist of seventy-seven handsomely bound volumes of manuscripts, plus several boxes of materials. Included are an autobiographical sketch to the year 1826, in the form of a fifty-page manuscript addressed to Hon. J. P. Cushman, a Commonplace Book, chiefly for 1808, and several brief diaries for various periods (usually times of leisure). The other sets of personal papers, important for this work, in the Library of Congress, are those of Caleb Cushing, Andrew Jackson, Francis Markoe, John Bassett Moore, Franklin Pierce, James K. Polk, Guillaume Tell Poussin, and Martin Van Buren, and the Papers relating to Gideon Welles compiled by Henry Barrett Learned. Smaller sets of Marcy papers have been studied in many repositories, particularly the State Library, Albany, the Historical Society of Pennsylvania, the New York Historical Society, the New York Public Library, and the Massachusetts Historical Society. The Brown University Archives also proved unexpectedly fruitful for Marcy's student career. The other chief collections of non-Marcy materials consulted were those of George W. Newell (often called, incorrectly, the Marcy Papers) and of J. V. L. Pruyn, in the State Library, Thomas W. Olcott, in the possession of Douglas W. Olcott of Rensselaer, N.Y., Horatio Seymour (typescripts), in the New York Historical Society, James Gordon Bennett, Azariah Cutting Flagg, and Samuel J. Tilden in the New York Public Library, John A. Dix and Peter D. Vroom, at Columbia University, James Buchanan, in the Historical Society of Pennsylvania, William H. Seward and Thurlow Weed, at the University of Rochester, George Bancroft, Edward Everett, and A. C. Washburn, in the Massachusetts Historical Society, and Francis Preston Blair and Benjamin F. Butler, at Princeton.

For Marcy's early career, the printed and manuscript materials at
the State Library and the records of the town of Sturbridge and of
Albany, Erie, and Niagara counties have been useful. For the Mexican
War, the best set of papers is contained in *House Executive Document
No. 60,* 1st sess., 30th cong. A number of other sets have been used,
however, as cited in the footnotes.

For foreign relations, the principal sources have been the department of state records in the National Archives. These are mainly the
instructions to the ministers abroad and the despatches from the same,
plus the notes to and from the foreign legations at Washington. These
items have been read for all the principal countries and many lesser
ones, although the printed volumes of correspondence, edited by
William R. Manning (see "Notes on Abbreviations") have for convenience been used in much of the work. The latter have been checked
against the originals, for completeness and general accuracy, and in
some important documents for accuracy in detail. The "appointments"
files, "special missions," and "reciprocity negotiations, 1848-1854,"
in the Archives, have also been useful. For the printed government
documents of the period, which have been employed fairly extensively, see the footnotes. As for foreign materials, the photostats in
the Library of Congress of the British Foreign Office Records have
been rather fully covered. (See the "Notes on Abbreviations.") They
have been an admirable source. For France, some of the materials in
the Archives des Affaires Étrangères, Correspondence Politique,
États-Unis, vols. 109-116, have been consulted at Paris through the
services of M. Abel Doysié, with the aid of Waldo G. Leland's *Guide.*
It will be noted that the excerpts from the original Russian and
Spanish records, respectively, in the articles of Golder (see "Notes
on Abbreviations") and of H. L. Janes, "The Black Warrior Affair,"
Amer. Hist. Rev., XII, 280-298, have also been very helpful.

INDEX

Aberdeen, Lord, premier, 317, 345

Abolitionism, in New York state, 97, 102-5

Accessory Transit Company, 243-4, 245, 370

Acton, Lord, viii

Adams, Elisha, 49

Adams, John Quincy, 34, Regency cool toward, 36-7

Africanization, fear of, 258-9, 332; *see also* Ostend Manifesto

Aix-la-Chapelle, meeting at, 330; *see also* Ostend Manifesto

Albany Argus, works for conservatives, 93; attacks Marcy, 274

Albany *Atlas,* 278, 281

Albany, city of, 1823, 32-3, charter election, 1832, 73; tariff meeting, 77; opposes abolitionists, 103; citizens of, buy lands for back taxes, 115n; "good old dutch city," 183; and Marcy funeral, 410

Albany meeting, love feast for Marcy, 1851, 198

Albany Regency, early leaders, 28; plot to win Federalists, 29-30; triumphant, 1820-21, 30; formed, 27-39; heyday in 1823, 32; abundant letter writing, 34; and election of 1824, 34-5; stalemated, 1824-28, 36; on economic issues, 36; triumphant, 1828, 39; leaders described, 39-40; character of organization, 40-1; use of state printer, 41; praised by Weed, 41; investments at Lockport, 49-50; relations with Jackson, 53; on tariff, 57; for Marcy, 69; well organized, 75; fear rift over slavery, 1836, 103-4

Allen, Elisha, chief minister to Hawaiian king, 390, 396

Allen, Stephen, 122, 136

Allies, 294; influence against neutral rights treaty, 297; occupation of, left U.S. free, 299; and Santo Domingo, 401; *see also* Anglo-French accord

Almonte, Mexican minister at Washington, 284

Amazon, efforts to open, 399

American politics, triumph of government "by" the people, 39

Andrews, Israel D., United States consul at St. John, and special agent, 249, 300; secret service funds, 251-2, 301, 308, 308n

Anglo-French accord, established, its vast naval power, Marcy questions its envoys, asks Buchanan to learn its aims, 290-1; *see also* Allies

Anglo-French declaration on neutral rights, 293

Annals of the American Pulpit, article on Messer by Marcy, 7

Annapolis, Marcy visits, 182

Antimasonic Party, 48, *see also* Masons

Army, size of, 141-2; staff little changed under Marcy, 142; ordered into Texas, 1845, then to Rio Grande, 143; efforts to enlarge, 144-52; officers shun temporary commands, 163; demobilization, 173

Article XI, 1848 treaty, 254, 284, 285

Astor, John Jacob, 43

Atchison, Senator David R., 207

Austin, James T., 61

Australia, talk of filibuster upon, 353

Austria, in Koszta case, 264-9

Austrian crown jewels, alleged role in Koszta case, 269

Avis Island, 315

Bailey, John, 27

Ballston Spa, 408-9

Baltimore Convention, 1852, 208-13; post-mortems on, 211-14

Baltimore *Sun,* 208

Bancroft, George, 92, 105, 134, 144, 151, 177; secretary of the navy, 139; history of U.S., Marcy on, 334

Bank of United States, *see* United States Bank

Banking in New York state, banks enjoy heyday, 82; monopoly banking, 82-3; Marcy proposes reforms in, 84-5; small bills ban, 85-6; temporary relaxation of, 94; free banking, 86, 88, 94; year of grace, 89-90; hard money policy, 90; resumption, 95; weakness of system, 83, 117

Barbour, John S., keeps Virginia delegation from Marcy, 211

Barnburners, 124, 128, 185 ff., 216, 224, 270, 272; threaten rift if Marcy chosen by Polk, 134; hostile to Marcy and Polk, 138, 140; revolt of, 175-83; support Marcy for president, 194, 197; and Nebraska bill, 275-7

Bay Islands, 243, 244, 357, 378-80

Beardsley, Samuel, 186, 187, 202, 203, 206

Bedinger, Henry, *chargé* to Denmark, 403-6

Belize, 242, 243, 247, 357, 374, 378, 379

Belmont, *chargé* to the Hague, 231, 236, 237, 325, 328, 342, 401-2

Bennett, James Gordon, Marcy's intrigue with, for governorship, 65-7; his paper for Marcy for 1852, 199

Benton, Senator Thomas Hart, 55, 57, 147, 162, 167; has ideas to end war quickly, 157; considered for command post, 161-2

Berkeley Springs, Marcy-Crampton negotiations, 249-50

Bermuda, H. M. Schooner, 314

Berret, James G., 203, 212, 227-8, 282

Bigelow, John, 198

Billé, Torben, Danish *chargé,* 405-7

Binghampton, 100

Birdsall, Ausburn, 206

Bissell, William H., 230

Black Warrior, and Happy Accord, 290; seized at Havana, 319; release of, 322-3; note to be presented, 332; affair settled, publication of papers, 338; amount due, 340

Blair, Francis Preston, 139-40

Bliss, William M., Marcy's law patron, 13-4, 16

Bluhme, Danish foreign minister, 403-4

Bodisco, Count de, Russian minister to U.S., 289, 291

Boilleau, French *chargé,* 395-6

Borland, Solon, minister to Central America, 229, 246, 310, 311

Bouck, William C., 120, 124, 125, 128, 140

Brackenridge, Henry M., 119

Brady, Mathew, 409

Breckinridge, John C., 336

Brereton, Mrs., landlady, 119

"Britches bill," 72

British consuls, dismissed, 373

British Honduras, *see* Belize

British recruiting in U.S., 344-52, 362, 363, 372-3

Brodhead, John Romeyn, 399

Brodhead, Richard, 205

Bronson, Greene C., 45-6, 74, 227, 270-1, 309

Brown, Aaron V., 133

Brown, Jeremiah, trial of, 51

Brown, John P., 265

Brown University, admissions to, described, Marcy's years at, 6-11

Bruce, Eli, 48

Bryant, William Cullen, 62, 231

Buchanan, James, in Polk cabinet, 133, 148, 149, 160, 177, 180, 195, 293, 325, 326, 396; Polk's secretary of state, 138-9; and 1852 convention, 204, 205, 209-10, 219; on appointments, takes London mission, 223-32; and dress circular, 236-8; accepts commission, 245-8; characterized by Marcy, 248; his solution on privateering, 297; on Central America, 309-10; with extremists, 331; rumored about to change places with Marcy, 334; tainted with Ostend, 355; "delicacy about," 355; becomes Democratic favorite, 367, 371; nominated, 374-5; deserts Dallas' pact, 380; gloomy *re* Hawaii, 390; and tolls, 403; inaugurated, 408; settlement of isthmian troubles made easier, by Marcy's work, 411; his relations with Walker, 411

"Bucktails," 26

Buel, Jesse, 81

Buena Vista, 164-5, 170

Buffalo, 101, 106, 196

Bulwer, Sir Henry, 243

Burritt, Elihu, 384

Butler, Benjamin F. (of New York), Regency leader, 39-40, 45, 47, 77, 91, 104, 132, 133, 135, 181

Butler, William O., 168, 172, 198

Butts, Isaac, 192

Byrdsall, Fitzwilliam, 194

Lane, Jacob L., 32
Lane, William C., 255
Larned, James, 119
Larned, Ruth, 3; *see also* Marcy, Mrs. Ruth Larned
Larned, William, 3
Latimer, Mrs., landlady at Washington, 144
Law, George, 202, 204
Lawrence, Cornelius W., 140, 224
Lawrence, William Beach, 225, 375
Lawyers, three years' clerking required, 13
Learned, Henry Barrett, on Marcy, vii, viii
Learned or "Larned," the name, 3n
Lee, William L., 394-5
Leggett, Aaron, 185
Legitimist party, Nicaragua, 359
Leicester, Mass., academy, 5
Leonard, Zenas L., 5, 6
Lewis, Clarence O., authority on Morgan affair, 48n, 51n
Liberal party, Nicaragua, 358-9
Liholiho, Prince, 391-4
Lincoln, Abraham, 302
Linn, Lewis F., 105
"Lithographic cities," creation of, 82
Loan law of '34, its success, 76
Lockport, 49, 115
"Loco-foco," 86
Loco-focoism, 96
Loco-focos, 86-7
London *Telegraph,* on privateering letter, 385
London *Times,* on U.S., 361; on privateering letter, 385; on dress circular, 236
Louisiana Purchase, debate on, 9
Louisiana sugar producers, 396
Lumley, J. S., British *chargé,* 347
Lynch, W. L., 316
Lyon, Oliver, 17

McCauley, Charles S., 339
McClelland, Robert, 221, 222, 286
McKay, Captain, 291
McLane, Robert M., 237
McManus, William, 18
McPherson, John D., 195
Madison, James, accepts idea of war, 18
Manifest Destiny, 231; European distrust of, 332-3; fails, 411

Mann, Abijah, 65, 84
Mann, Ambrose Dudley, assistant secretary, 225-6, 233, 250, 253, 269, 328, 336, 341
Marcoleta, 360, 413n; *projet* of, 310
Marcy, Miss Cornelia, daughter, 110, 184, 253, 335, 387
Marcy, Mrs. Cornelia Knower, wife, 114, 119, 145-6, 208, 253, 335, 348; characteristics, 109
Marcy, Mrs. Dolly Newell, wife, 19-20, 42
Marcy, Edmund, son, 110, 215, 220, 253, 264, 269
Marcy, Jedediah I, grandfather, 2
Marcy, Jedediah II, father, 1-3
Marcy, Jedediah III, brother, 173
Marcy, John, 2
Marcy, Moses, 2
Marcy, Mrs. Ruth Larned, mother, 1, 173
Marcy, Samuel Newell, son, 42, 109, 115, 159, 184, 215, 226, 264, 335
Marcy William G., son, 42, 109, 159, 228
Marcy, William L.

General Items

appearance, 23, 221, 408; *attitudes on foreign affairs:* mildly anti-British, nationalist, respects international law, 247; not expansionist, opposes island acquisition, 261-2; never insults foreign powers, 268; *autobiographical sketch,* 112; *callous* to criticism, 342; *card playing:* whist, 111, 173, 249; not skilled at poker ("brag"), 184; *carriage & horses,* 283; *characterized* by Buchanan, 221; *culture,* 111; *reading,* 108, 110-1; library of, 110, 110n; *common sense,* 42; *conservatism,* 76, 83-4, 99, 121, 123; conversational charm, 111, 195, 413; *corrupting influence of office,* 113; *failure to study and work on public problems when out of office;* uninformed, when subject first arises, 145, 192; *industry,* 413; *integrity,* 67n; *investments* and finances, 83, 115-6, 116n, 193, 408; *law, weak in,* 46; *a life of "learning trades,"* 250; *living in the past,* 1845-6, 146; *loyalty to party* and associates, 42, 55; *opinion of,* by twentieth century scholars, 194; *pamphlet-*

early 1854, his negligence on the Greytown instructions, 310-2; he defends
the bombardment, 313-7; inattention to
Central America, in rest of 1854, 317;
on Cuba: his criticisms of Soulé, 318-9,
322; his anger *re* the *Black Warrior,*
319-20; revival of purchase proposal,
321; his *Black Warrior* note, 323; the
plan for a conference of ministers,
325-6; warns emperor *re* V. Frondé,
326-7; "spats" with Sartiges over Dillon, etc., 327, 327n; disgusted at
notoriety of envoys, 328, 333-4; role
in November, 1854 campaign, his
difficult relations with Pierce, 328-30;
wins control, after Ostend, 332-3; less
busy, after Ostend, 335; is praised,
on the Ostend affair, 338; abhors "robber doctrine," 339; helps check Quitman, 340; Spanish affairs, the last
phase, mid-1855 ff., 340-3; and
Horatio Perry, 341-3; British problems
his chief concern, late 1855 ff., 344;
shocked *re* recruiting, is led to think
it has stopped, 345-6; sees hint that
ministry had authorized it, 347; makes
strong demands for amends, 348; goes
to Old Point Comfort for 1855 vacation, 348; summoned to capital, learns
of evidence of Crampton's part, 348-9;
desires to hit Britain hard, 352; role in
curbing the Kinney filibuster, 1855,
354-5; sends virtual ultimatum to Britain, 355-7; angry private letter, 358;
declines to recognize Walker, tries to
stop flow of recruits, 359-60, 370-2;
angry reaction to British squadron, asks
speedy reply on enlistment, 361; shifts
to softer line, 362; feels age and pressure of affairs, late 1855, 364; will
back Pierce's renomination, 366; partly
identified with Kansas policy, 366; relations with Buchanan, 356n; has host
of admirers, but will retire, 367-9;
entertains Buchanan, 371; accepts
Clarendon's note on recruiting but ap-
proves Crampton's dismissal, 372-3;
firm but conciliatory instructions on
Central America, 373-4; on Cincinnati
convention, 374-5, 374n; praised indirectly by Cincinnati convention,
1856, 375; London reacts favorably to
his instructions, 377-8; he insists on

improvement of Dallas-Clarendon *projet,* 379; his close attention to Dallas'
pact, its rejection, 380; gets Wheeler
recalled, 381; his letter demanding end
of seizure of private property at sea,
as price of abolition of privateering,
381-7; reception of Declaration of
Paris, 382; on large military establishments, 384; reception of privateering letter, 384-7; old and worn out,
spends 1856 summer at Grassland,
386-71; his estimate of Fremont, 387;
much support for Marcy's retention in
office, 387; on Hawaii, he favors annexation, doubts Allies will interfere,
learns offer of annexation was a trick,
negotiates vain reciprocity treaty, 389-
94; obtains U.S. ban on filibusters
against Hawaii, 395-6; his worldwide
policy for freer trade, plus recoprocity
near U.S., 398; little done in China
and South America, 398-9; appointment of Townsend Harris, 399-400;
gets consuls admitted to Dutch East
Indies, 401-2; instructs Bedinger on
Danish tolls, 403; delays on tolls till
1854, 404; declines U.S. participation
in conference, would pay for navigational aids, 405-6; final settlement,
1857, 407; in retirement, plans European trip, takes family to New York
state, has *angina pectoris,* his death,
1857, 408-9; eulogized by Develin,
410; elaborate funeral, 410; appraisal
of, as secretary of state; his personal
qualities, 411-3, 413n; helps revise
foreign service laws, 412; appraisal of
his career as a whole, 413-5; *see also*
Baltimore Convention, 1852, and Election of 1824, *etc.*

Marcy-Scott correspondence, 171
Marsh, George P., 266n
Mason, James M., 278, 287, 322, 374, 379
Mason, John Y., 139, 161, 166, 178, 179, 206, 221, 293, 331; minister to France, 229; wears fancy garb, 237; urged to "pulse" the French government, 261
Masons, and Morgan affair, trials of, 47-52
Maury, bark, 351
Meade, George G., 153, 174
Mechanics' and Farmers' Bank, 71